The
Powered
PARAGLIDING
Bible⁵

Jeff Goin

www.FootFlyer.com

The Powered Paragliding Bible[5]

Copyright © 2018 Jeff Goin All Rights Reserved
Published by
Airhead Creations dba FootFlyer.com

Fifth Edition
1st edition printed 2005
2nd edition printed 2008
3rd edition printed 2012
4th edition printed 2015

ISBN: 978-0-9770966-7-1
Library of Congress Control Number: 2017916995

Edited by
Tim Kaiser
Dennis Pagen
George Hawkins
Peg O'Keef

AIR HEAD CREATIONS
Polk City, Florida, USA

Email: *info@FootFlyer.com*

Photographs: Jeff Goin or Tim Kaiser except where noted.
Illustrations: Jeff Goin except where noted
Cover Photo: Jeff Hamann of himself with Luc Trépanier

For related materials, please visit **www.FootFlyer.com**.

The information is accurate to the best of our knowledge but errors may occur. This material is protected by U.S. and International copyright laws. No part may be reproduced or transmitted in any form or by any means, electronic or mechanical, without written permission from the publisher.

The reader acknowledges that powered paragliding, paramotors, wing handling, and related activities carry significant risk including dismemberment and death. You take this risk completely of your own volition and understand that the creators of this book assume no liability in connection with its contents.

Printed in the U.S.A.

Table of Contents

Table of Contents

Table of Contents

Table of Contents

Table of Contents

Foreword

Easy travel has given me access to our sport's greatest pilots and teachers. Their different styles and disciplines within the sport share one thing in common: a desire for excellence. Over the years we have collectively learned a lot and I'm happy to share that extraordinary wealth of knowledge, including new knowledge gained in many areas.

Paramotor instructors remain our greatest resource; this material can serve them as well

No book can instill a skill. We'll show how to do a task and what *practice* will turn it into a skill along. More importantly, we'll show how to minimize risk in the process. There is no way to learn a kinematic "feel" from reading, but knowing what exercises can help develop what skills will certainly help.

Is it Risky?

No Risk, No Reward. Know Risk, Know Reward.

Flight always involves risk. Our limited statistics suggest that risk is about the same as flying small airplanes or ultralights but we're likely to have more minor injuries. Being slow, stable craft helps but other risks, covered in this book, apply.

You could safely watch others live life through TV, but this sure is more fulfilling. As Wilbur Wright observed: "If you are looking for perfect safety, you will do well to sit on a fence and watch the birds." But then, even that can be dangerous.

How to Use This Book

Don't use this book for self-training! Absolutely nothing contained here should be tried without getting good instruction first—it's the best money you will spend on the sport. Our craft is a wonder of simplicity—graceful and capable aloft but ungainly and challenging on the ground.

1. **Section I** takes you from initial training through the first few flights, including terminology. Later sections will be more meaningful as you progress. It assumes that your instructor will take responsibility for determining appropriate gear, conditions, location and other minutia.

2. **Section II** covers the basic knowledge needed to head out on your own. Your instructor will make it more relevant to your location and situation. For example, if you live near a big city, ask about charts and airspace. If you live in mountainous terrain, dig more deeply into mountain weather.

3. **Section III** is for mastering the finer points. There are many. The amount of control available to those willing to really work at it is truly amazing.

4 **Section IV** is for the curious. It offers a more complete understanding of what's going on, especially regarding aerodynamics, while dispelling many stubborn myths.

5. **Section V** is for pilots buying their *second* wing or motor. New pilots should always choose an instructor rather than gear but there is a lot of benefit to understanding the tradeoffs. It may help avoid shysters who would try to fit their round-pegged gear into your square-holed needs.

6. **Section VI** offers suggestions on "what now?" Some are just plain fun but that's what this sport is about.

Companion Web Site:

Updated and supplemental information to this book can be found on **www.FootFlyer.com**. Videos and other material will also be placed there, too, organized under "Educational," like the book's chapters.

Thanks To

Many have contributed to my earliest and fondest memories of aviation and I am thankful for them all. Here are just a few.

Mom: *"It's a passing fad, you'll get over it."* Words that my 13 year old ears just wouldn't accept. Fortunately she not only relented, but eventually encouraged, and even joined my quest for flight. She's a wonderful human, a picky editor, an English Major, newspaper writer, flier of other things, and creative wordsmith. And to **Dad**, who tolerated all this with aplomb.

Eric Dufour: *"Don't look at the wing—it won't tell you anything you can't feel."* At my first fly-in, I watched this man finesse the craft in a way that showed me what was possible.

Michelle Daniele: *"It's a fly-in, if anyone gets mad at you for launching early, have them see me!"* After asking if it would be ok to launch at dawn during their first Balloon Fiesta fly-in. That was a concerto to my ears and permanently endearing.

Nick Scholtes: *"I thought you weren't interested."* After introducing me to the sport, I disappeared. The next time we met I had gotten training, purchased gear and couldn't get enough. We proceeded to gorge ourselves on airtime over the next few years.

Mark Sorenson: *"Power up to go up."* Words of my first PPG Instructor that I wish I would have heeded more quickly.

Jerry Daniele: *"We fly at the pleasure of the people; tick them off and eventually we won't fly anymore."* Sage advice.

Chris Bowles: *"Uh oh, it's on."* Words that ended the first USPPA officer meeting after soarable conditions developed.

Alex Varv: *"This is my baby, every now and then I like to come out and just admire it"*—Generous contributor of knowledge.

Rob Sutter: *"Jeff, you wanna to go in with me on one of these powered paraglider things?"* The question that started it all. He never did get into it.

Alan Chuculate: *"Just lean back and go for it!"* An admonishment from the instructor who really taught me kiting.

Jeff Williams: *"You might even like the soaring."* My first paraglider instructor whose patient wisdom guided me beyond the basics to a love for free flight. Yes, Jeff, I understand now, you can soar the heights without a variometer.

The Brothers Casaudemecq, Jose & Javier: *"It'll fly you just fine at that weight."* Advice on a used motor that would be my first and longest lasting. They were right on.

Elizabeth Guerin: *"Oh, you were the one that was never on the ground."* Comment made a few months after my first fly-in.

Bruce Brown: *"Wanna go play in the road?"* The enticement that preceded a memorable low-level romp near Albuquerque, New Mexico during my first fly-in.

Phil Russman: *"Is it over?"* Gifted crafter of content who always challenged me to excel. Yes, it's over—again.

Tim Kaiser—Indispensable emotional support human, editor, idea maker, continued pilot/photo victim, and "Enterprise" captain whose many miles at the helm has enabled many pages of work. Tim rocks. And he survived being my first student. Thankfully, he was mercifully easy.

Dennis Pagen—For getting me to do it in the first place, refining the content of the first two editions, and tolerating all of my non-standardness.

And to those who helped with material—you've improved this book enormously!

Mark Andrews	Maneuvers	Chris Lee	Aerial Photography
Bob Armond	Carts, Setup, Emergencies	Lance Marczak	Motor Man
Chad Bastian	Maneuvers, Emergencies	David McWhinnie	Shipping
Jeff Baumgartener	Homebuilding	Wayne Mitchler	Handling The Wing, Setup, Trikes
Steve Boser	Propellers	Mike Nowland	Cross Country, Motors, Wings
Bill Briley	Maneuvers	Steve Mayer	My "Paraglider Encyclopedia"
Chris Bowles	History, Engines, Setup	Scott MacMurray	Line Tangles
Stu Caruk	Towing information, Airspace	Betty Pfeiffer	Reserves
Alan Chuculate	Everything	Phil Russman	Aerial Videography
Francesco DeSantis	History, Homebuilding	Nick Scholtes	Motors, Trikes, Precision flying
Eric Dufour	History, Glossary	Tom Scott	Composite Propeller Repair
Dana Hague	Aerodynamics, Motors	Mo Sheldon	Carts, Glossary, Propellers
Bill Heaner	Glossary, Wing Handling	Geoff Soden	History
Rayiaz Khan	Photography	Alex Varv	Setup, Motor Maintenance

Preface

When my friend, Rob Sutter, first suggested powered paragliding, I thought he was nuts. "You want to do what?" I asked. He knew that I was a flying freak—I lived on an airport, had a hangar in my back yard, an airplane, a helicopter, and flew for a living. Ridiculous. So he figured that I'd be an easy mark for yet *another* flying contraption, even one I'd never heard of. I immediately thought of the guy who loosed himself over Los Angeles in a lawn chair with weather balloons. Not me. But Rob insisted, saying it was more refined and he wanted someone to share it with. So I went for a look.

What I found was astounding, revealing refinement and control that I never imagined. It became obvious that, besides fine control, it would not be subdued by a light wind's wily whirls. That got me fired up. It seemed too good to be true but I had to try. Having so few rules was even more exciting—I've spent my aeronautical life in regulatory hell and this looked like a way out—a really cool way out.

My mind raced—thoughts of moving freely about in 3D ignited desire. "There's got to be a catch" I thought.

The idea of running into the air was cooler still—stirring me like nothing else in aviation ever had. And I was already flying airplanes for work, for fun, and just got my helicopter license. That was all great but the paramotor seemed more intriguing. After all, I could take it *with* me.

I contacted local paramotorist Nick Scholtes who was welcoming and answered my many questions. He hung me in his little DK motor from some contraption in the shop (a tip of his iceberg, I eventually learned). We watched videos, talked endlessly and he allayed my fears. Yes, there's risk, but it was like others I willingly accepted.

That visit sealed my fate. Unfortunately, this was during Chicagoland's deep freeze—there would be no flying here and I wanted to start now! The recommended instructor, Alan Chuculate, was not available so I was steered towards another gem, Jeff Williams. After eight days, spanning two trips to California, I earned my USHGA (now USHPA) P2 paraglider rating for motorless flight, an experience that re-ignited a long-held love of soaring (I started flying gliders at 13). Then I went in search of propulsion. After a few calls, Aerolight in Miami satisfied my thirst for thrust as instructor Mark Sorenson, a fellow airline pilot, sold me a little direct drive unit that he had modified. Aerolight's Jose & Javier had just taken over the Fly line and were extremely helpful. Thankfully, training was included.

A week later it was at my house: Wing, motor, helmet—everything was there. And I was captivated. The prospect of launching from the grass at the end of my road was tantalizing. In the summer of 1999 I flew every single day the weather cooperated, sometimes both morning and evening. First the local area, then on to more distant locales, then on to 15-plus mile cross-country jaunts in whatever direction suited me. It was a freedom realized that I couldn't get enough of.

I started writing about it. Ask any of my high school teachers to peg the writers in their class and I wouldn't have even made the long list. But write I did; flights of fancy spilled into PPG newsgroups and eventually magazines, letting me relive these unbelievable experiences.

Passion exploded, taking me places I never dreamed possible. The simplicity, the freedom, the minimal regulation, it appealed to me like no other form of flight, including the helicopter. I wanted to help preserve it, to give it a voice, to help develop good training programs and to encourage others to embrace sustainable practices. This book is the culmination of that desire.

As before, there have been improvements in both techniques and equipment along with better ways to illustrate them. Many reader suggestions have been offered and incorporated for which I'm grateful. Here's to your life aloft.

And remember, "If there's air there, it should be flown in."

Section I

First Flight

Section
I

For most who undertake it, powered paragliding is the apex of personal flying, offering unprecedented freedom, simplicity, controllable safety, and low cost. There is no runway needed, no radio, no trailer. Just pull up, preflight, layout and launch.

A dedicated student, under competent instruction, can learn the basics in as little as three days. But to be comfortably flying on your own, expect five to eight days of moderately intense training and practice. In about a year of regular flying you'll build a confident autonomy. This section will help get to and beyond that first flight.

Ratings

Paramotoring in the U.S. does not require a license or rating unless you're flying tandems (two-seaters); see USPPA.org for the latest details. A rating may be required for insurance, flights from some places, and for some events.

Even if a rating is not required, it's helpful to measure personal accomplishment and progress. Ratings can also provide milestones during the learning process that will help ensure thorough, methodical training.

We enjoy the simplest path to flight of any aviation segment in the world, and it's up to us, as responsible citizens, *to keep it that way*.

What it Takes Physically

Physical requirements depend on whether you choose to launch on foot or wheels. Using a cart is much less demanding since you don't have to carry the motor or run. Even foot launching doesn't require athletic prowess, but you will exert yourself while learning. Flying itself can be relaxing, but the early stages of kiting and foot launching are a bit demanding.

Fortunately, as skills improve it gets *much* easier. Even after just a few sessions, newly recruited muscles adapt to their strange use and brute force gives way to finesse. A skilled "kiter," for example, can go for over an hour with minimal exertion whereas the neophyte will be winded in a few minutes.

Expect some muscles to bark during the first few days but, fortunately, it diminishes quickly. This well-earned soreness is to be relished!

by Angie Bateman

The Training Process

CHAPTER

1

No, a license is not required, but *skill* certainly is.

Powered paragliding may epitomize aerial simplicity but without proper training, it can be a painful, arduous, and vexing pursuit. Quality instruction will guide you carefully through important milestones while making the process safer and *far* more enjoyable.

With proper care and appropriate gear, mature children can learn to paramotor. Instructor Russ Bateman is shown here helping his son on an early flight.

Skimping can easily cost more in equipment repair and/or medical expense than is saved on instruction—many just give up without proper training.

Plus, flying in anyone's national airspace system is not trivial. Given societal fears, heading aloft without knowing the rules is irresponsible folly. Fortunately you've taken a huge step by using this book—let your instructor bring it to life.

Finding an Instructor

We do this because it's fun—the training should be too. Seek out an instructor you can get along with, who is thorough, known for quality teaching, and has access to good flying sites. Training is a lot of work for both of you, though; don't expect to be pampered, but do expect to be treated with respect. If you're willing to immerse yourself into the program, then you will probably get along with just about anyone out there. Most instructors teach because they love the sport, certainly not for the fame and fortune! Even with decent profit margins on gear there is not enough volume to make it big business. Instructors are the sport's national treasure.

A good resource is personal recommendation by a trusted pilot, especially someone in the community with nothing to sell. If possible, visit potential instructors, talk with them, and watch them train—you'll learn a lot about their demeanor and style.

Students should get tandem air time in *something* before going up alone—something that lets them actually make control inputs. The closer to what they'll be flying the better. There are a very few people who react poorly to piloting—it would be good to know that *before* their first solo.

Wheeled tandems are ideal but rules can make it difficult. In the U.S., for example, wheeled tandems must be done under the more restrictive Sport Pilot rules whereas foot launched tandems are allowed under less-involved exemptions granted to organizations such as the USPPA.

If you have no direct knowledge of an instructor or school, make sure they're certified for PPG as opposed to less relevant ultralight types like powered parachutes (PPC's). While government certification is not required in many countries (except for tandem), it does show that they have demonstrated some minimum knowledge and skill. Not only do they meet standards established by a national organization (USPPA in the U.S.) but they enjoy the training resources of that organization.

Be leery of instructors who have only been flying for a year or so themselves—they won't be well versed on the intricacies of student issues. Just about any pilot can explain how it's done, but experience provides the depth of understanding to better recognize and correct student problems.

Ask your instructor to use the syllabus from a national organization to help ensure important information is covered. Not all do even if they're certified. Ask if it's current—an old syllabus may not include important improvements.

Don't worry about equipment and be leery of sales pitches. There are some legends in their own minds out there. When you start hearing that this or that is the "best," step back and look around—the most vocal are frequently the least desirable.

Like all of aviation, there are trade-offs. Make sure you get matched up with appropriate gear for your size, weight and intended take-off elevation. Flying at high elevations means different choices than flying at sea level. A reputable instructor will do this matching within the line of gear he is authorized to sell. Your success has far more to do with your attitude and choice of *instructor* than your choice of gear.

Choosing a School

The person doing your instruction is the most important factor is choosing where to learn but here are some other considerations.

- *Large schools* are not better because they're bigger but they are more likely to be full time which makes scheduling easier. You'll be able to train multiple days in a row—a concentrated environment that allows rapid progression. You'll have to travel, though, and support will largely be by mail and phone.

- *Smaller schools*, usually one-person affairs, can offer equally good training but it may be spread out over more time. Frequently that means weekends. Being local, though, helps since you'll enjoy close support for training, equipment, places to fly and probably a ready community of other pilots. If you have a local instructor and he's qualified, be thankful—most don't.

- Some instructors will come to you, but find out what expenses you'll be paying, it could be much less of a value. Also consider how you'll get service after they leave. The benefit of having the instructor come to you is that they'll be able to help you pick out local sites, identify local weather patterns and airspace issues.

- *Location, location, location.* Any school should have access to a sufficiently open area to fly. They should also have appropriate training aids (*see next spread*) and examples of the various equipment available to buy. It is expected that they will prefer only a few types of wings and motors which is OK—they've figured out how to train on that gear and should be able to support it.

- *Rental Gear.* Schools that offer training on their equipment let you learn with far less initial cost. You will obviously be on the hook for any damage and can expect to make a significant deposit. Some schools only train those who buy gear from them which is another reason to choose an instructor rather than gear.

- *Ratings.* If you plan on getting insurance or flying at locations or events that require ratings, make sure they're actively offered. Of course you must pass a skills test so it's never a given.

If the school offers tandem introductory flights, that's a great way to see if the sport is for you while, at the same time, seeing how they operate with minimal commitment. Another good option is to find a school that will train you on their gear through first solo, then let you decide what to do. Be aware that you're nowhere near ready to set out on your own after such an introduction.

Different Methods of Instructing

There are many different ways to learn, and one size does not fit all. Some instructors are laid back. Some are intense. Some are more aggressive, and some are conservative. Drill sergeant types using military style discipline may have a serious demeanor but can be very effective.

Schools in mountainous areas may teach free-flying first. That's fun on its own and will expose you to a different type of flying. But it takes more work in many ways since the weather must fit a narrower window. You will learn "parawaiting"—hanging out until the weather improves.

Flatland schools tend to teach motor flying only, sometimes incorporating tow or tandem flights. A few don't offer either one—your first time aloft may be your first motor flight. That is not ideal, but with strong guidance, very good kiting skills, proper practice on the simulator, reliable communications, and a huge open field it can be done with reasonable safety. Using a stable wheeled platform improves your chances for early success even more.

All methods can be effective but the best instructors adapt to an individual's learning style. Of course some adapting is necessary on your part, too, for best results.

There must be a balance in pacing. For example, if you or the instructor pushes too hard, you'll tend to skip necessary information or rehearsals—overlooking critical steps. On the other hand, going too slowly means re-learning prior lessons, leading to frustration. There is a difference between rapidly paced and carelessly quick. With proper precautions, a quicker schedule can be reasonably safe.

For example, there is a benefit to working with higher wind in order to be prepared for it. So if it's somewhat windy, you can be learning how to deal with it.

Your first flight is just a beginning; much more remains to be learned and practiced with the instructor's guidance.

We are given much leeway in both regulation and required training. But those regs protect others, *not* us. So it's up to you to continue learning—not only for self preservation but also to understand the national airspace system in which we operate.

Like all freedoms, PPG flying requires responsibility—we either accept that responsibility or lose the freedom.

Learning to kite in stronger winds is a benefit of having sites with consistent, smooth wind.

1. Phil Russman getting pulled by Michael O'Daniel and Jeff Goin in strong winds on a Mexican dune.

2. Brad Weiss working with a student learning to soar some low dunes in FL.

3. Eric Dufour goes over last minute details before the student's first solo flight. Some schools start their students on wheels then transition them to foot launching.

Towing For Training

Towing is a great training tool if done carefully. Methods vary based on the mission, but they all share common elements: a proper towline, pilot's tow bridle with release mechanism, line tension control, a way to cut the line (like a hook knife), and usually a weak link to break before the paraglider does. Pilots must rehearse releasing and hook knife use.

Towing requires extreme care—you must execute the instructor's commands regardless of what may be happening. It requires a well trained, preferably certified, tow operator since the risk is not obvious.

Special procedures and gear make towing safer: visual signals, sound practices, a "tow assist bridle" (engages the speed system if the wing falls back too far) and reliable radio communications. Pilot response usually comes from kicking the legs fore and aft for "yes" or waving them left and right for "no."

Stationary Winch

1. Stationary winch towing uses a powered drum to reel in tow line fast enough to fly the connected pilot. Tow operators control reel-in speed with a throttle. They're reasonably affordable and can be run by the instructor alone; although it's better to have help.

Stationary Winch
with Turn Around Pulley

2. A Turn Around Pulley lets the instructor be next to the student during launch but is more risky since the student is going *away* from the instructor. It's harder to see how much distance remains to the pulley, and flying past the pulley is bad. Low tows, less than 10 feet high, are somewhat safer.

Vehicle Payout Towing

3. Truck or Boat towing uses a pay*out* winch to reach higher altitudes, commonly over 2000 feet, depending on line, location, and wind. It requires a longer run so that more line can pay out.

The truck (or boat) starts moving, paying out line and pulling the pilot with a controlled tension. It may be moving 40 mph but is paying line out at 20 mph so the effective pull is 20 mph. Line length quickly increases. The operator controls how fast the line pays out by controlling drum resistance (tension). Once the pilot releases, a motor winds the line in.

Some instructors use low power vehicles (quads) and short lines. In the right hands this can be done safely but is inherently very risky because a short line and lack of tension control makes *lockout* (next page) crash more likely.

More wind means more altitude, just like if you were pulling a kite. Experienced tow operators use their expertise to prevent excess climb by metering payout rate and keeping line tension within limits. Gliders and tow bridles can be overstressed although a proper weak link at the pilot should prevent catastrophe. Weak links are important since, if the payout drum stops, the line suddenly starts moving at the vehicle's speed which would impose enormous loads at the glider.

Boat towing typically nets the highest altitudes which is why it's used for maneuvers clinics or acrobatic (acro) practice. Extra precautions, such as flotation, must be in place in case the pilot goes for a dunk. Boat tows can be a bit bumpier if the water is rough since wave action gets transferred through the line.

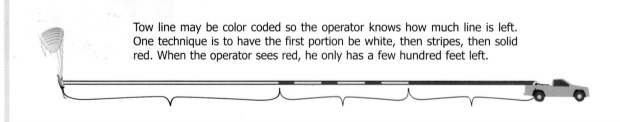

Tow line may be color coded so the operator knows how much line is left. One technique is to have the first portion be white, then stripes, then solid red. When the operator sees red, he only has a few hundred feet left.

Certification

Seek out instructors who are certified by a respected national organization that has a thorough paramotor program. Anyone can hang out a shingle but not everyone can demonstrate the skills and knowledge. There may be good uncertified instructors but then the onus is on you to determine competence and thoroughness.

Make sure they use a recognized syllabus to ensure everything gets covered.

Be aware that requirements for getting certified vary dramatically by organization. What minimums apply? What skills have to be shown to become rated? An instructor can hardly teach skills they don't possess. The USPPA has a thorough program but, even then there is variety in who is good at *teaching*.

No ratings program is perfect; they all rely on human instructors and, regardless of organization, there will be variety. This same diversity bedevils even government certification programs.

Training Aids

Training aids for paramotoring are marvelously simple and surprisingly effective. All reputable schools use some form of simulator and most have other aids to grease the wheels of learning.

One invaluable aid is getting students airborne and in control of *something* before the first powered solo. It can help alleviate first-flight anxieties and attendant problems. It can also reveal those very few people who react poorly to flight. If your school does not offer a method to do this (towing, hill launch or tandem), get at least one dual training flight in whatever craft is available—a powered parachute or other ultralight. The fewer sensory firsts, the better.

Towing

Towing uses an experienced tow operator to pull you up like a kite, have you control the craft briefly, then glide down for a landing (see preceding page). Increasing skill allows for higher flights although a few instructors do high tows from the start.

Towing is also used to get free flyers high enough to catch rising air currents (thermals) and soar without power. Payout winching is more common for that because it offers releases well above 2000 feet. Under the right conditions, soaring pilots can then fly for hours. You need more advanced skills for the more turbulent conditions but it offers a different sensory reward.

Low tows, less than 10 feet, have some safety benefits but still require extreme care since you'll be continuously close to the ground where small mistakes can be...impactful.

With some breeze (5-10 mph), hand towing is possible with appropriate precautions. It gives some minimal feel for the wing, flying, and landing flare. Don't take it lightly, though—the puller must know exactly what he's doing. Like other towing, it can quickly go awry if not done properly.

Hills

Bunny hills are small hills that allow ground-skimming free flight. You can practice launching, flying briefly and landing before ever strapping on the motor—a nice benefit. Light-weight harnesses make trudging up the hill easier. This is how most

Use your reader's QR code interpreter to bring up the USPPA's list of schools.

usppa.org/schools-training/

Lockout

During tow, if the pilot gets off heading, the towline's pull makes him want to bank more in that direction, aggravating the off-heading condition. Without correction the sideways pull can exceed his ability to correct: lockout.

It is more likely with inexperienced pilots, tow operators, or while using a turn-around pulley (see opposite page).

⚠ *Caution!*

Never, ever have a non-instructor pull you up with a rope (even by hand) or tie yourself to a stationary object while hooked into your glider. There are dynamics that make this weirdly dangerous.

Unsuspecting flyers have died trying this since it looks so easy. Lockout (above) is one of several maladies that can end with you arcing off sideways and down into a deadly whack. Beyond a certain point, the controls are insufficient to recover.

Wheels are a bit easier to learn on.

Tandem foot launching requires the instructor to wield a motor powerful enough for both occupants.

students learn to paraglide (without the motor)—launching from shallow hills at first then progressing up to bigger hills where soaring flights are possible.

The hill's slope should be about 4 to 1, where it drops 1 foot for every 4 feet forward, so that you can pull away from the hill once in flight. Your flight time (and height) can be metered by how far up the hill you start. Winds must be just right but most schools in hilly areas will have several sites to choose from.

Tandems

Tandems get you airborne with an experienced pilot at the helm of a two-place unit. Going up dual offers a valuable opportunity to experience flight, gain a basic understanding of the craft's handling, and give the instructor an opportunity to gauge your reactions to being aloft. That's good for both of you.

In most countries, tandem pilots adhere to extra equipment and pilot certification requirements since ultralights were intended for solo flight. In the U.S., tandems operate under an exemption from that and are for training only (see USPPA.org).

Wheeled tandems fall under more stringent regulations, at least in the U.S., where a government issued pilot's license is needed.

Control feel on Tandem rigs is heavier, and performance is sluggish, but the principles and directions are the same.

Wheels

Starting on wheels with a highly stable cart is another good method to learn. Some schools have students solo on wheels before moving on to foot launching. It will still take as much time to achieve the requisite skills, especially wing handling, but there's less chance for equipment damage early on. Foot launching is, of course, quite different from wheel launching (see Chapter 6).

Simulator

A simulator (opposite page) may be *the* most important piece of learning equipment. You sit in your motor unit, hanging by its intended hook-ins, and rehearse responses to important instructor-induced situations. It can be as simple as straps around a tree limb or an elaborate device with brake lines, bungees, and special riser spreaders. The more accurate, the better.

Critical aspects of flying will be learned from this simple setup. Besides certain normal flight drills, you will rehearse emergencies in which solutions are not always obvious and must be practiced. **Rehearsal is the only way to ensure learned responses will be performed when required.**

You will learn to react to instructor directives on the radio while coping with a flood of strange sensations. On that first flight, you'll be glad you paid attention in the simulator.

Throttle simulator

Chapter 3 lists what goes into making this simple practice throttle in case your school does not provide one.

Handling the wing is challenging enough—adding a throttle to the mix can make it feel like you're all thumbs. A throttle simulator is a regular throttle, possibly with cable, that feels and behaves just like its connected cousin. You get used to wing handling *and* working the throttle before putting on a motor. Otherwise, your first time with the motor—a difficult transition already—will be that much harder.

More advanced versions have a kill switch that beeps when pressed so the instructor knows you're pressing it—a critical reaction to learn. But even just practicing while holding a throttle-sized stick can help acclimate to the extra complication.

Weighted Frame

You may use a motor frame (no motor) for early training then progressively add weight as you improve. This great technique lets you learn kiting with the bulky motor and harness but without the full burden of its weight.

Multimedia

There are some highly useful videos: *Powered Paragliding Essentials, Risk and Reward, Instability II,* and the *Master Powered Paragliding* series, among others. *Airspace and Law for Ultralights* clarifies this difficult topic with live action and motion graphics. These tools, though, cannot begin to replace thorough instruction.

Radios

Being a solo craft makes communication critical. Good radios allow the instructor to give directions while you learn launching, flying and landing. If something goes wrong, or conditions change, the instructor can provide guidance. You'll either have to purchase or be provided with a helmet that works with the radio or comm system that your instructor uses. A few allow two way, hands-free communications.

Getting to that First Flight

As with all training, attitude drives success, enjoyment, and safety. Listening intently and reacting properly is key. It's not always easy; new pilots struggle to process instructions amidst the cacophony of sensory overload during early flights. Having an open mind and willingness to listen will help immensely—the instructor wants you to succeed but must be confident you'll respond. Be prepared to work. Even if the training seems harsh at times, or slow, it's due to progressing in a metered, orderly fashion.

In all likelihood you will cement a relationship with your instructor that will be enjoyed for years.

Simulator

1. Airlines know the value of good training aids. This $16 million 737 simulator lets Southwest pilots master skills they will never likely encounter.

2. Rob Catto's advanced virtual 3D simulator accurately models the unusual pendular behavior of a powered paraglider in pitch, power & roll.

3. On some simulators, you can practice taking radio directions while experiencing the noise, vibration and feeling of full power. This invaluable rehearsal helps ensure responses are swift and correct when it really counts. Emergency procedures should be rehearsed either with the motor running or other distractions until the response is automatic.

4. The most effective simulators allow manipulation of risers, brakes, and throttle. A practice reserve can be added also.

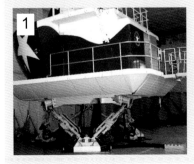   

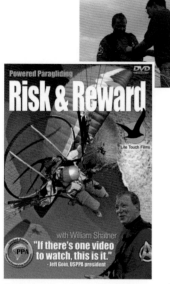

A must-see video is "Risk & Reward" which exposes where the risk is and how to avoid it. Watch it with your instructor. Ask about anything that's not clear but, far more important than watching, is rehearsing!

The video was a collaborative project of myself, Phil Russman and a number of USPPA instructors.

William Shatner, who appears several times in the video, got 12 flights of instruction in California then, several years later, asked for help flying into a Chicagoland charity event.

As a certified airplane pilot he knew the importance of training, recency of experience and personal limitations. Nick Scholtes agreed to be the instructor and we all worked together to make it happen safely. Below is Mr. Shatner flying East over the Northern Illinois landscape, accompanied by Nick (on the right), myself (shooting the picture) and several other Illinois pilots. The mission was a success. Score one for the Federation.

How Long Will It Take?

Training time will vary a lot depending on weather, equipment, location, and personal ability. If flyable conditions prevail, expect to solo in 2-5 days of solid training. A solo flight, with assistance, can be done quite early when extra precautions are taken.

Under rare circumstances you may get an assisted solo on the first day, possibly using wheels. It's a bit riskier since you wouldn't be prepared for emergencies.

Training time depends on your stamina, too. Being able to ground handle the wing (kiting) is the most important skill for launching—and it takes practice. Newly minted muscles will make their presence known after day one.

Learning is way more demanding than flying. Once equipped with the necessary skills, you'll only bear the motor's weight for a few minutes before launch transforms it into your magic chair. Expect at least 20 hours of "kiting" to get good enough—an investment that will return *years* of benefit.

Getting to the pilot level (PPG2 in the U.S.), where you can reasonably go out on your own, will nearly always take at least 8 days of training and 25 flights. If you only get a few days, you're not ready to be alone yet. Either fly with experienced pilots willing to be mentors or find another instructor.

Weather Dependent

We love *flying* in still air but it's not so great for early training where you want a 6 to 12 mph wind. Gusty winds, common at mid-day, are as bad for learning as they are for flying. Beaches usually serve up sweet sea breezes almost every warm afternoon. That's perfect for learning ground handling of the wing.

Winter weather is good if you can stand the cold. Low sun typically leaves smoother winds which is good for kiting, plus it's mellow for more of the day.

Progression

If you must travel to a distant school try scheduling at *least* 3 consecutive days—5 is better and a week improves your chance of acceptable weather. Depending on the location and time of year, that can be tough. Count yourself lucky if the school is within daily driving range but be prepared to be cancelled due to weather—call first.

When you arrive on the first day, you'll likely be introduced to the people, the school, and yes, the paperwork. Have a full pen and strong glasses—the forms are many and the print is fine. Of course there's risk (see Chapter 19) but don't be put-off by the dreadful sounding waivers—the sport has proven safer than they would lead you to believe.

Depending on what the school provides, expect to buy a few things. This book and the videos mentioned earlier were hopefully among them (kudos to your instructor). A kiting harness and helmet are common first purchases. It is far better not to buy gear in advance unless requested to do so by the school—each instructor has reasons for using what they do beyond profit margins. It's frequently compatibility with their training style or gear. Hopefully you can decide on a motor and wing by the time training has completed. Most motors and wings are just as good for flying as they are for training—so your best bet is to purchase the gear on which you learn. Then, after gaining a year or so of experience, you can better judge other brands.

Expect to be kiting in the first hour of your training if conditions cooperate. You'll need to practice this essential skill on your own but get rudimentary training first to avoid picking up bad habits. Since mid-day conditions are usually too rough for flying, expect to use that time for simulator or other ground work.

After gaining proficiency with wing handling using a kiting harness (15 - 25 hours is considered ideal), you'll add a throttle simulator, and then the motor (not running). You may do more practice in the simulator with the instructor on radio, possibly with the motor running.

The big day for your first flight will probably include some dress rehearsal and review of emergency procedures before actually going aloft. The solo may be "assisted," which can get you airborne earlier but in a less-prepared state. There is nothing wrong with that as long as you remain committed to further training.

For those able to do training in stages, learning to kite during an early visit is valuable so that you can then go home and practice. Mind the cautions given by your instructor—life-changing dangers lurk whenever you're hooked into the wing.

One common frustration is when you seem to reach a learning plateau or, worse yet, go backwards. It happens. One day everything is great, and the next day you're all fumbles. Maddening, but normal. Keep at it; success will come.

Previous Experience

So you're an airline pilot (or helicopter pilot or sailplane pilot or fighter pilot, etc)? That won't help much here. Past knowledge *will* prove useful for airspace, general aerodynamics, and a few other relevant bits but the reactions required of paramotoring can make a mockery of prior experience.

The critical maneuvering responses of this sport are vastly different than anything you've likely experienced. While not difficult, paramotoring deserves the same attention and respect as your first "V1 cuts" (or auto-rotations or spot landings or hydraulic failures or whatever).

This warning is most pertinent for skydivers who suffer negative transfer. There are, after all, two toggles in your hands, but don't be tempted to think of the paraglider as just an efficient jump canopy. Some maneuvers done by skydivers are nothing short of deadly in a paraglider. One experienced skydiver-turned-PPG instructor tells how he nearly killed himself this way. Flying may, in fact, be easier, but un-learning certain behaviors will be harder. Pay close attention to the limits of brake pull and low, steep maneuvering—give the craft great respect, especially at first.

The worst thing you can do to short-change your training based on perceived existing capability. Such arrogance has preceded the demise of many who took this approach.

Training will be frustrating yet invigorating. It will have highs and lows but should provide an experience like none other, whose value will far exceed the effort.

Regardless of past experience, treat this sport with great respect. Safety is almost entirely up to the pilot's attitude. A cocky approach can race past obnoxiousness and become lethally dangerous.

1. A skilled skydiver can expend his excess swooping energy over many yards after a long dive. But don't try this in a paraglider until you've mastered control and realize the limitations and dark corners.

Eric Dufour (below, wearing hat) works with the History Channel's Josh Bernstien, an outdoor adventurist who learned powered paragliding for fun and for his show.

Josh enjoyed the fruits of their combined labors. He had the right attitude, listened intently to his mentor, and excelled. After five-days of training he had nearly 10 solo flights under his belt.

Instructor Score Sheet

An instructor is your most important choice. This tool help appoint higher values to qualities of higher importance. They vary by individual, but it's a good starting point. Some will require either a visit or personal recommendations.

Notice how *un*important gear selection is—success depends more on quality instruction than brand. A *good* instructor will know what works even within the brand he sells.

_7_ 10 points. Can he fly to the level you're seeking? For new students that just means consistently launching, landing, solid *basic* ground handling, and maneuvering.

If you're moving on to precision flying, handling high winds, competition, or acro, then the instructor must have those skills. Not that many do.

_3_ 10 points. Can he teach? This involves demeanor, personality and the ability to convey ideas clearly. The best test, whenever possible, is a personal visit.

_8_ 8 points. Do your schedules match? It's a practical but important concern: you have to connect, preferably with high frequency, especially in the early stages.

_8_ 8 points. Does the instructor emphasize quality and thoroughness? If his talk or advertisements are all about being cheap and quick then don't expect.

_6_ 6 points. Does he use a syllabus from the national organization or licensing body? This is the minimum to ensure you're covering what's considered necessary.

_5_ 5 points. Is he seasoned? Has he flown a wide variety of equipment in a wide variety of conditions and locations? One year is not much seasoning but it could be depending on what was done in that year.

_0_ 5 points. Can he support you with spare parts and know how?

_3_ 3 points. Is he professional: certified, responsible, reliable, prompt, etc.?

_1_ 3 points. Is he efficient? Does he maximize students' time by having them practice when conditions are good and do ground work when they're not? If they could be kiting but are not, or he's flying while he should be training, he's wasting time.

_3_ 3 points. Can he issue a license or ratings? The importance of this varies based on whether or not you want insurance or plan to fly at sites/events that require them.

_3_ 3 points. Does he have a good place to fly? Kite (steady winds)? That can be a big problem and your safety is proportional to the size of the training field.

_3_ 3 points. Does he have good training aids? At least a simulator with working brakes and riser system and a throttle simulator for kiting practice.

_0_ 3 points. Can he get you airborne using either hill, towing, or tandem flights? If he does towing, is he certified? Towing is weirdly dangerous, especially in the hands of marginally trained tow operators (called tow techs).

_2_ 2 points. Will he test fly your gear? It's important that he knows what you face.

_2_ 2 points. How much? The importance of cost obviously depends on your finances but skimping on training rarely turns out to save money in the long run.

_2_ 2 points. Does he *rent* gear? Grant this more points if you want to learn without making the big financial outlay for equipment purchase.

_2_ 2 points. Will the training site reflect where you'll fly? If you'll be flying in Denver (high elevation), learning in Florida (sea level) may be less ideal.

_2_ 2 points. What success rate does he have? In the U.S., you can see how many ratings an instructor has issued at USPPA.org. But the best measure of success, by far, is seeing competent prodigy out there mastering their craft.

_2_ 2 points. What kind of gear will you train on? Lighter is better but you do have to have enough thrust (see Chapter 28). Some choices make it harder to learn on.

Of course, it isn't just numbers but these warrant consideration. A lot will depend on the vibe you get when talking to a prospective instructor. Unless you live next to a highly respected school, it's not likely to see a perfect score. A good instructor will frequently become a friend and resource for your entire flying career. Choose carefully; it's an incredible adventure.

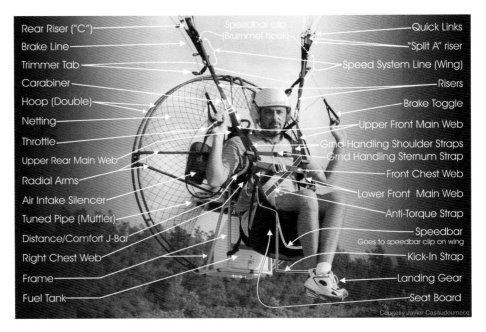

Rear Riser ("C")
Brake Line
Trimmer Tab
Carabiner
Hoop (Double)
Netting
Throttle
Upper Rear Main Web
Radial Arms
Air Intake Silencer
Tuned Pipe (Muffler)
Distance/Comfort J-Bar
Right Chest Web
Frame
Fuel Tank

Speedbar clip
(Brummel hook)

Quick Links
"Split A" riser
Speed System Line (Wing)
Risers
Brake Toggle
Upper Front Main Web
Grnd Handling Shoulder Straps
Grnd Handling Sternum Strap
Front Chest Web
Lower Front Main Web
Anti-Torque Strap
Speedbar
Goes to speedbar clip on wing
Kick-In Strap
Landing Gear
Seat Board

Courtesy Javier Casaudoumecq

Gearing Up

If only the Wright Brothers could see our stuff now. This overview covers the strange collection of gear that gets us airborne. A more thorough treatment of gear is in Section V, and maintenance of gear is covered in Chapter 12.

The Wing

The paraglider is your most important component. While it can suffer numerous individual failures and still fly, it degrades with time and use. When a wing wears out or fails an inspection, it must be repaired or replaced.

During flight, air goes into leading edge (front) openings, then through internal holes, to create a very slight internal pressure that keeps the shape against tension in the lines. Tension is always pulling outward, front to back and tip to tip.

We share almost identical technology with soaring (free flight) pilots who launch from hills or get towed up. Purpose-built motoring wings may sacrifice some amount of efficiency for speed and heavier load carrying capability.

Standard and Reflex Gliders

Standard paragliders, favored by soaring pilots, are optimized for efficiency. Reflex gliders, more common in motoring, are optimized for speed and collapse resistance at higher speeds. Reflex models are usually more complicated and may have special handling requirements, especially at their fastest speeds.

Fabric

Most modern gliders use a coated ripstop nylon that is nearly airtight. Additional coatings improve longevity at some expense in weight and launch ease. With care, a wing will last 300-500 hours but abuse or neglect could halve that. Lightweight models, or *mountain wings*, sacrifice durability for very low weight and launch ease.

Not all motors have all features, but these are common. It has high hook-in points and uses *underarm*, or *comfort* bars, to keep harness webbing away from the pilot's body.

Webbing is what we call the large load-bearing straps.

Why Is It So Expensive?

The main answer is that our gear is not mass produced with lots of robots. It is mostly hand-made, welded in jigs and assembled by human craftsmen one at a time.

Prices derive largely from labor, and building a paramotor or wing is time consuming. Wings may be cut with a laser but the sewing is still labor intensive. Engines, which constitute up to half the cost of a new paramotor, are also largely hand-built, even if parts are made by CNC machines.

Secondly, they are built in relatively small quantity.

Wings don't like heat, sun, dampness, harsh chemicals, sharp objects, gnawing insects, or snagging on things. "Ripstop" just means that tears don't spread *easily*.

Ultraviolet (UV) light causes nearly invisible degradation that weakens the fabric and makes it porous. Many manufacturers consider 300 hours of direct UV the maximum lifetime exposure. Thankfully, limiting sun time to early morning or late afternoon lowers total UV so it may last much longer than that.

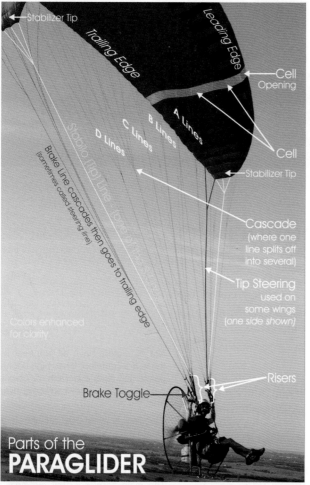

Parts of the
PARAGLIDER

⚠ *Caution!*

A line can break, undetected, inside its protective outer sheath. Sharp bending is the most likely cause, usually from yanking on a wing that's stuck on something.

To find such breaks run the line through your fingers, feeling for a "lip" where the Kevlar core has separated. If you find one, the line is unable to bear any significant load and must be changed. Brake lines are woven from a single material and have no Kevlar core.

Higher performance gliders may have completely, or partially unsheathed, lines. That reduces drag at some expense in durability.

Lines

Suspension lines (A, B, C, & D lines) support the pilot and motor, of course, but they also form the wing's primary airfoil shape. Shorten the rear lines, for example, and you pull the rear wing down. Forward lines, the "A's," bear most of the weight, followed by the next row (the "B's") and so on. Reflex gliders are even more heavily loaded on their A lines. Some wings, especially those used in free flight (no motor), have 3 rows, aka *3 line gliders*, while others have 4 rows. A very few competition soaring wings have only 2 rows of lines. Line *cascades* reduce the total number of lines and therefore drag.

Each line individually carries relatively little weight but must be strong enough to handle sudden "pops" in case part of the wing folds down then "pops" back to shape.

Most gliders have small loops sewn into the wing where the lines attach for easy line replacement. A very few models have lines sewn right into the wing—not good when lines need to be replaced.

Main lines (*not* brake lines) are made with a strong bundle of finely spun material, frequently Kevlar, and are usually sheathed in a thin protective outer weave. This is very strong in the stretch direction (high tensile strength) but degrades quickly if bent sharply, heated excessively, or put away wet. Avoid walking on or hooking lines in a way that could bend them sharply.

Brake and Tip Steering Lines:

Brake (or *steering*) lines run from the trailing edge (back of wing), down through a brake pulley and into *toggles* held by the pilot. Brake lines are more flexible to better handle bending at the pulley and have less tensile strength since they carry no flight load.

They pull one side of the trailing edge down, causing drag that slows that side down. The pilot swings opposite which actually causes the bank.

Most reflex gliders, when flown fast, are not intended to be steered with their regular brakes. Instead they have *tip steering* which pulls only the tip's trailing edge to cause a turn without affecting the main airfoil shape.

Risers

Our cool, variable geometry wings are partially managed in flight through strap-like *risers*. Their primary job is transfering and spreading load from the carabineers to the lines. A riser has individual risers, lettered A through D (or C for 3 riser systems) that may be color-coded although the colors are not standardized.

Wing lines go from the wing down to the risers which connect to your carabiner. Each row of lines attaches to a riser through *quick links* (also called *maillons*) to keep the lines apart and easier to work with.

Changing the length of a riser or line changes the shape of the wing (not recommended.) Wings and risers are certified together so optional riser sets should only be installed after verifying compatibility. The most common reason to switch risers is to put motor risers on a free-flight wing. This adds *trimmers* and makes it easier to reach the brakes and lines when flying high hook-in machines.

Trimmers

Most wings intended for motoring have a strap-slider attached to each rear riser that, when extended in flight, increases airspeed by letting the back of the wing up (reducing *angle of incidence*). That confers a 10% to 35% speed increase with the biggest increases on reflex models. Going faster requires more power to fly level or incurs a higher sink rate when gliding. *Reflex* wings usually have a longer trimmer range.

Split A's

Some wings have Split A's (Fig. 2.5) where the outer A line has its own riser. Among other things, it's easier to reach up and pull down just that line to collapse the tip in a descent maneuver called *big ears* (covered later).

Quick Links

Metal fittings (*maillons*) between fabric elements are commonly used to reduce wear and make changes easier. In this case, metal quick links connect the riser to paraglider lines and a rubber O-ring keeps the lines tightly together. When lines are replaced they are removed from this fitting on the riser and the wing.

Speed System

A speed system comes with most wings. The speedbar line on each riser connects to a harness-mounted, foot-activated speed bar. Pushing the bar lowers the leading edge by lowering the A lines mostly, the B's somewhat less, and the C's even less. How much each one is lowered depends on design since it changes the airfoil shape.

The wing portion of a speed system connects to the harness-mounted speedbar using *sister clips* that are made to be easily attached/detached. They employ 2 pulleys which act like block and tackle to give mechanical leverage. It takes more speedbar

Speed Control

Trimmers and speedbar are different approaches to speed control. Basically, speedbar lowers the leading edge while trimmers raise the trailing edge. They may also deform the airfoil in different ways. *Neutral trim* is usually considered whatever puts the quick links straight across as shown on the first risers at right.

Trimmers can be set while the speedbar must be held out, using 10+ pounds of push, with your feet.

Not all wings have both systems: soaring wings tend to only have speedbar while motor wings tend to have both.

Sister Clips (shown below), also called Brummel or Inglefield clips, connect the harness's speedbar to the wing.

Here is how to attach a standard looped line to one sister clip, then connect the clips together before flight:

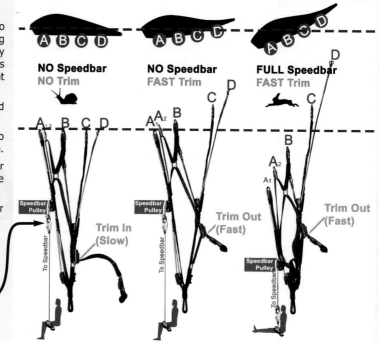

NO Speedbar NO Trim

NO Speedbar FAST Trim

FULL Speedbar FAST Trim

Speedbar Pulley

To Speedbar

Trim In (Slow)

Trim Out (Fast)

Trim Out (Fast)

Here is a reflex cross section. It allows a wing to fly faster by effectively reducing area. Trade-offs may include efficiency and control complexity.

Reflex

A   B   C   D   Brake

Normal

A   B   C   D   Brake

travel but is easier to push.

Speedbar is typically more effective than trimmers, and it can be released immediately by letting off the considerable foot pressure. Trimmers stay set.

On standard (non reflex) gliders, it is usually best to avoid speedbar use *and* fast trim, especially in turbulence (see Chapter 18 on *front tuck*). Many reflex gliders *can* be flown trimmed fast and on speedbar with certain precautions. Some models may even be *more* collapse resistant this way but should be steered using tip steering—special toggles that only deflect a small part of the paralider's tip. Always consult the wing's manual.

Not all motor harnesses have the necessary footbar connection points and pulleys, but they are easy to retrofit (see Chapter 18). Even if it is equipped, most schools will not have it hooked up for your early flights.

The Harness

The *harness* supports you and your motor in flight, making it the next most important piece after your wing. It's usually mated to a specific motor frame and has at least a seat with leg loops, waist strap, and a way to connect to the motor and wing. But there is a *lot* more than meets the eye.

Wheeled craft frequently have just a seat and belt, but offer multiple wing attachments to allow balancing; you want a slightly nose-high hang angle. Simple add-on carts may use the paramotor's harness but must provide additional support for ground operations.

Harnesses are usually overbuilt with webbing capable of sup-

These two harnesses detach easily from the motor for practicing wing control (kiting) and easy transport.

Courtesy Kati Harris

porting many times their rated loads. But steep turns or turbulence can push those limits, and UV exposure, chafing, chemical or other damage can reduce margins further.

During launch the wing first lifts the motor's weight then your weight by the harness's leg loops. You wiggle a bit, kick or push out a seat, and sit back until ready for landing. The harness must be adjusted properly and be comfortable—mostly it must not block leg circulation which could leave you numb for landing.

Numerous adjustments (see Chapter 12) allow fitting your weight, height, and desires, so expect your instructor to spend some time getting you situated with it. Among other things, adjustments determine how your motor will hang, how it will handle torque, where the brakes will be and how to best get into the seat (not always a simple matter). Adjustments are critical—failure to do them properly could yield a dangerous or un-flyable machine.

On a few brands, you don the harness first, then the motor.

Diagonal Anti-Torque Strap

Propeller torque causes numerous turning evils, so some harnesses add a strap that transfers pull from one side to the other to help alleviate it (see Chapter Cover).

Machines with *weight shift* (shifting one riser up and the other down to help turn) do not use this strap because it reduces weight shift. Plus, it reduces only one small element of torque's effect. Chapter 23 has more on twisting's causes and cures.

Ground Handling Straps

Ground handling, or *carry straps*, are made to better carry the motor around on the ground. They bear no flying loads and may include a chest (sternum) strap to keep the motor from sliding off your shoulders. Some may allow easy loosening once airborne for more comfort in flight.

Over-Shoulder J-Bars

Nearly all machines have some kind of *spreader system* as shown at right. High hook-in systems that use over-shoulder bars impart less wing motion to the pilot which feels smoother in turbulence. There is no difference in actual collapse resistence but it feels better.

Systems that hook to the wing via a metal bar usually add a backup D shackle to carry flight loads in case the bar breaks.

A more modern variation uses pivoting or floating J-bars that allow enough movement to give some feel for the wing and allows some amount of weight shift. This keeps the pilot hanging in the same way as regular over-shoulder J-bars but without being as stiff. J-bar machines are considered high hook-in systems since the wing attaches above the pilot's shoulders.

Underarm or "Comfort" Bars

Underarm bars are another way to prevent motor thrust from pinching the pilot against its front straps. Like J-bars, they transfer force to the forward harness straps that are under the pilot's arms. The bars may swivel up and down to provide weight shift steering. At least one brand allows them to swivel outward for easier ingress and egress but **they must not be allowed to swivel *inward!***

Harness Styles & Spreader Systems

Spreaders transfer the motor's thrust forward to keep the pilot from being squeezed between the backrest and front harness webbing.

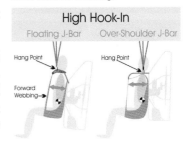

High Hook-In
Floating J-Bar   Over-Shoulder J-Bar

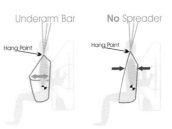

Underarm Bar   No Spreader

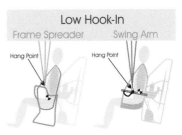

Low Hook-In
Frame Spreader   Swing Arm

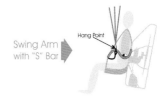

Swing Arm with "S" Bar

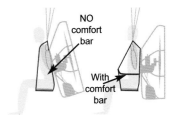

NO comfort bar

With comfort bar

Fig. 2.10 Quick Release Buckle

Simple Rectangle Buckle

Buckles should be quick release to allow for quick egress in case of fire or ditching (water landing). Simple rectangle buckles are not quick release.

Diaper Buckle

Fig. 2.15

courtesy Alex Varv

If the chest strap is hooked up, at least one leg strap is, too. Forgetting both leg staps can be catastrophic.

Releasable Motor

Carry Straps

Floating J Bar

Pull Rings release motor

An uncommon feature on this older design allows the motor to be jettisoned in case of fire or water landing. In Germany, where it originated, that used to be a requirement.

On some systems, carabiners attach right to the spreader bar—usually to more closely mimic low hook-in free-flight harnesses and to mate better with soaring wings which have longer risers. Machines with pivoting arms will have hook-in points that allow effective weight shift steering. Those without pivoting arms are *not* intended to have much weight shift capability.

Soft Harness

Only the simplest harnesses, mostly on older, direct drive units, don't use separating (spreader) bars at all. These would only be suitable for smaller pilots.

The Buckles

The vast majority of harnesses have quick release buckles (Fig. 2.10) with pinch buttons on the side. They are not designed to be released while under tension.

In an effort to save weight, you may find a few harnesses with simple rectangular buckles (shown at left). The small rectangle goes through the larger one at an angle. Pulling it tight flattens the pieces together in a strong hold. These should be avoided due to being treacherously difficult to disconnect in an emergency.

Get in the habit of fastening your leg loops first—it may be a life-saver if you start free flying (without a motor) where launching without the leg straps fastened can be fatal. With a motor it's normally just embarrassing unless you try to hang on and take off. Always buckle at least one leg loop, even when you're just wearing the motor, to avoid accidentally taking off with both leg loops unbuckled.

Make sure the buckles are properly fastened too—try to pull them apart. If they're not solidly fastened you could fall out after liftoff. The chest strap keeps the motor from falling off backwards during launch or abort.

Some harnesses help prevent forgetting the leg straps. These "diaper" styles (Fig. 2.15) make the chest strap fasten into a center piece that comes up from between your legs. If the chest portion is fastened then at least one leg is fastened too. Some may also use a central connection point where all the straps come together and fasten with one action. On those, make sure there is no way to accidentally unbuckle since you would fall out when getting out of the seat for landing. Their advantage is rapid escape in case of emergency (water or fire).

The Motor

The motor unit includes engine, frame and harness. On some units the harness can be detached easily enough to use for kiting practice. Harnesses are usually designed with a particular frame in mind but some work on many models.

Any good school will match the pilot to a motor based on his size, weight and expected launch elevation. Chapter 27 has details on options. Expect a 2-stroke engine with 80 to 320 cc's (cubic centimeters of piston displacement).

Training success has little to do with brand as long as your instructor is familiar with it. If you bring your own gear, then there may be a learning curve while the instructor learns its nuances. If you bring unacceptable gear (too heavy, too little power, dangerous, etc.) then the instructor, rightfully, may not be willing to train you on it.

Carabiners

Carabiners provide the connection from wing to motor/harness. They are like mountain climbing hardware but use a locking gate to prevent accidental opening. Most still allow one-handed operation.

Almost none allow releasing under tension like sport parachute systems. Ours must be deliberately unclipped. In fact, releasing under tension is nearly impossible. The need to ensure staying connected while flying outweighs the advantage of a quick disconnect. Even after a reserve deployment, we don't "cut away" from the paraglider as skydivers do.

The strongest carabiners are made of steel but lighter aluminum versions have proven sufficient if not abused. Strength is rated by how many Kilonewtons (KNs) they can bear without deforming while the gate is closed. One KN is about 225 pounds. 18 to 22 KN is typical for aluminum whereas steel carabiners go up to 28 KN. They usually list the much lower strength rating for when the gate is open but should never be flown that way.

Nearly invisible scratches and cracks can dramatically degrade the carrying capability of carabiners, especially aluminum ones, so treat them with care. Some instructors recommend periodic replacement, especially if they've been dropped.

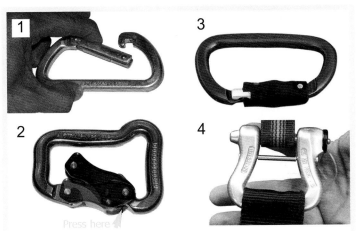

1. Avoid non-locking carabiners for flying: the gate can open by accident.

2. Press-gate carabiners have a self locking mechanism that can be operated by **one hand**. Pushing at the arrow both unlocks *and* opens the gate.

3. Another locking gate style where you push the green button and twist the gate to open. Requires 2 hands.

4. This uncommon style opens by pushing the small button in the load pin to remove it. Requires 2 hands.

Most carabiners are made of aluminum with a strength of at least 18 Kilonewtons (KN). Slightly heavier steel models go up to 28 KN.

This *Quick-out* model can be released (opened) under load—great if you're getting dragged, not so great if it happens accidentally while flying. It does take very specific motions so that's *very* unlikely. These are rarely used in powered paragliding.

Kiting Harness

Don't skimp on a kiting harness—you'll spend a lot of time in it. Given the importance of wing handling skills, it should be portable, convenient and comfy.

Some motors have easily removed harnesses for kiting practice—otherwise, it's not worth the hassle. Harnesses with only high hook-in points will cause back strain after a short time.

Paramotor Kiting Harnesses

Purpose Built: Kiting is different from flying so you'll be most comfortable in a harness made for the purpose. There's a lot of variety. Make sure the harness allows for low hook-in points and has strong carabiners: you may get lifted in a gust and need it to hold.

Free Flight Harnesses work, especially lightweight models, but are less comfortable than the best purpose built models and are more expensive. Full size versions are safer for flying but cumbersome for kiting.

Other Harnesses, like those for mountain climbing and utility work, can be used. Try to have separate attachment points about 4 inches above your waistline. **Detachable paramotor harnesses** range from perfect to acceptable depending on style.

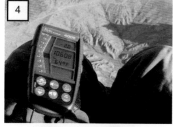

1. A mirror to see how cool you look flying this thing. And yes, it shows fuel level too.

2. Tachometer and Cylinder Head Temperature (CHT).

3. Wrist altimeter shows altitude, vertical speed, compass, and barometric pressure. It tells time, too.

4. Variometer for climb and descent. It also gives happy beeping for climb or sad buzzing for descent.

5. You can even get fuel flow, fuel, and flight time remaining.

Instruments

Simplicity is the sport's hallmark but some instruments are useful. And history shows that, if it can be carried, it eventually will. Start small, though; extra stuff adds weight, can foul moving parts, and fancies propellers. Anything that *can* fall off, *will* fall off, and it *will* go through the prop.

EGT and CHT

Exhaust Gas Temperature (EGT) is taken from the motor's exhaust stream at roughly its hottest point. Above-normal readings are generally the first indication of a lean fuel-to-air mixture and an impending outflow of dollars. Drilling into the exhaust can shorten its life.

Cylinder Head Temperature (CHT) uses a washer-like pickup at the spark plug. Since the metal has to heat up, it responds slower than EGT but is useful for the same reason: telling whether the engine is running too lean or not getting enough cooling. Normal EGT but hot CHT suggests poor cooling.

Tachometer

Motor RPM is the most common metric of power because it's easy to measure and highly relevant. Our props are fixed pitch, meaning the blade angle never changes in flight, so more RPM equals more thrust. Most tachometers count electronic pulses to the spark plug and display that as RPM. A few models work optically (see Chapter 28) but those are mostly for working on motors.

Altimeter

An altimeter reports altitude using atmospheric pressure (or *barometric pressure*) since air pressure decreases as you go up. Depending on initial setting, it can display altitude above mean sea level (MSL) or, if set to zero before launch, displays height above ground level (AGL) during flight.

Altimeter watches are generally accurate to within 20 feet, plenty good for us. An altimeter is essential near restricted or controlled airspace, but make sure it's set to launch elevation before takeoff.

Altitude from GPS devices is less accurate although they don't have to be set. GPS units with a 20 foot lateral error will likely have a 100 foot vertical error.

Variometer

A Variometer gives vertical speed—how fast you're climbing or descending. Most models beep faster in proportion to increasing climb rate and buzz with lowering pitch in proportion to increasing descent rate. They're most helpful for soaring but are not terribly common with paramotor pilots.

Phone apps (see opposite page) can provide altimeter and variometer functionality depending on hardware model. Very inexpensive out-of-date smartphones (now just called phones) can connect to Wi-Fi, download the apps and maps, and use its onboard GPS without paying for service.

Multi Instruments (right) provide several parameters in one device. This one has variometer, tachometer, and cylinder head temperature.

Accessories

So many gadgets and so few places to put them. But remember that, if you bring it, you've got to launch with it, muck with it in flight, and keep it out of the prop. Below are some of the basics with more in Chapter 28.

Navigation

You might think it's hard to get lost at 25 mph, but you'd be surprised. It's easy to lose track while exploring your new 3D reality—engrossed in the cool perch—and forget about position.

Dozens of GPS navigators make navigation a snap but used, GPS-equipped, smart phones are another inexpensive solution. Applications have been created for free flight and motoring that, among many other features, can tell wind direction at your altitude by doing one level circle.

Chapter 28 has more hardware suggestions, and usage is covered in Chapter 13.

Helmet / Hearing Protection

Most schools will wisely require a helmet for brain protection. Use one for kiting, too, where you can get tossed around near the ground. Full face helmets protect you during "face plants"—the non-flattering result of falling forward—but they restrict head motion which can limit vision, mostly because they're bigger.

Many PPG helmets have quality hearing protection with audio and a microphone. The quietest designs avoid having a chin strap go through the ear cups. Most have a push-to-talk (PTT) switch on an ear cup or, rarely, on a coil that goes out to your hand.

Communications

There are *many* choices but, unfortunately, no standards.

In the U.S., low quality FRS (Family Radio Service) radios are common for both training and pilot-to-pilot conversation. These usually include some channels in the GMRS band which allow more power but require an FCC license.

Bluetooth comm systems have gained popularity especially since they may also allow using cell phones or other inputs without wires. Cell phoning aloft may be illegal and creates a huge distraction.

Some schools, clubs or pilot groups use 2-meter radios which are far more reliable. They do cost more and require an amateur (HAM) license, but that only takes passing a multiple choice test. Morse code is no longer required, at least in the U.S.

Check with your instructor since helmets and radios rarely play well together (see Chapter 28). Schools may have a specific model they use for communications and will usually provide it.

Aviation radios can be used, especially if you plan to fly from airports. Regulations may require a Radio or Pilot License; check your country's laws. Frequencies used depend on location and purpose; check FAA AC 90-50D for frequency allocation. No license has been required in the U.S. since 1996.

Used, no-plan, smart phones can serve as inexpensive navigators, Db meters for sound level, wind indication, and more.

There are also applications for paramotoring that cater to our specific needs.

Courtesy PPGps.info

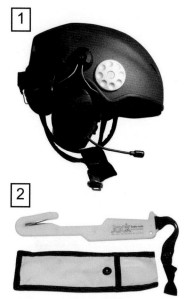

1. This purpose-built helmet for motoring has been fitted with a Bluetooth hookup to work with a variety of radios or even cell phones.

Plugs are not standard, even those that look alike, so Bluetooth, in spite of its own compatibility woes, may be a better solution.

2. It's hard to cut yourself with a hook knife but easy to cut through harness webbing or lines in an emergency. It should be mounted in a readily reachable area.

Footware

In most cases boots help prevent ankle injuries while running for launch or landing. They're more beneficial on rough surfaces and benefit free-flyers more since their launch sites are frequently strewn with nature's rocky randomness. Choose boots that allow easy running—in light winds, you'll be thankful. Favor those with laces or loops instead of hooks which can catch paraglider lines during inflation.

If you'll be training in grass, have something that's waterproof. Otherwise, bring many changes of socks.

Hook Knife

It's unlikely that a hook knife will be needed, but if you're getting dragged or pulled under water, it may be the only way out. It can quickly slice through lines and harness webbing with minimal risk to yourself.

Reserve

Reserve, or rescue, parachutes offer a last-chance survival option for major wing malfunctions, midairs, or structural failures. Without proper installation and understanding, a reserve can add more risk than benefit mostly due to the possibility of accidental or improper deployment.

Reserves go in a pouch attached to the motor's frame. Bridles (risers) then attach to the paramotor harness in such a way as to avoid entanglement during deployment. The bridles connect near the paramotor's normal carabiners to insure sufficient strength to endure opening shock while providing proper hang angle (tilt-back of the motor). Some motor harnesses have special reserve attachments, usually above the main carabiner hook-in. The reserve's pouch has a handle with pins that must be installed and inspected to prevent accidental deployment, a very serious situation (see Chapter 12).

Most paramotor schools do not use reserves during initial training because of the extra weight and the risk of accidental deployment. Schools that teach free flight first *do* frequently put new students on reserve-equipped harnesses if they will be flying high enough for it to work.

This is the only time a pilot ever wants to see his reserve outside its container. Chapter 28 has more choices, Chapter 12 has more on installation, and Chapter 19 covers deployment.

A built in-reserve container is under the seat. That makes launching a bit harder because the seat is forced away from the frame.

Steerable reserves may allow the pilot to glide away from dangerous obstacles like water or power lines. On initial open they descend vertically, but when the pilot releases its steering lines, gliding starts. They go about 2 feet forward for every foot down.

This is the most common type of reserve. It's made to open quickly, reliably, and have a relatively slow descent for its size.

By Remy Swaab

Handling the Wing

"But officer, I'm just flying my kite."

Ground handling the glider, or *kiting*, is getting the wing overhead and controlling it in a breeze. Fortunately, it's fun too since ground handling is our sport's seminal skill. It's also the most challenging one to really master.

A Kiting War puts kiting skills to the test against other pilots as each one tries to be the last one up.

The initial goal of kiting is to keep the glider overhead while standing mostly in one place, then ultimately, to make it go where *you* want with the least amount of effort. To master kiting is to master launching—it will help you succeed, make you look good, and spare much costly aggravation.

Finesse and higher-wind skills come with practice which, thankfully, can be done in any open area having a smooth, steady breeze. Be careful, though, it is surprisingly risky without proper instruction.

Your site should be big, free of fabric-tearing, line-snagging protrusions, and be upwind of buildings or other obstructions that would cause turbulence (a *wind shadow*). You also want smooth terrain downwind—space you're willing to get dragged through if the wind picks up. A wing's powerful pull in a gust can easily be overpowering.

Use your instructor. He can save enormous frustration with sometimes important and seemingly trivial tips. Once the basics are down and you understand the limitations of when to kite, doing it on your own will hasten the training process dramatically. Repetition greases the wheels of progress.

Few students will want to attempt kiting in more than about a 10 mph breeze and it takes at least 7 mph to practice effectively. As skill develops, you may be able to handle winds as light as 5 mph and as much as 14 mph.

Rear Riser Pull

Wing is Depowered

> ⚠ **Caution!**
>
> In even moderate conditions, be ready to handle the wing as soon as you hook in. A sudden gust can quickly unravel your tenuous balance. Practice deflation methods in moderate conditions to be better prepared for ugliness.

Brake Positions/Pressures

References to hand positions use the descriptions below. Learn to equate them to brake *pressure*, not position. They vary by glider; one glider's position 2 may do very little, while on another it's highly responsive.

0   1   2
UP   ¼

3   4   5
½   FULL

Deflating the Wing

A wing in a wind has a mighty pull; before learning to control it, you must first learn how to depower/disable it. Here are some techniques.

- The common method is to pull both brakes hard until the wing comes down (see pg. 36). First reduce brake pull so that it surges overhead. Just before it starts moving back, pull hard so the wing comes quickly down through the power band (highest pull force).

- Reach up and pull the rear risers (D's on 4-line gliders) as far as possible. Hold them. They may be hard to find while being dragged, so rehearse doing this under more controllable conditions. Rear risers are easy to find which is handy if you're about to lose control. On some wings the C's (see pg. 36) may be more effective but are harder to find in a hurry. Plus, with the rear risers, the wing is more likely to stay on the ground once it's down.

- As a last resort, pull only one brake hard then keep pulling that brake line hand-over-hand if necessary, until you're holding tip fabric. The wing may flip over and swirl around, twisting the lines, but keep pulling. You'll be happy to be wearing decent gloves.

If the wing is pulling hard, try walking or running towards it to reduce the relative wind. Your goal is to grab tip fabric, then keep pulling it, hand over hand by the upper surface, until holding approximately the center cell.

Brake Positions/Pressures

We'll reference brake positions using a fractional position or a number from 0 to 5. Zero is hands up and five is the maximum brake pull possible without stalling the wing (flying stops, dropping begins). Forearms are kept vertical through 4.

Think of control inputs as *pressures* more than positions. If it takes 5 pounds of pressure to get position 3, remember the 5 pounds. Every wing is different too, and lower hook-in motors tend to have lower hand positions than motors with higher hook-ins. When trying a new wing or motor, be particularly careful about excessive brake pull. If possible, adjust your brake lines so the following positions work—they offer the most brake travel.

- Position 0: Hands up, no brake pull, toggles are stowed or at the pulley.

- Position 1: Starting to feel brake pressure, around ½ pound.

- Position 2: About the weight of your arms. An extended thumb would be near ear height on most configurations, but see where it is by resting your arms.

- Position 3: Intermediate.

- Position 4: About shoulder height. your forearm is kept vertical in this position. It is the most brake pull that should ever be used for normal flight.

- Position 5: Anything beyond position 4 should only be used for landing flare, managing strong turbulence, or advanced maneuvering. Use with extreme care.

These positions depend a bit on your glider but it should be adjusted so that these positions generally work. Beware that a glider *can* stall well before reaching position 5 under some conditions.

Preparing To Practice

You've got a wing, harness, helmet, and gloves—it's time to practice. If there's more than about a 6 mph wind you'll probably do a *reverse inflation* (pictured right); otherwise you'll do a *forward inflation* where you run with the wing coming up behind you. Forwards, as they're called, are much harder, primarily in very light wind. That's what we'll start with.

Unless you're doing a calm wind demonstration, don a helmet before clipping in; kiting is one of the most likely times to need it. Pilots have been seriously hurt after getting caught by a big gust. "Helmet on before hooking in."

If possible, have (or make) something to simulate a throttle (practice throttle). After learning basic kiting, start using it in whatever hand your motor uses. It will grease the transition to motor launching but, sadly, not all instructors use them.

Reverse Inflation
Bringing the wing overhead while facing it.

Forward Inflation
Used in light or no wind, you run with the wing behind.

Cable Stop
Compression Spring
Fuel Line
Spring Hook
Throttle Simulator: from hardware store and bicycle shop.
Bicycle Shifter/Brake Cable
Bicycle Brake Assembly (used)
PVC Pipe

Untangling Lines: Taming the Dips and Loops

One way to keep risers together.

Prevention is easier than untangling. Keep steering toggles on their keepers, put risers together (as shown at left) or in a riser bag, and keep the risers from going into the lines when finished.

Tangles still happen, and these steps can help remove them. Whatever you do, don't disconnect anything! Find a clear, open area to lay out the wing like a forward launch. As you're able, kiting it between steps may reveal a solution.

Pull loops through
Rats Nest

Rubbing the risers back and forth. See step 6.

1. Snap the brakes into their retainers and separate the risers. Pull them away from the trailing edge as far as possible and shake them to clear the easy stuff.

2. Make sure there are no line overs where a line goes over the leading edge. If so, bring the rogue line(s) back underneath (pull the wing through if necessary).

3. Untwist the riser. It might be difficult to tell which way to do this early on, but keep making sure they're untwisted as you proceed. Shake the riser and try teasing lines apart as you go.

4. Remove sticks and ensure nothing is caught in the riser pulleys or brake handles.

5. Pull apart any rats nests as much as possible. Look for and remove loops. Clearing one loop (dip) can de-puzzle the whole mess.

6. While holding the risers up and outstretched, tension them slightly while sliding them back and forth so the lines rub on each other.

7. Hold the cleared A's up with some tension to help sort out remaining tangles. Then try tensioning and separating the individual B, C, and D risers.

8. If it's still tangled, start from the wing. Pull the innermost A until the riser is hanging by that A line and let everything else drop below. Orient the A riser properly and, while holding some tension to the wing, it will be more obvious what needs to be done. You'll probably have to put the riser loops through some of the outstretched lines. It may require twisting the risers around to sort things out.

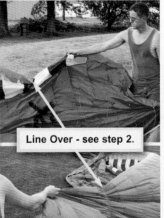

Line Over - see step 2.
Line overs can be difficult to see, check from behind.

Forward Inflation: Setup

Here is a step-by-step guide to to the potentially confusing setup for a forward inflation. Follow your instructor's guidance since he may have a different twist on it.

1 Lay out the wing in a slight **"V" pattern** so the center inflates first

2 Nothing can be on top of the A's, they must be clear. WIND   A riser

Pictorial Guide

1. Good launches begin with good layouts. Spread the wing out properly, lines clear, and on non-snaggly ground. This reduces the chance of it coming up crooked or not at all.

A slight "V" pattern helps get the center to inflate first. You don't want the tips coming up in a horseshoe shape. Too much "V" will slow inflation down.

2. Clear the A's. Nothing can be draped over the A riser and lines out to the wing.

3. Clear the brakes to ensure they're not caught on on anything. Don't deform the wing, pull just enough to see the trailing edge move an inch or so.

Move out towards the tip, as he is doing, to provide for an even pull on the trailing edge and make sure all the brake lines are free.

4. Setting the risers out this way, with the A's up, *every time* helps insure proper connection. This is surprisingly easy to do wrong. While picking up a riser, make sure the A stays pointed upward/forward to avoid confusion.

5. As you bring the riser up, keep the A's and speedbar pulley facing forward (or outward depending on harness).

6. Ease the riser down so that its *brake* is pointed forward or outward and there are no lines draped over the connected brake. Clip to carabiner then repeat for the other riser.

7. (opposite page) Strap on your practice throttle. Run your hand down the riser, over the trimmer, and pull each brake off its keeper. Spread your arms out to reveal a triangle, formed by your arm, risers and brake line, that should look like this. The *Brake Check* ensures there are no lines hanging over the brakes and that the risers are on properly.

3 Clear the Brakes
1. Hold Riser
2. Pull Brake Line
3. Tug *slightly* at trailing edge
4. Lines should all be on TOP

4 **With a Clean Layout**, A's facing up, stand between the risers and pick up the right one. Hold it up, A's forward as shown in the next frame, then let it down.

5 A riser forward
Speedbar pulley is forward
Carabiner

6 Trimmers
Brakes

Brake Check
You're almost ready...

1. (Practice) Throttle in hand
2. Brakes in hand & clear
3. Trimmers out/forward & set

Practice Throttle

Clear Triangle

Clear Triangle

Brakes
Clear to pulley

Trimmers
Out/Forward

Brakes
Clear to pulley

A Risers

A Lines
Twist around
other lines here

7

8a

8b

8c

8 Gunslinger A-Grab

Ready!

Trimmers
are facing up. If this gets confusing, imagine how it will look when the wing comes up.

A Riser
Should be forward of, or on top of, throttle. It's this feel that makes using a practice throttle so helpful.

Brake Toggle

Other Risers
and lines will be draped *behind* and over your arms. ONLY the A risers (inner A on some wings) are held.

Throttle
cable is in front of arm.

A Lines - Must be clear to wing with no other lines draped on top of them.

8. This simplifies the process of getting the "A" riser in your palm properly. Order is important. Get the throttle, then the brakes (7), then the A's. If your glider has split A's, it's usually best to use only the inner (center) A's.

Everything has been done properly if it looks like "**Ready!**"

This is the pilot's perspective (no throttle simulator is used here).

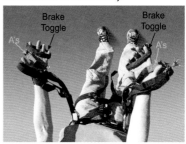

Brake Toggle   Brake Toggle
A's   A's

Centering & Clearing

After getting setup as shown on the previous pages, step forward until you *just* feel some tension. Don't pull the leading edge over.

From here, look down the A's. They should be "clean" to the wing with no lines draped over. Nothing.

Move left and right to make sure you're centered. That slight line tension should feel equal.

Most wings don't require *grasping* the A's, rather they will slide through your open palm (below). Larger or more sluggish wings may require a firmer grip like that shown at right. Your instructor or the wing representative will have suggestions.

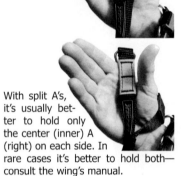

With split A's, it's usually better to hold only the center (inner) A (right) on each side. In rare cases it's better to hold both—consult the wing's manual.

"Turtle" position

This can happen if trying to forward launch in too-strong a winds.

Calm or Light Winds (Forward Inflation)

Calm winds are great for PPG *flying* but a challenge for *launching*. Unless you're at a beach, most early flights will probably be in light or calm winds. That means lots of forward launch practice, a skill you'll be mighty thankful to have.

The basic technique is similar to what free flyers use and can be practiced at home with no motor. Other techniques use power to differing degrees.

Avoid forward launches in stronger winds. The breeze may yank you backwards as the wing inflates, unceremoniously dropping you into the "turtle" position.

The Run

You're standing there centered, holding the brakes, a throttle simulator, the A's, and are pointed into whatever wind may be present. A light crosswind, up to 30°, is ok if it's less than about 2 mph. Don't accept *any* tailwind.

The instructor is invaluable here and will help with the *many* nuances.

Take one step backwards toward the wing and plan the direction you'll start to run. It should be directly away from the wing. Find a distant object to look at and plan your run towards. Here we go.

1. **Inflation. When you go for it, go hard.** Lunge away from the wing, arms back leading with your chest to quickly tension the lines. Once it takes shape, **then** pull more A's as necessary. It initially inflates quickly but then imposes enormous resistance. Keep driving, and **now** pull the requisite A's. Not too much—on most wings that's only an inch or two.

2. **Rise.** Drive hard through the resistance, with just enough A pressure to keep the wing coming up. Too much A pull will cause a *front tuck* (leading edge folds downward). Not enough A's will allow the wing to fall back. Your instructor will let you know. Consider using open palms to let the A's slide up, thereby limiting how much you can pull.

   On some wings, especially older or larger models, you may need to hold the A's for quite a while, until you've gathered some speed, the wing is fully overhead, **and** you're moving. Such wings take more A-pull but are less likely to overfly you and front tuck.

   The bigger the wing the longer it takes to come up and the more A-pull it probably needs.

3. **Damping.** Keep forging forward with your body—speed is life. As the wing

nears overhead, let go of the A's and pull some brake pressure so the wing doesn't overfly. If it's coming up quickly you'll need to let off on the A's and pull brakes sooner. That's called "*checking* the wing" or "damping" it. If it's hanging back you'll need to stay on the A's longer, waiting until it's fully overhead and you're moving before pulling any brake.

4. **Control.** You're running with the wing overhead. Speed is life, but this will get tiring *very* quickly if there's no wind. You will use all your 1 person power to generate the full 6 mph or so to keep it flying.

If the wing leans right, run right *just enough* to get under it while pulling a *little* left brake—it's easy to pull too much brake and have the wing fall back.

5. **Finish.** After some seconds of running you'll be done. Before collapsing in a sweaty heap, turn around, walk backwards (if you're on a super-smooth field) and pull on the brakes so the wing lands more neatly on its trailing edge.

In very light or no wind, don't bother with turning around but do pull brakes while still moving forward. That avoids getting draped in line spaghetti, where the wing falls down on your head.

While running, you will learn to detect a subtle pull, left or right, from the tensioning lines. If the wing starts pulling you to the left, go left enough to keep under it while driving forward and, if you have enough speed, pulling slight right brake. Looking up at the wing too early can slow you down. Consider turning your head left or right, looking at the tip instead of looking straight up.

Later on, when doing this with a motor, you'll be leaning back into the thrust, For now, though, you'll need to lean forward to get enough oomph. In completely calm wind, the initial run will feel like you're pulling a limp rag with little resistance. Keep driving forward: speed=success.

With even a couple mph breeze, the wing will snap to attention much faster than in a dead calm. It will try to stop your forward momentum then come up quickly and want to overfly; be ready to pull on the brakes *briefly* to slow it down while moving forward then let off the brakes. The vast majority of blown forward inflations can be traced to insufficient speed, releasing the A's too early, or *checking* with too much brake. Even a slightly crooked inflation can be managed if you get enough speed and get under the wing while minimizing brake (usually none) pull.

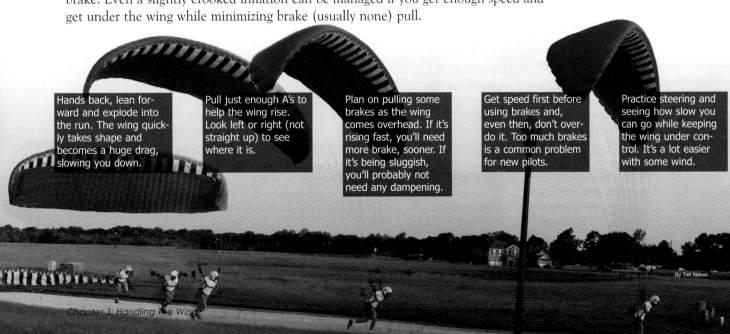

Hands back, lean forward and explode into the run. The wing quickly takes shape and becomes a huge drag, slowing you down.

Pull just enough A's to help the wing rise. Look left or right (not straight up) to see where it is.

Plan on pulling some brakes as the wing comes overhead. If it's rising fast, you'll need more brake, sooner. If it's being sluggish, you'll probably not need any dampening.

Get speed first before using brakes and, even then, don't overdo it. Too much brakes is a common problem for new pilots.

Practice steering and seeing how slow you can go while keeping the wing under control. It's a lot easier with some wind.

Reverse Inflation: Setup

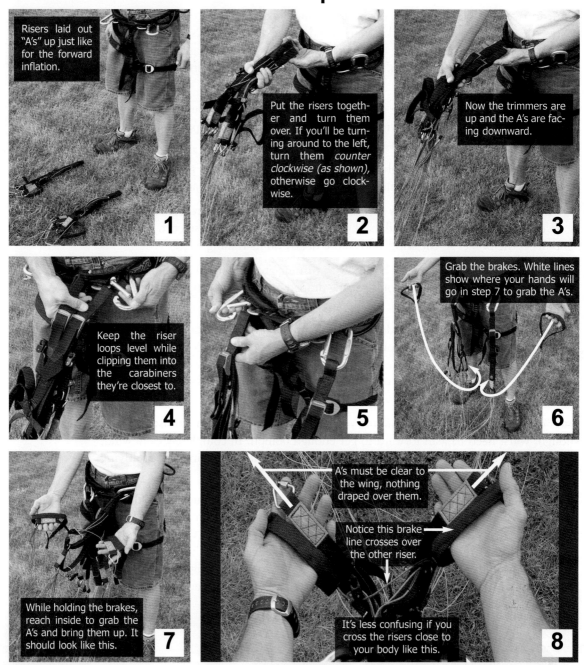

1 — Risers laid out "A's" up just like for the forward inflation.

2 — Put the risers together and turn them over. If you'll be turning around to the left, turn them *counter clockwise (as shown)*, otherwise go clockwise.

3 — Now the trimmers are up and the A's are facing downward.

4 — Keep the riser loops level while clipping them into the carabiners they're closest to.

5

6 — Grab the brakes. White lines show where your hands will go in step 7 to grab the A's.

7 — While holding the brakes, reach inside to grab the A's and bring them up. It should look like this.

8 — A's must be clear to the wing, nothing draped over them. Notice this brake line crosses over the other riser. It's less confusing if you cross the risers close to your body like this.

Free Flight & Kiting Reverse Hook-In: This method, using one hand per A, is the most common reverse inflation technique for kiting and free flight. Notice there is no mention of a throttle simulator (practice throttle). That's because this method is not good for motoring. If the throttle gets caught in a line during inflation you could suddenly go to full power—an unexpected 100 pound push from behind. That rarely ends well.

For motoring, the best technique is to hold both A's in one hand and the throttle in your other hand (shown later). It's the same through step 7 then, in step 8, instead of grabbing one A per hand, you grab and hold *both* A's with your non-throttle hand. It's covered in Chapter 5 and some instructors will have you doing it right away so you're comfortable with it. In that case, use a throttle simulator. If your motor has a left hand throttle, plan on turning around to the right (see opposite sidebar). So you would hold both A's in your right hand, leaving your left hand with only the throttle and left brake.

For kiting, the one-A-per-hand method offers more control that will come in handy later if you choose to advance beyond ground handling basics.

Move Under the Wing

This is as unnatural as it is necessary: you must move under the wing while running or forward kiting. If it goes right, you must move right. In calm wind, don't pull any brake while gathering speed; then, once moving with the wing nicely overhead, use just enough brake pressure to steer and keep it from overflying. This won't come easy. Fight the instinct to pull against the wing—it always wins.

Through inflation you'll keep the A's in your hand, pushing them up and forward to help the wing come overhead. On some models, you must stay on the A's (keep applying pressure) until it is fully overhead *and* your body is moving nicely forward. Then let off on the A's and pull just enough brakes to keep the wing from overflying you.

Speed is life. The goal is to keep enough speed (airflow) for control using brakes alone. More airflow equals better control. If the wing goes left or right, move with it, but only as much as needed. Turning your body too much can thrust you to the other side and start a zig-zag oscillation that worsens. You run right and the wing goes left in a series of increasing oscillations that end in a fall or worse. Use *small* direction changes and small brake inputs to ease back into position. It's a fine dance that requires practice, but it's oh so fun when mastered.

Remember that, when you're doing this with a motor, after inflation you'll need to stand up straight and let the motor push.

Forward Kiting

Most wings need at least a 6 mph breeze to become controllable, and more is better, up to about 12 mph. The value of some breeze becomes painfully obvious after a few tries dragging 20+ square meters of wing overhead. It's good that you *can* (and should) practice this in no wind, but it's a lot of work.

Forward kiting reveals a critical behavior of the wing—if you move your body left, the wing goes right, and will continue to the ground. It reinforces why staying centered under the wing is so important. It also means that you can make the wing go right by first moving slightly left then following the wing as it goes right. That'll be important later on when we explore advanced ground handling.

Wind Over 6 mph (Reverse Inflation)

Much of your early learning will involve reverse kiting. You'll need at least a 7 mph wind to do so. Some schools may teach how to kite the wing without the harness, a useful skill covered in Chapter 15.

Hooking In Reversed

Some free flyers hook in forward then turn around while lifting one riser over their head. That's tough with a cage so we use other techniques. There are surprisingly many ways to hook in reversed but we cover the most common (opposite page).

It seems complicated but, when you pull the wing to life and turn around (you'll turn left using these instructions), it all sorts out magically. The correct hand will already be in the correct brake.

After you're hooked in, make the two risers cross each other near your body; then, while keeping hold of the brakes, grab an A riser with each hand like in figure 5

1. If the **body** goes left... **2.** The **wing** will go right.

Which Way To Turn Around?

Plan to turn around opposite of your throttle hand. If your machine has a right hand throttle (as shown), plan to turn to the left. Later on you'll find it helpful since you can hold the A's longer during the turn-around as shown above.

Riser Loops from right side

Tip: An alternate hook-in method for reverses is to treat it like the more obvious forward method. Step up to the wing like a forward launch but stand *beside* the risers instead of between them (1). Pick up both risers while facing forward and lift them over your right shoulder (2). Remain facing away from the wing and hook the left riser to your left carabiner and the right riser to your right carabiner just like you do for a forward. Don't twist them. Envision how they will be in flight when the wing comes up.

(3) Once clipped in, the risers and lines are draped around your right side. Now turn right to face the wing—you're ready. After inflation, you'll turn to the left. Reverse the actions if you prefer turning right.

Both A's in one hand method for reverse inflations.

and on page 30. Alternatively, and for motor launches, you'll put both A's in your left hand (left). On wings with split A's you may be holding four risers although it's usually best just to have the inner A's on those wings. Eventually you'll also have a throttle in that right hand (or left depending on the motor setup). Repetition fixes the inevitable confusion. There are many ways to teach this—go with what your instructor is most familiar. You're now ready to build a "wall."

Construction: Building a Wall

Having the wing partially inflated while it sits on the ground in a moderate breeze (it needs at least 8 mph) is called "building a wall." It helps to:

- Ensure being properly hooked in and positioned to bring the wing up centered.

- Quickly spread out the wing and expose tangles or snags.

- Get a feel for the wind strength and direction.

Having a good, level wall helps the success rate for reverse launches in addition to being a great exercise in wing handling.

"Building a wall"

4. This is a common stance for reverse inflations with a motor. For a right-handed throttle, plan on turning around to the left as shown.

Start with the practice throttle, then grab the brakes, followed by putting both A's in your non-throttle hand. It feels awkward at first but does get easier. You'll use the same order with an actual throttle.

5. It's not always possible to "build a wall" like this but, whenever possible, it's helpful.

To build a wall, spread out the wing and hook in, holding the brakes as shown on page 30. You should be holding the brakes with an "A" in each hand.

Be prepared to pull brakes *immediately* if the wing tries to billow up before you're ready. In a stronger wind it will want to snap to attention and come up.

Get some tension on the risers with your body, step forward once and then lurch backwards while applying some upward pressure on the A's. If there's enough wind, the wing will start to come up. Just as it leaves the ground, let go of the A's and pull *just enough* brakes to bring it back down. Not too hard—you want to leave the wing standing there "at attention" with the leading edge a few feet above the ground. Do this several times—at first it's confusing just *finding* the two A risers but practice really pays off. It feels like work for a while.

Once the wall is built, you can modulate how tall it stands by stepping towards or away from it. Leveling the wall is done by stepping sideways toward the higher side. You can also practice holding both A's in your non-throttle hand to be ready for adding power. Get used to going for the A's, pulling the wing up mostly with your body, and then bringing it back down using brakes. Timing is a challenge; you want it to come just off the ground and then bring it right back down again—the trailing edge should never get more than a few feet high. Once you have gained some experience you can do this without the trailing edge even leaving the ground.

Use your body, not the A's. After the wing billows out *then* help it with the A's; if

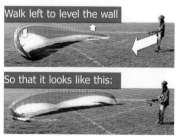

Walk left to level the wall

So that it looks like this:

the leading edge deforms, you're pulling them too hard. The wing must see pressure more evenly on the lines, especially if there's barely enough wind. On some wings, you do not need any pull on the A's at all which improves your feel for the wing's pull. There's more in Chapter 15.

Reverse Inflation

Once the wall is level and looking good (if there's enough breeze for a wall), lower it slightly then be prepared to lurch backwards. When ready, take several steps backwards, letting your body pull on the risers as your hands (or hand if using one hand) pull *just enough* on the A's. This action should be more of a fast snatch than a walk. Otherwise you end up dragging the wing along the ground. Use your body, not just the A's.

As the wing comes up, keep some A pressure until it's nearly overhead, then let off. Walk backwards, if necessary. Be prepared with some brakes—you will need to "check" the wing (pull brakes) if it's coming up fast. With much wind you'll get a rapid inflation and must be ready to release the A's earlier and jab in some brakes. Then reduce brake pull so it doesn't fall back.

If it's lumbering up limply then you'll need to hold the A's all the way up, waiting until it's nearly overhead before even thinking about going to the brakes. You'll need to be walking backwards to keep it coming overhead.

In a stronger wind it wants to come up quickly on its own and may even try dragging you downwind with it—be prepared. Shortly after it starts up you may not be able to avoid getting pulled for several feet. Let yourself slide and be ready to check an overshoot with brakes. If it lifts you when braking to stop it, let up on the brakes until you get turned back around to control the wing and bring it down; hopefully you've rehearsed how to deflate it. These conditions are way too strong for a new ground handler.

Reverse Kiting

Once the wing is happily overhead you want to use the least amount of input to keep it there. We'll refine this more later, but for now, the steps to successful reverse kiting are:

Both A's in one hand method for reverse inflations. This is how you'll launch with a motor.

One A Per Hand is good for kiting practice and free flight because it allows finer control. It is not good for motoring since it's easy to accidentally squeeze the throttle.

• Stay under the wing's center cell. If it moves left, immediately walk left until you're directly under it, and another foot more. Same if it moves right.

• If the wing goes left, pull the brake in your left hand (yes, *left* hand), if it goes right, pull the brake in your right hand, always returning the other hand up to near the brake pulley. So if the wing drifts to the left, walk left, pull left, but only as much as you need. Walk as little as you can get away with but move aggressively at first. Lead it—stop pulling as the wing approaches the desired position.

1. **Move with the wing**. While reverse kiting, if the wing starts falling right: step right and, with your right hand, pull some brake which goes to the opposite trailing edge. If the wing starts falling left, step left, pull left. If it tries to overfly you, pull both brakes.

• Be light on the brakes: you'll 1) avoid over-correcting, 2) be less likely to have the wing fall back down, and 3) work less. If the wing keeps falling back, use less brake pull and walk backwards to increase airflow.

• Take a few steps backwards whenever the wind dies and control feels soft.

If it wants to sag downward, let up the brakes and walk backwards to give it more airflow.

The goal is to stand in one place, using the least amount of brakes possible to kite it overhead. Move your body if needed but work towards being able to just stand there, kiting, without over controlling.

When input is needed, go one hand up, and one hand down. Always be moving towards the center cell until you're brake handling is good enough to keep the wing centered overhead with*out* moving your body.

Another benefit of having minimum brake pull is that you're less likely to get lifted. If the wing is hanging back and you've got the trailing edge deflected (as you will with pulled brakes), you are vulnerable to gusts. It's like sticking your hand out the window of a fast moving car—if the hand is angled up, airflow pushes it up and backward, but if it's streamlined, there is less effect.

2. "Straight Riser" kiting should not be used, if at all, beyond your first day. That's because you'll need to learn crossed-riser kiting in order to launch.

In a light wind you may need to walk backwards to keep decent airflow over the wing for good control. After all, if the wind isn't blowing enough, then *you* need to generate it with your motion. Airflow (airspeed over the wing) is life—the more the better for control.

Wing falling left?
walk left,
brake left.

and move back
a few steps.

If the wing tends to fly past you (*overfly*), apply both brakes; if it drops back, reduce brakes and walk backwards (away from the wing). By modulating these inputs and movements you can become quite adept at making the wing stay where you want it, even in light winds. Wings that inflate easily tend to front tuck more.

Practice kiting until it's second nature. Besides being fun to master, good wing handling is the crux of being a good launcher. It is what will determine the conditions you can handle, especially stronger winds. More advanced techniques are covered later.

Alternative Training-Only Method: Straight Risers

The normal way of kiting while reversed can be confusing at first, so a very few instructors use a straight-riser method (pictured left) to quickly get the student kiting. But the regular method must eventually be learned so use this only briefly if at all.

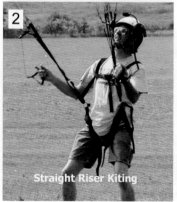

Straight Riser Kiting

The risers go straight out to the wing without crossing or twisting. The drawback is that brake input is backwards from what you'll eventually learn. It *is* quicker to get some basic feel for the wing and how to stay centered.

Hook in without crossing the risers, A's facing up. Grab the brake closest to each hand from the outside; there should be nothing crossed. With the brakes in your hands, reach up to hold the A's and inflate the wing by stepping backwards, using your body while pulling slightly on the A's to help the wing rise.

As the wing comes overhead, dampen it with brakes so it doesn't overfly you. Then modulate the brakes to keep the wing there just like the other methods. In light winds you'll have almost no brake pulled most of the time. If it wants to fall back, walk backwards to increase the wing's airflow and reduce brakes. If it starts falling left, step left and pull some brake with the right hand and vice versa if it falls right *then let up*. Only left/right steering is opposite to the normall method.

Whether kiting with crossed (normal) or straight risers, **watch the trailing edge move** and visualize it slowing down that side which is exactly what's happening. This will make the wing's behavior and response more clear.

The Turn *and Move*

Once you are reliably kiting the wing overhead, your next step is to turn around to the left (if hooked in as described here) and kite it forward. Start moving immediately after turning around.

While keeping the wing centered overhead, take a step backward (into the wind which is at your back) to get the wing moving, turn around quickly then *keep moving forward*, especially in light winds. Lean forward if necessary but remember that, with a motor on, you will stand up straight and throttle up to keep moving. If you'll be turning left, it's beneficial to have the wing slightly to your left (while reversed) before turning around so you're turning towards the wing.

You must turn and *move*. Speed is life since the wing needs airflow for the brakes to be effective. A common failure is the wing falling back or sideways while its pilot stands there pondering the meaning of life. Move right away, and fast, to prevent this. Once you've got the wing under control *and* moving forward, you're doing forward kiting as described earlier.

Bringing the Wing Down

You could just let it flop down in a heap but you're aspiring to greater things. So work on letting it down gently, level, and leading-edge up. It will be easier to re-inflate or put away. Plus you'll look good.

Assuming you were forward kiting, turn around to face the wing, walking backwards slowly if needed to keep it powered. If you turned left for inflation, turn right when bringing the wing down. That will leave the risers crossed just like they were

Even in light wind, practice the "turn and move." Bring the wing up; then, just as it reaches overhead, back up, turn to face forward and start walking or running. You'll need to generate more speed in less wind. While running, keep your hands back and up to avoid pulling too much brake.

Your goal is to use the least amount of brake and body movement to maintain control.

Practice turning back around to face the wing and setting it back down neatly.

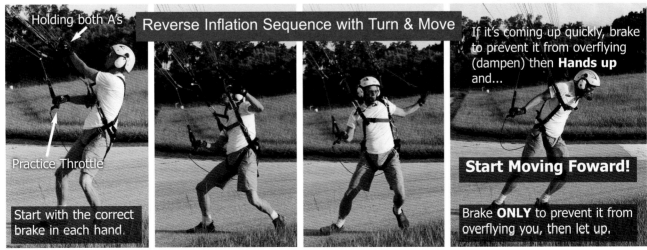

Holding both A's — Practice Throttle — Start with the correct brake in each hand.

Reverse Inflation Sequence with Turn & Move

If it's coming up quickly, brake to prevent it from overflying (dampen) then **Hands up** and...

Start Moving Foward!

Brake **ONLY** to prevent it from overflying you, then let up.

    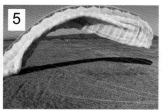

1,2. The standard deflation is to just pull brakes. They are, after all, already in your hands.

Finesse tip: If the wing wants to come down hard, about 5 feet before it hits, let *off* the brakes. Timed properly, the wing decelerates and lands gently on the ground. You look like a hero and the wing says "ahhhh."

3, 4. This is the "C" line kill for depowering a wing in a wind. Find the C's (3) and pull them down as far as you can (4). Using the "D's", (rear risers), as shown earlier, is generally easier because they're easier to find, and the wing tends not to snake up as much.

5. What the wing looks like when you pull the "C" risers.

⚠ **Caution!**

More serious injuries come from getting body parts into a spinning prop than any other cause. Use extreme care when handling a motor and do not start it until given specific instructions.

during inflation (good for re-inflating and going again). You can turn the other way, but it's easier to habitually use the same direction every time so you're ready to re-inflate in the familiar manner.

Once you're facing the wing, pull enough brakes so that it falls back evenly. Just as it touches down, take a step towards it so the leading edge lays back nicely. This makes it somewhat easier to re-inflate or fold up.

If it's windy, you can bring the wing down on its side. Use whatever inputs are necessary to get the wing to go crooked then let it fall onto a tip. This reduces its tendency to re-inflate. A strong wind can make it difficult to bring the wing down at all (see also Chapter 15.) The strong-wind solutions listed earlier should be rehearsed.

The best one to practice is the *Rear Riser* deflation. You can also use the B or C risers (B's or C's) with varying effectiveness. Practice with each. For one thing, it's good to see just how hard it is to *get* to the B or C risers while you're kiting. Some wings tend to "snake" around if their B's or C's are pulled down, making them hard to disable. If that happens, go for the D's.

Adding the Motor

Hopefully you've been kiting with a practice throttle. Otherwise you'll be surprised at how confounding this simple addition is. Have your instructor present before starting the motor!

The following description is for a right-handed throttle. If yours is left handed then you'll hold the A's in your right hand. Which side the throttle is on doesn't matter much, but if you have a reserve, its better for it to be opposite the throttle.

Learn where the kill switch is and practice pressing it. Make it two distinct steps: 1) release the throttle, 2) press *and hold* the kill switch. You want that to be automatic for when things turn ugly—a still-spinning prop carries big risk. There will be times where the wind has its way with you and being quick on the switch will save many shekels. While kiting with the throttle simulator, practice hitting (and holding) the kill switch whenever the wing goes awry. **At the first sign of trouble, kill it!**

After proficiency is gained with the throttle simulator (which happens quickly), put the motor on and practice kiting in short bursts. This will be tiring so don't do it for long. Some schools use frames with weights to help build up to the full motor weight—a cool tool.

Learn to "turn and run." That is, once the wing is mostly overhead and moving forward, turn right away and start moving. Your instructor may pull or push you to simulate the motor's thrust. You must be able to control the wing with the motor pushing before even *considering* flight. The motor has a lot of inertia so when you turn around it will tend to continue twisting. It's just a matter of feel to turn fast without letting it swing you much past forward.

With these skills reasonably in hand, you will start the motor (there are some significant "gotchas" to know about) and go through these exercises with it running. Note that it is eminently possible, probable even, for lines to go into the prop without due care.

Before hooking in, get used to the basic controls on the motor by running it up and feeling the range of power. Practice going for the kill switch.

Storing the Wing

Wings like it cool, dry and dark. Heat or chemicals can degrade the material strength while dampness and its moldy cousins can rot holes in the nylon. UV from sunlight (or other sources) weakens the fabric and makes it porous—all bad. With their 300-hour average lifetime measured mostly in UV exposure, and $3000+ price, basking in sunshine costs about $10 per hour.

Before putting the wing away, try to make sure there are no bugs inside. That's best done by folding or stuffing it right away. If grasshoppers or other critters get trapped inside they'll make a hole one way or another, either by chewing to freedom or by leaving their acidic little remains—caustic chemical carcasses can cause carnage.

If you notice crawling things already inside, find a reasonably bugless place and shake the trailing edge so that they fall out the leading edge openings. This can be done inside but you'll be amazed at how big the wing is. In that case, leave half of it folded while you attend to the other half. Ribs have big holes in them for the air to spread out but they also make fine bug highways.

Before putting the wing away, clip the riser ends together with a small carabiner or other clip. As you put it away, don't let the riser ends go through any lines. Keep them well separated to reduce the likelihood of tangles when pulling it out again. That's the purpose of a riser pouch if you have one.

Rosette

When finished with the wing, hold its riser pair with your left hand, grab all the lines with your right hand (vice versa for southpaws), sliding it out towards the wing. At full extension, coil the lines into your riser holding hand. Don't let the riser ends go through any lines. Slide your right hand out again and repeat until it reaches fabric, leaving you with a big, easy-to-carry *rosette*. If there's a wind, turn around once so the fabric doesn't billow.

Stuffing

Stuffing the wing into a wide-opening *stuff sack* is quick and easy. Put it away the same way each time, with risers pointed down from the wing's center, so when you get it out again, you'll know which way it goes. A riser pouch is great, if available, or you can clip them to the sack's carry handle. Most importantly, make sure the risers are situated so that no lines will get mixed in.

Stuffing isn't better or worse than folding, although stuffing will leave more wrinkles. Newer wings with special leading edge rib reinforcements benefit from an *accordion* (or concertina) fold where the leading edge cells are all kept flat.

1. A *rosette* is a good way to carry the wing—just throw it over your back.

2. Before stowing, clip the risers together or put one end inside the other. Most importantly, make sure they remain clear of all other lines.

3. This light weight stuff sack comes with an integral riser bag for protection and to reduce tangles. Before launching, stuff the stuff sack into its riser bag and put the whole thing under your paramotor seat. Now you've got a wing bag in case of an out landing.

4. An *accordion*, or *concertina* fold keeps the leading edge rib reinforcements from getting creased or bent.

Folding

Folding takes a bit more time but allows for a much smaller package that's good for shipping and leaves fewer wrinkles. Methods abound but the one below is quick and easy even if you're alone, although it's obviously quicker with two.

First off, be loose. Tight folding stresses the stitching and weakens the seams if done repeatedly. Avoid sharp bends of the leading edge rods (Mylar layered reinforcements on older gliders) so they stay shapely for better performance. These stiffeners help keep the cells open during light-wind inflations and hasten recovery from in-flight deflations (collapses).

Lay the wing out flat with the lines laid in the same position as for a forward launch (without any "V" of course). Pull the riser loops away from the trailing edge and lay them, A's up, on the ground then fold it as shown.

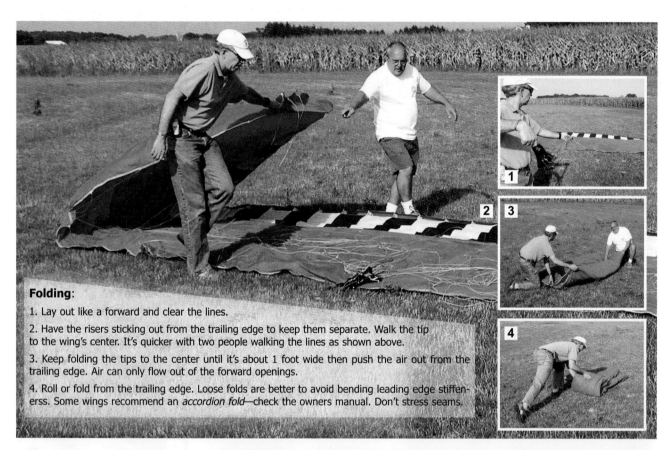

Folding:

1. Lay out like a forward and clear the lines.

2. Have the risers sticking out from the trailing edge to keep them separate. Walk the tip to the wing's center. It's quicker with two people walking the lines as shown above.

3. Keep folding the tips to the center until it's about 1 foot wide then push the air out from the trailing edge. Air can only flow out of the forward openings.

4. Roll or fold from the trailing edge. Loose folds are better to avoid bending leading edge stiffenerss. Some wings recommend an *accordion fold*—check the owners manual. Don't stress seams.

Daisy Chain / Braiding

You may come across this method for storing lines but it's not recommended by paraglider line makers (Cousin Trestec) due to tighter line bends. It's more common with skydiving canopies whose lines are made to accommodate higher opening forces.

The technique shown is just the basic idea. Done wrong, it can leave an impressive tangle.

Preparing
for First Flight

4

Above: Your instructor will help ensure a proper connection, but it's a combined responsibility.

First solo can be an overwhelming concoction of sensations and emotions that overpower normal reason. Early flights have proven to be a risky time, especially with insufficient or low quality instruction. These steps, along with *good* instruction, can help it be the highlight of your training.

Now that you can handle the wing, we'll add power to become an aircraft under control. Expect it to feel awkward and tiring at first, but the results are well worth the effort. This chapter is all about being prepared.

Adjusting the Motor

You will start with a simulator *hang check* to adjust the motor (harness) for flight (see Chapter 12) and let you get seated easily. The propeller, when aligned vertically, should be tilted back between 5° and 15° (upper tip back). The harness must be comfortable and have no straps, bars or frame parts pushing uncomfortably. If it has a kick-in strap you should be able to reach it while hanging there to get into the seat. The motor should not "scoop" you (force your legs out front) excessively as it lifts.

Getting into the seat is surprisingly critical. Harness leg straps are not designed to hang from for more than a few minutes. Doing so can render your legs uselessly numb, a definite drawback on landing.

Practice getting into the seat while in the simulator and, if your equipment requires using a hand to do so, *don't forget to let go of, and stow, the brakes*—a potentially fatal mistake. Ideally, you can get in the seat just by lifting your legs and sliding back while wiggling. The second best method is using a kick-in strap which should be heavy enough to hang down in the slipstream.

Siphoning Fuel

Siphon hoses use gravity to pull fuel up out of the source (gas can) and into your paramotor tank which must be *below* the source.

Here are two ways to start the siphon.

1. Submerge the hose in your source can until it fills completely with fuel. While keeping one end submerged, block the other end with your thumb, hold it, then lift that end out and into your paramotor tank. You now have a hose, full of fuel, running from the source can to your paramotor tank. Release your thumb and the fuel should flow.

2. Use a "wiggle pump" as shown above. Submerse the pump end into your gas can and the other end into your paramotor tank. Wiggle the pump end up and down for a few seconds to start the flow.

Once started, fuel will flow until the source tank empties or you pull it out.

Gas Cans & Fueling

After fueling, put the cap back on your *motor's* tank first. Otherwise, you *will* eventually forget and try to take off with fuel splashing everywhere, including the exhaust.

Gas cans like this come from dirt bike suppliers and work well if you can transport/store a tall container. Their long, flexible hoses reach the tanks of most paramotors.

5 Gal From Dirt Bike Shops

⚠ **Caution!**

Before filling a can, place it on the ground to avoid an explosion caused by static electricity.

Fueling

Most paramotors have two-stroke engines which require a proper mix of gasoline and 2-stroke oil. It can be mixed right in the fuel tank but most pilots use a different container 1) for convenience, and 2) it insures only mixed gas goes in the motor's tank—that's *really* important! Put the oil in first to improve mixing.

Running a 2-stroke for even one flight with gas that's not mixed **will ruin it.**

Do your preflight inspection *after* refueling to catch the common and dangerous mistake of forgetting the fuel cap.

Don't over fuel since you have to lift it; mixed fuel weighs 6.2 lbs per gallon.

When pouring premix (mixed fuel and oil) into your motor, a long skinny funnel, like a transmission funnel or a siphon hose is handy (see left sidebar).

Fuel Selection and Storage

Fuel that's left exposed to air for over a couple weeks may degrade and cause motor problems. If stored in an airtight container (it hisses when you open the lid), fuel may last several months although some engine gurus recommend fresh fuel regardless of storage.

Use what the manufacturer recommends but, absent that, use mid or higher grade auto gas, preferably with no Ethanol (better for rubber parts). Higher octane ratings reduce knocking, a premature rapid combustion that puts holes in pistons. Gas stations that sell pure gas can be found on websites like *pure-gas.org*.

Aviation fuel (avgas) is preferred by some makers but it leaves lead deposits. The common 100 "low lead" (100LL) is actually heavily leaded by modern standards. Avgas formulations *are* more consistent throughout the year (auto gas varies) plus it doesn't stink. Avgas can be purchased at small airports where it is sold by Fixed Base Operators (FBO's) for about 30% more per gallon than auto gas. Tell them it's for your ultralight.

New Avgas formulas, such as one by Swift Fuels (no lead and no ethanol), are increasingly available.

Mixtures

Two types of *mixtures* get discussed: **fuel/oil** mixture relates how much oil goes into a gallon of gas and **fuel/air** mixture is how much fuel is mixed with air in the carburetor. The proper fuel/air mixture is managed through carburetor jets, orifices and needle valves. When you hear the term *lean*, it means too little fuel in the fuel/air mix which can overheat the motor.

Oil Selection & Mixing

2-stroke motors derive all their lubrication from what oil gets mixed into the gas and it must be mixed in the correct proportion.

Modern 2-cycle oils work well with a ratio of gas to oil around 50:1 which means there are 50 units of gas for each 1 unit of oil. Lower ratios (more oil) are frequently specified for the first few hours of a motor's life, the *break-in* period. A mix chart in the Appendix can be used to determine how much oil gets added to your fuel. Since many oils come in metric units (liters or milliliters), those units are included in the Appendix chart. Most 2-cycle oil bottles have a chart printed on the container for other ratios as well.

You'll hear nearly religious fervor when seeking advice on oil selection and ratio—go with the manufacturer's recommendation, if available. Otherwise, make your selection based on the following priorities:

• Use two-cycle oil, never four-cycle oil such as that made for cars.

• Use two-cycle oil that is made for *air-cooled* motors. Marine varieties are made for cooler running outboards and may break down at our hotter temperatures.

• Use synthetics which are commonly recognized as having better characteristics at higher RPMs and hotter temperatures. They also leave fewer deposits.

• Use oil that is dyed so that you can tell whether a particular batch of fuel is mixed. If using clear oil, develop a fool-proof way to track what fuel is already mixed. The phrase "I thought it was mixed" follows many a piston seizure.

Avoid mixing synthetics and mineral oils. A very few brands may not mix well and could form gel-type clumps in the tank. This was more common years ago.

Preflight Inspection

A preflight inspection is done before each flight. It must be (1) **consistent**—start from the same place and do it the same way each time, (2) **thorough**—don't skip items; touch each one as you check it, and (3) without **interruptions.** If you are interrupted start over at the carabiners.

Motor

There's little reason to skimp—preflighting a paramotor takes less than a minute on most machines. Resist the temptation to crank & go, and never, *ever* start it without ensuring the throttle-carburetor linkage is at idle and free moving with easy access to the kill switch.

Start the preflight by pulling at the carabiners. That will bring out harness webbing to expose potential problems and allow inspection of the critical carabiners and harness. Check the webbing, fabric, straps, and any attached connection hardware. They must be free of excessive fading, tears, cuts, badly worn sections, or other damage that could affect integrity. Here are other items to check:

• Look for small cracks in the **carabiners**; they could lead to a catastrophic inflight failure, especially on some aluminum models.

• Squeeze the **throttle,** watching for lever movement at the carburetor, making sure it's at idle. This reduces the harrowing possibility of it suddenly going to high power on startup. Skipping this check causes more serious (and sometimes debilitating) injury than any other cause.

• Make sure any cruise control is off and SafeStart, if equipped, is on.

• Walk around the machine, moving parts for security, and looking for loose bolts or other parts. Loose prop bolts, even one or two, can set up a vibration that tears the prop completely off its mount, possibly taking the engine with it.

1. Start your preflight from the front and do it the same way every time, uninterrupted. Avoid leaving the machine with anything unflyable (bolts loose, fuel cap off, etc).

2. This engine overheated and melted a hole in its piston, testimony to the value of thorough preflighting. You can catch problems before they make great sucking sounds on your wallet, not to mention how unwelcome an inflight motor failure is.

Anything that causes the mixture to run lean, from a clogged fuel vent to loose exhaust system bolts, can lead to overheating (see Chapter 12).

1. The most important preflight action is to move the throttle while observing that the carburetor linkage returns to idle.

Float bowl carburetors hide the throttle mechanism inside a housing—on these machines, just make sure the throttle freely moves to idle.

2. This style of prop mount has a center bolt. If there is any play in the prop (wiggling fore and aft), this bolt may be loose.

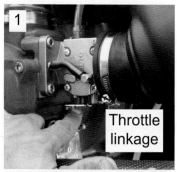

Throttle linkage

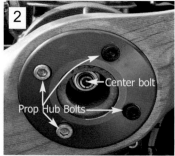

Center bolt
Prop Hub Bolts

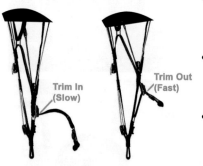

Trim In (Slow)
Trim Out (Fast)

Setting Trimmers

Trimmers must be set for takeoff. Most wings have a recommended position, frequently a number or sewn line.

If they're pulled in too far (set slow) the wing is sluggish to come overhead. If they're let out too far (set fast) the wing tends to front tuck and requires more running.

• **Mufflers** cause many problems. Look for cracks, loose or broken mountings, fiberglass packing inside, missing rivets/screws, and general security. Put safety wire, or other restraint, on anything of consequence that can loosen.

• Check **redrive** belts for proper tension and position.

• Check **motor mounts and nuts** for security along with reduction drive bolts.

• **Spark plugs** loosen and fall off, especially on inverted engines. Check for general security.

• The **fuel system** needs a clear vent to allow air into the tank and a supply line running up to the carburetor. Check for tank security, line condition, and turn on the appropriate valves. Some have an off valve for the vent—it must be open (on). If left closed, or the vent gets plugged, the engine will run for a while until diminishing fuel lowers the tank pressure, possibly collapsing the tank. Eventually the fuel pump can't suck any harder and the motor quits.

Tighten the lid and vent (if removable).

• Check the **propeller** for condition. Small nicks are generally OK but long splits must be repaired. Fortunately many prop maladies can be repaired in the field without removal (see Chapter 12). Check that the hub and center bolts (if equipped) are tight.

• Align the prop vertically then push the top tip fore and aft. It should have less than about 1/16th inch (1.5 millimeters) of play. Check the motor mounts when doing this to see that they flex but have no cracks or excessive looseness.

• If the prop has been removed since its last flight, check that it's not on backwards. This embarrassing mistake will be felt when the motor produces about half of its normal thrust. The curvy surface faces forward, in the direction of flight. Another way to remember is that the fatter part of the prop, the leading edge, is more forward.

• Check the **cage** for security and complete assembly. If the motor has a clutch (the propeller spins freely without the motor running), spin the prop around to insure sufficient clearance from the hoop and cage parts.

• Ensure that accessories are secure and straps are out of harm's way. Nothing should be able to touch the exhaust or get into any moving parts. Close any zippered compartments.

• If equipped with a reserve, ensure its bridle routing remains unobstructed, attached, and the reserve pins are secured properly without being pushed all the way through (see Chapter 12).

Wing

With a breeze of at least 6 mph, checking the wing is easier. The most minimal preflight is to kite the wing up for a look. Always check that:

• Lines are connected, kink-free, and sheathed (outer covering intact).

• The fabric has no structural tears or holes.

• The risers have no visible damage, quick links are closed and tight, trimmers are set for takeoff, brakes are in their holders and the speedbar system is free. Brake lines must go straight through their pulleys which must be free spinning. A stuck pulley will wear the brake line quickly to failure.

A more thorough inspection should be done periodically (every 25 flights or after rough handling). Lay out the wing flat in a calm location and do the following:

• Field strength test. Find the most faded areas of fabric which will usually be on the top surface. Pull the fabric taut with your hands about 3 inches apart then push your flat thumb into the spread as if trying to poke a hole. It should hold with about 3-5 pounds of pressure.

• Run each line between your fingers from the quick-link to the wing (or cascade). Feel for thin spots which would reveal broken Kevlar inside, rendering the line unusable. Having one line broken may not seem like a big deal, and usually isn't, but it stresses the remaining lines. It's even more critical for inner A or B lines.

• Check overall condition of the risers, quick links, and brakes. Try to pull the risers apart at the stitching with about 20 pounds of pull.

If you leave something for later, it's likely to be forgotten—maybe not this time, but eventually. Take the fuel cap, for example. If you leave the machine, even for a moment, secure the cap. Before walking away from your motor, try to leave it in an airworthy condition. If unable, use a reminder, like a wrench on the seat. Interruptions of routine contribute to aviation accidents of all kinds.

Starting the Motor

Wait for your instructor to show you proper starting, especially how to avoid propeller injuries. Treat every start like it will go to full power, an all-too-common cause of tragedy. Unfortunately, most cages are designed to protect *lines* from the prop, not people.

Advise bystanders to stand clear and keep them away from the propeller arc, check that the throttle is at idle, and shout "CLEAR PROP." Never, ever start without a cage—its minimal protection is still way better than nothing.

The safest way to start is while it's secured on a stand. Next best is on your back. A good electric starter *can* be safer, provided it allows starting on your back. If using a pull starter, have another pilot pull it for you unless you can pull it yourself with the motor on.

The least desirable and, unfortunately, most common method is to start the motor by yourself while standing in front of it; be ready for unexpected thrust!

Consider using some form of "Rope Trick" (right) or other protection if it's available on your motor. Ask about added cage protection (left) if your motor only has a single hoop. Chapter 27 has more safety suggestions under "A Better Paramotor."

Making it Go

Chapter 12 has more on troubleshooting but any gas motor requires fuel, air, spark, and spin. An electric starter makes the spin easy but requires some extra care itself. Specific details of priming, choking, master switches, and fuel/air valves depend on model and will be described by your instructor or seller. If there's an owner's manual, be thankful and read it thoroughly.

Kite the wing by hand to quickly look for line problems, holes, unusual wrinkles or anything else that just doesn't look right.

Rope Trick

Also known as the "Prop Stopper," this can reduce risk on clutched machines.

1. Using a sufficiently stout 4-foot rope, create a loop in one end.

2. Before starting, wrap it around the frame and prop as shown. Make sure it's tight and far enough out on the prop to avoid getting wrapped in the prop shaft.

4. Start the motor and strap in.

5. Before runup, pull the rope's free end and stow in a safe place that can't get into the prop.

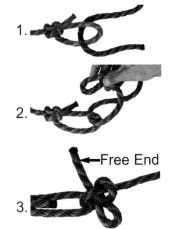

1.

2.

3. ←Free End

Tip: 2-Stroke Tuning:

There are many carburetors and many techniques for getting them to run just right. The owner's manual, if available, is the best place to start. Chapter 12 contains a troubleshooting guide and Chapter 27 explains adjusting (*tuning*) the most common 2-stroke carburetors.

Tuning is frequently required after big changes in temperature or elevation. But if the motor ran fine the last time at a given elevation and temperature, tuning will not likely help.

Throttle linkage at carburetor must be **free moving** and **at idle** before starting.

Don't let thrust push on **more throttle.**

If you *have* to start the motor like this, hold it:

1. to keep quick access to the kill button, and

2. so the throttle cannot be actuated accidentally. A surprise burst of power could push your hand in a way that squeezes even more throttle.

It's far safer to start it on a rack or on your back. Also use the "Rope Trick" or other risk mitigation.

If starting by yourself here's how to reduce the odds of a prop puree: 1) hold the throttle by its stem in a way that can't be accidentally pushed by a thrusting motor and make sure the kill button is accessible. 2) If unable to start on a rack, brace the motor with your free thumb hooked around a solid frame part and pretend that a gorilla is about to push against the propeller. 4) Position your body to be ready for the gorilla's push. 5) If the machine has a clutch, use the "rope trick" (see page 43). Take it off once the motor is idling.

Make sure the ground area is clear of loose objects that could get sucked into the prop. Loose straps or cords must not reach the prop or exhaust. And be mindful of where the prop blast is going—even at idle it can disturb things nearby, especially paraglider wings.

Don't let the motor idle for too long, carbon builds up on the spark plug, cylinder head and other parts (called *loading up*). After idling for more than a few minutes, run it up to 50% power for about 10 seconds to *clear* the motor.

Have a Plan: Patterns, Areas and Altitudes.

Before soloing, you need a plan, including signals, to use in case of radio failure. The USPPA has adopted a set of common ones but your instructor's my differ. You will fly a rectangular *pattern* (see Chapter 5) that helps judge landings, provides a known path that other pilots can easily search, and gives a way to describe location.

All patterns are based on taking off and landing into the wind which lowers ground speed. It is simply a rectangular path around the field to position yourself for landing. After reaching a safe altitude and getting into the seat you will turn left or right to go crosswind and continue climbing. The next turn is downwind and positions you for landing back at the launch site in case of a motor-out. Even if you're not landing right away this is a good path to fly before heading out of the immediate area. As a new solo student you will likely continue climbing so as to stay within gliding distance of the launch area.

Your instructor will tell you where to fly and what maneuvers to practice. If you cannot get into the seat he will direct you to come in for a landing. You cannot keep flying while hanging from the leg straps—it's too uncomfortable and may cut off circulation to your legs, making them go numb. If everything is normal then you will just fly around and enjoy your accomplishment for a half hour or so. When you come back in, you will most likely enter the pattern for landing.

⚠ **Caution!**

Most propeller injuries occur just after start. Ensure the throttle linkage is at idle and free moving before start. Body contact with a spinning prop is the most common cause of serious injury.

Electric starters reduce this risk but must be disabled when not flying. Re-rig any motor where the starter handle comes out the side—a dangerous design on older machines that led to many mishaps. Hands can quickly dart into the propeller.

Start the motor on a stand and, if it has a clutch (the prop doesn't spin at idle), use the "Rope Trick" to prevent unexpected thrust. See page 43. But assume the rope won't hold, maintaining great respect for the prop.

Make sure there is no way, even with difficulty, for the throttle cable to sneak through an opening on the cage. If that happens, the prop can pull a hand/throttle back into its arc.

Taking Instructions via Radio

You'll be up there alone but with instructor guidance—filling in blanks or insisting on immediate responses. New sensations make concentrating difficult but concentrate you must. This is why simulator practice is so valuable, especially with the motor running and controls in hand. Some instructors may not run the motor in their simulator (which involves some risk of its own) but should still have you go through the drills while causing other distractions. It could save your life: *prior rehearsal is critical!*

You will be required to pull brakes, add power, reduce power, and kick your legs in response to radio instructions. Front/back kicking means "yes" and left/right scissor motion means "no." Follow instructor commands explicitly. You may not know why, but he will. Responding right away will reduce how dramatic the response needs to be.

Reaction and Overcontrol

Because you hang below the center of roll, your instinctive reaction to swings is exactly opposite to what it should be. Plus, it is common for new pilots to pull too much brakes. This combination can result in an increasing oscillation, especially on non-beginner wings. **You must use deliberate, *smooth* inputs *and* hold them for at least 3 seconds, resisting the urge to correct each swing.** Listen and respond intently to the instructor: your life depends on it.

Rehearsing

If you have to think about a response, don't count on it. Reactions must be rehearsed and automatic. For example, the reaction to a forward surging wing is applying some brake for a couple seconds then letting up. The reaction to a wing falling back is to immediately reduce power and reduce brakes while preparing to "catch" the impending surge with brake pull. Throwing a reserve is another action that must be rehearsed—if it's needed, you won't be calmly contemplating your navel.

Any good instructor will have you rehearse, in a simulator, what you'll do in flight, preferably some of it with the motor running. Rehearsal is key to ensuring necessary reactions. You must get to the point of responding to commands instinctively in the simulator.

You must rehearse taking instructions, especially for those early flights. Then, as experience is gained, add other situations. When hell is breaking loose, rehearsed reactions win the day.

Handling Emergencies

These can be rehearsed in a simulator. Some are best done with the motor running (or other artificial distractions) since the flight environment is so loud and foreign at first. Simulator practice makes it less so.

Distraction and reaction can be worse than its cause or consequence. So when something does go pop, take a deep breath and deal with it methodically.

These are common hand signals used by many instructors and others. They supplement radio communications and can be effective in emergencies or when the radio fails.

Courtesy Jerry Starbuck and USPPA.org

Situational emergencies, where the pilot has more time, are covered in Chapter 19 and include thought processes and options to be considered.

Above All

Following your instructor's radio commands is paramount, but a few common priorities apply to all emergencies:

- **Maintain Control.** Regardless of what happens, keep flying the craft. Use **"reduce power, reduce brake, then steer"** in uncertain situations. Steer essentially straight with the least control input possible, avoiding large movements—rash actions almost always do more harm than good. Panic destroys the reason that preparation prevents. Situations needing immediate action are rare.

- Be smooth and hold brake inputs **for at least 3 seconds** to avoid oscillations.

- To the extent possible, **get on a safe course and altitude**. When something happens, *look* towards a safe course, *steer* that way and climb slowly, if appropriate.

- Once control and flight path are established, **deal with the problem.** Look around at what you've got. Loud noises are rarely good. It's almost always better to land rather than trying to "limp" home if the landing can be done safely.

- **Land into the wind** and away from wind shadows (created by wind-blocking obstructions) unless it's for a really good reason. A downwind beach landing, for example, might be better than an upwind water landing. Hopefully you already had a plan. Be essentially level before touchdown *and flare.* See *landing priorities.*

Throttle Cable Caught

After launch, while bringing your hand up, the throttle cable snags on something. It works but your hand is stuck.

Maintain control! This simple problem is a non-event *unless* you panic. Use normal brake input of the other hand (make shallow turns in that direction), look forward and keep climbing; you may be in a shallow torque turn. Once at a safe height with a safe flight path, move the throttle back, away from the motor and up. Make turns to stay near the launch site. It will probably be a simple matter of looking down to see the obvious solution then executing it.

If it remains snagged, plan on a power-off landing. Get over the landing area with plenty of height and shut off the motor. Then pull your hand out of the throttle and do a regular power-off landing.

Radio Failure

Your instructor's input is important but radios can quit. Have a plan in mind. Usually that's to continue around the pattern, climb out above the field to get some feel for the machine, then come in for a normal landing near center field. You should have rehearsed this in the simulator and be able to recite back a detailed description of climbing up, getting into the seat, pattern and landing.

Use hand signals, maneuvering to see your instructor and respond accordingly.

Brake Line Failure or Tangle

A brake line can come untied, break, get cut off by the prop, tangle, or become disconnected, but there is plenty of steering authority in the rear risers. As with all emergency situations, *fly the aircraft first*. Use available control to steer while climbing to a safe altitude.

Most likely it's a loop of brake line fouling the pulley. You may be able to undo this in flight but get up to a safe altitude first (at least 300'). Remember, if the brake is stuck, it will still pull the rear riser its attached to albeit less effectively.

Like any abnormal situation, don't do anything rash; it's normally benign. If possible, climb up higher than usual, carefully get into the seat (if able) and establish level or slightly climbing flight. Once on a safe course you can deal with the problem.

It's usually obvious what needs to be done—reach up and fix it while being mindful of flight path. You can safely land without the brakes, but it's obviously better to regain their use.

If the brake line is just stuck, you may be able to use it by reaching *above* the pulley, especially if you have shorter risers and/or a low hook-in machine.

If you cannot use the brakes normally, plan on using the rear risers for steering and flare. Don't use one brake and one rear riser, use both rear risers. Do some practice turns and flares to get a feel for how much pull it takes to turn and slow down. It takes a lot.

The rear risers can also be used for landing but won't be nearly as effective as the brakes. Allow for a longer, straight-in approach.

At the point where you would normally use the brakes to flare, pull harder on both rear risers and be ready for a firm touchdown. Landing power-off is generally preferable to avoid prop/cage damage but a fall is still more likely without use of the brakes. With experience you can land power-on. That allows a softer, but still fast, touchdown at some increased risk to your gear.

Avoid the temptation to pull the D's too hard since response is dramatically slower. Limit pull to just what you need to lessen the possibility of pulling into a *parachutal stall* where the wing descends vertically (see page 52).

Engine Failure

This is normally a non-event unless you're over bad terrain. Slow landing speed allows many options from all phases of flight *provided* you stay within gliding range of safe landing sites. Keep track of wind direction to allow landing into it.

A quick response is only needed if the failure occurs during initial climb or while

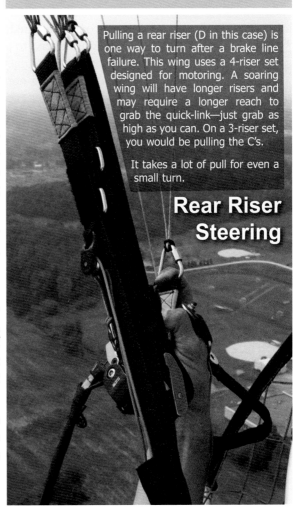

Embarrassment Avoided

Right after liftoff, during an impromptu demo flight for some police who showed up, I discovered the right brake was stuck (bad preflight). Not wanting to look bad in front of our new observers, I came back around and landed using the rear risers to flare. They had no idea that anything was amiss and I wasn't about to tell them.

"Wasn't that cool?" I asked while quietly fixing my brake. "Here, I'll go again." And I took off uneventfully this time.

They probably wondered why that flight was so much longer.

Pulling a rear riser (D in this case) is one way to turn after a brake line failure. This wing uses a 4-riser set designed for motoring. A soaring wing will have longer risers and may require a longer reach to grab the quick-link—just grab as high as you can. On a 3-riser set, you would be pulling the C's.

It takes a lot of pull for even a small turn.

Rear Riser Steering

ENGINE FAILURE
During Takeoff or At Low Altitude

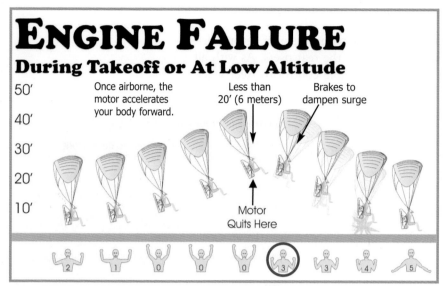

50'
40'
30'
20'
10'

Once airborne, the motor accelerates your body forward.

Less than 20' (6 meters)

Brakes to dampen surge

Motor Quits Here

Above: A motor failure *just* after take-off requires dampening the surge immediately by pulling brakes. That prevents diving into the ground.

With more height, 30 feet (9 meters) or so, dampen (brake) less aggressively, establish a brief glide, then do a normal landing.

Not doing anything would let the wing surge forward followed by you swinging back under it (the faded flyer).

Smaller wings (higher wing loadings) require more altitude.

The Spectator Question

You'll hear this a lot: "What do you do when the engine quits?"

For best effect, answer "plummet and die." But the real answer is actually quite mundane: "Not much," at least if you're above 200 feet.

If it happens closer to the ground things get more urgent as shown above.

flying low (under 20 feet) as shown at left. Steeper climbs beget stronger surges.

After that initial surge is controlled, ease your hands up to accelerate for a normal flare. Less than 10-20 feet, the brakes should just be held with a flare at the normal height. There won't be much brake left for flare but it beats coming off the brakes and diving into the ground.

A motor failure from more than 50-100 feet gives plenty of time to turn into the wind for a normal landing.

If you have enough time (more than a couple hundred feet), get established in a landing pattern, *then* try to restart. Always attend to piloting before dealing with the motor. Try different throttle settings. If you *do* get it started, maintain the same power setting until reaching a point where a normal power-off landing pattern can be made. Plan the landing with no power even if you let the motor idle.

Concentrate on the landing once you're below 200 feet.

Landing Priorities

Landing into the wind (upwind) is a big thing but it's not the only thing. Be level, on the best surface, and with a good flare.

Always flare! Even if you're not quite into the wind, do a good flare where you swing out to get the slowest possible forward and downward speed before touchdown (impact). If you've pulled too much brake, or too early, you'll have nothing left to flare with.

As covered earlier under "Above All," priorities change based on circumstance but only accept an off-wind landing if your into-the-wind options are much worse. The stronger the wind, the more important landing into it is.

Turbulence - Non Reflex

On non-reflex wings if conditions turn bumpy, set trimmers to slow and increase brake pressure to about level 2 and let it ride. *Pressure* is key. If a brake handle tries to yank upwards, let it, while maintaining the same pressure. Likewise, if a toggle goes limp, let it go down. When throttling off, increase brake pressure slightly, almost to 3. At low power settings, slowing down is generally better, but be careful—too much brake has proven more dangerous than not enough.

You'll be swinging around some but don't try to correct for individual swings. If you need to turn, *hold* some brake input for at least 3 seconds, and turn slowly. This avoids inducing or worsening pilot-induced roll oscillations. In almost all cases, newer pilots who try to counteract oscillations (active piloting) make them worse. If you *do* start oscillating, ease up pressure, hold both arms steady, and ride it out.

Keep a good posture with elbows in to further minimize over-controlling.

Flying this way reduces the chance of various wing maladies where the leading edge tucks under, causing a brief but rapid descent and possibly a serious turn.

Chapter 16 covers active flying but trying that before you're ready will only make matters worse due to the unusual pendular action of our craft.

Turbulence - Reflex

Reflex wing handling in turbulence depends on wing design and pilot experience. Some reflex makers suggest handling turbulence by letting the trimmers out (fast) and only using tip steering. Others suggest putting the trimmers slow and flying like a traditional glider as just described. Always follow the wing's manual.

Small Asymmetric Wing Collapse

Small wing collapses happen occasionally in turbulence and the wing usually snaps back before the pilot even knows what happened. Generally, just following the turbulence advice above will suffice.

Small collapses that don't come out immediately can normally be cured with *gentle* pressure on that side's brake. Just do what it takes to steer straight and the wing will likely reform quickly. A stronger, quick pull of brake on that side may also work but don't overdo it.

Large Asymmetric Wing Collapse

A severe asymmetric collapse, covered in Chapter 18, is where more than half of the wing tucks under. It is rare enough in powered paragliding that most pilots have never experienced it. With a motor, lines *could* wrap around the prop or a frame part. That's why flying in *big air* (strong turbulence) is best avoided.

If you get a large collapse, up to 55%, it's still flyable. The *initial* reaction remains to smoothly **reduce power, reduce brake pressure, then steer** about as fast as you say those words. That helps fight the tendency to over control which makes matters worse. Then carefully brake and weight shift (if your motor allows) to steer straight. Use about pressure 1 on the collapsed side (it will be limp) while steering to fly straight. Do what it takes to avoid a steepening bank, which may be a lot more brake, and be ready to let the collapsed-side brake come back up as its pressure builds.

Most collapse-related PPG incidents are from *too much* brake. If you're low to the ground or near an obstruction, do whatever it takes to steer clear even if that means a nearly immediate turn input.

Cravat

A cravat happens when part of the wing tip folds down and gets tangled in the lines, causing a turn. More fabric, more turn. A small cravat, like the one at right isn't bad, and if you can steer easily, just come around to land. Sometimes a quick brake pump to pressure 2 will clear it. It could require quick action if a turn suddenly develops. Use minimum brakes at first, but *do what it takes to fly straight* (or as straight as you can).

Consider pulling the stabilo (tip) line on the cravated side. Doing so may free the fabric if it's a fairly small cravat. The line is hard to find with so much going on which is why rehearsal in mellow conditions, or while kiting, is so valuable.

A large cravat, as covered in Chapter 18, is a *much* bigger deal.

> **⚠ Caution!**
>
> In any malady, do not accept an increasingly steep turn. After initially reducing brake pressure, use whatever input it takes to prevent a spiral dive.

Pilot induced 50% collapse is still easily controlled. Excessive brake use causes many, if not most problems.

Wily weather can do much worse: don't be fooled.

This happened during a competition run while flying on speedbar (accelerated flight). The pilot was able to continue steering straight and the fold came out on its own.

Small Cravat   By Tim kaiser

Riser Twist

If you feel yourself starting to twist during launch, abort. Do so at the first sign of any uncontrollable turn. Before trying again, figure out why it happened and find a cure. Torque issues are covered in Chapter 23.

If a twist starts after launch, *immediately, smoothly,* **reduce power, reduce brake pressure, then steer.** Reducing brakes helps avoid a stall/spin and ensures they're not pulled if you go into a full riser twist which could trap them.

With reduced thrust you should swing back around and resume forward flight. The glider will actually fly just fine regardless of which way you're pointing as long as you relax power and brakes. Once facing forward, throttle up only to what's necessary. An immediate landing into the wind may be your best option if terrain allows.

Riser twist almost always happens on launch. Trying to continue at full power can spin you around into a crash. Even without going all the way around, if you point left, thrust will push you left which causes a right bank (motor induced lock out). The only solution is reducing power—trying to stop the twist with brakes alone can lead to spinning and dropping.

How Torque Bites

This shows a belt-driven machine which yaws (twists) the pilot left causing a right turn. Gear driven models twist right, causing a left turn.

1, 2. Just after liftoff, various forces conspire to cause some left pilot yaw. If the wing is slightly right as you lift, that left yaw is aggravated by *loaded riser twist* (see chapter 23).

3. Once twisted, thrust now pushes your body left and the wing into a right bank.

4. Pulling excessive left brake in an effort to stop turning right may cause a spin and rapid descent as shown.

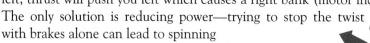

Kill Switch or Throttle Failure

Your runup should have tested the kill switch, but if it fails in flight, you won't know until landing. If you haven't rehearsed alternative methods of shutting it off inflight (see below), make a normal landing with it idling. After touchdown, carefully turn around, bring the wing down to keep lines out of the prop, and have your instructor shut it off using other means. Another option is to climb up and run it out of gas but you'll need lots of room, time, and of course, a power-off landing.

Getting the throttle cable chopped off in the prop has several ugly possibilities. It can trap your throttle at a high setting *and* disable the kill switch (see more in Chapter 19). Worse yet, it can pull your hand in the prop.

You may get stuck climbing. Hopefully, your motor has another pilot-accessible shutoff method such as a choke or primer bulb. Rehearse reaching for these in the simulator. What seems obvious while standing comfortably over the motor can be perplexing in the noisy adrenaline-pumped aftermath of a chopped throttle.

One hapless pilot who had this happen on a first solo wound up circling into the chilly heights above a large city. She climbed through controlled airspace until finally running out of fuel after several thousand feet of climb. Fortunately the instructor guided her to a successful landing.

Unfastened Leg Straps

In free-flight paragliding, forgetting to buckle your leg straps can be tragic. It is equally dangerous for motor pilots if they try to hang on and "take care of it in the air." Plus, many motor pilots eventually wind up free-flying, so it's helpful to get into the habit of buckling your legs first and *un*buckling them last. Use the checklist in the Appendix *every time* to prevent this problem.

If you do forget one (or both) leg straps you'll feel it quickly on launch as the motor tries to lift off without you. If that happens, let off the power smoothly and abort! Swallow your pride and quietly buckle up before another try.

Reserve Deployment

Reserve deployments in motoring are rare but there have been "saves," usually following botched aerobatics, midair collisions, strong thermal turbulence, or huge changes in wind. Free flyers are far more likely to "toss the laundry" in strong lift or aerobatic exuberance.

Situations that warrant throwing your reserve must involve nearly complete or impending loss of control: a mid-air collision, a serious collapse, or other malady that won't recover. If you start to spiral, act fast—G-forces can build so quickly as to leave you un*able* to deploy at all. Follow the steps below deliberately to get the reserve out within 3 seconds.

1. **Kill** the motor. You don't want your "last chance" being chopped by the prop. You may be getting tossed around so this must be automatic.

2. **Look** at the reserve handle to avoid wasting time reaching endlessly for a handle that's not there. At least one pilot hit the ground while grasping wildly for the reserve handle on his right side—it was on the left.

3. **Pull** the handle out in a forceful "Z" pattern to help pull both pins positively. The reserve sits at the end of a foot-long line. It can be difficult if you've never rehearsed it in a moving simulator. Let go of the brake before pulling to avoid throwing it into the brake line. Some instructors suggest putting both brakes in one hand before tossing with the other hand.

4. **Clear.** Find a clear direction that is free of wing lines and paramotor. Be deliberate but quick.

5. **Throw** towards clear air, down and outward of any turn. It will be like tossing a 5 pound rock at the end of a foot long cord. Yank on the bridle to help open the parachute if it doesn't deploy immediately.

These actions must be rehearsed and performed with purpose. Commit this to muscle memory: "**Kill, Look, Pull, Clear, and Throw.**" Say that line over and over, making the motions, until it's automatic.

Once the reserve opens your glider may reinflate, *downplaning* and pulling the reserve sideways, reducing its effectiveness. It's generally best to disable the glider, possibly by pulling hard on the "B" lines so it cannot degrade your descent. Be aware that, while pulling lines, it can yank powerfully out of your hands, causing burns.

If everything is stable, and you're not very high, consider leaving it alone to prepare for landing.

Practice Reserve Toss

Courtesy Dave Purdin

1. This pilot is doing a reserve clinic and was surprised that his first "toss" barely moved the reserve. By the third try (pictured), he succeeded at getting it out with good force.

Throwing a reserve is much like throwing a 5-pound weight from the end of a foot-long cord.

2. A save. After launching into rough air, the pilot took a major collapse and tossed his reserve. It worked. That's never a guarantee, and the landing may be in a very bad location, but it beats the alternative.

Hold both brakes in one hand if that's how you rehearsed.

Practicing reserve tosses in a simulator being shaken by the instructor.

Parachute Landing Fall
By Dennis Pagen

1   2   3   4   5

Parachute Landing Fall

Landing under a reserve will probably be pretty hard. Depending on your weight and reserve size, the descent rate at touchdown will be the equivalent of jumping off a 4-6 foot table depending on reserve size, your weight, and wind conditions. The bigger the reserve, the softer the arrival.

Many years ago, military paratroopers devised a way to get their soldiers down with fewer injuries—the Parachute Landing Fall (PLF). It works well for landings under reserve or any hard landing.

The idea is to transfer vertical energy into horizontal energy. For a motor pilot, the frame will usually intervene during the roll which is good. Some instructors advocate lifting your legs and letting the frame take the impact. While that may work, be very mindful of protecting your spine. Success depends on your motor's frame bottom. Consider that a broken leg beats a broken back.

Once you recognize the need for a PLF, put your legs together with knees slightly bent. At touchdown roll in whatever direction is natural, absorbing some with the knees, then hips then the frame should take the rest. Allow yourself to roll it out and end up on your back (or frame, more likely) as depicted.

If you remember nothing else, make sure your legs are together with knees slightly bent and toes slightly down.

When approaching the ground, look at the horizon and prepare for the *Parachute Landing Fall* (PLF), a tried and true method for absorbing high impact forces. Put your legs together with knees slightly bent. You'll hit hard but try to orient yourself such that you can roll to one side or the other. It should be feet, knee, hip, then shoulder, ending in a rolling motion. Use the motor to absorb some impact if the frame is below you. Protect your spine at all costs. Pulling your legs up to hit on the motor's frame may reduce the chance for leg injuries at the expense of your spine. Use the frame (lift your legs) only if you *know* it will give sufficient protection.

Parachutal Stall/Spin

A wing goes parachutal when it stops flying forward and starts descending vertically like an old round parachute. The wing, which remains fully inflated, may seem to fall back as forward airspeed slows. It usually involves several factors, including too much brake, turbulence, power, or a combination thereof. Many of these turn into spins, where the glider rotates due to one side having slightly more drag (from brakes or turbulence). See Chapter 19 for more details.

Parachutal stall is far more common under power because thrust keeps the paraglider stalled where it would otherwise recover on its own. Most PPG accidents involve the pilot impacting at full power under a fully inflated wing and frequently spinning. But it can also be caused by simply pulling too much brake, such as when slowing down to make a landing spot.

Recovery is simple but must be done *immediately* and fully upon feeling the wing slow down or the airflow stop. Thankfully, the default emergency reaction will normally work: "**Reduce Power, Reduce Brakes, Then Steer.**" In this case, reduce *all* power, let *completely* up on the brakes and be prepared to dampen a surge when the wing recovers into flight.

In the *extremely* unlikely chance that it's *still* not flying, and you're well above a hundred feet, then: reach for the A's, palms forward, thumbs down, grab and twist the A's down about 2 inches. This is called *tweaking the A's*. If you happen to have your feet on the speedbar (not likely), then push it. If a full vertical descent had established, recovery can be violent. Letting out the trimmers could also work.

Be aware that during recovery, the wing may surge violently forward, followed by you swinging below it. With too little altitude, that might be worse than landing from the parachutal stall. So if you're below about 60 feet, it's probably better to ride it down and prepare for the PLF.

The Flight

5

Time to fly.

It's not always some momentous event, but rather a converging of skills and conditions that find you ready. You've learned essential kiting skills, rehearsed the flight and know what to expect. You've been practicing, waiting for the right conditions (see Chapter 7), and now they have arrived.

This day's flight adds new and significant elements into the mix: Sensation and adrenaline—don't underestimate them. That is why you've practiced so much. In the face of kinematic newness, you can't think things through. Anything not rehearsed will likely be done wrong. Like airline trainers, PPG instructors know of this human shortcoming and have found repetitive practice to be invaluable.

Your first flights should be on a beginner wing! History has shown that more advanced wings are unforgiving of certain, relatively common, beginner mistakes. Your first mission is to not get hurt.

Launch

Variations in technique exist to accommodate different equipment, conditions, experience and simple preference; do what you've learned to minimize surprises. Listen intently to your instructor. Be prepared to abort quickly and nothing gets fed to a hungry propeller.

Unlike other forms of flight, launch is literally and figuratively the biggest hurdle. You'll spend more time on this one area than all the others combined.

Let's begin. After preflight, check that the throttle is at idle and free moving. Say "clear prop," wait a second, then carefully start and warm it up then shut down.

Lay out your wing as instructed (see Chapter 3). A good layout is critical to launch success in light winds. Start the motor again and strap it on, fastening all the harness straps, starting with the leg straps. It's best to start with the legs because forgetting those has the worst consequence, especially if you ever go free flying. Get the throttle

Below: Airlines use checklists for good reason: they work. Skipping the checklist for expediency or omitting items has proven deadly.

In comparison to a Boeing 737 our checklist is mercifully brief. It is no less important though. An easy-to-use set of checklists is in back of the book.

Before launch, do the checklist (inside back of the book). Mind where the prop blast goes and keep the propeller plane away from bystanders in case it sheds pieces.

1. Ready for inflation: Throttle, A's and brakes properly held, the other risers draped over your biceps or forearms and the throttle trigger is free. You must be able to get to the kill switch immediately if something goes awry.

2. Pulling too much A's causes the leading edge to fold downward or *front tuck*. It doesn't like that.

situated comfortably in your hand then hook in like in Chapter 3. With everything now connected, do a pre-launch checklist from memory to cover the basics (see Appendix - Checklists).

You'll do just as you've rehearsed, but now with the motor's throttle, thrust, and weight, it will feel different. Hopefully you practiced with a throttle simulator.

Just before launch, determine the wind direction (See Chapter 7). Your face is best suited for this if the prop isn't spinning (clutched machines), otherwise use whatever wind indicators are available. If the wind has turned significantly, you'll either need to wait or move. When it's light and variable, waiting may be the better course. As the day wears on, thermals increasingly come through and can change the wind direction dramatically from minute to minute. About the time you get it laid out into a new direction, a thermal comes by, changing it again.

Rehearse the abort: "Release throttle, press *and hold* kill switch."

Inflation—Light or Nil Wind

Launching in zero wind is our toughest task, and there are many variations. We'll present two techniques and a variation; they all start with a nice layout as described in Chapter 3. Tension the lines slightly without curling the leading edge, get centered, be perpendicular to the glider and take one step back. If the A's are split, use the centers. Don't make a running start—it tends to cause crooked inflations.

Regardless of technique: start with your arms back, leading with your chest. Once the glider takes shape, *then* pull an appropriate amount of A's. Some gliders require more, some less, and some glider/motor combinations require holding your arms up more. A good instructor will know. And he will earn his entire keep in that moment.

1. Partial Power Forward.

This is a reliable method, but it's not for all machines, namely larger pilots on bigger wings and/or with powerful motors. For those, use a no power forward (shown next.)

Using too much power initially can make it go wrong quickly—cages give, the wing darts overhead too fast, or once it comes overhead, the sudden acceleration pushes you over onto your face. They're all expensive. Partial power means holding about 25% power before starting the run. See below for a description.

Partial Power Forward: Most effective method if your cage can take it

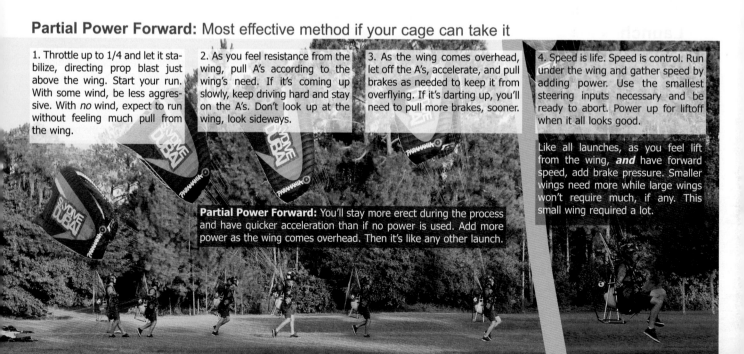

1. Throttle up to 1/4 and let it stabilize, directing prop blast just above the wing. Start your run. With some wind, be less aggressive. With *no* wind, expect to run without feeling much pull from the wing.

2. As you feel resistance from the wing, pull A's according to the wing's need. If it's coming up slowly, keep driving hard and stay on the A's. Don't look up at the wing, look sideways.

3. As the wing comes overhead, let off the A's, accelerate, and pull brakes as needed to keep it from overflying. If it's darting up, you'll need to pull more brakes, sooner.

4. Speed is life. Speed is control. Run under the wing and gather speed by adding power. Use the smallest steering inputs necessary and be ready to abort. Power up for liftoff when it all looks good.

Like all launches, as you feel lift from the wing, **and** have forward speed, add brake pressure. Smaller wings need more while large wings won't require much, if any. This small wing required a lot.

Partial Power Forward: You'll stay more erect during the process and have quicker acceleration than if no power is used. Add more power as the wing comes overhead. Then it's like any other launch.

2. No Power Inflation

On a no-power inflation, it's all you. This is more difficult with large wings due to their higher air resistance while coming up. It's even more difficult if the wing feels a slight tailwind up at 15 feet (3 meters).

You'll start just like you did in Chapter 3, leading with your chest, then arms, pulling A's as needed by the wing. The challenge is coming in with power just as the wing comes up past 60° or so. You must throttle up but not while the lines are still pushing against the cage. This is the most vulnerable time; the wing is likely to fall back or sideways because it's feeling so little airspeed.

2a. No Power Inflation – Variation

A variation is to throttle up to 50% or so before starting your run. Let it stabilize then lunge forward, but *just* before reaching full line extension, throttle off. This way the motor propels you quickly into inflation without too much risk to the cage. It's good for small wings and may prevent lines from catching on some cages. Then it's just like a regular No Power Inflation.

On All Launches

Every launch is an inflation into a controlled run. As the wing comes overhead, add power. If the wing is coming up quickly, dampen it with brakes then let up so it doesn't fall back. Add only enough power to stay in a controlled run. Speed is life, speed is control, but don't try to fly before you're stable. Don't try to jump in the air—keep running until your feet are churning air. On lower powered motors some instructors may have you go to *full* power as the wing comes overhead.

Once in a controlled run with the wing overhead—tracking in a safe direction and under control—throttle up for takeoff. Think of takeoff as the reward for good control. You can't dawdle–that has its own problems–but stabbing at the throttle of a thrusty motor can provoke it into a riser twist. Be smooth. Stand upright; let the power push.

There's a lot going on during these early flights and this level of control will be tough. It's one reason why high thrust is not always best and why becoming adept at ground handling, especially with a practice throttle, is so helpful.

Be primed to abort. If anything starts to go wonky, *immediately* release throttle and hold the kill switch so nothing gets fed to the prop.

During inflation, if you must look at the wing, look to the side. As the wing comes overhead, looking up tends to slow you down. In calm or light wind concentrate on getting speed quickly. Speed is life!

Older gliders or those with shrunken lines may not come up all the way. Try setting the trimmers faster. See "Troubleshooting" on the next page.

No Power Forward: Most common method taught

1. Take 1 or 2 steps back and start with everything you've got. In no wind and/or on small wings you'll need to run and won't feel as much resistance. Speed is life.

2. Glance at the wing sideways, not upwards which tends to slow you down. Stay on the A's. As soon as the lines clear your cage, stand upright and power up.

3. Lean back into the power so you aren't leaning forward too far when the thrust kicks in. Throttle up enough to get into a controlled run.

4. From here it's like the partial power launch described on the opposite page but you get to relish your success a bit more. And no cage pieces get fed to the prop.

No Power Forward: It was the same shutter rate as the partial power forward. You can see that acceleration is slower. He stands up and throttles up the moment the wing lines get high enough.

Troubleshooting *Forward* Launch Problems

Some are contradictory because they address different problems. Follow your instructor's advice: he *sees* what's happening.

Symptom 1: Wing comes up crooked.

1. You're not starting or continuing the run exactly centered and perpendicular to the wing.
2. If the wing always comes up to the left, point your body, and run slightly to the right.
3. Start from a clean surface with a good U or V shaped layout and be pointed exactly into whatever whiff of wind is present.
4. Be more aggressive to build speed faster. Speed improves control. This is easier with a relatively small wing.
5. You're pulling too much A's or pulling them unevenly. Lead with your chest (arms back), then A's, then power.
6. Lines are catching on the cage (right). Install smooth tubing around the offending cage hoop and ensure there is nothing to snag on. Don't use line holders for foot launching. Holding your arms up higher or wiggling the A's during the initial inflation doesn't help much since it's usually the rear lines that catch.
7. A brake is tied too short or there is something caught in the lines.
8. Use the center A's if they're split.

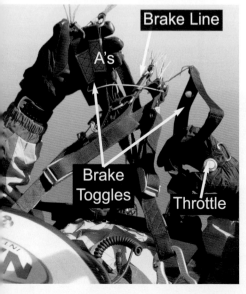

Symptom 2: The wing doesn't come all the way overhead, especially when there's no wind.

1. Stay on the A's longer and delay going to the brakes. Some wings, especially older gliders, require lots of A pull during inflation *and* acceleration. Also, gather good forward speed before applying any brakes.
2. Make sure you're not pulling brakes inadvertently. Try this: After letting go of the A's, touch the risers before pulling any brake.
3. You're pulling *too much* A's and curling the leading edge. Have your arms back to start the inflation *then* apply A pressure.
4. Not enough power or not throttling up early enough.
5. Your initial run needs to be more aggressive. It's common to slow down when looking back at the wing—keep driving forward.
6. Let the trimmers out (faster setting) some. This will require a faster launch run, though.
7. Don't look up at the wing; look sidewise while continuing to drive forward.
8. Some pilots *may* benefit from looking up at the wing as they throttle up if it forces them into a more correct upright posture.
9. The brakes are tied too short or the rear lines have shrunk. See Chapter 12 on line stretching.

Symptom 3: The wing tends to over-fly me then collapse, especially with some wind.

1. Get off the A's earlier and dampen with brakes earlier. Apply enough brakes to dampen then let off.
2. Make sure the trimmers are in their slowest setting (pulled in).
3. If using power, use less. Prop blast aggravates the problem.

Symptom 4: I Can't get airborne in spite of running my fastest.

1. After initial inflation, stand up straight as you ease into full power. Concentrate on letting the motor push you as fast as your legs will go with long strides before adding more brake. You may need brake to take off but then ease them up to climb.
2. Make sure the trimmers are in (set neutral or slow), your motor is producing normal peak RPM and you're into the wind. If the motor is making full RPM but it's not pushing hard enough, make sure the prop is not mounted backwards.
3. Adjust your harness for the least amount of tilt-back possible so the wing's lift doesn't force you to run while tilted back.
4. If it's calm, try going the other way. It's possible the wind at 15 feet is oozing the opposite direction.

Symptom 5: I tend to go side to side before lifting off and almost fall.

1. Once you get the wing up overhead and moving, use just enough power to keep moving, steer the wing overhead straight, then go up to full power for lift off. Never takeoff with the wing off-center—it must be almost exactly overhead before throttling up.
2. Don't change running direction much. Only correct *half* as much as you think.
3. Master forward kiting through an obstacle course—steering the wing then following it.
4. Stand straight up early in the launch run. If you're leaning forward, then the wing lifts you into an upright run; precession will impart a twist. Consider using less power for initial climb.
5. Adjust your harness to minimize torque affects (see Chapter 12); primarily, decrease any tilt-back.
6. Make sure the wing is either exactly overhead or slightly left (right for geared machines) just as you lift off to prevent *loaded riser twist*.

Symptom 6: I tend to sink back down to the ground and land on my butt.

1. Keep running until you are churning air. Don't get in the seat until well clear of the ground and established in a climb.
2. Don't let off the brakes too quickly after liftoff. Ease them up slowly to accelerate into a climb.
3. Adjust the harness to prevent the seat from kicking you into the air too early. Be less tilted back.

Reverse Inflation—Stronger Conditions

Anytime you can stand there and kite the wing, do a reverse inflation. With enough wind, build a wall as described in Chapter 3.

You'll be facing the wing holding everything as shown at left. With the A's in one hand and throttle in the other, lean a bit towards the wing. When ready, snap back using your *body* to pull the wing up with just a *bit* of pull on the A's. Get it stable overhead and moving into the wind (walking backwards) before turning around. You want the wing to have some forward momentum before turning around. Then as soon as you are facing forward, *move forward*. Turn and move. Throttle up in the turn to help keep forward motion.

Your instructor *may* have you hold off throttling up until you're walking for-

Troubleshooting *Reverse* Launch Problems

The reverse launch can vary from easy to frustrating depending on conditions. Here are some possible cures for your troubles.

Symptom 1: Wing doesn't come up even when the wind should be strong enough.
1. Take one step toward the wing before moving backwards to build momentum when you back up.
2. Only barely pull on the A's until most of the fabric is mostly inflated; then pull primarily with your body.
3. If there is enough wind, building a "wall" helps make sure it comes up straight and quickly.

Symptom 2: The wing falls back when I turn around.
1. With the wing overhead, step backwards to get it moving, go hands UP, turn around and start moving forward immediately.
2. Throttle up during the turn so there is less delay in getting forward momentum.
3. Try to turn around only when the wing has forward momentum (into the wind).
4. Do a forward inflation instead.

Symptom 3: The wing falls over sideways when I turn around.
1. Ensure the brakes are up when you turn and the wing is tracking straight in the same direction as your movement.
2. Avoid stepping significantly sideways as you turn. If you step left, the wing will fall to the right.

A's in one hand

1. Building a wall is best if there's enough wind. Wing layout must be such that your back is square to the wind.

2. Snap back hard with your body, applying pressure to the A's as they allow. Keep walking backwards, if necessary.

3. Use no brakes as the wing comes up unless needed to slow it. Move left or right with the wing. Pull the A's as necessary.

4 & 5. Use minimum or no brakes while turning around and throttling up. A quick transition to forward motion is key. Add brake to prevent a frontal.

ward with the wing stable. That reduces the chance of having the wing overfly and collapse into the prop but is more difficult in lighter winds. As soon as you've verified that the wing is under control, add *some* throttle and move.

Another approach is to go strictly by feel: turn around and throttle up while looking forward *and moving*, responding to the small left or right tugs from the wing. Obviously this takes practice.

If the wing tends to fall back, you're applying too much brake or not moving enough. It needs airflow for control so keep moving. As it comes overhead, reduce brake pressure but prevent it from overflying you. If it's coming up fast, you'll need to dampen (pull some brake), then ease up, turn, and move.

During the turnaround, your hands go mostly up to avoid engaging any brake. Plus, you must move forward immediately after turning around. Don't just stand there; get moving. The wing needs airspeed, feed it. Once moving and under control, it's just like a forward launch.

As with forwards, be quick to abort if it isn't going well—kill the motor and turn around. Trying again is better than "parablending" your wing.

When everything looks good, you're running in the right direction with the wing overhead *and* tracking straight, throttle up and hold it. Stand up straight and let the motor push while taking increasingly larger strides. Sideways glances at the wing are OK, but concentrate on running and steering. If the wing tries to pull right, steer it back to the left with *just enough* brake.

As the wing lifts, but while you're still running, steer it slightly left (right for geared machines) to reduce torque twisting effects (*Loaded Riser Twist*). Approaching your fastest run, add brake pressure, easing off after liftoff.

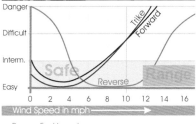

1. It's in the body, not the arms. Pull a bit of A's while staying loose on the brake (right hand) and be primed for the kill switch.

2. This chart helps select a launch method based on winds. Light wind reverses increase the chance of falling backwards while high wind forwards increase the chance of being pulled back into a "turtle" position. Trike flying is covered in the next chapter.

Getting Seated

Rehearse getting seated in the simulator; it's not always easy and may require a particular technique that your instructor will cover like in the picture above.

Regardless of how you do it: **Don't pull brakes while getting into the seat!** Students have stalled their glider by reaching down for the seat with brakes still in their hands. Your instructor may have you show an open hand *before* reaching down to make sure you aren't holding a brake toggle.

Also, be careful letting go of a brake. It can get sucked into the prop. If a kick-in strap is used, a bar that hangs down about 6 inches below the seat lip is ideal. Elastic is nice so that it stretches out when needed, but stays close to the seat otherwise.

How the Seat Board Moves

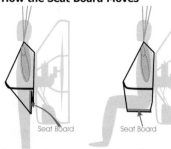

Standing/Launch   Seated/Flight

> ⚠ **Caution**
>
> If you must reach down for the seat, **let go of and stow the brake(s) first!** Do it slowly, too. On some configurations it's possible for the brakes to flail into the prop.

Climbout

Use minimum brake while climbing out: "Hands up to go up." And when you do use brake for turning, always pull and hold **for at least 3 seconds**. This piece of advice may save your life—it prevents getting into pilot-induced oscillations.

All motors *torque*, which causes a turn, but use minimal brake to counteract it. If possible, let it turn in the direction it wants to go. If you feel any twisting in the risers, *ease* off the power by half immediately even if your climb rate will suffer. If you *must* turn against the torque, do so gingerly. Too much brake will cause a *spin* (see Chapter 18).

If your body starts twisting one way but the wing is banking the other way, you are entering a *motor-induced lockout* and *must* reduce power immediately.

Climb up to at least 300 ft above the ground while keeping your landing area within gliding range. Altitude is your friend; it provides options and avoids obstacles—you can't hit something below you.

Reaching a safe altitude, reduce power. Avoid long-term use of full power whenever possible, for the motor's sake.

Getting into the Seat

This action turns out to be surprisingly critical. After liftoff, you'll be hanging uncomfortably by the leg straps. If you cannot get into the seat easily, without letting go of the brakes, keep climbing. Tough it out until at least 50 feet high or advised by your instructor, but you must land within about 5 minutes.

If it's easy to get seated with*out* letting go of the brakes (may require a kick-in strap), get in the seat once a safe climb is established. Some machines, when adjusted properly, require just lifting the legs while wiggling to become seated.

If you *have* to reach down for the seat, be ready for a motor failure; new pilots sometimes hit the kill switch or get the throttle chopped off when it loops back towards the prop.

If the harness is not setup properly, especially if the leg straps are too loose, it may be impossible to get into the seat.

Machines equipped with a *kick-in strap* or bar let you keep the brakes in your hands while kicking in. If the bar is hard to reach with just a foot, carefully stow the non-throttle brake toggle and reach down to position the strap for your foot. Then kick out the seat.

The next best way to get seated is by using one hand to push down on the back of the seatboard. Carefully stow your non-throttle brake toggle or, if possible, put it in your throttle hand. Then reach down with your free hand.

The least desirable way is using both hands. *Carefully* stow the brakes in their keepers then, reach down. Make it two distinct steps: stow the brakes (some machines may allow just letting go) ensuring that they can't go in the prop, then go for the seat. Using your thumbs, grasp the outer part of the seatboard (where the front strap attaches), pushing down and forward. On some motors, it's easier to push down on the back part of the seatboard to pop it "under center." Be careful not to press the kill switch.

Tightening the leg straps makes it easier to get into the seat on most machines but more difficult to run. Tighten them all the way, then loosen a couple inches. Setting it up properly may allow you to wiggle into the seat. Get several successful launches under your belt before trying the wiggle, though, since its contortions can result in killing the motor.

If it proves too difficult to get into the seat (this *can* happen on some equipment), return to land promptly so your landing gear doesn't go numb.

Rehearse getting into the seat while hanging in a simulator, preferably with the motor running for realism. Do it until the action is automatic.

Flying Around

Now the reward: You're flying! Once up at altitude, everything gets much easier; it's time to relax a bit and enjoy the view. Your instructor may have you try a few things after a while. Normally the flight should last no more than about a half hour to make sure you have no numb or tired parts (like arms).

Having an Out

Your first flights will be a sensory flood, drowning out many normal thought processes. That's why rehearsal, and an instructor on the radio, is so beneficial—but there are still some things you must think about.

1. Where would I land if the motor quit? Allow enough altitude to get back and set up a pattern. 500 feet is generally about right. Always have an out; the engine *will* eventually quit.

2. What is the wind doing? Where are the wind shadows and rotors (see Chapter 7)? Winds may change during your flight, possibly even reversing, and you must always plan on landing *into* it.

3. How much fuel/time do I have left? Noting your launch time and knowing your endurance is one way to avoid running out of gas. But it's also good to check the fuel level using a visual means such as a mirror. Even if you started with enough fuel, it is possible for a leak to dramatically reduce your flying time.

Posture

Keeping good posture does more than make you look good—it helps avoid over-controlling. Primarily that's elbows in, legs together, head upright, and never holding the risers. Holding the risers is like grasping the dash on a car—it may feel good but doesn't do much for control.

Turns

Before turning, use "Look, Lean, Pull, then Power." **Look** where you're about to turn (*clearing the turn*), **lean** if you are using weight shift, **pull and hold** brake to turn then add **power** to hold altitude in the turn. Others will see your intentions, too, if your looking is deliberate. Start with a **shallow** turn, then look **up** and **down** in the direction of turn, and finally, turn.

Pulling one brake means first relaxing the other brake slightly. Pull brake

"Having an out" means having a good landing option. Always be assessing where you'll go when the motor quits.

The "Bump Scale:"

Here is a common reference to help when relating "bumpiness" to other pilots:

0 Completely smooth

1 Getting jostled, no real change in flight path.

2 Causes small changes in flight path. The most that new pilots should fly in.

3 Causes body swings of around 3 feet with no control input.

4 Causes moderate changes in flight path and body movements of around 5 ft. Significant surging & retreating with small tip collapses on high performance wings.

5 Very active air. Causes small tip collapses even on beginner wings.

6 Causes 50% collapses on high performance wings.

7 Causes 50% collapses even on beginner wings.

8-10 Increasing levels of dangerous air where 10 is completely uncontrollable.

in the turn direction slowly and *hold* it for at least three seconds or longer as needed. Start with position/pressure 1. Learn how much pressure it takes to get to position 1 and use that feeling (pressure). When pulling the brake initially, you will swing out, then swing back to a stable shallow turn. Don't try to counteract that swing—hold the brake for 3 seconds *minimum*. Don't try to damp oscillations yet either; just use measured, steady pressure and wait for the turn to develop. Too much brake will spin the glider (see Chapter 18).

To level out of the turn, let up the brake *slowly* (take about 3 seconds). It needs to be released slower than the glider's natural swing rate (pendular period). Letting off too quickly will cause a left/right oscillation. Keeping your elbows in and forearm vertical will naturally help prevent over-braking.

Wake Turbulence

Planes and paragliders fly by pushing air down as they move through it. They spin off powerful little tip vortices along the way that spread slowly, drifting with the wind, and settling about 300 feet per minute (see Chapter 22).

Turning more than about 180° may result in flying through your own wake, a potentially startling ripple in your universe. It's not prop blast either, which is a disorganized burble of minimal effect.

Altitudes

Altitude means options; you stay above obstacles, have time to handle unhappy engines, and can reach more landing sites.

Pattern altitude is about 200-300 feet (about 90 meters) above ground level (AGL), high enough to easily make it back to the landing site and land into the wind while avoiding obstacles.

Cruising is best done between 200 and 500 feet which is below most other aircraft (except crop dusters, pipeline patrols, military, etc.) yet above most obstructions. If you're flying near an airport, learn about airplane patterns and altitudes (Chapter 10); avoiding them is legally *our* obligation.

At higher altitudes more visibility is required (see Chapter 9) but, even down low, we can't ever fly with visibility less than 1 mile.

Glide Ratio & Wind

As part of always having an out (somewhere to land), you must know how far you can glide. This *glide ratio* is how far you'll travel per unit of altitude lost. Our craft typically achieve about a 6:1 glide ratio (pronounced "six to one"), meaning that you go 6 feet forward for every foot down.

Wind affects glide. A 10 mph headwind cuts glide in half for a craft that flies 20 mph. So you'd only glide 3 feet forward for every foot down or 3:1. Conversely, a tailwind helps glide. That same 10 mph wind from behind means you're going 30 mph over the ground while still dropping at the same rate, yielding a glide ratio of 9:1 (9 feet forward for every foot down).

Wingtip Vortices

Energy & Injury

In an accident, energy and injury are powerfully intertwined. A fact of physics is that energy dissipated in a collision increases to the square of the speed: doubling the speed quadruples the energy (i.e. damage).

Consider a mere 7 mph wind and a typical flying speed of 20 mph. Hitting something while flying into the wind is a 13 mph collision. Hitting it while flying downwind is a 27 mph whack: far more dramatic, having over twice the speed and more than four times the energy!

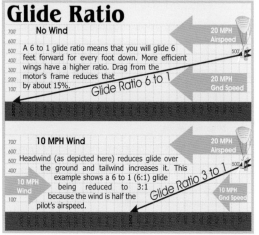

Glide Ratio

No Wind

A 6 to 1 glide ratio means that you will glide 6 feet forward for every foot down. More efficient wings have a higher ratio. Drag from the motor's frame reduces that by about 15%.

Glide Ratio 6 to 1

20 MPH Airspeed

20 MPH Gnd Speed

500'

10 MPH Wind

Headwind (as depicted here) reduces glide over the ground and tailwind increases it. This example shows a 6 to 1 (6:1) glide being reduced to 3:1 because the wind is half the pilot's airspeed.

Glide Ratio 3 to 1

20 MPH Airspeed

10 MPH Wind

10 MPH Gnd Speed

500'

Think of your landing options as a cone spreading out below you (see Chapter 19). Wind will move the cone of options downwind. As you go higher, the available area gets bigger since you can glide farther. Allow room for maneuvering and unexpected sink, too.

Ground Track

You may get aloft and notice that you're flying sideways after turning crosswind. That is because the wind is blowing you "downstream." Your wing is still flying through the air like it always does, but the air is moving over the ground and so you are—drifting with the wind.

Ground track is the line that your flight path draws over the ground. If the goal is to be flying directly into the wind, as you will on landing, then turn into the "current." If you're drifting right (sliding sideways to the right), gently turn left. Don't just pull the brake and release it, but hold the gentle turn until drifting stops. Practice this input when you're up high so it doesn't surprise you on landing. You'll want to minimize sideways drift on landing.

Reflex Wings

If your first flights will be on a reflex wing, start with the trims set to neutral (0 on some wings) and leave them. It might be a good idea to tape them to avoid accidental activation. Brake use and response will be similar to any other glider at this setting. When trimmed fast, especially with speedbar applied, these gliders prefer to be flown using their tip steering system instead of the brakes. **Consult the glider's manual.**

Before adjusting the trimmers, practice using any provided tip steering controls (toggles or balls) while trimmed neutral. When you're comfortable with that, grab the tip steering controls in your hands, stow the brakes (if necessary), *then* set the trims to fast. Some of these gliders are more collapse resistant at their higher speeds. As a beginner you should *not* be asked to do this.

Since tip steering doesn't do much in pitch (fore/aft) control, when you're ready for landing, pull the trims back to neutral (0) and return to using the brakes for normal handling.

Landing

Beyond the mechanics and concepts, landing can't be simulated well. That's why tow, hill or tandem training is so beneficial. As covered earlier under "Landing Priorities," strive to land level, into the wind and with a good flare—enough to have some swing-out before touchdown. A good instructor will be invaluable to help with timing. With just a bit of effort, landings can be reliably smooth and always on your feet or wheels.

Always choose a specific landing spot to aim for—something the size of a Frisbee. It will take plenty of practice to actually hit it, but always be trying. Don't try so hard, though, that you stall or spin. Chapter 16 and 17 have more on landing for when you're more experienced.

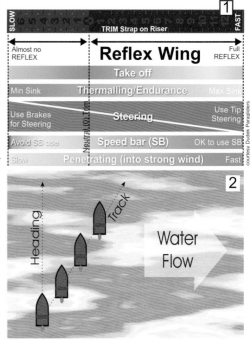

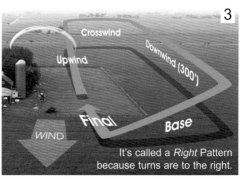

1. Reflex Wings have long trimmer travel to manage their wide speed range. But *heed the maker's manual!*

This chart shows some typical trimmer usage scenarios. For example, under steering, use the brake toggles while trimmed slow and the tip steering when trimmed fast.

2. Ground Track: Picture yourself in a glass-bottomed boat. The river's bottom is ground and the water is air. Relative to the water, you're just rowing straight forward. Relative to the river bottom, you're drifting downstream.

3. Landing patterns provide approach consistency that makes landing easier. Doing "S" turns on final is frequently done to lose altitude but should be straightened out and into the wind, by 50 feet Above Ground Level (AGL).

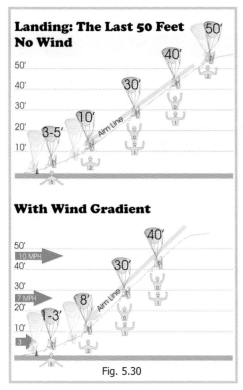

Landing: The Last 50 Feet No Wind

With Wind Gradient

Fig. 5.30

With a calm or *steady* wind, the spot that you're going to hit will not be changing angle, just getting bigger. That is your "aim line" and hopefully it's also your target.

By 50 ft be out of your seat, ease off the power, then shut off the motor. The wing will surge forward slightly as thrust quits and you'll stabilize in a descent. Keep your hands mostly up, between pressure 0 and 1.

At 10 feet, flare slightly. That will start a swing out, slowing both your forward speed and descent speed. At 2-5 feet, with one foot forward, knees bent, smoothly do a full flare. Be ready to take the weight and run. With some wind you can flare later and less. This technique varies somewhat by wing model.

With wind there's probably a wind gradient where it decreases near the ground. Descent angle steepens because the wing is diving to regain lost airspeed.

> ⚠ **Caution!**
>
> Look at your desired flight path, **not** nearby obstructions! Numerous accidents stem from *target fixation*, where a pilot looks at an obstruction, fixates on it, then flies into it.

The Landing Pattern

Landing patterns provide for an orderly arrival, plus they let you:

• plan the approach by giving common reference points;

• scope out the landing field for wind and obstructions;

• keep the flow of traffic in one direction and project where to expect other pilots—good for collision avoidance.

Initial pattern segments are named according to their relationship with the wind (see Landing Patterns graphic previous page). The downwind leg is about 300 feet away from the runway and 300 feet high. Leave the motor idling until reaching 50 feet or so in case a go-around is needed.

Patterns are either right or left according to the turn direction. A right pattern has all turns to the right and a left pattern to the left. Standard patterns for planes are to the left, but for us, direction will more often dictated by wind and terrain.

Enter on the downwind leg, flying level at about 300 feet AGL. Pass beside the desired landing point (abeam) and continue until it is about 45° behind you then ease off the power and turn onto base leg. Here is where to judge whether you are high or low. If it looks like you're low and might not make the spot, turn towards it. If you're high, angle away from the spot to lose altitude before lining back up.

Never turn completely away from the landing spot—you can quickly get too low or not make it back directly into the wind. Plus, losing eye contact with the desired spot can be disorienting.

Final Approach

Turn final and point yourself towards the landing spot; then extend your legs so as to be hanging by the leg loops. That action should fold the seat back to where it was on launch. Make small corrections to keep aimed at the spot. Don't over control; make only *small* brake inputs, **hold for at least 3 seconds**, then ease up.

Once it's obvious that you'll make the landing area (not overshoot or undershoot), press and hold the kill switch until the motor stops completely. If you release it early, the motor may restart. You want the prop stopped no later than 50 feet.

Be mindful of drift. If you're drifting to the left it means a wind from the right is pushing you. Ease in, *and hold* enough right brake to correct to the right until the drift is almost stopped then *ease* off the brake. Look at your wind streamers to verify wind direction.

Below 100 Feet

Below about 100 feet, disregard the spot to concentrate on landing wing level and into the wind for a good touchdown. Use minimum brakes. By 30-50 feet have your hands nearly all the way up (minimum brakes) in preparation for flare. That improves brake effectiveness (maximum speed) for the flare. Flare as shown in Fig. 5.30.

If you feel left/right swinging (like a pendulum) do nothing! Make no left/right corrections. If you're above 30 feet, ease *both* brakes up to position/pressure 1 *and hold*.

Pendular dynamics are such that attempting to correct will all but guarantee a hard landing. Let the wing sort itself out. It's much better to accept a small pendulum than to try correcting it at this stage.

If you notice a drift while flaring, beware of a nearly irresistible urge to extend your downwind hand as if to protect yourself from a fall. That's exactly the *wrong* input! Practice correcting for drift up high. Imagine yourself drifting left, pull and hold a *bit* of right brake for 3 seconds then ease up. Of course you cannot be aggressive on the brakes at this point but want to minimize drift, not pendulum—if it feels like a "swing," then don't do anything.

Flaring is the process of slowing forward speed and sink rate as you reach the ground. It must be started from a nearly hands-up posture. It's not the pulled trailing edge, it's the forward swing that does most of the work, angling the wing up to momentarily produce more lift and slow down. (See preceding page margin).

A two stage flare also works well. Start with only a couple inches—just some pressure to get your body swinging forward, then reaching max swing, pulling more brake to arrive at the ground with nearly full brakes. Run a few steps forward then turn around and pull both brakes to quickly get the wing on the ground. If it's windy, walk towards the wing and grab a wingtip.

Before touchdown, your feet should be positioned for running—one slightly in front of the other. Touchdown with knees slightly bent, ready to absorb a potentially firm arrival. Fortunately our slow speeds and descent rates make this no big deal. Going to your knees during early landings is somewhat common, and proper posture makes that a non-event.

Controlling Glide

The touchdown point can be predicted while gliding straight ahead. If it appears to be rising (you increasingly must look up) in your field of view then you're going to land short. If it is falling below (you increasingly looking lower) then you will pass over it. The stationary point is where you're going to land. You've actually been doing this for years when walking or driving but in a horizontal direction: the stationary spot in your windshield or visual field is where you're headed; everything else slides by your periphery.

Gliding for spot 3, put your shoe up to the spot. If the spot rises as you descend, you'll land short. If the spot sinks below your shoe, you'll overfly it.

When trying to stretch glide *against* a wind, be hands up with trimmers out for more speed. Even with the higher sink rate, you'll cover more ground.

courtesy Lowes.com

1. Stowing equipment properly can be extremely important in some settings!

2. Readily available vehicle platforms, and modified bike racks, are common transporters for those without a truck or van. See Chapter 31 for more ideas.

As covered on page 60, glide is steeper (worse) when flying into a headwind and shallower with a tailwind. In a headwind you can steepen the descent by slowing down, but don't overdo it. Use no more than about a quarter brake (position/pressure 2) until you're *very* familiar with the wing. If you do slow down, ease up the brakes (take 3 seconds) to speed back up by 50 feet AGL (15 meters) so as to have enough speed left for an effective flare. As you let the brakes up, expect to drop 20 feet (6 meters) or so while regaining speed.

You can also do small S-turns to lose altitude and effectively shorten a glide. Keep them shallow, though, and get yourself steadily back into the wind by 50-100 feet.

Go Around

If something is amiss with your landing, do a *go-around* to climb back up. Use two steps: throttle to half power *and wait* 3 seconds, you'll swing out then start to swing back, now *smoothly* throttle up to climb power, usually full.

After Landing

Run out the landing enough to keep the wing from overflying you; it should come down behind you. As you stop, turn around quickly and apply brakes so that it falls on its top. This makes bundling or folding easier, offers less chance for the lines to become tangled, keeps lines out off of the motor, and looks more refined.

Unclip quickly to avoid letting a gust catch the wing and pull you off balance. Wearing a motor makes this both more likely and more expensive.

Postflight

Get the wing covered to reduce its UV exposure, even with clouds. Either fold, bundle, or put it in the shade and away from sandy, dusty, or gravel areas.

Check out the motor and harness just like a preflight inspection. It's far better to discover problems now so you can fix them before your next session. Even if it was running fine when you landed, parts loosen, props get nicked, and gremlins gnaw on flexible stuff.

Cleaning

Cleaning the machine after each flight allows detection of cracks, crankcase leaks, and other problems that can hide under a cloak of grime. For example, if you see a large increase in the amount of black goo squirting onto the prop, suspect problems; that's hard to detect with a dirty machine.

Gasoline, WD-40, and mineral spirits are good for wiping down motor parts. Carburetor cleaner is great on un-painted surfaces but is brutal on paint. Avoid getting citrus-based cleaners on aluminum. Fabric sprays that offer other protection work well and help preserve the gear but don't use them on wing fabric. If possible, cover the motor during transport to prevent UV damage to the harness; it fades pretty quickly when exposed to sunlight.

Clean the wing by draping the trailing edge over a clothes line hung high enough to keep the leading edge off the ground. Spray clean water (no solvents) on the outside and up into the cells. Dirt and debris will run out. Let it air dry, preferably out of the sun. Dust and sand abrade the fabric, shortening its life.

Adding Wheels

CHAPTER

6

Wheels add a whole new dimension to Powered Paragliding, enabling more people to fly and providing another layer of fun. They can be anything from a simple add-on cart up to heavier, purpose-built machines with integrated motor and seat.

There will be more weight and drag so speeds are higher, climb rate is less, and fuel burn is higher than the same foot-launched craft. Bigger motors are preferred since there's no help from your legs during initial inflation.

Carts do impose limitations; mostly they don't like uneven ground or strong wind. They're more difficult in some respects—you can't step sideways during launch—but are overall easier, especially in nil winds or high elevations where groundspeed is higher.

Just like foot-launching, more skill means more capabilities. A good wheel pilot can handle nearly as much wind as a good foot launcher—it mostly depends on wing-handling skill. The practical wind limit for most pilots is 8-10 mph since reverse inflation is very difficult on wheels (see Chapter 15).

Tandem operations (See Chapter 8 for legalities) with wheels are easier and safer since little is required of the passenger/student. In foot launched tandems, the student must be active which is asking a lot for a first flight. Wheels allow the student to take it all in while only getting involved as the instructor sees fit.

Large, soft, and slippery wheels are preferred since they act like shock absorbers and roll better on rough or soft surfaces. Being able to slide helps reduce the chance of flipping over since they don't grab in a sideways drift. Thinner wheels work OK on hard-packed surfaces. A wide wheel base, four vs. three wheels, lower center of gravity (CG), and lower hook-in points reduce tippiness.

Elisabeth Guerin launches an add-on PPG trike that uses a paramotor and its harness. Like most, you steer with your feet using pegs which are connected right to the axle. So ground steering is opposite to how certified aircraft work but the transition is quick. Aircraft-style steering is so uncommon that it makes jumping into other PPG carts more difficult. Chapter 28 has more on steering.

Wheel brakes are rare due to our low speeds; but be careful, there is more mass than you think—it's just masked by the wheels.

Fresh Breeze's Xcitor is a hybrid PPC—heavy and powerful like a PPC but with hand controls and elliptical wing like a PPG. The wing has multiple-line attachments.

Multiple line attachments behaves like A-assists.

Paratour's "PPCg" is a lightweight hybrid PPC with a moderately powerful motor and hand-controls. Its paraglider-like wing uses multiple-line attachments like a PPC.

Fly Products Flash Trike is a cable-braced, highly portable PPG trike. It uses regular riser attachments. You supply the paramotor and harness.

This Fresh Breeze pedal-powered cart doubles as a PPG trike. During launch, manual steering is locked out—the front wheel moves in response to wing pull.

Paracruiser's PPG Quad uses paraglider wing attachments, foot-launch paramotor *and* harness (check legality in your country).

By Bob Armond

Blackhawk's LowBoy quad has an integral seat but uses paraglider wing attachments and you supply the paramotor.

By Chad Bastian

TrikeBuggy.com's unit has an integral seat but uses paraglider wing attachments and you supply the paramotor.

By Terry Lutke

The "Timber Trike" may be the cheapest way to roll but you still better know what you're doing.

1

2

1. A trike *can* be reverse launched with high end wing handling skills: see Chapter 15.

2. This inexpensive trike uses an off-the-shelf 4-stroke generator motor. Affordable parts are readily available but it's heavy. A huge prop improves thrust, although that requires a large cage. It uses a regular, large paraglider and employs hand controls so it is more PPG than PPC.

Wheeled Types

Powered parachutes (PPC's) are high-powered craft with parachute style, draggy wings. They trade efficiency for ease of operation. High control forces necessitate foot steering—a primary difference from PPG's. PPC wings generally have very long risers or, on a few units, have *multiple line wing attachments* where lines attach at several points on each side.

The distinction between PPC's and wheeled PPGs have blurred, but if it's hand-flown using brake toggles and a hand throttle, then these techniques will work.

Hybrids are basically PPC's with hand controls—they are not intended to be foot launched, even without the wheels. Some of these have multiple-line wing attachments that don't unclip quickly. *Standard* wheeled PPG's use foot launchable paramotors and paragliders.

Wheeled PPG's have other distinctions such as the number of wheels. 3-wheel *trikes* are popular due to their simplicity while 4-wheel *Quads* are more stable. *Buggies* derive their name from kite buggies—low slung carts propelled by a paraglider-like kite. They usually have their own seat rather than use the paramotor's harness. *Collapsible cable-braced* carts are highly portable via their fold-up structure. A very few carts are *jettisonable*, but that's risky to others *and* the cart. Hook-in position, high or low, is another difference. High hook-in lessens in-flight wobbling of the cart while low hook-in resists tipping on the ground.

Setup

Before flying, do a hang check to make sure it balances so the rear wheels are slightly lower than the nosewheel—a 5 to 15° nose-up angle is best. If the nosewheel hangs below the rear wheels it will *wheelbarrow* on takeoff or landing, making a rollover far more likely.

Adjusting clip-in position must be done for each different pilot weight to assure proper balance. A heavy pilot will be nose heavy (very bad), and a light pilot will tend to be tipped back (not *as* bad). All tandem and most solo carts allow moving the attachment points to get a good hang angle.

Set the motor angle so that, on the ground, thrust blows just *above* the wing. That minimizes ruffling the fabric at idle and lets the cart start rolling before wing inflation. If the wing inflates before you get moving, it can cause a tug-of-war where thrust pushes against the wing which pulls back on the cart and nothing moves.

Hook up the A-helpers, if installed (see photo next page). They pull the A's during the wing's first 70° of upward arc, then become slack.

Launch

Nearly all cart launches are forward inflations. See Chapter 15 for the advanced technique of doing reverses. Layout is just like a forward foot launch.

The wing and cart must be centered and directly into the wind. Lines should drape over the line holders, if installed, and be clear of the rear wheels (see image 3). Before starting, roll the cart forward, barely tensioning the lines to insure everything is centered. A slight tension keeps the lines from getting sucked into the prop. Some instructors recommend rolling it back a few feet to allow some speed build up on launch, but not if the prop is likely to suck in lines.

The basic launch sequence is **Power** (partial or full as required), **A's** (if required), **Dampen** the wing as it gets overhead, **Reduce** Power, **Taxi**, then **Takeoff** if everything looks good. Of course timing is everything.

1. Start the motor, get in, and buckle up. Go through your pre-launch checklist. A little wing ruffling is OK as long as it doesn't ruin your layout. Strap the throttle onto your hand, grab the brakes, then put the A's between your thumb and palm (if no A helpers). Put your feet on the steering pegs.

2. Look around to clear the area then throttle up. How much throttle depends on your gear. Powerful units on smooth surfaces with small or easy inflating gliders do better with partial power.

   How much A's you hold depends on the wing. Most require some A-pressure while a few larger models require a lot. It also depends on the cart's seating arrangement and whether you can get a good hold of the A's. Machines with A helpers pull the A's for you.

3. Look back at the wing—it's easiest to look left or right. A mirror can be helpful, too. As the wing comes overhead let off the A's and be ready to pull some brakes briefly to prevent the wing from overflying. Stay on the power until after dampening. Reducing power early or not dampening enough will let the wing overfly you and dive expensively into the prop.

   If the wing rockets upwards, get off the A's early, dampening it sooner and with more vigor. Stay on the power though—when the wing comes up quickly it usually stops the cart. Be just as quick to let off your dampening brake pressure as the wing comes overhead.

   If the wing is hanging back or coming up slowly, you'll need to stay on

1. Wing lift effectively raises the center of gravity (CG), making it surprisingly easy to topple a trike with the wing up and a bit crooked.

2. A natural reaction to tipping is to put a hand out as if to brace against falling. That pulls the wrong brake *and* may break the hand, too.

   Rehearse reaction to a rollover: practice keeping your hands inward and feet firmly on the pegs.

3. Adjust to keep the back wheels below the front wheel(s) in flight.

4. Wood planks for soft sand.

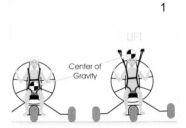

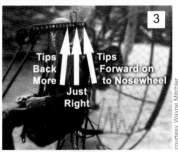

the A's longer. Once the cart has accelerated to a good kiting speed, throttle back enough to prevent further acceleration. Don't take off yet.

If the wing comes overhead crooked, minimize brake pressure, keep up enough speed to kite, and turn *slightly* towards it. Too much turn will start an oscillation. If the wing gets more than about 20° off center, abort. As you build finesse—*lots* of finesse—you can redeem surprisingly crooked inflations.

4. Taxi the cart/wing combo mostly by steering the cart straight and keeping the wing overhead. **Turn by first steering the *wing* in the desired direction then driving the cart below it.** Keep enough airflow (rolling speed) over the wing to do this. It is imperative that the wing be tracking with the cart, centered and stabilized before accelerating for flight.

5. Once you and the wing are tracking together, smoothly throttle up and hold it through liftoff. Use minimum brake inputs and, if the wing gets very far off, abort.

A mirror can help to see the wing during initial inflation.

If you're on thick grass or other soft surface you may need brake pressure to lift off the ground, but once airborne, slowly reduce brakes to accelerate. Climb rate is almost always better with *less* brake. At high density altitudes you may be un*able* to climb if holding excessive brakes.

The worst carting sin is lifting off in an oscillation. If you feel the wing going side-to-side, slow down, straighten it out or abort. Cart dynamics make matters worse; as the wing careens overhead in an oscillation, it unloads the cart which then accelerates rapidly to the other side, pulling the wing even more powerfully into a bank the other way. Getting airborne like this can result in returning to earth with a mighty thwack.

Crosswind Takeoff (Opposite Page)

Taking off in a crosswind should be avoided until you've mastered steering the wing during taxi. It's tricky and increases rollover risk, but can allow flying from sites like beaches and runways.

1-3. Inflate into whatever wind there is, if possible.

4-5. Once the wing is overhead, you've dampened it, and are moving nicely, turn the *wing* towards the runway then steer yourself under it.

6. Now keep the wing exactly overhead, pointed somewhat upwind (crabbing), as you do what it takes to track down the runway. More crosswind=more wing crab.

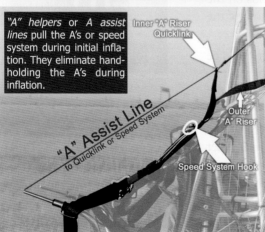

"A" helpers or A assist lines pull the A's or speed system during initial inflation. They eliminate handholding the A's during inflation.

Inner "A" Riser
Quicklink

"A" Assist Line
to Quicklink or Speed System

Outer "A" Riser

Speed System Hook

At liftoff the cart will twist to match the wing. It's a disconcerting and vulnerable transition that leaves you just over the ground, moving quickly, pointed sideways. Touching back down may cause a flip or severe oscillation. So before liftoff, gather speed and reduce brakes; once you get light on the wheels, apply enough brake to liftoff solidly and quickly, gaining a few feet right away. Don't overdo the brakes though, lest you settle back to the ground.

There is a technique, covered in Chapter 15, for inflating in a crosswind but it requires a bit more finesse than even this. That technique describes foot launching but it works just as well on wheels.

Flying

The main difference in cart flying is a slightly higher airspeed and somewhat heavier control inputs. Carts bobble around a bit more due to having higher mass and having it spread out more. Torque is less noticeable because the center of gravity is lower and the motor is usually more vertical (not tilted back so far).

Low altitude maneuvering must be done with care and planning to account for a slower climb rate. Visibility is frequently slightly restricted by framework so you may have to move your head around somewhat to keep an eye out for traffic. Skimming the ground is fun since your eyeballs are so low.

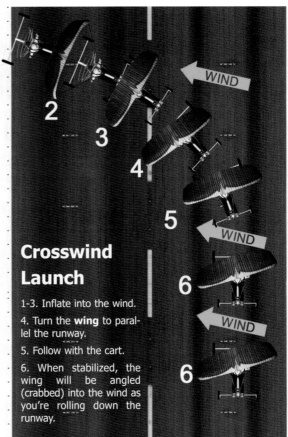

Crosswind Launch

1-3. Inflate into the wind.

4. Turn the **wing** to parallel the runway.

5. Follow with the cart.

6. When stabilized, the wing will be angled (crabbed) into the wind as you're rolling down the runway.

Landing

Wheel landings are easier than foot landings since you don't have to run it out. A little more speed, or a little heavier machine is no big deal.

Do a normal pattern then, if room permits, add some power to shallow the descent during the last 50 feet and *hold the power steady* to a touchdown. Use brakes like a normal landing then shut off the power. As always, if a left/right oscillation develops on final, ease up both brakes and *do not* try to correct it.

A power-off landing is the same as on foot but your eyeballs will be a bit closer to the ground. Glide will be slightly faster and steeper due to the extra weight and drag. Land into the wind to avoid a sideways touchdown which could flip you over.

While rolling out after landing, slow down then get the wing to fall over sideways. Turn slightly towards it to unload it and avoid dragging fabric. In breezy conditions, use minimal brake input as the wing comes down. You may need to pull one brake in, hand-over-hand, to disable it. If the wing falls straight back, you may get pulled backwards and end up flipping or tipping onto the cage and rear wheels—a *turtle* (see next page). After landing with much wind, be ready to unbuckle, get out, and secure the wing.

In the U.S., wheeled solo craft are ultralights regulated under the minimalist FAR 103; whereas tandem wheeled machines are considered Sport Pilot aircraft, requiring certification of both craft and pilot.

In some countries even *solo* wheeled craft are regulated more than foot launchers; check your local regs.

Risk Comparison

Cart flying is about the same risk as foot launching with one exception: prop injury, which is much less likely on wheels. The motor is on a more stable platform during start and hands stay farther away from the prop.

In comparison with flying foot launchers, cart pilots tend to:

- Rollover instead of fall. This does occasionally break limbs that get extended as an unfortunate reaction to imminent ground contact. Keep those things in.

- Takeoff in a left-right oscillation and hit the ground.

- Get lines in the prop slightly more often.

Hard landings are less likely to result in injuries to cart pilots, but they're surprisingly rare for foot flyers, too.

The worst cart accidents happen when pilots expect too much performance, namely climb rate, and fly into something (water, trees, power lines, buildings, etc.) Exuberant hope can't trump lackluster performance. Water is equally lethal if flotation is not used.

The safest carts have rollover *resistance* (quads or a wide wheelbase), rollover *protection,* and enough shock absorption to handle vertical impacts. Other safety concerns are identical to foot launching. One nicety of wheels is that it's easier to carry a reserve parachute since you don't have to heft it.

Tandem operations are safer on wheels but may not be legal (check your country's regulations). Tandem foot launch includes the significant risk of the student/passenger sitting down early, imposing more weight than the pilot, who's still running, can bear. That usually means a face plant for the student and equipment damage. Thankfully, injuries are rare.

Walk or Roll

Besides making easy work of calm conditions, wheels add impressive carrying capabilites. We'll all be rolling at some point if we want to keep flying into our sunset years. So, even for those who only plan on foot launching, take a good look at your wheeled options; they're pretty good.

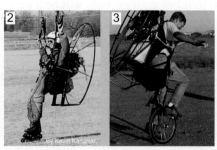

No tandem rating is required but keep the pooch perched—you don't want a stray cat to upset the cart. This canine, *Boots,* is right at home.

There's always someone at the extremes. In this case it's either too many wheels—Jeff Goin flying with inline skate wheels, or too few—Mo Sheldon riding with a paramotor on one wheel.

Carts can be *turtled* too, usually in a breeze. It happens either during initial inflation or just after landing as the wing inflates or deflates. Thankfully, if you get to the kill switch quickly, nothing gets damaged.

Section II

Spreading Your Wings

Section II

Spreading Your Wings

You've left training and have a world to explore. Now what? Learning is far from over!

This Section covers what you'll need to know before heading out on your own. Work with your instructor and other knowledgeable pilots to better understand these subjects. A willingness to learn from others is far more helpful than prideful distance. Be careful though, some input will be useful, some will be useless, and some may even be harmful. If something sounds fishy, ask your instructor or a trusted pilot before acting on it.

Ideally, you will practice on your own for a while, then visit your instructor to vanquish any acquired bad habits and refresh proper techniques. Better yet, you can delve into more advanced techniques and refinements to continue improving.

If ground schools or ratings clinics are held in your area, these are great ways to further your growth in the sport too.

If you haven't seen USPPA's "Risk & Reward," you should. It covers some of this material in an entertaining, easy-to-understand format.

Weather Basics

CHAPTER

7

The weather information needed for safe flying is available on local TV and the Internet. This chapter covers the basics needed to enjoy your newfound freedom and help make the critical go/no-go decision. It's the bare minimum knowledge to grasp before setting out alone. A more thorough treatment is found in Chapter 24 with comprehensive coverage in Dennis Pagen's *Understanding the Sky*.

It was good that he didn't fly. Soon after this picture was taken, a gust front blew through with 25+ mph winds.

One way we learn about local weather is by talking with local ultralight pilots. They have probably formed some useful observations on what to look out for.

The Perfect Day

In general, we want calm or steady light winds with little change expected during our flight. For inland flyers, that means mornings and evenings during stable weather with no fronts. We can glean all that from general forecasts about clouds, wind, and rain. Beaches can be flown all day but have their own risks.

Obviously rain is bad. It's uncomfortable, hard on vision, degrades the wing's collapse recovery ability and makes parachutal stall (see pg. 52) more likely. Heavier rain can cause pooling in the trailing edge which is even worse. The motor doesn't think much of it either.

Rain *showers* are worse yet, coming as they do from large-enough cumulous clouds to cause dangerous gusts. The next time you're out there in regular life and feel a gratuitous gust, think how that would have felt while flying. Be a student of windly wanderings.

Pay particular attention to the wind forecast because abnormal changes mean something is amiss. A forecast calling for calm in the morning followed by 5 to 10

Notice no cu's over Lake Michigan

1

2

3

By Christiane Moisant

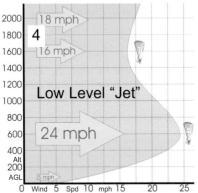

1. Cumulus Clouds (Cu's).

2. Cumulus Clouds gone bad. We don't even mess with these (thunderstorms) in Boeings.

3. Dust devils, created by strong thermals, are deadly to paramotor pilots. Conditions strong enough to generate such turbulence are best avoided. Don't even be hooked in when these are likely.

4. It's nowhere near as strong as a real jetstream, but can be quite surprising. This occasional phenomenon won't be found on aviation weather products.

mph in the afternoon and then calm in the evening is perfect. The wind normally increases during the day, a good reason to limit flying to the first and last three hours of daylight.

Be leery of any forecast exceeding 10 mph or having a large change in speed or direction. Wait until after the change so that you can assess its strength before taking off. Surprises belong to birthdays.

Thermals & the Daily Cycle

Every day Sol arises, heating the ground, which in turn, churns up rising air currents that gather strength as the day warms, peaking by around 2PM. These *thermals* are felt as turbulence when you're airborne and gusts while on the ground. Big gusts on the ground portend big turbulence aloft. They can be separated by 15 to 30 minutes so don't be fooled by a few minutes of calm while standing in the field.

Under many conditions, thermal turbulence can become dangerous. Fortunately it builds predictably, making for nice mornings and evenings.

Clouds don't stop the daily cycle, but they do dampen its power. Sometimes, a sunny afternoon will sprout cumulus clouds (fluffy white with a piled-up look) that mark thermal tops. Other days they build and spread out, becoming overcast.

Occasionally, on calm mornings, there can be a strong wind just a few hundred feet up (*see sidebar*). Thermals may soon mix with this fast-moving air causing strong, gusty surface winds. So if you launch early and encounter a strongish wind a few hundred feet high, expect turbulent conditions a few hours after sunrise.

Indications of Turbulence

Turbulence lurks in many places; fortunately, with a little knowledge, it can usually be predicted. Clouds are one important clue but dangerous atmospheric shenanigans happen in the clear, too.

Cumulus

Cumulus clouds—typical of warm, summer days—indicate a tumultuous atmosphere. Soaring pilots use them to mark rising air currents to stay aloft. More vertical development suggests stronger turbulence that warrants keeping well clear of.

Dust Devils

Dust devils are miniature tornadoes swirling near the surface. Created by strong thermals, they are the visible evidence of very dangerous air. While some are wide, slow, and soft, most are quickly rotating funnels of air that dine on paragliders. Dry climates see them more frequently because thermal action is stronger, and there is a source of visible matter to pick up. You don't even want be clipped into a wing, let alone flying, when one of these slices through.

Testing conditions

If you have any doubt about conditions, spend at least 15 minutes at your launch site feeling what the winds are doing and how much change is happening. Sudden shifts in direction or speed mean a bumpy ride aloft.

Another tool for testing is to kite your wing. You can use a harness or just use your hands (one reason the technique can be beneficial). Only clip into a harness if you're certain the conditions will remain benign. If you can easily and steadily kite your wing, or there isn't enough wind to kite it, then conditions are probably OK.

Be careful though. It *can* still be bumpy even when the surface air seems mellow, so don't use this test alone. It may be that gusts are simply farther apart than a 15 minute wait would reveal. Like dust devils that are sparsely spaced, you could be out there all day and never feel one. That's why we typically avoid mid-day.

Thunderstorms

Thunderstorms, nature's most violent atmospheric production, should not be trifled with. Flying anywhere near them has proven deadly, both from turbulence and from getting sucked into the freezing heights. Even small storms exceed 30,000 feet where temperatures fall below -40°F (which is also -40°C). Turbulence is far beyond a paraglider's capability to maneuver through.

Thunderstorms frequently produce gust fronts that precede the actual storm by up to 20 miles. The sudden wind change from such a gust front can be violent and impossible to outrun.

Don't be tempted to fly immediately after storms pass either. It seems innocuous at times—the thunderstorm rages through, followed by a quiet calm and benign-looking clouds. Don't fall for it. Give time for the wind to shift and see what upwind stations are experiencing to insure there are no surprises. A localized, individual cell that is not associated with a front may leave flyable conditions but you should still wait at least an hour.

If there is severe weather behind one set of storms, even if it is many miles behind, don't fly. While it *may* indeed remain mellow enough to fly, we can't tell. Going up is a dreadful gamble in such conditions.

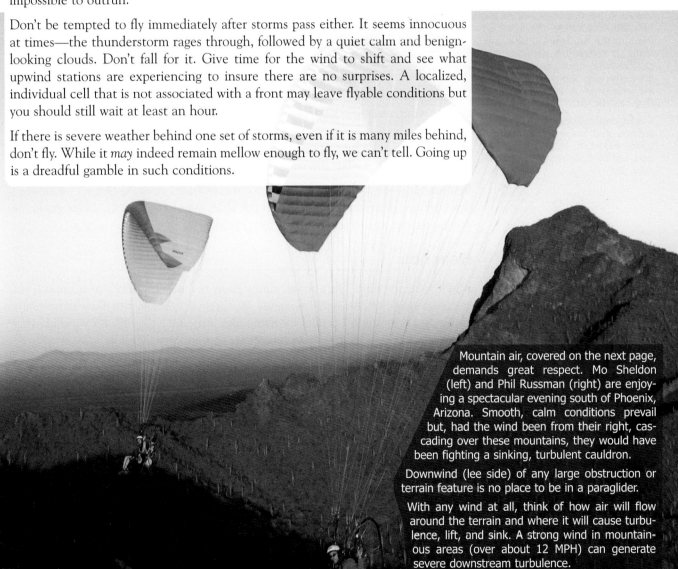

Mountain air, covered on the next page, demands great respect. Mo Sheldon (left) and Phil Russman (right) are enjoying a spectacular evening south of Phoenix, Arizona. Smooth, calm conditions prevail but, had the wind been from their right, cascading over these mountains, they would have been fighting a sinking, turbulent cauldron.

Downwind (lee side) of any large obstruction or terrain feature is no place to be in a paraglider.

With any wind at all, think of how air will flow around the terrain and where it will cause turbulence, lift, and sink. A strong wind in mountainous areas (over about 12 MPH) can generate severe downstream turbulence.

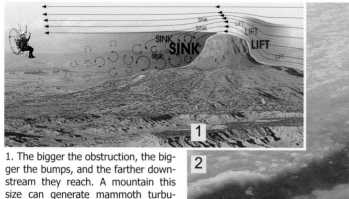

1. The bigger the obstruction, the bigger the bumps, and the farther downstream they reach. A mountain this size can generate mammoth turbulence and sink for miles downwind.

2. Clouds expose how airflow around a mountain behaves like water flowing around a boat's bow. Smooth (laminar) airflow makes it more pronounced.

An inversion is present here where the air aloft is warmer than the air below which is why the stratus clouds have formed in the first place. When the turbulent flow behind the mountain mixes up the two layers, a clear area forms. It reveals the nastiness that can be found downwind of obstructions. This also shows how far away the effects of a large geographic shape can be felt.

Soaring pilots will appreciate the rising portions of airflow well away from the source mountain. Motor pilots could save fuel by flying along the lines of rising air.

Mountains

Wind in the mountains means turbulence in their lee (downwind). It can be completely calm at your launch site because of a wind shadow, but up a few hundred feet, it's a nasty cauldron. Local knowledge and looking up forecasted winds aloft will help avoid such air.

For example, if you're launching at 4000 ft in an area surrounded by mountains, and the winds aloft at 6000 feet are forecast to be over 20 knots, expect strong turbulence. If the winds are forecast to be westerly then make sure you're flying on the west side of the hills. If possible, it's hugely valuable to get to the top of a hill and see for yourself what the winds are doing up there.

Mountainous areas also have unique local conditions because of cool air flowing downhill and warmed air wicking up the sides (see Chapter 24). Even gradually sloping terrain will have local daily flow cycles from this effect.

Beaches

Beach air is the best. On normal, sunny days, heated land sucks in a smooth *sea breeze*, lasting past sunset. Unfettered by thermal heating, this flow is normally steady and consistent—perfect for flying. But if the forecast calls for wind blowing off shore, look out: that is a *very* dangerous condition to fly in.

Check weather at an inland station to see if it has off-shore flow (a *land-breeze*—from land to sea). If so, and it's on-shore at the beach, that could be trouble. At some point these winds meet to form a *convergence zone*. At best it will produce uncomfortable turbulence; at worst, the outflow (away from land) could take over, blowing you out to sea. This is hard to forecast and can quickly turn a benign wind turbulent, let alone possibly blowing you out to sea (see Chapter 19).

Whenever conditions diverge from normal, or from the forecast—winds seem different, clouds are forming too early, temperatures are unseasonal, etc.—be suspicious.

Sea Breeze:
The Good Stuff

Whenever There's Wind

From the air, use flags, smoke, trees, and other vegetation to reveal when the wind has picked up. Crops can be used to tell direction along with other methods shown at right and covered on the next page. Here are some common, significant phenomena that show up whenever the wind blows.

Mechanical Turbulence and Rotor

Just like a rock in a stream, whenever air blows past an obstruction it becomes turbulent (bumpy) downstream. More wind or bigger obstructions mean worse turbulence extending farther past the obstruction and even *above* the obstruction. Rotor, wind shadow, and mechanical turbulence all have specific meanings (covered in Chapter 24); the latter two are mistakenly referred to simply as rotor.

Wind Gradient

Friction slows airflow as it rubs against the ground. In the morning, when cool air sits at the surface, it can be calm while only a few hundred feet above it's blowing 20 MPH. As the ground heats up in the morning, that fast-moving air aloft mixes with the still air below, and a bumpy surface wind develops—be ready or be landed.

Wind Shear

A dramatic change in wind speed or direction from one altitude (or area) to another is wind shear. The transition is a *shear zone* and will likely be quite turbulent. Wind shear associated with thunderstorms have brought down airliners.

The forecast winds aloft give some indication of a shear's presence as do clouds moving in different directions at different altitudes. Days that are brewing thunderstorms can portend dramatic windshear in many directions, even without storms nearby.

Pilots experience it most often during climb; passing through some altitude you get strongly bounced around (hopefully that's all) and then notice that you're now drifting over the ground in a different direction, possibly even going backwards. Look for this when it has cooled a lot from the previous day's high temperature and the forecast winds aloft are strong (over about 15 mph).

Telling Wind Direction

You'll want a windsock or streamers at your launch site especially since wind direction may change while flying. Having an indication 15 feet up may reveal a very slight breeze at wing height even though it's calm at the surface. Chapter 28 has more, but here are several types of wind indications, both intended and natural:

- Lakes are calmer on the upwind side. Bigger waves mean more wind with whitecaps starting at about 12 mph. Boats anchored off shore will be pointing into the wind.

- Flags flap downwind of their pole, but be careful; big flags require a big wind to wave. What looks light on a big flag may be quite strong.

- Smoke is the most sensitive indicator. Plus it shows direction at different heights, but never, *ever*, fly in the updraft created by a large fire which can spew extreme turbulence several thousand feet up.

1. Anything that sticks up into the wind will cause down stream turbulence—from mountains to trees and buildings to buses. Not only will there be turbulence on the lee (downwind) side, but there will be sink—descending air that may make it impossible to stay level.

2. While away from your windsock, still water is one of several ways to tell wind direction. It will be calmer next to the shore on the upwind side.

3. Smoke, steam, and blowing dust also work well for wind indicators. But if you see blowing dust, be ready for a ride. And don't fly through smoke plumes—they may harbor horrendous turbulence depending on their source.

Windsocks can be confusing. To land into the wind, think "Eat the Carrot."

WIND

1. Many wind indicators spaced around the field are helpful especially when it's light and variable. Surveyors tape or similar material, known as *tell-tales,* work well and are easy to place.

2. It took 13 - 15 MPH to get this big flag waving.

3. Marketing flags can work as wind indicators provided they're free to pivot. Many aren't. They're useful for telling wind speed, though—fast flapping means more wind.

Thin Mylar streamers

- Crops and vegetation can show direction, intensity, and gusts. It's quite interesting to watch a gust form on a crop and spread across the field.

- Moving cloud shadows work but can only tell the wind at cloud height.

- In desert areas, blowing sand and tumbleweeds show wind. Visible blowing sand suggests a strong, bumpy cauldron.

- Ground track can reveal the wind speed and direction at your altitude (see Chapter 10) as can some phone applications.

- Helium party balloons with lightweight streamers expose *very* light breezes.

Lift & Sink

When air flows up over an obstruction it produces lift in front of the obstruction and sink behind it (*lee side*)along with rotor and turbulence. The strength of each depends on the shape of the obstruction and strength of the wind. Soaring pilots make use of this lift (called ridge or Orographic lift) to stay airborne, but it must be given great respect—any lift powerful enough to keep a pilot aloft can also produce deadly turbulence if you end up in the wrong place.

Acquiring Aviation Weather

There is great value in *aviation* forecasts—they tell winds at altitude, estimated times for frontal passages, wind shifts, and other useful info. The same call can be used for finding out about airspace restrictions too (see Chapter 9).

In the U.S., our Federal Aviation Administration (FAA) funds a valuable resource through Flight Service Stations (FSS). These privately run facilities offer pilots a ready source for official aviation weather. Don't be daunted by the sound of that; it's not hard, and they don't mind hearing from you (they helped edit this section).

To make it easier, have the following info on hand before calling:

- Launch location relative to an airport or VOR (if flying cross country.) They primarily have airports and navigation aids charted. For example, if you're 10 miles south of your city's

Universal Time: Converting to Zulu

Aviation uses *Coordinated Universal Time,* abbreviated UTC, which is also known as *Zulu Time*. It's the time in Greenwich, England and does not recognize Daylight Saving Time (DST) so the conversion is different in summer and winter. Standard Time (ST) is unadjusted.

In the U.S. DST runs from the second Sunday of March to the first Sunday in November. In Europe it's called Summer Time where it runs from the last Sunday in March to the Last Sunday in October. Convert to Zulu time by adding the following hours to your local time.

Zulu is:	Pacific	Mountain	Central	Eastern
In Summer (DST)	Local+7	Local+6	Local+5	Local+4
In Winter (ST)	Local+8	Local+7	Local+6	Local+5

The Flight Service Station (FSS) Briefing Made Easy

Here is a sample briefing for an early morning flight using 1-800-WX-BRIEF (U.S. only). Listen to the recording and select the appropriate menu options to get a human. The briefing also includes Temporary Flight Restrictions. Have a pen and paper handy; they talk pretty fast. It will go something like this:

Pilot:

"Hi, I'm ultralight pilot Fred Flyer," (Briefer write/types this down to record an activity). "I'll be flying from a field 8 miles northeast of Aurora Airport for a couple hours starting at about 7AM local and would like a *standard briefing* (includes things the FAA consider are necessary)."

You can also ask for an *abbreviated* briefing which has only the main weather. If you do so, make sure to ask for any relevant Temporary Flight Restrictions (TFR's).

Briefer:

"How high will you be flying?" (Because you didn't mention that)

Pilot:

"No more than 1000 ft AGL (above ground level)."

Briefer:

"OK, You've got high pressure over the area with a cold front well to the north... (describes an overview)"

"Currently Aurora is reporting sky clear, visibility 6 miles in haze, winds are 220 at 7 knots, altimeter setting is 29.92 and the temperature is 22 with a dewpoint of 14." (temperatures are given in Celsius)."

"The Aurora forecast calls for clear skies, winds light and variable until 1400Z then becoming 230 at 10."

Pilot:

"What time is that local?" (If you don't know, ask, but it's better form to know the conversion before calling).

Briefer:

"That's 8am local. Then after that, calm."

"The winds aloft in your area, Joliet, should be 280 at 16, temperature +12 at 3000 feet."

"There is a NOTAM for taxiway closures at Aurora (in following a standard format they have to include information that may not be of much use) and the VASI to runway 26 is out of service"

Pilot:

OK, thank you very much; that will do it for me.

1. Wind direction is always given as the direction it is *from*. Nearly all aviation reports and forecasts use the 360 degrees of a compass rose relative to true north. Magnetic north is where a compass points and true north is what lines on a map are drawn with.

So a south wind would be given as 180° and a West wind would be 270°.

2. Flight Service personnel have access to many tools that give them a more complete picture of the weather, notices about airspace and other issues affecting flyers. They are not meteorologists but can provide a wealth of information.

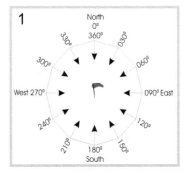

courtesy Leidos Flight Service

airport, tell them that.

- Approximate launch time and how long you'll be flying. Although they work with the worldwide standard time, Universal Coordinated Time (UTC) they can translate to local; just be sure to say "local."

- Your planned maximum altitude above mean sea level (MSL). You can also use your height above ground level (AGL) but tell them that ("I'll be less than 500' AGL").

Be wary of changing conditions or incorrect current weather. If the forecast for right now listed south winds at 5 knots but it's actually northwest at 12, be suspicious of the entire forecast. See what's coming by checking upstream stations where the weather is coming from.

While on the phone, ask for another useful FSS product, the "VAD" (Velocity Azimuth Display) winds report. Winds are derived from special radar that uses airborne particles to determine winds aloft over a wide area. They're actual winds too, given in thousand-foot increments instead of 3000 feet for the regular winds aloft forecasts. You do have to ask because they're typically only used by balloon pilots and, of course, paramotor pilots.

Other Weather Sources

The Internet provides several great sources for information. Flight Service is good when you're out in the field (use a cell phone) or need to get NOTAMS, but consider looking at web sites that show surface winds throughout the day. FootFlyer.com lists some good sources for both motor flying and soaring.

Air flows over the cool, wet ocean, gathering water vapor and condensing into a low cloud layer. It gets pushed up the mountains where moisture is spent making these clouds thicker. By the time it gets a few miles inland, there's little moisture left. So when the air starts descending back down the other side, it warms and immediately goes back into invisible water vapor again.

It is valuable to compare forecasts though. Most of them get their data from the National Weather Service but may apply different interpretations. If one forecast calls for a big change in winds and another does not, someone may have old information. Be suspicious.

Having a smartphone provides a whole range of useful tools, especially for local winds. Look at applications for balloon pilots and sailors in addition to those for flying.

During the first major U.S. powered paraglider gathering, held in 2000, clues of a gust front went ignored. As pilots prepared to launch for a new record number of PPGs aloft, a line of cumulus clouds was massing upwind. Some didn't like the looks of it and stayed put.

One pilot offered to call Flight Service. He was rebuffed—the clouds just didn't look that bad. Someone launched and lemmings soon followed. Sure enough, ten minutes later, with 15 or so already airborne, a strong gust front came through.

Several didn't make it back to the field, landing in various places downwind. A few suffered minor injuries in the resulting high-wind fracas and only one made it back to the launch area. They were *all* quite lucky.

What they missed by skipping that call to Flight Service, was a newly formed and very local cold front. The forecast (we called afterwards to see what it said) cautioned that a 20 knot wind shift was expected. Yup, it was right.

By Tim Kaiser

Common Sense & the Law

8

We operate at the pleasure of the people—a nervous and sensitive people who enact laws on everything from noise to disturbing animals. Even if no prohibition exists, if you annoy enough of the right people, one will be enacted. That's not surprising; if a neighbor starts running his chainsaw at 3 a.m., for example, you'll want a law.

Aggravating people is rarely good—there are more of them (non-flyers) than us, so *we* must minimize aggravation, police ourselves, and encourage others to do the same. Entire states have banned flying on their beaches due to the inconsiderate actions of one pilot. Don't be that pilot. And when you see him, bare your disgust.

Keeping a Low Profile

Avoid over-using any one area if there are neighbors. Even if you have permission—launch and leave whenever possible. If confronted, try to work it out and don't flaunt our minimal regulation—the sport's crown jewel.

Animals have people and vice versa. Annoying either can be downright expensive. For example, if you spook someone's million-dollar horse into an injurious rampage, expect a visit from the riled owner and/or his lawyer; the possible loss of that flying site may be the least of your concerns.

Fly quietly. Stay high, use minimal thrust in noise sensitive areas, and quiet your machine—air intake silencers, mufflers, and big props all help in this regard.

Don't take the approach "It's my land; I'll do what I want." That may be true but only to a point—neighbors don't always need to be right next door to cause problems—they just have to convince the right people that you're either violating some existing law or they will try to enact a new one. Numerous laws have blossomed for exactly this reason.

Like any human interaction, treat law enforcement with respect. You may be legal, but if they dislike your presence they'll find a way to make it difficult. They *may* just be curious about your strange flying machine.

In one case, an officer showed up at a pilot's flying site and the pilot got all defensive. Turns out the officer was a pilot just checking out his launch technique.

While the FAA (Federal Aviation Administration) governs U.S. airspace, locals govern local launch sites. Many municipalities have laws that prohibit launching any type of human-carrying flying machine from within their jurisdiction except airports. Just as often the locals are unaware of those laws. Don't force them to figure it out!

 This video uses live action and animation to help clarify the gloriously brief but sometimes vague US Ultralight Regulations.

Regulations

In the U.S., a simple two-page Federal Aviation Regulation, FAR 103, covers ultralights, defined as any powered single-occupant aircraft (termed vehicle) weighing under 254 pounds; that obviously includes us. The most recent version can be found at www.faa.gov. Its intent is that only participants incur risk, not others. So every interpretation of your flying must conclude that you weren't endangering anyone else. Advisory Circular AC 103-7 expands on the rule's intent.

The absence of specific training requirements is no excuse for ignorance of the law. Flying in any country's national airspace system is a privilege to be taken seriously. What a travesty it would be for someone to buy gear, train enough to get airborne, then crash into an airliner. Besides the obvious tragedy, public pressure to shut us down would be extreme. We must not only learn the rules and follow them, but must help our fellow flyers do the same.

Perception is important: looking like you're doing something dangerous will draw undesirable attention. Not getting reported to police solves many problems. Not looking dangerous may help with survival too. "Showing off" by flying close to gatherings is one way to get noticed, possibly unfavorably. While we *can* fly close to objects, we must do so with discretion.

One common misconception is that we must maintain 500 ft away from anything on the ground. That may be advisable at times, but is *not* the law (as it is for fixed-wing aircraft). Being able to legally fly down a fence row at 5 feet is a fantastic freedom that we should cherish and preserve.

Right of Way

All certified aircraft have the right of way. That means if we see an airplane or helicopter, we have to stay clear or move, even if we're unpowered. Plus we must not create a collision hazard. Know where airplanes are likely to be and steer clear. Fortunately, we usually operate below their altitudes so it's easy, but near airports we have to be extra vigilant.

Among ultralights, the only rule is that powered craft must give way to unpowered ones. Common aviation practice, even though not regulatory, recommends:

- PPG's approaching head-on should each steer to the right.
- Overtake on the right.
- Landing pilots have the right of way; although, when a field is crowded, landing pilots should let launchers go. Standing there while awaiting repeated touch-and-go's gets old quickly.
- The craft to the right has the right-of-way.

What is Congested?

It's the million dollar question. In the U.S., FAR 103.15 tells us "No person may operate an ultralight vehicle over any congested area of a city, town, or settlement, or over any open air assembly of persons." There is no altitude that allows overflight and no definition of congested—it's intentionally left to the eye of the enforcer. Some regional FAA offices consider even one house to constitute "congested," while others say that 6 houses qualifies, and others have no set number.

1. In the U.S., you can fly an additional 30 minutes before sunrise or beyond sunset by using a strobe that's visible for 3 miles and staying within class G airspace. Essentially that means staying below 700 or 1200 feet (as charted).

2. Crossing fences and trespassing signs is bad enough, but crossing into this area would defy any definition of common sense. Not surprisingly, the area is near a military installation.

3. Even with the houses, ultralights have been flying out of this field for years and have had no complaint by any FAA officials. Those white hangars (yellow circle) belong to members of an ultralight club. Credit the responsible behavior of club pilots that it lasted well beyond the buildup of houses.

The rule makers crafted a simple but broad wording, and the term, *congested area*, has many possible meanings. We will inject some practical experience into the interpretation that should be defensible by both the letter and intent of the law. Again, this is merely an interpretation, a *congested area* is:

• Any group of occupied buildings where there would not be enough room to easily launch or land. Remember, this defines the level of congestion, not the operational conduct. It should not be construed as suggesting flight over a congested area just because you have a good landing option nearby. You can never fly *over* a congested area at any altitude. But, if it is not sparse enough to easily land there, it should be considered congested even for overflight.

• An open-air assembly of people is any gathering of two or more people. That includes golfers, beachgoers, sporting events, parties, and spectators (even at *fly-ins!*) Again, flying high enough usually avoids the problem because you don't appear threatening and spread very little noise—nobody is likely to report you.

• One interesting situation is roads. There is much precedence that suggests overflight of roads is OK, but with caveats. There are fields with approved (by FAA control towers) ultralight flight patterns that go over major roads, even interstates like the OSH example at right. They usually specify some minimum altitude (300 feet is common). At major fly-ins there are ultralight flight patterns that go over well-traveled roads as well. But it requires reason: if you distract, annoy, or endanger a motorist, then they may call the area congested. If there is enough traffic that something falling off your machine would likely hit a car and damage it, then it might be called congested. Your best bet is to climb to at least 300 feet AGL before crossing roads and do not operate in a manner that disturbs the groundlings or brings undue attention.

Case Law & Other Issues

Verdicts handed down to pilots who ran afoul of the law warrant study. Even though U.S. flyers abide by Part 103, cases involving violations of other air regulations have been used as precedent for ultralight pilots—used to impose fines (or other sanctions) by virtue of their definitions.

In one case, a definition of congested was given by saying that: "30 to 40 homes, located on relatively small and adjoining lots, constitutes a 'congested area' within the meaning of the regulation." Unfortunately no dimensions were given but little is needed; there's no doubting that most suburban developments would qualify.

Another case is even less encouraging. It is a bit more complicated because it involved an agricultural airplane that operates under different regulations but is not allowed over congested areas. The judge labeled the following as congested: An area 0.6 miles long and 0.3 miles wide (about 115 acres) with 60 houses—at nearly 2 acres per lot that's pretty sparse by most definitions. This definition was used to say a PPG pilot was flying over a congested area.

An FAA web site offers some relief regarding the definition of congested. It says that an operation (this was given for aerobatic pilots) can be done

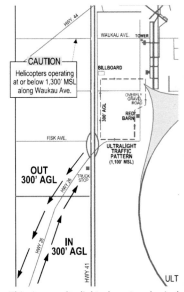

This is an ultralight departure/arrival corridor for use during the world's largest airshow in Oshkoth, WI. It's an FAA approved procedure that clearly shows a flight path over roads, including the well-traveled Highway 41. But pilots *have* been violated for flying over roads at times when the roads were considered "congested."

Flying high makes you much less noticeable. It's not so much whether you are violating the law as it is whether you *look* like you are violating the law. Sad, but that's how it works.

Flying over congested areas is prohibited at any altitude. David only *looks* like he's over Chicago because a zoom lens was used. This is one way that people get falsely accused of flying "over" congested areas.

over an area as small as an acre, even if surrounded by houses. That means flying along a right of way, beside railroad tracks, or a path that keeps you away from buildings would be allowable. Just don't fly over nearby houses and avoid flying in ways that make people complain. It is worth reading and heeding these rules; each violation carries a fine of $1000 or more and can get your equipment confiscated.

Endangerment & Dropping Objects

Anything you do that might endanger (or be perceived as endangering) another person would violate FAR 103.9(a), a catch-all regulation that says don't operate "in a manner that creates a hazard to other persons or property." Nearly every country has similar verbiage.

FAR 103.9(b) uses similar language, prohibiting dropping anything *if* it "creates a hazard to other persons or property." That's why bean-bag dropping contests are legal.

What is "Flying Over?"

1: He is not flying directly over any houses but certainly an observer might think otherwise. Avoid those who may be hostile to your presence.

Either be up high or make sure that nobody can prove you were over their house. Being higher does not allow overflight, but reduces your chance of being accused.

2: You can drop things provided they don't endanger property or people on the surface.

When are you "over" a prohibited area and how far away do you need to be? By one measure you must be *directly* over it. But if an observer *thinks* you are too close to something, then you will be labeled as "flying over." For example, houses may be well to your right, but to an observer on your left, you may *appear* over them.

So here's a measure to use for keeping a reasonable distance horizontally from off-limits places: Use the distance you would travel in 5 seconds of flying time. At 20 mph we go about 30 feet per second. So in 5 seconds we go 150 ft. Higher up increase that to maybe 10 seconds at 300 ft. So if you're flying alongside a road that is busy enough to worry about, stay at least 5 seconds of flying time horizontally away from it. Also, don't let the trajectory of potential falling parts endanger people.

Like so many aspects of life, attitude can be the difference between a lip lashing and enforcement action. If local authorities question your operation, be respectful and explain how you were doing your best to follow the pertinent air regulation—they may not be aware of the specifics but can look them up later. And don't come off as arrogant—they *may* be quite knowledgeable. Offer to avoid the area and, if it seems appropriate, ask where a good alternative launch site might be.

Have a copy of the regulations, an altimeter, an air map excerpt of the area (sectional chart in the U.S.), and know how to read it. Having it on your phone is one easy solution. If confronted and it feels appropriate, show them how you were staying within the law. It may be enough.

If you wind up being investigated or have to answer a letter of investigation, be prompt, be honest, but *be minimal!* It's quite possible that your response to that letter is the best thing they have against you. The vast majority of FAA folks that I have encountered are not "out to get" pilots. They are trying to do their job appropriately and with the least amount of effort. If you are belligerent, though, your prosecution may *become* their mission.

Digging Deeper

FAA Advisory Circular AC 103-7 spells out many details under which FAR 103 was concocted and gives some interesting background. It reveals the why of the regulation's restrictive stance. It is available at www.faa.gov.

Commercial Use

Commercial use is prohibited in Part 103 but not directly.

The rule just says our activity must be *only* for recreation or sport. That makes the stroke very broad and difficult to avoid. Don't confuse it with other rules such as those prohibiting private pilots from commercial activities—our rule is far more limiting since it defines what we *can* do. Flying for movies or photography missions is questionable even if no payment is made for the flying. A law judge must only decide that your flight was not for recreation or sport.

Regulators figured that, with no license given, there is little accountability and few safeguards to the public, so ultralight flying would not be appropriate for commercial, or even practical use.

Where the payment issue comes into play is when defending the "sport or recreational" nature of a flight. Getting paid makes it difficult to justify that purpose.

The most common question is about aerial photography. The temptation is to say that you are not getting paid to fly but rather are selling a service and just happened to have pictures from your PPG. If you were out flying for fun, taking pictures, and later discovered a really cool shot, it would technically be valid to sell it. If you flew solely to get pictures then it's not even the selling that's illegal, it's that the flight's purpose is not allowed.

The people most likely to report your activity are those who do aerial photography, aerial advertisers, and the like, who use expensive certified aircraft and pilots. They have a lot to lose if someone drains away their business with inexpensive, unregulated capabilities, and may they already be sensitive about competition from commercial drones.

Instructing

The only way to get paid to fly is by giving tandem instruction, if allowed to do so in your country. Experienced pilots can go through an approved program that allows them to fly students using two-seat craft. Such flights are done under a special exemption for instruction only. In the U.S., approved programs are run by member organizations such as the U.S. Powered Paragliding Association (USPPA), and do not fall under the far more-involved Sport Pilot regulation which applies to heavier craft.

You can also get paid to teach PPG from the ground—there is no restriction on that. Of course there are many pitfalls to instructing which is why going through a thorough certification process is important. We also recommend our book *Paraglider & Paramotor Instructor.*

Getting Someone Else to Pay

While you cannot get paid for flying, you can offset your flying costs by having a company buy your wing or motor for you. You can have their logo and text emblazoned on it, but they can't tell you when or where to fly it. It has nothing to do with getting paid—if you fly for the purpose of gaining exposure, it is a violation of the rule. If you're thinking that would be hard to enforce, you're right. But do something blatant where the purpose is obvious and you'll bring scrutiny.

Tandem instruction is one way to get paid for flying—teaching flying in this case. You can give introductory flights too, but must have some form of certification in nearly all countries including the U.S.

In the U.S., wheeled two-seat operations fall under the Sport Pilot Rule which excludes foot launched PPG's. Tandem PPG operations are only allowed under an exemption from the single-occupant rule in FAR part 103. That exemption, administered by organizations such as the USPPA, must be renewed every other year. See FootFlyer.com or USPPA.org for the current status.

Writing on the wing and having your sponsor buy the wing is one way to get someone else to help pay for your flying legally.

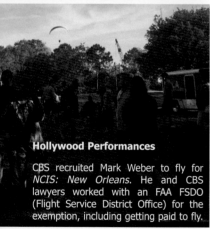

Airshow Performances

by Eric Farewell

Flying in airshows is possible with an exemption. The Paradigm Aerobatic Team flew at Airventure, the world's largest airshow, by operating under the EAA's existing exemption. And they were a huge hit. Above, Ethan Martin works the crowd after a show.

by Eric Farewell

Hollywood Performances

CBS recruited Mark Weber to fly for *NCIS: New Orleans*. He and CBS lawyers worked with an FAA FSDO (Flight Service District Office) for the exemption, including getting paid to fly.

by Joe Ruscito

If I Violate the Rules?

Professional pilots have the most to lose: FAA officials will go after their certificates because that's easy and effective. A good aviation attorney is a must there.

Generally the FAA is obliged to investigate any complaint, and, once that train has left the station, it's hard to stop. However, if handled amicably, the event may be settled with minimum fuss.

The first indication will usually be obvious: police show up and take a report. They don't always contact the aviation authorities but will certainly do so if motivated. Be polite! And don't assume they're unaware of our rules. Be sensitive, but it's possible they may accuse you of violating rules that don't apply which can work in your favor later. You'd rather avoid having a "later."

This is where flying with a copy of the regulations, air map and an altimeter can help show you're trying to be responsible. Don't be arrogant and only offer the rules if you think it could be effective (the official is being reasonable). Otherwise, they may find something else to use. Offering to show them the chart may be a better approach if it's airspace issue.

Protecting Yourself

Besides being familiar with the rules and having a chart, consider recording your ground track with a GPS. That's easy on most phones: make sure the GPS is on, download an app, and turn on its recorder. Now, if you get accused of a violation, the track could exonerate you.

Exemptions

It is difficult but possible to get exemptions from FAR 103 rules providing equivalent safety is maintained. For example, airshows commonly let pilots fly in ways that would otherwise be illegal but, by virtue of a waiver, are allowed under certain guidelines aimed at protecting the public. The airshow organization is trusted with setting rules to that end.

Any hope for success hinges on providing evidence for how the public interest is served while maintaining equivalent safety.

Our freedom is a double-edged sword that *can* cut deeply.

When one PPG pilot ran afoul of local law, police contacted FAA officials. The case went all the way to trial, and FAA lawyers used prior rulings (left) to prosecute the pilot. Even though those judgements weren't directly about FAR 103, they did include a reference to *congested*.

The pilot was fined over $1000 and had to pay his legal fees. There is, unfortunately, little recourse in such cases and one avenue, the National Transportation Safety Board (NTSB), is not likely to help.

Airspace

"Can I launch here?" you ask. Probably, but there are some things you should know.

In the U.S. our freedom is broad; we can fly just about anywhere with few restrictions and no certification requirements. But, like all freedoms, that privilege carries great responsibility; namely, knowing the airspace and adhering to its limits. Launching into a sky full of airliners without knowing the rules is pure folly; a risk for you, others, and ultimately, the entire sport. You don't need to be an expert, either—this chapter provides the essentials.

Instructors at local airports are a good resource on local airspace, but they probably won't know much about ultralight rules. That's OK. Explain that you're an ultralight pilot and ask if they would share advice on good areas to fly and areas to avoid.

Become familiar with the Aeronautical Sectional Chart for your flight area. These are packed with necessary airspace boundaries and much more. Bigger cities also have detailed VFR (Visual Flight Rules) Terminal Area Charts.

While describing airspace we will dispense with height limit descriptions, such as "up to but not including." Using "Above" or "below" will suffice. The full U.S. air regulation, including cloud clearance minutia, is available on FootFlyer.com.

Unless you go above 10,000' MSL (Mean Sea Level), we mostly use only two sets of cloud clearance and visibility requirements. They are abbreviated here:

- **5,1,2&3** means **500** feet below, **1000** feet above, **2000** feet horizontally away from the clouds with **3** miles visibility (most Class E airspace).

- **CoC&1** means "**Clear of Clouds**" and **1** mile vis. (most Class G airspace).

Sectional charts can be purchased from some local airports, viewed for free on the Internet, or loaded into a smartphone application.

They come out every 6 months with the latest changes although a call to Flight Service is the only way to be completely current.

This phone is on Skyvector.com, but some applications show your location on the chart—quite handy for checking airspace at impromptu launch sites. They may not be current but can be a great resource.

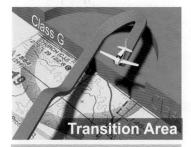

Transition Area

Altitude Abbreviations

Here are the common abbreviations when referring to airspace.

AGL is Above Ground Level.

MSL is above Mean Sea Level. It is used interchangeably with ASL, Above Sea Level.

Refer to the chart below. Positions ❷ & ❿ are both over 10,000 feet and have identical minimums even with 2 in E and 10 in G airspace.

Positions ⓿, ❻ & ❽ have the lower Class G minimums, being below 1200 feet AGL.

You can fly below B and C airspace (❶ and ❼)—you'll launch in G and climb into E airspace until reaching the overlying B or C airspace.

You can fly at position ❾ too, with only a mile visibility but need more cloud clearance. Position ❿, being above 10,000 feet, requires much higher visibility. Position ❻ points to a transition area where the floor of E drops from 1200 to 700 feet.

Airspace Types

Air Traffic: Airspace rules were implemented to control air traffic in busy areas while allowing maximum freedom. It's classed as A through G but not F—think "F for Forgotten." What's called "controlled airspace" is everything but G.

Security airspace is intended to keep air traffic away from nationally sensitive sites such as the Capitol, military installations, events with large crowds, politician's residences and others. They include Temporary Flight Restrictions (TFR) that pop up whenever a dignitary swoops in, and can be issued with very little notice. Prohibited, Restricted and Alert areas are shown on charts whereas temporary airspace information comes via Notices to Airmen (NOTAMs). These are accessed via computer or by calling a Flight Service Station (see Chapter 7).

Wilderness: Some national parks and other public areas have altitude minimums for overflight. Even if you fly legally according to air regulations, disturbing wildlife may run afoul of other rules. While it's true that the FAA governs airspace (in the U.S.), they don't define "disturbing" as it relates to animals.

Other: Special airspace restrictions can pop into being for a variety of reasons, including tethered balloons, high powered rocket launches, and disaster areas.

The ABC's of Airspace

Airspace isn't as complex as it may seem. Picture a 1200 foot thick blanket of G airspace covering the whole country. Above that is E airspace up to 18,000 feet MSL. Above that is A. In populated areas or near airports, the G is only 700 feet thick. These *Transition Areas* (*above left*) are marked on charts by a shaded magenta line; they accommodate air traffic descending lower to make approaches. We fly in G and E—that's essentially the entire country up to 18,000 feet MSL! Busy airports have specially controlled airspace around them as depicted below.

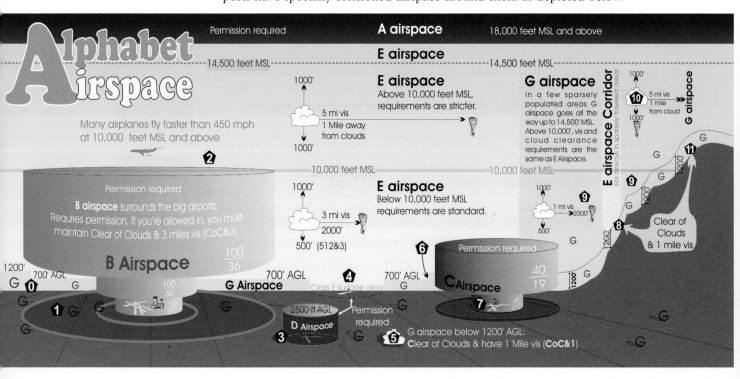

So Class **G** is next to the **G**round and E airspace is essentially **E**verywhere else. The difference is that E requires more visibility/cloud clearance to make "see and avoid" more effective up where traffic flies faster.

If you live in a smaller city that has an airport but no control tower, there is probably no restriction on flying, although it might be a good idea to talk with the airport manager about any special traffic flows nearby.

If you live near a city with more than about 50,000 people, there is probably a nearby airport with a control tower and surrounding D airspace (requires permission). Bigger cities have bigger airports and more restrictions.

The Letter Meanings

Basic airspace definitions are recognized worldwide as shown on the "Alphabet Airspace" diagram (preceding page). The letters go down in severity of restriction as they go down the alphabet with details that vary by country.

A airspace is above 18,000 feet MSL. Requires special equipment, an instrument flight plan, and talking to air traffic controllers. Think "**A for Above.**"

 Access: Authorization is required through ATC and a special wiaver, obtainable for record attempt flights or similar. Contact NAA.org or USPPA.org in the U.S.

 Coverage: Entire Country and up to 12 nm (nautical miles) from shore.

 On Chart: Not depicted.

B airspace is associated with the biggest airports. Layered like an upside down wedding cake, it is marked with solid blue lines and tops out around 10,000 feet MSL. We can fly below the layers but so too can everyone else—expect a lot of traffic and fly *well* below the bottoms. Think "**B for Big & Blue.**"

 Access: Authorization is required but is unlikely, even with an aircraft radio. You must maintain CoC (clear of Clouds) and 3 miles visibility.

 On Chart: Solid blue lines with numbered altitudes for segment floors and ceilings.

C airspace is a mini version of B with less traffic. Some major airlines and lots of commuter airlines fly into these airports along with business and private airplanes. The airspace typically extends 10 nm from the airport and goes up to about 4000 feet above the airport. Think "**C for Commuter.**"

 Access: By permission which is marginally likely. You'll probably need an aircraft radio. Requires 5,1,2&3 (500 below, 1000 above, 2000 to the side of clouds, and 3 miles visibility).

 On Chart: Similar to B airspace markings but with solid magenta lines. On the Chicagoland excerpt, MDW is the inner area of its class C airspace.

D airspace surrounds essentially all airports with an operating control tower (see Chapter 11), typically extending 5 miles out and 2500 feet above the airport's center. If the control tower is not operating then it usually reverts to **G Airspace.**

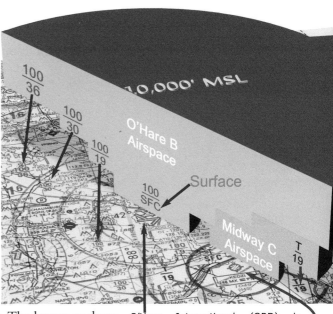

O'Hare International (ORD) is Chicago's big airport with runways outlined in blue. Its rings of Class B airspace radiate outward with increasingly higher bottoms as shown in this cutaway. We can't fly within the center ring but *can* legally fly below the outer layers. Finding enough uncongested area will be a far bigger problem.

Midway (MDW), Chicago's 2nd busiest airport, sports the smaller Class C airspace. Like O'Hare, you can't launch in the center, but you can launch under the outer ring. It happens to be the same floor as O'Hare first ring, 1900 feet MSL.

However, these areas will be extremely congested with air traffic operating below the main airspace. If you do find a field, stay less than 500 feet AGL to avoid most air traffic (expect helicopters).

100 =10,000' MSL top
30 =3000' MSL floor

If a picture is worth a thousand words, imagine what 30 pictures per second is worth. Animation and live action brings these difficult topics to life while covering far more than what's possible in two chapters. It's aimed at ultralight flyers with our simple rules in the U.S. Available at FootFlyer.com.

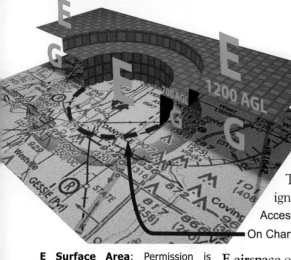

E Surface Area is unusual in that only we ultralights are restricted. It may be an extension from Class D like Thousand Oaks (Position 2 below). Or it may be like Vermillion Regional at left. Certified airplanes don't need to even be talking with anyone, but ultralights need permission and there's no upper limit.

This is what FAR 103.17 calls the "surface area of Class E airspace designated for an airport."

Access: By permission only, They may require an aircraft radio but usually not.

On Chart: Dashed magenta lines.

E Surface Area: Permission is required and pilots must maintain 5,1,2&3 (see right margin) inside its lateral boundaries.

E airspace overlies G airspace starting at 1200 feet AGL (or 700 feet in places). It covers most of the country except for some sparsely populated areas.

Access: Access allowed. Requires 5,1,2&3 for cloud clearance and visibility while below 10,000 feet MSL, more above that.

On Chart: No designation except in very sparse areas. A blue shaded line means no E airspace at all on the sharp side of the line—class G goes up to 14,500 feet.

G airspace is what's there if no other airspace is depicted. It's where we launch. Most of the country is covered with G airspace from the surface up to the overlying E airspace which is normally 1200 feet AGL but, in a few sparsely populated areas, is up to 14,500 feet MSL.

Can I Fly Here? Refer to the Thousand Oaks excerpt below.

1. Yes, you can fly here. It's G airspace with E starting at 700 feet AGL. You must remain CoC&1 (clear of clouds and 1 mile vis) until above 700 feet AGL (E airspace) when you must have 5,1,2&3 (500' below, 1000' above, 2000' beside the clouds, and 3 mile visibility).

2. Requires Permission. It's Class E surface area. Must have 5,1,2&3 even if permission is granted.

3, 4, 5, 6. Requires permission. It's D airspace. Must have 5,1,2&3 even if permission is granted.

7. Yes, this ring denotes equipment required for airplanes. We don't need it (a Mode C Transponder allows the radar controllers to "see" airplanes better and know their altitude).

8. Yes, this is just like 1.

9. Yes, you'll launch in G airspace, climb into E at 700 feet AGL but must remain below 7000 feet MSL which is where this piece of LAX's class B airspace starts.

K. Same as 9 except that the class B airspace starts at 5000 feet MSL.

It's Almost all G Airspace!

(Which is Where We Launch)

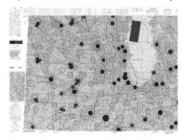

Everywhere on this chart has G airspace at the surface except for the blue and magenta areas (added for clarity). Even there we can fly with permission.

Blue denotes control tower airports with their D airspace and magenta denotes E surface areas.

We launch in the G, and climb into the E at 1200' AGL or 700' near airports.

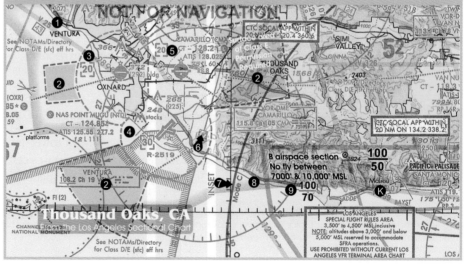

Access: Access allowed, requires at least CoC&1 below 1200' AGL (clear of clouds and 1 mile visibility).

On Chart: No specific designation. If there is nothing on the chart, G airspace is assumed.

Security Airspace

Most flavors of military airspace are off-limits to us. Sometimes it's only closed during a specified time or altitude range, and sometimes it's just advisory. "Military operating areas" (MOAs), for example, are advisory—they don't use the airspace enough to close it but want users to know about their possible presence.

Air Defense Identification Zones (ADIZ) and Flight Restricted Zones (FRZ) protect national borders, capitol cities (including the U.S.), and a few other extremely sensitive sites. Penetrating one could get you shot at.

 Visual and Instrument military routes (VR and IR) depict courses the military uses for practice and transit. While we're not prohibited, time on these thin, gray lines should be minimized. Military aircraft have no speed limit and may be moving over 400 mph. We're told that they don't have radar tuned to pick up paramotorists.

Prohibited and Restricted areas keep airspace closed during certain published times as depicted on sectional charts. Times vary but you can call Flight Service to find out their "hot" (active) times. Chapter 7 addresses the call.

Alert areas, Controlled Firing areas and MOA's do not actually prohibit flight; rather they serve as a warning that military operations will be conducted and pilots should "look out." Keep in mind that some military training involves low-altitude flying (called "nap-of-the-earth") where they follow the terrain, staying below a couple hundred feet AGL, right in the middle of our favorite altitudes. *We* must avoid *them*.

Temporary Flight Restrictions (TFRs) are put up anywhere various government agencies deem them necessary. Some have been up for years while others pop up whenever the President or his people appear. Some pop up with no warning—don't be surprised when dignitaries show up. TFRs also appear during or after disasters.

Regulations prohibit flying near large events such as major sporting events, conventions, and many other public gatherings. Some facilities that might be considered terrorist targets are off limits. Even when there are no specific restrictions, the regulation admonishes pilots not to "loiter" at sensitive sites. Doing so may garner a special reception, possibly by helicopter, at your return.

Knowing the rules is important but so is common sense. If an area looks like it might be considered sensitive from a security perspective, either find out first or avoid it altogether. Put yourself in the protector's shoes.

Wilderness Areas

Many public parks, like the Grand Canyon, have areas preserved for their natural, quiet separation from civilization. Some are protected by special rules prohibiting launch and even overflight. In most cases these areas are not strictly prohibited but pilots are admonished to avoid overflight below 2000 AGL.

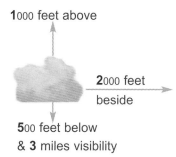

5,1,2 & 3 means

1000 feet above

2000 feet beside

500 feet below
& **3** miles visibility

CoC & 1 means

Clear of Clouds &
1 mile visibility

Several websites offer graphical depictions of current Temporary Flight Restrictions (TFRs). The most reliable way to get them is a briefing from Flight Service which also puts you on a recorded line as having checked from an "official" source. TFRs can pop up with *very* little notice.

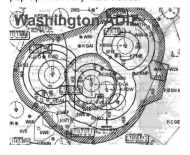

Digging Deeper: What is "Mode C"

Around most class B airspace is a 30 mile ring that says "Mode C." It means that regular certified aircraft must have special equipment but does *not* apply to ultralights in the U.S.

These equipment requirements change as new technologies evolve. ADS-B, for example, is a satellite-based technology that is replacing radar as the primary means for tracking aircraft.

Wilderness & Restricted Areas

Ocotillo Airport (arrow) is a popular ultralight field nestled in a charted wilderness area. The 2000 foot AGL minimum "request" applies there. Don't take this lightly, they can issue expensive fines for violating noise ordinances or disturbing habitat.

More important are Restricted areas just a few miles Southeast. The whole area with the blue hash marks is R-2510A. It goes from the surface to 15,000 feet. R-2510B sits atop the northern half of R-2510A, going from 15,000 feet up to 40,000.

The magenta Kane West MOA outlines a Military Operating Area that we can fly in but at elevated risk.

The details for all these areas are printed in the margin of the LAX sectional chart pictured above.

**Digging Deeper:
The Nautical Mile (nm)**

Aviation's standard measure of distance is the nautical mile (nm). It is one minute of one degree of the earth's circumference. There are 360 degrees, 60 minutes per degree, and 60 seconds per minute in the coordinate system.

Read nautical miles as the tic marks on Sectional Chart's vertical lines (lines of longitude).

One nm equals 1.15 statute (regular) miles.

Flying in national parks is prohibited. It's a big deal, too; violations could land you in jail facing big fines with your gear confiscated.

Wilderness areas are indicated on charts by a blue dotted line. Some (like the Grand Canyon) have special restrictions outlined in Special Federal Aviation Regulations (SFARs) while others are covered in Notices To Airman (NOTAMs). Before flying in a popular park or famous site, contact the FSS and ask if they know of any restrictions. There may also be some local restrictions that apply—check with Park administrators for that. Ask about overflight rules too.

NOTAMs

Whenever airspace is put off-limits, the FAA issues Notices to Airmen (NOTAMs). They cover natural disasters, dignitaries, military needs, rocket launches, and others. It could be a small area or, as on September 11, 2001, an entire country.

The NOTAM's location is usually referenced to a navigation station, such as a VOR, with direction (radial) and distance from the station. Radius is how big the area is. Obtain NOTAM information from FSS like a weather briefing (see Chapter 7). If not offered, ask for any pertinent NOTAMs in the area.

Here's an example (reference "Digging Deeper" next page): A truck carrying paramotor fuel explodes on the highway northeast of Vermillion, IL. FAA managers, at the behest of local officials, close the overlying airspace by issuing a NOTAM—prohibiting overflight below 2000 and within 2nm of the DNV 043 at 12.5nm. In this example, the closed TFR area is shaded red for clarity. It is expected that, once receiving this NOTAM, you will get your chart (or computer or phone) and plot it out. Locate the DNV VOR (Danville VOR, what #3 is pointing to) then follow its 043° radial (the line at #4) northeast out 12.5 nm.

The same or similar method alerts pilots when a dignitary's presence closes off airspace. Airborne or ground assets may be protecting the area.

Visibility & Cloud Clearance

We always need at least one mile visibility and clear of clouds—a minimal requirement that's only allowed in G airspace and then only below 10,000' MSL.

As we fly higher (above 700 feet AGL), the chance of encountering airplanes increases and, not surprisingly, so do the minimums. This makes sense given that an airplane may be going 300 mph or 440 feet every *second*. At a half-mile away you're only *six seconds* from colliding—precious little time to recognize the threat, determine that it's on a collision course, do the right thing, and actually get out of the way in time. Realistically, it's too late. Better visibility allows more time for you or the airplane pilot to see and avoid.

Above 10,000 feet MSL, airplanes go as fast as they want (they're limited to 250 knots below that) so visibility and cloud clearance minimums are higher yet, which makes sense. With jets commonly going over 400 mph, they need a lot of room to see and react to a PPG pilot. They punch through those innocuous looking cumulus clouds too, which is why the horizontal cloud clearance requirement goes up to a mile and visibility goes up to 5 miles. Even then, a jet popping out of the cloud from a mile away is only 9 seconds from impact.

Magenta Airport
No control tower, almost always Class G up to 700' AGL then Class E. Solid circle means paved runways.

Blue Airport
Control tower, Class D up to 3800 MSL then Class E, permission required within dashed blue lines.

Legend

VOR Transmitter

Reading The Charts

Charts depict our world. A legend adorns panel one, but *real* detail lurks in the downloadable *Aeronautical Chart User's Guide*.

Airports with paved runways are shown with the runway orientation so you can better predict where airplane traffic will be. Runways are numbered in the direction of takeoff, so runway 27 means the pilot is taking off to the west (270° Magnetic).

Relatively few areas are closed to us. In the Danville, IL excerpt below, that's only the TFR and the Vermillion Surface Area of Class E which *is* available with permission.

Danville, IL (Vermillion Regional)

Let's consider Danville with an eye to launching. Airport details, including who to call for permission, are in *digital chart supplements* (d-CS) for the airport (DNV). These used to be called Airport Facility Directories (A/FD).

Position 1: You want to launch from the arrow's tip.

Launch? You're in G, with E airspace starting at 1200 feet AGL.

Need: CoC&1 (clear of clouds and 1 mile visibility) until climbing above 1200 feet AGL then it goes to 5,1,2&3 (500 below, 1000 above, 2000 horizontally from the clouds and 3 miles visibility).

The Danville VOR (what position 3 is pointing to): Notice it's just inside a magenta vignette. That means the E Airspace floor dropped from 1200 to 700 feet.

Launch? Yes, you're in G airspace with E above starting at 700 feet (that's what the shaded magenta does—lower class E from 1200 to 700 feet AGL).

Require: CoC&1 up to 700 feet AGL, then 5,1,2&3.

Position 5 is just inside the "Surface area of Class E" which is off limits to us at any altitude without permission from air traffic control (ATC). The authority is usually an Approach Control or ARTCC facility ("Center") for that region. In this case the d-CS tells us it's Champaign Approach Control.

Digging Deeper: VOR

VHF Omnidirectional Ranges (VORs) make up an old navigation system whose remains still make up waypoints used for aviation. Pilots can determine a direction (radial) from the VOR where 0° is north, 90° is east, and so on. We care because:

1) These stations concentrate traffic, especially in areas where pilot training is prevalent since they may still practice using VOR's.

2) They serve as reference points for airspace, airways, including routes that don't even rely on the VOR's, and notices to airmen (NOTAMs).

Below is a temporary flight restriction placed on the 043° radial at 12.5 nautical miles with a 2 nautical mile radius.

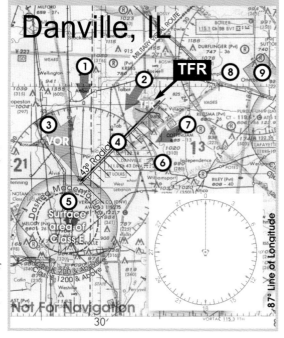

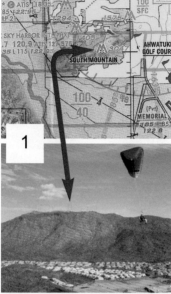

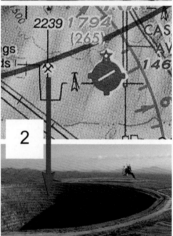

1. South Mountain is a high point just south of Phoenix. Being festooned with towers makes it a great landmark and cross check of altitude. The chart shows the towers, depicted with the double blue teepees, to be *3047* MSL. You can set your altimeter to that. The magenta flag indicates that it is also a reporting point where airplanes radio their position to Phoenix approach control. The 100 over 40 means that Phoenix's B airspace starts at 4000 ft MSL and goes up to 10,000 ft MSL in that area. Expect heavy airplane traffic there.

2. Some charted features can be inconspicuous on paper. The mine symbol just west of Casa Grande airport doesn't do this hole justice. This abandoned copper mine is the most prominent landmark within 20 miles.

Launch? No, unless you have permission. Call FSS for to get the phone number. You'll sound like a hero if you tell them you've already looked at the Airport/Facility Directory (A/FD) and that it's Champaign Approach.

Require: If you *do* get permission (probably will) it would require 5,1,2&3.

TFR: The NOTAM that creates the TFR will give other information as to altitudes, restrictions, and times of effectiveness.

Launch? Not unless specified in the NOTAM verbiage.

Require: Whatever they specified in the NOTAM.

The Boiler VOR (a mile northwest of position 9): Purdue University, a control tower airport, is 8 nm southeast of here. We should be vigilant for airplanes flying instrument approaches from the VOR into Purdue airport—they may be down low.

Launch? Yes, you're in G airspace with E airspace starting at 700 feet AGL.

Require: CoC&1 up to 700 feet AGL above which you must have 5,1,2&3.

Chicagoland, IL

Red shaded areas have been added for clarity to show where you can*not* go without permission, but there are many areas where you *can* fly

Position 1 is just outside the outer ring of ORD's class B airspace.

Launch? Yes, you're in G airspace with E starting at 700 feet AGL. In big city areas expect that.

Require: CoC&1 then 5,1,2&3 climbing above 700 feet AGL..

Position 2 is just inside the outer ring of ORD class B airspace. The label to its right shows the B airspace "shelf" goes from 4000 feet to 10,000 feet MSL, so we can't fly there between those altitudes.

Launch? Yes, you're in G airspace with E airspace starting at 700 feet.

Require: CoC&1 then 5,1,2&3 if you climb above 700 feet AGL.

Concerns: Aircraft funnel through this area so they don't have to talk to O'Hare. Expect heavy air traffic above about 600 feet AGL.

Position 3 This is just inside ring 2 of ORD class B airspace. The B airspace "shelf" goes from 3000 feet to 10,000 feet MSL.

Launch? Yes, you're in G airspace with E airspace starting at 700 feet AGL.

Require: CoC&1 then 5,1,2&3 above 700 feet AGL.

Position 4: This magenta dashed line, just beyond ARR's Class D airspace, outlines an extension that takes class E airspace to the surface. The blue dashed line outlines Aurora's Class D airspace associated with their control tower.

Launch?   No, unless you have permission from Aurora tower.

Require: If you get permission, you need 5,1,2&3.

Position 5 is inside DPA's (DuPage) Class D airspace.

Launch?   No, unless you have permission from DuPage tower. The tower frequency is 120.9 (that is on the airport information block above position 5.)

Require: If you get permission, you must have 5,1,2&3.

Notes: Airspace-wise you could fly above DPA's Class D (top at 3300 feet MSL) and below ORD's Class B (base at 4000 feet MSL) without talking to anybody. You may be violating FAR 103.13(b), though, by creating a collision hazard.

Position 6 is outside of the B airspace overlay and on the "Mode C" ring which doesn't apply to us. It's also just northeast of the Joliet VOR.

Launch?   Yes, you're in G airspace with E airspace 700 feet above.

Require: You must have CoC&1 then 5,1,2&3 if climbing above 700 feet AGL.

Notes: Expect more airplane traffic related to the Joliet VOR above about 800 feet AGL. You can climb as high as you want but there will be jet and other traffic shuttling into the side of both ORD and MDW's airspace.

Positions 7 & 8 are below MDW's C airspace which starts at 1900 feet MSL and goes up into the overlying ORD B airspace (that's why the "T" for Top instead of an altitude). Obviously most of this airspace is off-limits due to being congested.

Launch?   Yes, you're in G airspace with E airspace 700 feet above.

Require: You must have CoC&1 then 5,1,2&3 if climbing above 700 feet AGL.

Notes: Expect high density airplane traffic to be skirting underneath and around MDW's airspace. This is a bad place to be more than about 500 hundred feet in a PPG although helicopters operate close to our altitudes.

Other Uses For the Charts

What's available on the internet (think Google Earth) is impressive. It eclipses what these charts present, but paper charts are still handy for the large area they reveal at once and, when folded, make great fly swatters.

Topographical

A useful chart feature is showing elevation for airports and obstruction tops. Sometimes obstructions add AGL which can be subtracted from their MSL height to get elevation at the base.

This is an obstruction pair.

Top is at:	386' MSL
It's this tall:	261' AGL
So the base is:	125' MSL (386 - 261)

Contours give elevations in 500 foot (sometimes 250) increments—not terribly precise but good for general knowledge. You can generally estimate your height visually to within a couple hundred feet. Of course, if you used GPS to locate yourself on the chart then it should also show your altitude within a few feet.

Don't be this guy!

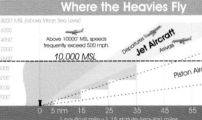

Where the Heavies Fly

Above: Airplane traffic gets concentrated around predictable arrival and departure paths, both vertically and horizontally. Jets depart steeply and arrive at a shallower 300 feet per mile from the airport or about 3 miles per 1000 feet of altitude loss.

Piston aircraft follow a shallower departure and arrival path.

So at 10 miles away from the airport you can expect jets to be about 3000' (10 * 300'). If you're flying at 10,000' MSL, expect jets to be about 30 to 40 miles away from their landing airport. Fast aircraft spend more time at 10,000' MSL than most other altitudes because they must slow down before going lower. Controllers do sometimes descend airplanes earlier—this is just a guide.

Above: Terminal Area Charts are more detailed than the more-common Sectional Charts which cover a far wider area.

We may not *need* airports to launch, but they sure are nice to use. Pay particular attention to traffic patterns though; airplane pilots and airport managers are not very forgiving of ignorance.

Below is a typical left pattern. Overlay it on the sectional chart runway to visualize where to expect airplane traffic. Like us, they prefer landing into the wind.

Left patterns are standard because most airplane pilots sit in the left seat.

Right turns are indicated by "RP" (Right Pattern) like Lowell airport below. The open circle means that the runway is not paved. RP 18 means a right pattern is used for runway 18.

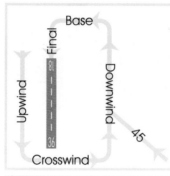

Finding Sites

 Ultralight strips are usually paramotor friendly and occasionally soaring schools will tolerate us. Some private airports are friendly too, so it may be worth asking. Small airports, especially grass ones, are pretty welcoming as are some sky diving airports. The latter is already used to seeing canopies although usually the canopies aren't going back up. Skydiving airports are marked by a little parachute symbol. On the chart, sailplane operations show a sailplane symbol with a G, hang glider sites show up with an H, and ultralight strips use the letter U. Sadly there's no paraglider symbol.

Airports that accept Federal Aviation Airport Improvement funds include grant assurances that obligate them to welcome all aviation, but there are loopholes. Ssee page 100. Cooperation is always the best long-term solution.

Things Look Different Out West

Primarily the colors become more brown to show higher elevations. You'll also find the rare G airspace poking above 1200' AGL, up to a maximum of 14,500' MSL (blue vignetted line around 1 below). You still need a mile and clear of clouds to launch but can have that limited visibility up to 10,000' MSL. Cloud clearances remain 5,1,2.

Here are some other highlights.

Spot 1's are in that rare "G up 14,500 MSL feet" area discussed above.

Spot 2 is in an area where the G goes up to 12,000' MSL.

Spot 3 is the surface area of E as indicated by the dashed magenta lines. You need permission to launch here and must have 512&3.

Spot 4 is the transition area where G goes up to only 700' AGL.

Spot 5 is another example of G all the way up to 14,500' MSL. As with everywhere else on this excerpt, E is above that up to 18,000' MSL (abbreviated FL180 for Flight Level 180).

You can launch almost anywhere here without airspace permission and need only a mile visibility to start. This allows visualization of the boundary between G and E. We need a mile and clear of clouds in G, with more when climbing into E just like everywhere else.

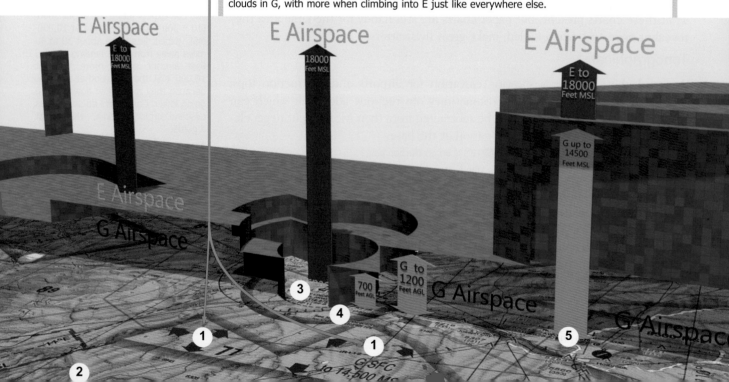

By Scott Johnson

Flying from Anywhere

10

What a treat—running aloft from the most unlikely locales and setting off for parts unseen. This awesome capability carries enormous challenge and extra risk, too.

Choosing a suitable launch site is crucial to safety and success; heeding a few basic rules can prevent catastrophe, whether the site is a wide-open prairie airport or a tight little mountain clearing.

Being *able* to launch from anywhere, however, doesn't mean that you *should*. Both safety and permission can be showstoppers. There's nothing worse than being all suited up, motor idling and wing laid out, only to have someone come up shaking their finger at you. Or worse. In a country brimming with great sites, permission to use them can be elusive.

Any prospective site must be 1) in legal airspace, and 2) must match your skill. It should not require trampling through crops, climbing fences, or ignoring "No Trespassing" signs. Public property, such as state or federal lands, frequently prohibit any kind of flying. Parks are notoriously difficult because they usually have specific prohibitions and the staff to enforce them.

Needing to maintain an emergency landing option puts many forested areas out of reach, same with swamps. Even in these areas though, if you can find a sufficient clearing to launch from, it's fun to just climb up high over the landing zone (LZ) and check things out. Many otherwise boring views sprawl into gorgeous panoramas with a bit of altitude.

Nevermind the DOG Beware of OWNER

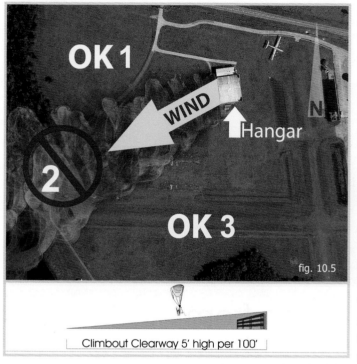

Climbout Clearway 5' high per 100'

fig. 10.5

Choose a launch site with plenty of room that is appropriate for your skill level. Small or otherwise innappropriate sites contribute to many accidents, especially among newer pilots.

Know your limits by measuring your regular field and comparing any new locations to that. Google Earth's measuring tool is the easiest way to do that, but pacing the edges works well enough. Realize that conditions may still make a site impossibly difficult so have some margin.

Avoid launching downwind of tall obstructions like the swirling areas shown above. Dangerous mechanical turbulence and sinking air lurks there.

As skills improve enough to accurately steer the launch, you can consider long, narrow spaces.

Choosing the Site

Size Matters

Bigger is, in fact, always better. Depending on your skills and conditions, a congested site with trees or wires can be deadly. Those early, unsupervised flights require *much* more space. For one thing, you probably have little experience telling field size, knowing climb angle, etc. Another factor that determines acceptability is your climb technique—newer pilots should only accept fields that allow a straight-out climb for the first 100 feet of altitude.

A smooth 500' x 500' area, inside an obstruction free 1200' x 1200' area, is generally good for newer pilots. If there's water nearby, make sure your paramotor has automatic flotation.

That seems large, but when launching in still air, distance goes by quickly. Past incidents have shown that new pilots need more than they think. And don't be fooled by training experiences where you got airborne in a hundred feet—launch distances can triple under hot, high (altitude), or calm conditions, and it's easy to underestimate requirements.

One way to size up a field is to pace it off. Find your stride's length by walking a known distance then dividing that by your footsteps. Even easier is using the mileage ruler in Google Earth. Plus that allows getting a lay of surrounding terrain and, in some areas, obstructions.

Don't guess—wires, trees and buildings are unforgiving, and the distance is hard to judge. When in doubt, pace it out.

A small field is OK providing the obstructions would let you plow through them harmlessly if things go awry (beans, wheat, tall grass, etc.) As experience improves directional control during the run and liftoff, you can decrease field sizes, especially width, to where launching on a road, even in a crosswind, is doable. Even with good control, though, be leery of mechanical turbulence, mentioned below.

A skilled pilot can launch from anywhere that's long enough to get airborne and circle over. That ensures it's big enough to land in should the motor quit. But realize that wind can make a small, obstructed site dangerous at *any* skill level.

Mechanical Turbulence and Obstructions

As covered in Chapter 7, air burbling around obstructions creates *mechanical turbulence* downstream that must be accounted for.

Some locations work well for certain wind directions only. In Fig. 10.5, launching at 1 or 3 is OK but not 2. With less than about 5 mph wind, mechanical turbulence will be present but should be manageable. Look out, though, if the wind picks up as it tends to after sunrise—it can quickly turn nasty. Look at the forecasted wind direction and speed.

As wind increases, turbulence will extend many times the obstruction's height. At

10 MPH, for example, it extends at least 4 times the obstruction's height. Tall obstructions in moderate winds leave a lively wake.

Mechanical turbulence can and has caused large collapses or altitude loss at the worst possible time (when you're down low). Wind shadow, the calm area just behind an obstruction, must also be avoided.

Slope and Surface

Launching downhill is always best for two reasons: (1) you can run faster and (2) the ground falling away acts like having more lift from the same running speed.

Downhill *landings* aren't so good since the ground is falling away as you descend making them tend to be long. But landing uphill is *really* dangerous with the potential for a very hard impact due to both the slope and sinking air. If wind is coming down the hill, try landing cross hill (and crosswind) instead.

Smooth surfaces are far better than rough ones. In fact, tall grass, soft sand, or a rutted surface can add so much leg drag (see Chapter 17) as to prevent a launch. They also make tripping and falling more likely.

Site Permission

"It's better to beg forgiveness than to ask for permission" is a well worn statement that can get us in trouble. Permission is always preferable! Even if you *think* a particular site is OK, at least mind these guidelines:

• Never climb a fence or cross a "No Trespassing" sign to get there.

• Never do any property damage in your effort to get to the site or while preparing. This is especially true for crops—destroying crops doesn't sit well with either the owner or his brother, the sheriff.

• Never set up where somebody lives or has a presence. If there is somebody to ask, you must ask even at the risk of refusal.

• Never use a park or other facility where known rules prohibit flying. Almost all state and federal parks prohibit launching aircraft and ultralights except at airports. You can probably use the airport. Be mindful that many parks have a minimum altitude to fly over. Don't quibble over who controls the airspace (probably another agency); they can always get you for disturbing the animals.

• Avoid lingering. Launch then fly away to minimize attention from surrounding communities or neighbors.

• Fly a minimum noise profile. Use low power to get away from people; then power up when clear of any noise sensitive areas.

High Elevation Fields

High elevation fields require longer launch runs and better climbout options. More power and/or a bigger wing may be necessary to launch *at all*. Smaller or faster wings may require so much groundspeed to get the necessary airspeed as to exceed your ability to run, even with full thrust. Chapter 17 offers techniques to improve success in this situation.

1. Learn your own takeoff distance by setting out four cones, 50 foot apart, in your launch direction. Then see how far it takes you to liftoff in nil wind.

Learn your circle radius by flying to a soccer field of known dimensions (they're not all the same) and seeing how far out of it you fly when circling. Google Earth is a good way to measure the soccer field size.

2. It looked good from the road but didn't measure up. The pilot nearly impaled himself on a fence post trying to launch from here. Pace off potential sites and be conservative about launch distance estimates.

3. Surfaces can be deceiving. Do a test walk without your motor on to make sure there is traction and support. This type of surface can hide quicksand.

It doesn't look like much but this dirt road got us airborne. We planned it so as to turn well before the highway. This entire area is landable leaving plentiful engine-out options.

Obviously, roads must be nearly abandoned, have no wires, and the pilot must be capable of steering during his run. That is an advanced skill that is well worth mastering.

As always, make sure your site has an "out" that allows for an unexpectedly shallow climb and doesn't require climbing over obstructions or hills. That's tougher at higher elevations. Have at least one climbout route that allows clawing your way to altitude without having to traverse any obstructions, especially wires.

Unless there is some wind, the launch surface will need to be smooth. Ruts or tall growth can easily keep you from generating the requisite speed. Roads out in the boondocks are good as long they have no power lines. Beware of barbed wire fences, which do surprising canopy damage and aren't much good for skin, either. Avoid parking your vehicle *on* the road.

Flying at or near Airports

Uncontrolled airports (no control tower) can be a perfect PPG playground. Unfortunately, getting permission can be tough. Airports with control towers are usually too busy but *can* be used with the right equipment (see chapter 11).

General aviation (non-airline) un-controlled airports normally sit in G airspace with E airspace 700 feet above. Functionally that means you only need 1 mile visibility and clear of clouds (CoC) with stricter requirements higher up.

Right of Way

FAR 103.13 obligates us to stay out of *their* way.

That essentially means we must avoid getting near heavy concentrations of certified air traffic in a way that could interfere. Airport traffic patterns qualify, and most major cities also have published jet routes that must be avoided. Fortunately they're high up, almost always 3000 feet or above. Check with local pilots in your area.

A popular misconception is that airports accepting federal grant funds *have* to let us fly (Airport Grant Assurance #22). They can, and frequently do, prohibit us based on perceived safety issues. But the safety question must be answered by FAA officials, not the airport. Still, airport managers can impede access so much as to make it impractical for us. It pays to get along.

Many licensed pilots and airport managers are quick to condemn having us mix with their traffic. That's unfortunate since a knowledgeable, conscientious PPG pilot probably adds less risk than a general aviation aircraft: we're extremely slow, highly visible, and have no need to ever use their patterns. Another reason for the occasional cold-shoulder (and probably a big one) is our lack of financial contribution. Airplanes based at the airport pay rent and buy fuel. Paramotor pilots, even if they do buy fuel, contribute almost nothing.

So it's hugely beneficial to get along and work with management and other users to show how easily we fit, and how our flying can have minimal impact on other operations. Explain our capabilities (to those willing to listen), then follow through with consistently responsible flying. Launch away from airplane traffic and remain clear of their patterns.

We must avoid becoming a collision hazard. Beyond complying with local and FAA rules, we must not annoy people, create a hazard, or even have the appearance of such.

When planning regular operations from an airport, contact the airport manager to find out the best places to operate. Explain how you plan to avoid conflicts with existing users. Ask about gates, codes, areas to avoid, noise sensitive areas, and other location-specific needs, then comply with those requirements.

About Runways & Patterns

You must know where air traffic is in order to stay clear. The patterns are fairly well defined but, unfortunately, they don't always get followed.

Understand runway numbers—they indicate magnetic heading for aircraft taking off or landing with the ending "0" removed. So north is 0 or 360 (runway 36), east is 090 (runway 9), south is 180 (runway 18) and west is 270 (runway 27). If the runway were aligned east/west, then the *approach* end of the runway for aircraft landing west (270°) would be 27. Taking off or landing in the other direction, 090°(to the east) would be runway 9.

Standard traffic patterns are to the left—meaning turns are made to the left. Runway 27 in the diagram below uses a left pattern; runway 9 uses a right pattern.

Right patterns are only used for a reason, like to keep noise away from sensitive areas (noise abatement). They may indicate pattern direction using a large, highly visible segmented circle near the runway complex. It has little "L"s oriented to the runways they depict, showing the turn direction from base to final. The segmented circle quickly shows what pattern direction is appropriate for each runway. If no indicator is present, left patterns apply.

Normal pattern altitude for airplanes range from 600 to 1500 feet AGL depending on aircraft type; jets and larger twins use the higher altitudes. Pattern size varies greatly based mostly on aircraft speed with faster aircraft flying larger, higher patterns. Jets may fly downwind leg 2+ miles away from the runway while slower aircraft may be within a half-mile and other ultralights even closer. PPG patterns will be the closest to the runway (around 300 feet away and 200 to 400 feet high).

One technique for crossing runways is to fly over the runway's middle, maybe slightly closer to the beginning, at around 400' AGL The depicted PPG is doing just that: He takes off into the wind then gains 400 feet in a left turn before heading across the runway.

Make sure the airport management approves of your plans. Otherwise, don't cross any runways at all—go around the ends, down low and at least a mile away.

On a standard glide slope, airplanes will be approximately 300 feet high for every mile away from the runway. Some airport managements ask us to be *above* pattern altitude before crossing the runways.

Watch out for aircraft wakes which descend at about 500 feet per minute (fpm) and can linger up to 2 minutes.

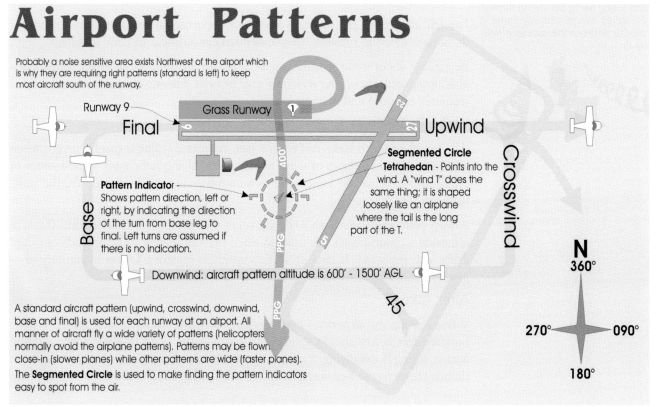

Airport Patterns

Probably a noise sensitive area exists Northwest of the airport which is why they are requiring right patterns (standard is left) to keep most aircraft south of the runway.

Runway 9 — Final · Grass Runway · Upwind

Segmented Circle
Tetrahedan - Points into the wind. A "wind T" does the same thing; it is shaped loosely like an airplane where the tail is the long part of the T.

Pattern Indicator -
Shows pattern direction, left or right, by indicating the direction of the turn from base leg to final. Left turns are assumed if there is no indication.

Base

Crosswind

Downwind: aircraft pattern altitude is 600' - 1500' AGL

A standard aircraft pattern (upwind, crosswind, downwind, base and final) is used for each runway at an airport. All manner of aircraft fly a wide variety of patterns (helicopters normally avoid the airplane patterns). Patterns may be flown close-in (slower planes) while other patterns are wide (faster planes).
The Segmented Circle is used to make finding the pattern indicators easy to spot from the air.

N 360°
270° — 090°
180°

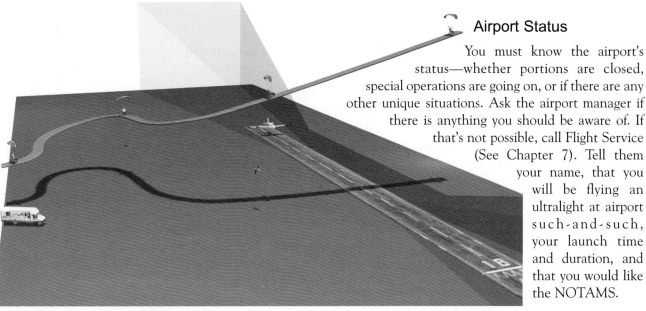

Airport Status

You must know the airport's status—whether portions are closed, special operations are going on, or if there are any other unique situations. Ask the airport manager if there is anything you should be aware of. If that's not possible, call Flight Service (See Chapter 7). Tell them your name, that you will be flying an ultralight at airport such-and-such, your launch time and duration, and that you would like the NOTAMS.

Above: The reddish shape shows typical corridors flown by aircraft landing or departing at an airport. It's our job to avoid them. This PPG pilot climbs while away from the runway then flies over the center at a sufficient height.

Below: Wingtip vortices are little tornadoes generated by any aircraft that's producing lift (flying). They are worse following heavy, slow, aerodynamically clean airplanes. Give such craft a wide berth; blundering through one would almost certainly cause a collapse. Between the vortices is sinking air.

Airplane pilots normally choose the runway based on wind but not always. Sometimes they'll do a long, straight-in final approach to a different runway even if it has a tailwind (for convenience). PPGers must be on the lookout for this—5 knots of tailwind isn't as big a deal to an airplane on a long runway.

How to Mesh

Now that you have the airport information and know where its patterns are, it's fairly easy to stay out of the way. And indeed you should avoid where aircraft are likely to be.

Launch away from the runways and their departure/arrival corridors. Plan your flight path to avoid runways, their extended centerlines, and any buildings.

Be vigilant about noise sensitive areas: If the airport management gets noise complaints caused by you, your welcome may be brief. Staying clear of congested areas (required anyway) will frequently suffice.

Wake Turbulence

All aircraft produce wake turbulence (see chapter 22) but it can be severe when generated by an airplane, or even worse, a slow-flying helicopter. A helicopter in cruise throws about the same wake as an airplane but, as it slows down, the wake turbulence worsens.

Always plan your flight path to be above, or well beside, another aircraft. If you're following a ground track, be upwind since the turbulence sinks, spreads out, and drifts with the wind. It lasts up to two minutes, lingering longer in smooth air—just when we like to fly most.

After Takeoff

When leaving the airport it's best to stay well below aircraft traffic patterns. Four hundred feet below should suffice, but balance the need to keep a safe landing option open. If overflying a runway is absolutely necessary, go over the center, slightly closer to the beginning at 400 ft. AGL. There is less likelihood an airplane will be flying there.

If climbout near the airport is necessary, do so away from any pattern in use. But realize that airplanes may overfly the airport from any direction, usually from pattern altitude, up to 500 feet above it. They do this to check things out before landing, a fairly common practice.

See and Be Seen

If you see an airplane that you suspect does not see you, *turn*. Not only will the motion make you more visible, but the changing aspect on your wing will help as well. If you need to escape, the only thing a paramotor can do quickly is descend.

The other obvious need is to keep a look out for others, especially when you're flying up where other air traffic may be. We have the best view in the world with nothing but a pair of risers between us and the visible planet—use it.

Be Heard

Aviation radios that can transmit and receive on the airport's frequency (called Unicom) are beneficial. Even a receive-only radio helps—you can hear where other radio-using traffic is. The airport frequency is found on air charts (122.8 pictured).

Keep any talk to a minimum but be listening for other traffic. When you're ready to go (if able to transmit), announce your intentions, "Powered Paraglider 1, just south of runway 5 approach, launching northeast then turning south, remaining south of the airport."

Represent Us Well

We are the sport's ambassadors and, in the environment of an airport, a conscientious appearance does double duty. Our future access and acceptability will be based on our behavior. So, above all: Be polite, don't annoy anybody, fly quiet and, by all means, fly safely.

Places to Look

It's strange that you sometimes have to go near cities to find launch sites. We don't want to be *in* the city, but near its perimeter where the humans are frequently building things. That's good since they tend to clear the land before building on it. Many industrial areas have a long way to go before build-out and, in the meantime, they tend to keep it nicely mowed for potential customers. This can be perfect for us.

Private farms with a co-located home can be good too, given their frequently launchable grass areas and agreeable owners.

Incomplete residential or commercial areas can be great sites. Play nice with the neighbors.

While it's great that we can launch from so many places, always consider "what if." Besides the obvious engine-out concern, try to account for wind forecasts or trends. Launch sites that require an upslope wind, for example, may not allow a return if the wind shifts.

This site would only be feasible in a wind coming from the pilot's right.

Safe Havens

One beauty of our sport's uniqueness is that it's easy to make friends who share the passion. And the best places to fly are those that have already been pioneered by a local pilot. Locals will likely know where other pilots commonly fly. Most PPG schools have their own sites and will let others fly there providing they respect the site and its surroundings. Not surprisingly, these schools may require a membership or some form of payment from those who didn't train with them.

Almost any site where pilots fly regularly has rules which, among other things, help keep their neighbors happy. Follow them closely to maintain your welcome.

Also, every site has at least one unhappy, noise-hating neighbor. It doesn't matter that busy railroad tracks are in their back yard—they'll still call the cops on you. Steer clear for the sake of the site's regulars.

Telling Wind Direction from Flight Path

If you choose to alight somewhere that has no wind indicators, you'll need to know wind direction. Chapter 7 has tips on using ground features but, in the absence of those, here is one method to use while you're aloft. Descend to about 200 feet and do a slow 360° turn while watching the ground (or look at your GPS groundspeed). When you're moving the slowest over the ground, you're going directly into the wind. If there's much wind at all, you'll notice drift. If you're drifting left, the wind is from your right—turn into it until the drift stops and that's the wind direction.

There are phone apps that can do this also, requiring the same thing—a slow, steady 360. Of course the wind at the surface may be completely different, but this is a good start. In thermally conditions, of course, expect it to be variable and turbulent.

The owner of this palatial launch site discovered powered paragliding and shared it with friends. He kept the lawn clear so that foot drags were possible for nearly the entire perimeter.

Find out where the locals fly and respect their sites by adhering to any special requirements. It's good to be invited back.

Flying from Controlled Airports

CHAPTER

11

There have been ultralight clubs flying from controlled airports, mixing it up splendidly with others, for years. Foot launching adds another dimension but can certainly be done safely.

As learned in Chapter 9, airports with control towers have class D airspace around them for air traffic control (ATC) and, therefore, require permission. It's not hard to get, but it's easier if you have an aircraft radio. Most towered airports will require it. See Chapter 10 on flying from airports.

Telephone

If your launch site is within class D airspace, but not on the airport, you may be able to get permission via telephone. Even if you're using an aircraft radio, phoning first lets you explain your plans, your weird craft, and accommodate any special needs they may have.

Before calling, figure out where you'll launch relative to the airport. Using a sectional chart or phone app, plot out a bearing and distance in nautical miles. Google Earth can be a great resource too, by using its ruler function. If there is a VOR (see Chapter 9) nearby, you can plot out a radial and distance from that. Know the airport's elevation, where the runways are, and their traffic patterns. ATC will try to keep you away from known air traffic. Have a route that will let you exit and re-enter their airspace quickly (as much as we do "quickly") .

Tower numbers can be hard to find. Try Acukwik.com. Or it may be listed under Government, Department of Transportation, FAA Control tower. Failing those, call Flight Service (800 WX-BRIEF) and explain that you need to talk with the "local controller" or "tower cab" for flight permission, and they should give it up.

During my first summer flying PPG I wanted to fly it everywhere. As a professional pilot, I'd spent years arriving on large airports' long ribbons of concrete with a 150+ mph chirp, now I wanted to land on one by foot. What a mesmerizing experience: running down the first stripe, then lifting back into the air.

Before taking off I had called the tower via telephone so they knew what to expect. That was exceedingly helpful. Of course I took my camera because it just seemed so unnatural.

A Note About Call Signs

You make up your own descriptive call sign for use with aviation radios; there is no need to register it with anyone. "Ultralight Papa Gulf" is one example.

Rules for aviation transceivers vary by country. Generally, if the equipment is used as intended, nobody will ask questions but check your country's rules.

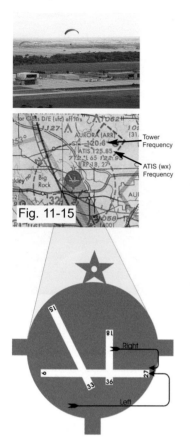

Fig. 11-15

Aurora airport's control tower is at 120.6 Mhz and the Automatic Terminal Information Service (ATIS) is broadcast on 125.85 Mhz.

The picture above was from a flight of three paramotor pilots who trekked into this Class D airport while one talked on the radio and the others followed.

We were instructed to make "Right Closed Traffic" for the grass North of runway 27 and remain east of runway 33. The enlarged airport above makes it clear what these instructions mean. We followed the right pattern, depicted above, meaning that our turns to final were to the right. Airplanes were using the standard left pattern.

Being instructed to remain East of 33 meant that we had to plan our climbout carefully to give that runway a wide berth. Airplane wake, just like our own wake, drifts with the wind and sinks. An encounter with that while down low could be messy.

Ask for the *Tower Chief*. Arranging this a few days in advance because, if you can't reach him and have no aircraft radio, it may not work. Explain that you:

1. Would like to launch your "ultralight, a powered paraglider" (that may take some explanation) from location x.

2. Will stay below 500 feet AGL (or some acceptable altitude) as you exit or enter their class D airspace.

3. Have (or don't have) an aircraft transceiver and a transponder (used by radar controllers to identify specific aircraft.)

4. Will be flying between certain times.

Ask if they have any special requests. Permission is much better than forgiveness in this case, especially for certified pilots.

If you *do* have a radio then tell them you'll call on the tower frequency once airborn. Even if the airport has radar service, they will still probably want you on tower, but ask to be sure.

Towered Airport Talk

If you fly from the towered field itself then have an altimeter that can be set to field elevation and an aircraft radio—Chapter 28 has more on the hardware. Also, have a working knowledge of runways, how they're numbered, airport markings, and traffic patterns. Chapter 10 can help, especially before talking with the airport manager about access and launch space.

Choose an easily understood, brief, and descriptive call sign like "Ultralight Papa Golf." It's easily picked out from other aircraft and conveys immediately that you're a low speed craft.

When talking with airport management in person, have pictures or a video to show. On the phone, describe yourself as a "foot-launched powered parachute." They'll get the idea.

ATIS

Most controlled airports have a continuously repeating weather recording—**A**utomatic **T**erminal **I**nformation **S**ervice, or ATIS, that gets updated every hour. It includes airport weather, runways in use, and other relevant bits. To ensure pilots have the latest information, each update is labeled with a different letter. So the first hour's recording may be information "Alpha" (A) and the second hour's would be "information Bravo" (B) and so on. The tower wants to know that you've listened to this and will expect you to let them know on initial call.

The ATIS frequency is on sectional charts under the airport's name and control tower frequency (CT). See Fig. 11-15. Listen to this broadcast first then contact the tower via radio and mention it to them "…information Bravo" (if it's B).

Tower Talk: Launch

Communications are taken seriously, for good reason—when you're transmitting, it ties up the frequency. Nobody wants to deal with slow, uncertain transmissions. Plan your words, press the transmit button, then speak clearly and succinctly. Rehearse a few times.

Your initial call to the tower should include the facility name, your call sign, the letter of the ATIS recording (if one is broadcast), and your request. When you're ready to launch, motor running, A's in hand, then call the tower, saying that you're ready for launch. They will give you the winds, special instructions, and clear you to launch. They will probably tell you to "proceed as requested" or "at your own risk" since technically you're not on any clearance and aren't using a runway.

Complete your launch and comply with any instructions. If you delay more than a half-minute or so they will probably cancel the authorization and ask you to call them back when you're ready. If the launch doesn't work out, explain that you needed to abort and will call back when ready.

After you've launched and flown a few miles away, the tower may offer a frequency change; just respond with your call sign and "roger." You are not required to ask for a frequency change nor are they obligated to give you one once you leave their airspace.

Tower Talk: Landing

Before returning to land, listen to the airport's ATIS and note the letter (Alpha for A, Bravo for B, etc.).

Call the tower by saying its name and that you "have information such and such (ATIS letter)" followed by your request for a landing. They will issue instructions regarding patterns and runways. If you're coming into the airport you will need to tell them exactly where on the field you want to land.

Example Communications

Here is a sample communication for a paramotor pilot flying from Aurora airport near Chicago, IL. It's in Class D airspace at 600 ft MSL elevation (above mean sea level). Ideally you will have already talked with the tower by phone, so they know about the craft and where on the field you will launch from. Have a name for the place such as "in front of GF Aviation" (see sample diagram next page). Make sure you understand the airport's runway and taxiway layout along with its typical patterns.

In the examples, your transmissions use this font and *ATC transmissions are italicized.*

Here is an example of ultralights playing well with aircraft. The tower controllers, airport management, and club operators have agreed on this arrangement. It allows a very active ultralight pattern to be flown right next to the airport runway. Aviation radios are required but the ultralights aren't expected to mix with the regular traffic.

Tip: AWOS

Many non-tower airports also have recorded weather: Remote equipment that monitors conditions and broadcasts it continuously. It updates every few minutes, broadcasting current info on the listed frequency.

These Automated Weather Observation Systems (AWOS) are noted on the sectional chart along with their frequency. They also sometimes have a phone number with the recorded weather.

In this example, Casa Grande airport's recorded weather can be picked up on an aviation frequency 132.175 Mhz.

These recordings are also usually available via telephone or a phone app.

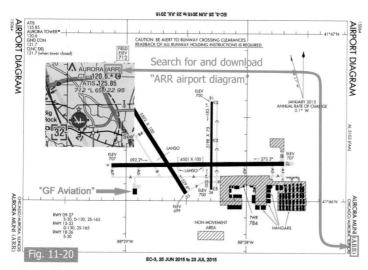

This is the Airport Diagram for Aurora Muni, identified as ARR. GF Aviation is a fictitious paramotor-friendly business we've added for our examples.

Digging Deeper

There are 3 primary types of airport identifiers. Bigger airports usually get the same basic 3-letter code. Not every airport has a code from every international organization.

1. The FAA (U.S.) uses 3-letter codes, like ARR, for most airports and 4-letter/number combinations for small and private airports like FA08 for Orlampa, better known as Fantasy of Flight in Polk City, Florida.

2. The International Civil Aviation Authority (ICAO) uses 4-letter codes that start with a unique country ID. For the U.S. that's "K", so ARR is KARR. Smaller countries have two-letter ID's and only the last two letters are unique. EB is Belgium, for example, so Brussels is EBBR.

3. International Air Transport Association (IATA) uses 3 letter /number codes mostly to be more obvious for airline passengers. Brussels, for example, is BRU. It's not perfect, though, Aurora, IL is AUZ.

Dial in the ATIS frequency:

"Aurora Tower information Charlie, time one four five three Zulu weather, wind 040 at 5, visibility 6 haze, scattered 35 hundred, temperature 24, dew point 18, runway 9 in use, runway 33/15 closed, caution for crane operating 600 feet east of the tower up to 150 feet, taxiway Charlie closed, tower and ground combined on 120.6, advise on initial contact you have information Charlie"

The above tells you that the wind is from the northeast at 5 knots and runway 9 is in use (airplanes will be taking off and landing towards the east). The weather observation was made at 1453 Zulu (see Chapter 7).

You are set up in the grass south of runway 9 near the GF Aviation building (Fig. 11-20), planning to head south. Call the tower when ready to inflate.

"Aurora Tower, Ultralight Papa Golf by GF Aviation is ready to launch, would like a south departure."

"Ultralight Papa Golf, remain clear of runway 9, southbound departure approved, proceed as requested, launch is at your own risk."

"Ultralight Papa Golf, will remain clear of runway 9"

After launch, turn south and head out. If the tower knows about traffic in your vicinity, they may call it out. Positions are given relative to your *ground track* using clock directions where 9 o'clock is off your left, 12 o'clock is in front of your flight path, and 3 o'clock is to the right of it.

"Ultralight Papa Golf, you have traffic at your 11 o'clock and a mile westbound at 1500 feet, he's on right downwind for runway 9"

Look for the traffic; it is given relative to sea level (not airport elevation) so 1500 feet means he's 900 feet above the ground. Your altimeter should be set so that it reads airport elevation at launch for this reason.

Stay below about 500 feet or as instructed and respond accordingly.

"Ultralight Papa Golf, traffic in sight" *or, if you don't see it,* "Ultralight Papa Golf, negative contact."

After you've flown out of the tower's airspace you are legal to change frequencies (no permission required). They may, however, offer the change.

"Ultralight Papa Golf, clear of my area, frequency change approved."

"Ultralight Papa Golf, roger."

When returning to land, listen to the ATIS again (note the letter—X in this case) to make sure there are no changes. Call the tower with your position and request. Since this is an initial request, use the facility name.

"Aurora Tower, Ultralight Papa Golf is 6 miles south, southeast, landing with X-Ray (the ATIS letter)."

"Ultralight Papa Golf, approach the field from due south, remain below 1200 feet, call 2 miles out."

When reaching 2 miles out, report your position.

"Ultralight Papa Golf is 2 miles out."

If there's no traffic, it's fun to do a "touch and go" on a runway. If it's not being used, you may be able to get permission.

"Ultralight Papa Golf, if traffic permits, request touch and go on runway 36."

"Ultralight Papa Golf, roger, can you keep your pattern south of runway 27?"

If you're absolutely certain, beyond the slightest shadow of a doubt, that you can safely comply, respond with "affirmative." Otherwise, say "negative." For this exercise we'll assume there is plenty of room.

"Ultralight Papa Golf, affirmative."

"Ultralight Papa Golf, keep your pattern south of runway 27, make right traffic for runway 36, report abeam the tanks."

When abeam the tanks (they pass by perpendicular to your flight path), report.

"Ultralight Papa Golf is abeam the tanks."

"Ultralight Papa Golf, cleared for the option runway 36, then make right traffic, remain south of runway 27."

This means you are cleared to land and stop, do a touch and go, or do a flyby of the runway. If you land and stop the clearance ends (you cannot takeoff again until cleared for takeoff) but if you touch and go, or fly by, make your pattern turns to the right while staying south of runway 27.

When you are ready to land back at your launch site:

"Ultralight Papa Golf is ready to land back in front of GF Aviation."

"Ultralight Papa Golf, remain south of runway 9, landing is at your own risk, proceed."

You will only be "cleared" to land or take off from a runway, not the adjoining grass or taxiways. Clearances, per se, are only issued when they involve the runway.

"Ultralight Papa Golf, roger."

Most instructions should be repeated (read back) to ensure you understand and will comply. All clearances relating to runways and taxiways *must* be read back. If you're only told to "proceed" then a full readback isn't really necessary; a simple "roger" will do. If you are asked to maintain an altitude it will be MSL so have a reasonably accurate altimeter available—most wrist altimeters work.

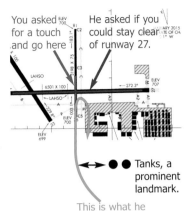

You asked for a touch and go here. He asked if you could stay clear of runway 27.

●● Tanks, a prominent landmark.

This is what he expects you to fly coming from the south, southeast with the instruction "keep your pattern south of runway 27, make right traffic for runway 36."

This control tower was closed, leaving G airspace. Look up the "Digital Airport Facility Directory" and enter the airport identifier to find this out. Had it been Surface Area of Class E you would have contacted the Southern California Approach Control (SoCal) by phone to get permission.

IMPERIAL BEACH
IMPERIAL BEACH NOLF (REAM) (NRS)
CT - 120.65 ★ ATIS 276.2
24 *L 50

Digital A/FD entry for NRS airport

AIRSPACE: CLASS D svc 1600-0630Z‡ Mon-Thu; (1500-0600Z‡ DL); 1600-0200Z‡ Fri clsd from 1800Z‡ day prior till 0800Z‡ day following gov holidays other times CLASS G.

Letter of Agreement

If you fly frequently from a site within D airspace, you may be able to get a letter of agreement from the controlling facility, usually a control tower.

Set up an appointment with the tower chief (or his appointed minion) and have a map that shows where you fly along with a picture of your craft. If approved, you will be issued a letter specifying boundaries, altitudes, and times where you can fly without contacting them. It can work for a club, too.

Digging Deeper: Phonetic Alphabet

Aviation radios aren't known for clarity so this pronunciation alphabet was developed to help, especially with B's, C's, D's, T's, etc.

A Alpha
B Bravo
C Charlie
D Delta
E Echo
F Foxtrot
G Golf
H Hotel

I India
J Juliet (*See R; someone had a sense of humor!*)
K Kilo
L Lima
M Mike
N November
O Oscar
P Papa
Q Quebec
R Romeo
S Sierra
T Tango

U Uniform
V Victor
W Whiskey (*strange choice?*)
X X-Ray
Y Yankee
Z Zulu

These numbers pronunciations prevent confusion in some languages:

3 Tree
5 Fife
9 Niner

A flight of five paramotorists flew right off the end of this airline runway. Sometimes all you have to do is ask.

Another person on the ground monitored air traffic control via aviation radio and stayed in contact with the PPG pilots. We stayed below the flight path of airplanes that were taking off and landing. Wake turbulence was a concern but moderately strong onshore winds helped there.

by Wesley Woo

Setup & Maintenance

12

"You're not a paramotor pilot, you're a mechanic who gets to test your work."

Unfornuately, reliability is not a strong point. Our machines look simple and, in most regards, they are, but some dark corners lurk. Proper setup and maintenance is critical beyond appearances. Follow manufacturer guidance, when available, then your instructor or dealer who is experienced with the brand. Improper adjustments, especially to the harness, can render a paramotor unflyable or dangerous.

Harness

A paramotor harness includes the critical liftweb. Its webbing (the structural straps), fabric, and padding, connects you to the wing, provides a seat, and supports the motor. It also has your most important adjustments—for hang angle, torque management, comfort, and other aspects of flight. Avoid UV rays, extreme heat, cuts, and harmful chemicals.

Riser Spread

The harness should provide a riser separation of 17 to 20 inches (42 – 50 cm) to keep most wings within certification. Your wing's manual may list other limits but few specify it. Be especially careful to avoid *less* than minimum separation which would accentuate *riser twist*, where the pilot spins around under the wing. Too much separation risks glider structural integrity and handling.

Setup

Setup *must* be done while hanging from the carabiners in a simulator (see Chapter 1). You can hang it from a tree limb, rafter, or anything high enough to get your feet off the ground. Try to find someone familiar with how the harness works.

You want the thrust line to point slightly downward (between 5° and 20°) from

This common low hook-in style frame connects carabiners to the S arms and, to prevent metal failure from being catastrophic, has a backup strap that goes to the fabric harness (black material).

Courtesy MacFly Paramoteur

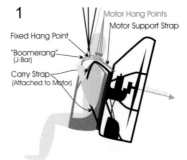

1

Motor Hang Points
Motor Support Strap
Fixed Hang Point
"Boomerang"
(J-Bar)
Carry Strap
(Attached to Motor)

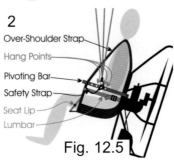

2

Over-Shoulder Strap
Hang Points
Pivoting Bar
Safety Strap
Seat Lip
Lumbar

Fig. 12.5

1. This *soft J-bar* style adjusts the hang angle by changing which "boomerang" hole the motor hangs from. The last hole is typically used, but moving to a more-forward hole gives a more upright hang position.

2. Low hook-in machines adjust the hang angle by choosing different holes in the weight shift bar (or rigid rail). Using a forward hole makes the motor hang back farther. Motors with no carry strap are normally launched with the main strap (over-shoulder) tight; then it's loosened in flight for comfort.

Tightening lumbar support (as equipped) moves the back of the harness forward. That moves the pilot, and therefore the CG, forward which tends to make the motor hang more upright.

Repairs to the liftweb should be done by a certified parachute rigger or equally qualified professional. Other harness repairs can be made with any strong thread such as for leather or carpet. The hooked needle helps push it through thick straps.

straight back (see Fig 12.5). A leaned-back posture may be more comfortable but it makes takeoff and landing more difficult. Sitting bolt upright is less comfortable but minimizes the twisting effect of torque and makes launch easier.

Adjust the hang angle by moving the carabiner hook-in point. On many harnesses, like those illustrated below, this is done by moving the carabiner loop along the upper front main web. Then adjust the upper rear main web (strap 3 in Fig 12.10) so that the motor or harness does not press against your body in flight. You should feel little or no harness pressure on your body—distance/comfort bars prevent that by transferring motor thrust to the forward harness straps.

If the carabiners clip into a bar or frame, selecting the appropriate hole or position is critical. Moving the carabiner forward increases tilt-back. Light pilots typically use the most aft positions (nearer the motor) to counteract the motor's weight. It's opposite if the *motor* clips into a bar (which is rare)—holes farther back make the motor tilt back farther.

Leg straps should be snugged up tightly then let out a couple inches. If they're too tight it's hard to run, and on most machines, if they're too loose it's difficult to get seated. A few models, however, are designed for the leg loops to be completely loose—check with the manufacturer.

The Anti-Torque strap (see page 13), if equipped should be tightened until it's snug but without forcing the carabiners together. This slightly reduces the effect of motor torque at some expense in weight shift. Many machines *made* to weight shift don't have this strap since weight shift can counteract some torque effects.

On machines equipped with a seat lip adjustment strap, it should be left loose for launch and landing. Pull it tight while hanging in the simulator to get some feel for how much tightening it takes and then let it loose again.

The front chest web (figure 1 at left) keeps you from falling out forward and prevents the risers from spreading out too far. Being over-tight might bring the risers too close together and will also reduce weight shift authority. The chest strap should be just barely snug.

Ground Handling Straps

Ground Handling straps, or *carry straps* (see figure 1) help keep the motor "hiked up" while preparing for launch. On over-the-shoulder machines they keep the bars off your shoulder. And they make forward launches easier by preventing the motor from wallowing around.

In flight, the ground handling straps can be loosened for comfort if needed. On harnesses where these straps pass through

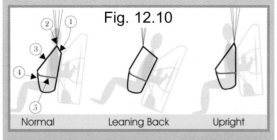

Fig. 12.10

Normal   Leaning Back   Upright

Balancing the weight of the motor and pilot keeps the prop disk (area created by the spinning prop) nearly vertical or hanging back slightly. Many harness varieties exist; the example above shows a soft harness type where the high hook-in can be moved by lengthening the #1 distance. That moves the motor's weight farther aft causing the motor to tilt back more, vectoring (pointing) the thrust downward slightly. It may be more comfortable in flight but challenges the launch and landing. More tilt-back dramatically aggravates the twisting effect of torque.

A good compromise in comfort and safety is about a 5° tilt-back which means the thrust line is also correctly pointed about 5° down.

a buckle, tie a knot at the end so the strap can't come all the way out and wind up in the prop.

A sternum strap usually attaches to the carry straps to keep them from slipping off your shoulders.

Machines without carry straps should have their main over-shoulder webbing cinched up reasonably tightly. You can loosen them in flight for comfort. These machines may also provide a side strap lumbar tensioner that can be tightened for launch and loosened in flight if necessary.

Kick-In Bar

A kick-in bar or rope is used to help get in the seat on some machines. It should be heavy enough (like an aluminum bar) to hang down a bit but must not interfere with walking backwards (for reverse launches). Normally it should hang a little over halfway down to your foot while sitting in the simulator.

Speedbar Setup

Once unclipped from its holder, a speedbar should ride just below the seat so you have full travel. If the machine has both speedbar and kick-in bar, the speed-bar should hang closer. Having it close allows more travel but makes it harder to get your feet into. Some harnesses have handy loops where the foot bar can be stowed during takeoff and landing.

Speedbar adjustment in a simulator requires that you attach the wing's risers and hold them up like you're in flight with the sister clips connected. Make sure the speedbar line is not so tight that it pulls the A's with*out* the bar being pushed out—that could be deadly. When fully depressed, the two A-riser pulleys should almost touch each other (see Fig. 12.10).

Make the line a bit longer than what the simulator suggests, then go test fly it. While flying, pull the bar up as far as you can, using its line, but still get your feet on the bar. Mark that spot then make adjustments after landing—that's how far the bar should hang below the seatboard.

Some "speedbars" have no hard bar; they're just thick line or a strap. They may also come with another strap that attaches to the seatboard for kicking out the seat.

Another style speedbar system uses two loops which allows for two-stage activation of the speedbar. Push out on the first loop to full leg extension, then go to the closer loop for yet more travel.

Hard Point Hook-Ins

On machines with low hook-in points there are usually hard points that the cara-biners attach to through a short strap as shown at right. Adjusting hang angle is a compromise between keeping the risers forward of the pilot's arms and leaning

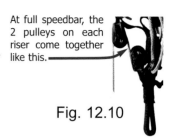

At full speedbar, the 2 pulleys on each riser come together like this.

Fig. 12.10

Hard Point Hook-Ins

Tilt angle is affected by where the carabiners attach: moving them forward means more tilting back.

Speedbar Setup

Hold Riser up to determine speedbar line length.

Built-in loops for pulleys

Velcro bar holders

Speedbar *usage* is in Chapter 18.

These over-shoulder floating J-Bars use hard point connections; carabiners attach directly to the bar which moves up and down.

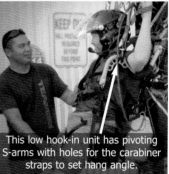

This low hook-in unit has pivoting S-arms with holes for the carabiner straps to set hang angle.

by Rob Whitaker

Collar

S-Arm

Some machines use a sliding collar to set hang angle. It's held in place with a set screw.

A lightweight pilot flying a heavier machine must hook the carabiners to the farthest point aft.

Some machines connect using a loop of webbing through an opening on the spreader bar. The proper holes must be used! Connecting *around* the bars and holes (likes shown in the inset at right) would allow the carabiners to slide forward, causing severe tilt-back and riser twist.

Hang Point Adjustment

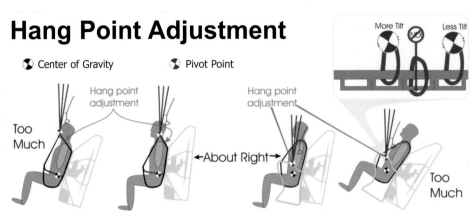

🜨 Center of Gravity   🜨 Pivot Point

Too Much   Hang point adjustment   Hang point adjustment ←About Right→   Too Much

More Tilt   Less Tilt

back too far. Leaning back is more comfortable but causes stronger torque effects.

If carabiners attach to a bar instead of the harness webbing, they use a safety strap that goes from the riser loop to the harness. That avoids a loose metal-to-metal contact point which is slightly more susceptible to fatigue failure.

Reducing Torque

Chapter 23 has more on torque effects but the two main components are riser shift (weight shift) and yaw (left/right twisting of the motor). Yaw is worse since it redirects thrust which then pushes you sideways and into a bank. It can easily over-power your turn authority. Here are some mitigation methods.

- Reduce the hang-back angle. This reduces riser twist due to the horizontal component of torque, especially for smaller pilots flying powerful motors.

- Use anti-torque aerodynamic thrust redirection (see Chapter 23), if available for your model.

- Make sure the motor cannot slide left or right on the harness which would cause offset thrust, the second most powerful twisting force. It's like having someone push on a shoulder blade with 100 or more pounds—you will twist. If you tend to twist right, (motor pushing on left shoulder) adjust the motor to push slightly on your right shoulder. Chapter 23 has a nice diagram of this. You could also move the hook-in point laterally (left or right) on one or both sides of the harness if your machine has fixed bars.

- Ensure that there is sufficient riser separation and the motor is held rigidly in place. Left-right swinging arms must never swing inward (outward is ok).

- Create a differential carabiner hang height. In other words, if the motor torque tilts you to the right (pulls down the right riser), make the left carabiner lower. That will make it turn slightly left during power-off glides, fly straight at cruise power, and turn slightly right during climb. This works best on higher hang point motors because the motor's center of gravity (CG) is well below the hang points.

- Move the hook-in point aft on one side (easier on motors with hard point attachments). This angles the thrust slightly so as to oppose its natural tendency. So if you tend to twist left during climb (wing banks right), move the hook-in point on the left side back (aft) and/or move the right-side hook-in forward.

Two-Cycle Motor — Troubleshooting Chart

START Does the starter make the piston move? → **No** → **Starter problem:**
- Pull start - check pawls, looseness.
- Flash starter - check main spring.
- Electric starter - power, engagement solenoid, motor, gears.

Yes

Does the motor have compression when you pull/crank it over?

→ **Too Much** → **Remove the spark plug. If there's still too much resistance to pulling, it could be:**
- Seizure (piston partially melts against cylinder wall).
- Bad pull or electric starter.
- Other internal problem.

Otherwise it could be:
- Clogged decompression hole (if equipped) - clean it out.
- Bad decompression valve (if equipped). Clean or replace.

Yes / **No**

Does the motor Start and continue to run?

Yes / **No**

No/Low Compression:
- Spark plug is loose - tighten.
- The piston has a hole in it - replace.
- If it has a decompression valve this is normal but you'll hear hissing during pull.

Does it fire at all? Make sure it's not flooded: remove the spark plug and ground it (to prevent coil damage), pull the starter or crank it, then replace the plug. A wet plug may indicate flooding.

Does it develop and keep full RPM?

Yes / **No**

→ **If full RPM does not deliver full thrust, then it could be:**
- The prop is on backwards - the curved side always faces forward (towards the motor).
- The belt or clutch (if equipped) is slipping.

Is the spark weak or absent?
Set the connected plug on the cylinder and look for a spark while pulling/cranking the motor. Don't touch!

Does it go to full RPM then fade or does the power vary without changing the throttle setting?

Yes / **No**

Is it overheating?
Use a CHT to tell.

No / **Possibly**

Spark is not being generated or is being shorted. It could be:
- Bad spark plug - Try a new one.
- Kill switch is shorted - disconnect it and see if it fires or verify the kill circuit is an "open" when **not** pushed. Some motors use the throttle sheathing as to complete the circuit.
- Coil or magneto (as equipped) is bad. Most use a magnet and coil to generate the high voltage required of the spark plug.
- Spark plug boot. Black soot means loose contact.

Tune the carburetor, check the reed valve, get fresh fuel.
Did that solve the problem?

Yes → **Go Fly!**

No

Is properly-mixed fuel getting to the carburetor? Try spraying starter fluid in the air intake. If it pops when cranked then fuel mixture is *not* being delivered.

Yes / **No**

Power Fade, Not Overheating:
- The prop is either too big or has too much pitch - "over propped."
- The mixture may be changing as the motor heats up (even though it's not overheating). Tune Carb.
- The cylinder and piston need to be de-carbonized.
- Bad or broken tuned pipe. The damage is usually not visible. Try replacing the pipe if able.
- Check for cylinder or crankcase air leaks.
- Throttle cable allows activation of the throttle without squeezing the trigger.
- Air leak (bubbles) in fuel line, especially at primer bulb or fuel filter, as installed.
- Contaminants in carburetor or inline fuel filter. They compress with time.

Has Fuel, Air, Spark & Compression; could be:
- Bad reed valve (if equipped).
- Excess internal carbon deposits.
- Bad ignition system (coil, plug, wire, boot). Even though you see it spark the strength may be inadequate.
- Exhaust is bad. Tuned pipes can make engines run rough if broken or improperly made.
- Ignition timing is off, call expert.
- Timing issue, loose/off timing mechanism
- Piston rings stuck or sticking.
- 100 other arcane possibilities. Assume the fetal position and cry, or consult an expert.

Losing Proper Fuel/Air Mix:
- Air leak in a fuel line. Replace line. This can sometimes be seen as bubbles in the fuel line.
- Blocked fuel filter.
- Fuel tank air intake vent blocked. This will cause the motor to run for a while then become lean and quit.
- Old fuel - it may last only a week if unsealed.
- Improper fuel. Small motors don't like Avgas or low octane fuel and some prefer Avgas.
- Pinched fuel line.

Overheating has several possibilities:
- The fuel/air mixture is (or gets) too lean, possibly from air leak into cylinder from exhaust flange, base gasket, cylinder head O-ring (or gasket), or crank case.
- Too little oil in fuel. This should not be a problem up to 50:1 fuel/oil ratio.
- Bearings have seized.
- The cylinder is scored.
- The piston ring(s) are stuck or sticking.
- Cooling fan failure or blockage.
- Head bolts loose.

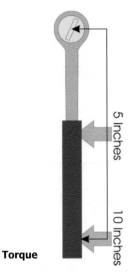

Torque

A torque wrench allows you to gauge how powerful you are twisting something. The farther out you push on the wrench, the more torque you exert. So 10 pounds of pressure at 10 inches produces the same torque that 20 pounds of pressure at 5 inches does—100 inch-pounds.

Units

The standard international measure of torque is newton meters (N m). The U.S. uses Foot Pounds-force (ft·lbf) or just foot pounds. A less-often used measure is kilogram-force meter (kgf m). 1 Ft Lbf = 1.36 N m = 0.14 kgf m.

Safety Wire, Tools and Bolts

Aircraft safety wire stays strong even after being twisted. Attach it to prevent the bolt or part from unscrewing or departing—parts are always seeking freedom and this is good escape prevention. The muffler springs below have been safetied so they stay put after breaking. Such projectiles can damage bystanders, the wing, or cage on their way out.

Safety wire comes in various sizes; thicker is better given our machines' vibration. Use the thickest size your application allows. Few bolts are made to accept safety wire and must be drilled through the head.

Motor

Getting into this sport means, to some degree, becoming a mechanic. Precious few shops—motocross and cart racing shops mostly—can work on our gear, and they may be reluctant once they know it's for flying (worried about liability). Local shops probably won't have parts so you'll need someone who specializes in your particular brand. In all likelihood, you'll need to ship your broken unit to a shop that knows the model. But if you want it fixed quickly, you better learn to do it yourself. There are, fortunately, some preventative measures that can keep little problems from blossoming into big ones that require repair.

Troubleshooting

All internal combustion motors need four elements in the right proportion and at the right time: spark, fuel, air, and compression. Ensure these are present and you'll likely solve the problem. Sometimes, just replacing the spark plug is all it takes. At other times you'll need full use of the preceding flowchart and more.

Start with the simple and cheap then progress to the more involved. If your dealer can't help, www.FootFlyer.com has a great troubleshooting section, and Internet discussion groups dedicated to your motor can also be a good resource.

Fortunately, these machines are relatively simple, fairly reliable, and easy to work on. Many "mechanically challenged" pilots, when faced with being grounded, have risen to the occasion.

Bolt Tightening and Force

There is a universal way to describe how much force is used to tighten bolts: the kilogram-meter or Foot-Pound (imperial units list distance first). It is how much force is applied and how far out on the handle it is applied. That's torque. If you hold a wrench way out on the handle, it doesn't take much force to get the bolt tight due to leverage.

1 foot-pound is 12 Inch-Pounds. Be careful with units: 50 foot-pounds is a *lot* more torque than 50 inch-pounds.

Over tightening bolts is worse than under tightening since you can easily strip threads, especially aluminum threads.

Preventative Maintenance

Spark Plugs may last as little as 10 hours before carbon deposits and other wear degrades performance. They should either be changed every 20 hours or at the first sign of trouble—primarily because they are so cheap, easy to change, and are so commonly the problem. Tighten them to the motor maker's, or spark plug maker's specs. Normally, about 15 ft-pounds is enough to flatten the washer that comes with most plugs.

Fuel Lines harden over time, making them more likely to develop cracks or holes and should be replaced before becoming stiff. Tygon brand line is the gold standard. Don't route it around sharp corners or let it touch sharp objects lest chaffing causes holes. The primary sign of holes is bubbles in the fuel line—that will make the motor run rough, lean, or not at all. Don't secure fuel lines with wire ties; their sharp edges can dig into the line creating a hole.

Exhaust system bolts, rivets, and springs are always trying to vibrate off—a serious problem if parts either deform or drop onto the fuel tank. Although a fire is still highly unlikely, this area deserves close scrutiny. Exhaust components, whenever possible, should be safety wired. Putting heat tolerant sealant into the springs helps prevent failure from vibration.

Head bolts should be checked with a torque wrench of appropriate units, especially when the machine is new. They tend to loosen up along with many other fasteners.

Reduction Drive

Most paramotors use a reduction drive to turn the motor's high-RPM into a propeller-friendly lower RPM. They either use a belt or gears.

Gear Drive

Most gear drives consist of 2 gears and 4 bearings in a sealed grease-laden aluminum housing. It's normally driven by the motor through a clutch bell.

Normal maintenance requires ensuring sufficient grease (or gear oil depending on make) and good bearings. They generally require very little attention; however, on rare occasion, little bits of metal can muck up the works. When that happens, the case must be split open and the debris removed.

1. After installing new fasteners or parts, put a dab of fingernail polish on the juncture. You'll be able to quickly see, during preflight, if it has loosened.

Any mis-alignment of the pulleys will cause the belt to either come off or break well before its time. With proper adjustment and a light propeller, a belt should last 100 hours.

On average it should be tensioned so that there is about a 1/4" of play when pressed at spot 1 below.

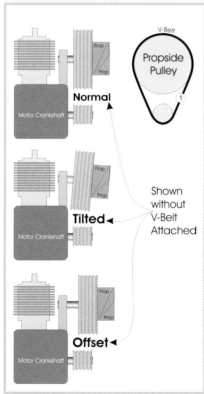

If you feel play in the prop, and it's not due to prop bolts, the bearings may be failing. Replacement requires splitting the redrive (gearbox) which is fortunately easy. Unscrew the bolts part-way then tap on their heads with something that won't do damage. Once the halves are partway separated, use a gear puller or prying tool (chisel or something wide that won't scrape the metal) to finish the separation. If the gears are damaged you may need a gear puller. If the bearings are bad, you'll probably have to heat the case to get them out. Be sure to replace any sealer around the edges to prevent leaks.

Belt Drive

The primary adjustment on belt-drive units is belt tension. Too loose and it slips—causing a "chirping" noise on each power stroke. Being too tight can bend the stand-off or stretch the belt. All motors have some way to adjust belt tension by changing the distance between pulleys. You must tighten new belts a few times since they stretch in the first few flight hours.

2. This is a common belt-drive arrangement. One good way to check belt tension is determining how much torque it takes to make the belt slip. Put a torque wrench on the center nut as depicted, hold the prop still and try to tighten the nut. The nut should stay put, but if the belt slips with less than 1.8 kg m (13 ft-lbs), then the belt is too loose. Tighten it and try again. The torque value will vary depending on the belt and motor.

Below: Flash starters have TWO springs, one to retract the cord and a big one to spin the motor. Have some starter pawls and a main spring on hand.

Courtesy Nayot Kurukitkoson

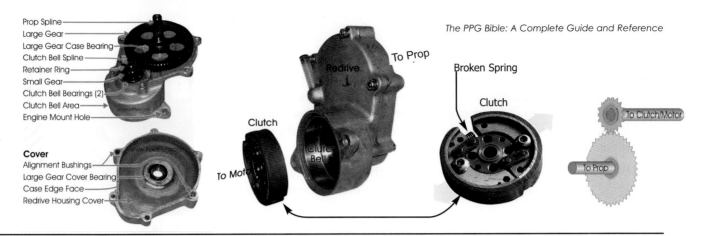

Prop Spline
Large Gear
Large Gear Case Bearing
Clutch Bell Spline
Retainer Ring
Small Gear
Clutch Bell Bearings (2)
Clutch Bell Area
Engine Mount Hole

Cover
Alignment Bushings
Large Gear Cover Bearing
Case Edge Face
Redrive Housing Cover

To Prop
Redrive
Clutch
Clutch Bell
To Motor
To Mot

Broken Spring
Clutch
To Clutch/Motor
To Prop

Gear reduction drive with clutch

The motor spins the clutch fast enough for clutch shoes (aka pads) to expand into the clutch bell which is part of the redrive's small gear. That then drives the much larger propside gear at a lower, more prop-friendly RPM.

The clutch pictured above on the right has one broken spring. So the two shoes spread out against the clutch bell too easily, causing the clutch to engage which makes the prop spin, even at idle. It should be stationary at idle.

The two pulleys must be aligned properly as shown on the previous page.

The belt should not squeak during power up; that's too loose. A heavy propeller (especially where the mass is out towards the tips) will aggravate slipping and may dramatically shorten belt or redrive bearing life.

Clutch

A clutch allows starting and idling the motor without spinning the prop. They are found mostly on smaller motors because larger motors need the prop's mass to act as a flywheel.

It's just like a mini-bike; at idle, springs hold the clutch shoes in. As you throttle up, the clutch shoes are thrown outward, rubbing against and grabbing the clutch bell. The prop is attached to that bell through either gears or a belt reduction drive. Make sure the prop is free-wheeling (no rubbing) with the motor off and that the clutch shoes are not too worn which would damage the bell.

If a clutch bell gets grooves worn in it, or is pitted from rust, it will quickly eat up clutch shoes and should be replaced.

Propeller

The propeller must be mounted with the curved side facing forward (direction of flight) and the bolts tightened evenly. The prop is held in place by friction with the plates, not the bolts. If there is torsional stress on the bolts, such as when they're too loose, they will break.

Do not drill extra holes in the prop hub to fit a different bolt pattern. The weakened wood could break, causing a catastrophic failure.

Use grade 8 bolts or better, and check tightness periodically. They should be torqued to approximately 5 Foot-Pounds (0.7 kg m); the goal is not to deform the wood. Tighten each bolt partway in succession, one at a time, on opposite sides, until getting to the desired torque just like a car wheel. Composite props can be torqued up to 7 foot pounds (1.0 kg m).

Rotate the prop to vertical and try to move the tip fore and aft while watching the engine mounts. A broken or nearly failed mount may allow enough flex for the prop to hit a frame/cage part and must be replaced. If the prop wiggles, check the center nut (on those motors that use it) and tighten if loose.

Balancing Act

Vibration is a paramotor's mortal enemy and props are close allies. There are many methods for balancing, but the most common, and fortunately the easiest, is static balancing. Less obvious is balancing out various aerodynamic maladies that can cause equally bad vibration.

Static Balance

The prop should balance exactly at the center of the hub. Special balancers can be purchased that will quickly reveal if the prop is heavier either spanwise (tip to tip) or chordwise (leading edge to trailing edge). Most balancers have a cylinder plug sized to fit snugly in the prop's center hole. The prop is hung from a single point right in the middle. If one blad (or side) droops then it's too heavy. A lawnmower blade balancer works OK too.

The cure is to put enough weight on the light side to bring it back to center. One method is to drill a hole opposite the heavy side and melt solder into it until balanced. Don't drill the hole all the way through so only one side has to be smoothed afterwards. Cover the hole with Super Glue™ (or equivalent) and baking soda mix then sand to match the wood contour.

Carbon Fiber props are different since they're hollow. Drill a hole near the tip and add epoxy or, in more extreme cases, melt solder in it (usually only necessary after a significant repair on the opposite blade). Seal the solder with epoxy and sand to shape.

Minor corrections to fix an imbalance can be done by spraying clear varnish to the lighter side. Several coats will be necessary as much of the weight evaporates off.

Aerodynamic Balance

If one blade is pulling harder than the other blade, it will cause vibration; it is aerodynamically unbalanced. Possible causes are:

- The propeller has a chordwise offset (see diagram on page 121), probably one or two bolts on one side are over-tightened, compressing the prop unevenly.

- The propeller is warped. This is more likely if it has been significantly repaired.

- One blade is longer or fatter than the other. That's relatively easy to correct by shaving off some length. One way to tell is to set shelf paper on the floor, put the prop on it, and carefully outline one half. Then put the other half over the outline and see if it's close. If not, reshape the larger half to match.

You can measure the angle of each blade by first setting it on a smooth, flat floor. Go 75% out towards the tip, hold a straight edge against the prop's flat bottom and measure its angle to the floor with a protractor.

Anytime a prop is worked on or reshaped, it should be statically balanced.

Tracking

If one blade tip passes by the same point in space at a different spot (either fore or aft) than the other blade, the tracking is off. The prop could be warped, improperly mounted (bolts unevenly tightened) or it could have an aerodynamic imbalance which would be more difficult to detect.

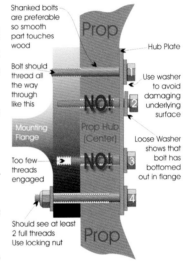

The curved surface mounts *towards* the motor so that it faces the direction of flight. Trying to launch with a backwards-mounted prop is embarrassing, at best. You'll have thrust but certainly not enough to fly. Looking at a paramotor from behind you should always see the prop's flat side.

The 4 bolt holes go through the *hub* which mounts to a *flange* on the motor—usually a redrive.

If prop tape does not adhere well to the curves, cut V's out as depicted here.

The tracking can be off by up to a ¼ inch with little effect. Any more than that, though, should be corrected by tightening the bolts evenly. If the prop is not causing vibration, leave it alone.

All propeller blades flex and twist a bit when under power—causing either more or less lift as they do. If one blade twists more than the other, it will cause a vibration even though the prop balances statically. A vibration that worsens may be caused by this. Poorly made, or thin, or props with large repairs are more likely to suffer from flexing.

Prop Tape

Special tape can be applied to the prop's leading edge to protect it from minor dings but it extracts some performance penalty. Also, if not adhering well, it can come off and cause an uncomfortable imbalance (it can generally be flown that way back to the destination).

Thin tape is better for going around the sometimes-difficult curves and tends not to hurt performance as much. Thick tape can sometimes be coaxed to work but may require small V-cuts or using a hair dryer to make it more malleable (see diagram at left).

Propeller Repair

Props will be sacrificed—to cages, to lines, to departing parts, and ground debris. Fortunately, many oops's are pretty easy to fix. Repairs must be done correctly to avoid pieces flying off with devastating consequences.

On all repairs, the surface should be cleaned first and sanded afterwards. If two-part epoxy is used, it should be allowed to fully cure before sanding; use a hard sanding block to prevent airflow-ruining bumps.

Repairing Wood Props

The quickest repair for small divots is Super Glue™ (or equivalent) and baking soda. Micro balloons, available at hobby shops, can be used in place of baking soda—they are lighter and easier to sand. Layer on the glue and sprinkle in baking soda. In the right proportion the mix may smoke a bit but should harden quickly.

Cylinder Style Prop Balancing

Here is a cylinder-style prop balancer in use. It allows balancing both lengthwise and widthwise.

The cylinder slides in the prop's center hole and then sits on the pointed stand. Any imbalance will cause the prop to tilt towards the

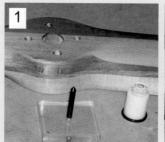

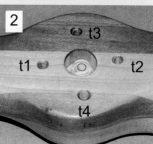

heavy direction. On this prop, the bubble is down and left meaning that it's heavy to the right and up. Weight has to be added down and left.

The t1 through t4 is what order the bolts should be tightened when re-mounting the prop. Barely tighten t1 then t2 then t3 then t4 then go around again until they are appropriately tightened.

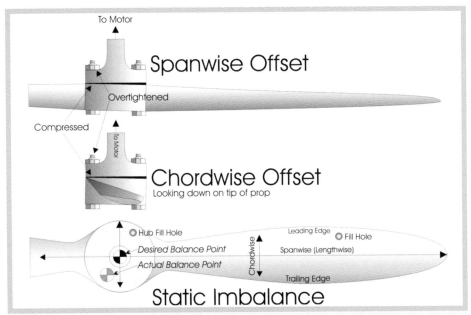

Spanwise Offset

To Motor

Overtightened

Compressed

To Motor

Chordwise Offset
Looking down on tip of prop

Hub Fill Hole   Leading Edge   Fill Hole

Desired Balance Point

Actual Balance Point

Chordwise

Spanwise (Lengthwise)

Trailing Edge

Static Imbalance

If a prop is not flat on the flange, the offset will cause some vibration. A chordwise offset is worse because one blade has more pitch than the other, pulling harder as it goes around.

Static balancing can be done by drilling a shallow hole where weight is needed and melting solder into it. Put a layer of epoxy on top to hold it in place then sand and varnish. The prop above (Static Imbalance) shows that weight needs to be added at the "Fill Hole" to counteract an actual balance point low and to the left. Use a fill hole on the hub when it is mostly a chordwise imbalance.

Repeat until the damage is filled then sand to shape.

Somewhat bigger gouges can be filled with epoxy and baking soda (or micro balloons). Use tape to follow the prop's contour in a way that you can pour the mixed epoxy in. That reduces sanding. Use an equal amount of epoxy and baking soda (by volume) to help reduce weight and make it easier to sand.

After it hardens use a hard sanding block to reshape it. It must be well cured before sanding; 5-minute epoxy, for example, must harden for several hours first.

Larger repairs, up to 30% of the length or width of one blade can be done with a variety of methods, one of which is depicted on the next page.

Once it's shaped and fine sanded, apply varnish, let dry and repeat until you're satisfied. Then balance.

Repairing Carbon Fiber Props

Carbon Fiber props are less forgiving of damage. Even after being repaired, they may harbor invisible degradation that could separate later, without notice, throwing shards. They should only be used when no risk to bystanders is present.

Carbon fiber props are usually hollow with a ½" thick or so foam core to keep the halves spaced appropriately. Lighter, but much more expensive than wooden props, they are also more challenging to repair. Don't expect them to look perfect after being repaired since fiberglass needs to cover part of the top for proper adhesion.

Simple cracks or holes aren't bad as they can be filled using epoxy. Force epoxy into the hole then use tape to form the prop's shape while the epoxy sets. Lay it so the

Static Prop Balancers.

These balancers are accurate, reliable, and simple to use: The prop's heavy side droops down.

1. A stand balancer checks only for lengthwise imbalance, the cause of most vibration. Put the cylinder through the prop's center hole and place on the green stand. This one, modified by Alex Varv, uses razor blades mounted on the stand to improve sensitivity.

2. The Xplorer string balancer checks for both spanwise and chordwise imbalance. Put the cylinder through the prop and hang from its string.

Both of these commercial versions take the hassle out of balancing props. You can, of course, make your own but these are inexpensive and already fit almost all props.

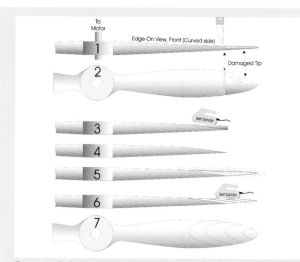

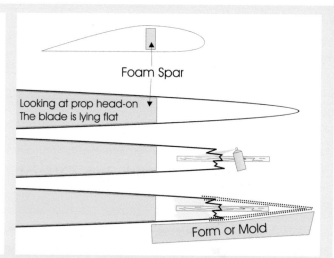

Surprisingly large repairs can be made on wooden props if done properly. A belt sander makes it easier but having a steady hand and some basic wood-working skill is a must.

Use a quality wood glue, spread evenly on 1/4" thick slabs of poplar wood (step 5). Make sure they're completely flat against each other and clamp firmly for overnight drying before sanding.

Sand to shape then varnish, sand, varnish, and balance.

Small repairs can be filled without stiffening. Anything over about an inch across or deep needs more. Always wear a respirator and goggles whenever working with fiberglass resin or sanding the hardened result. Anything over 3 inches should be repaired professionally and some carbon fiber prop makers strongly recommend against trying to repair their products.

Fiberglass is heavier than carbon fiber so balancing after the repair is especially important.

epoxy puddles against the tape while curing. You can also use putty-type epoxy.

More severe damage, such as when more than about an inch of tip is missing, requires another technique. You'll need fiberglass cloth and resin (available at some hardware and most marine supply stores). See the diagram for clarification of these steps.

Clean and sand the area within two inches of the damage to have a good bonding surface for the resin.

Spray foam (insulating foam is sold at many hardware stores) into the tip void for support. With worse damage, embed some reinforcement material (wood or wire) into the foam such that it extends beyond the foam. That will help hold the repair (next steps) in place. Let the repair set up overnight.

Trim the foam so that so it does not protrude into the repair area.

Mix the resin according to its directions—a finicky step that warrants practicing elsewhere. The mix must be just right. Cut up pieces of cloth, mix them into the resin then work the saturated pieces into the tip and around the mold. Longer pieces should overlap the prop's top and bottom upper and lower surfaces for the best bond.

Once hardened completely, sand to shape. A belt sander really helps to speed up the process but don't sand away where the fiberglass overlaps the existing prop. It won't look perfect, but is necessary for strength. Lightly hand sanding that overlap area helps smooth it out without decreasing strength.

Balance the prop and expect to add weight in the other tip.

The Wing

Paraglider wings require attention in proportion to how they are stored and used. Age and moisture tend to shrink lines which then must be stretched periodically, especially rear lines that don't get much load in flight. Conversely, loaded lines can get stretched, especially during steep maneuvering or abrupt re-openings. And lines weakened by heat or sharp bends (especially knots) can fail early.

Fabric can tear, become porous, moldy, or get chewed by insects and must be repaired. Most experienced pilots have found that beyond about 300 hours of strong UV exposure, the wing has served its time. Here are some tips to help keep your wing airworthy and even extend its life.

Replacing Risers

Unless they get damaged, risers should outlast the rest of your wing since they're quite over-built. When inspecting newly acquired risers, check their general condition; especially check that the stitching is done correctly. At least one set was shipped with the riser loop only tack stitched—an incredibly dangerous flaw that will likely fail on the first flight.

Risers can be separated from the lines to accommodate either a different model or replacement. Mostly this is done to put *motor risers* (shorter) on soaring wings to use with motors having high attachment points. Otherwise the soaring wing's brake position can be too high. Risers on soaring wings are longer to go with typical free-flight harnesses which nearly always have low attachment points.

A different riser set can dramatically change the wing's flight characteristics and usually takes the wing out of certification. Only use riser sets recommended by the manufacturer. Even then the wing may be out of certification if it wasn't re-tested with those risers.

You can remove risers by taking the lines off at their *quick links*.

Complete one side before doing the other side, starting from the A's, then proceeding back to the brakes. Put masking tape across a group of lines before detaching them and use a felt tip marker to note which side faces forward ("F" in the pictures) as well as what lines they are (A's, B's, etc.) including the split A, if equipped. Replacing the lines on one individual riser at a time is another good way to keep everything straight.

Here is one method for replacing risers in case you must do it all at once (such as sending them away for replacement). Start by marking the brake line knot location with a felt tip pen. Untie the brake toggle to pull its line through the brake pulley (or guide) then:

- If you have to cut away anything (like shrink wrap plastic) always cut *away* from the fabric. Be careful while using tools to avoid scratching the metal—that weakens it significantly.

- Pull the lines off and inspect any rubber O-rings that you remove. They keep the lines from misaligning or rubbing across the nut and threads. Replace old ones (plumbing supply outlets carry these) since they get brittle with age and break easily.

- If hard plastic shrink wrap was used, replace it with either electrical heat-

Don't change risers unless the manufacturer approves of the new set. Glider behavior and handling can differ dramatically with different risers. Picture 1 shows how risers affect relative line height, especially when the trimmers are up (fast).

2. Store the risers together either by clipping them to a small carabiner or by hooking them into each other like this.

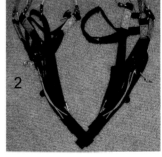

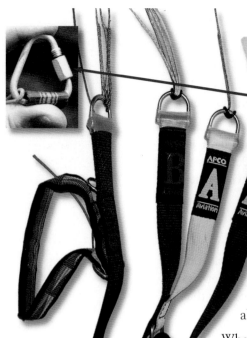

shrink tubing (from electronics supply stores) or electrical tape.

• Put the heat shrink tubing on the lines (if used), put the lines on the new riser, put the O-ring on with a figure 8 pattern (as shown), and then snug up the fastener.

• Snug to finger tight, then go an 1/8th turn more with a tool.

When completed, kite the wing before flying to make sure everything appears in order and it handles as expected. Additionally, make sure the brake lines get adjusted before flying.

Adjusting Brake Lines

Brake line length is a critical adjustment that should only be done by, or under the guidance of, someone familiar with the procedure. Brake lines that are too short will deflect the trailing edge—a dangerous situation that could cause a parachutal stall (see Chapter 4). Excessively long brake lines might allow a toggle into the prop and also may limit flare authority for landing.

This riser set is ready to have its lines removed.

On triangular quick-links (inset), if you have to use a tool to remove the connector, it's bent. Don't use pliers to force it on. You're better off replacing a bent one than flying with a compromised part. Over or under-tightening can cause structural failure under load.

The black rubber grommet is used to keep lines together and positioned properly on the quick link. It prevents them from snagging on an edge. These grommets should be replaced with new ones if cracked. On the riser set above, the C lines (rear risers on this wing) are missing the grommet.

When properly adjusted, with toggles at their pulley (flying hands-off), there should be some slack in the brake line with no trailing edge deflection. You'll see a slight arc in the line from its pulley up to the trailing edge. In flight, your hands should rest near position 2—that leaves enough flare authority while remaining comfortable. Having your arms hang lower may be more comfortable but sacrifices brake travel. Your bicep should be about horizontal when resting the weight of your arms in the brakes. A few inches can make a big difference in comfort.

Many free flyers set their toggles lower since they can take *wraps* (wrap the excess line around their hands) to have full authority. The throttle makes that difficult for motor pilots.

On those few wings that have two brake line pulleys to choose from, use the one that is most comfortable. Generally, with a low attachment motor, use the high pulley and for mid or high attachment motors use the low pulley.

Most wings come from the factory with the brakes set somewhat long to reduce the likelihood of a new pilot stalling. But that also limits control authority. To set the length, kite the wing and mark where the new knot should go. Untie the existing knot and retie it at the new location using the depicted brake line knot.

Brake Line Knots

The "8 Follow Through" is an ideal knot with low stress on the line. It is easy to tie since after looping through the brake toggle, it just follows itself back through the half-hitch.

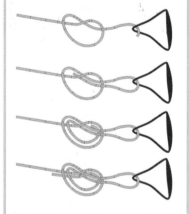

The Bowline (below) is commonly used for a quick tie but stresses the line more due to sharper bends and is not very secure.

Whichever you choose, keep the brake toggle and knot close together to prevent the toggle from flapping about in the breeze.

Repairing the Wing Fabric

Invariably you will tear the wing's fabric: either by pulling it too aggressively or mishandling. Sharp rocks and other protrusions are frequent culprits. Fortunately there is a lot of resilience and this doesn't always have to be a grounding item.

If the tear is structural then you'll have to bite the bullet and send it in for a full repair. Structural is where there is significant stress on the material at that point. The best example is just about any seam or anywhere lines attach to fabric. If the loop pulls out of the wing you'll have to send the wing to a shop for repairs.

Anytime wing meets spinning prop, get the wing inspected. Even repair magicians may not be able to put a torn mess back together but surprisingly extensive damage can be mended by qualified shops. Small non-structural repairs can be done on the field. Rip-stop nylon tape from camping stores, available in various colors, can work in a pinch. Cut it into an oval that covers the tear with about an inch of overlap. Make one for both sides of the fabric. Stretch the fabric out as much as possible, wipe it clean and dry, then press the repair tape on top. Press hard. It is best to line the pattern of little squares up with the wing material's pattern. Repeat for the other side.

Inspection

After 2 years or 100 hours of sun time on a new wing, it should be professionally inspected. After that, annual inspections should be done for hard-core flyers and biennual (every other year) inspections for everyone else.

Although there are many lines, a *cascade failure* is where one line breaks and transfers load to adjoining lines, which break in a cascade of many lines. It is rare but does happen, especially on wings that are "ridden hard and put away wet." That includes heavy maneuvering or aerobatics—such wings should see *at least* double the inspection frequency, much more if they're flown often.

Line Stretching

Don't tie a broken line together, especially the highly loaded A's; it shortens the line and reduces its strength by half—replacement is required.

Lines shrink with time, especially if they get damp, losing up to a couple inches in length. Kevlar lines shrink less than Dyneema (or Spectra). Since the A's and B's

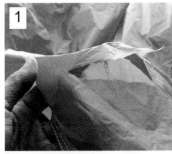

1. The hole.

2. The patch.

3. The real fix. Here is a typical inspection shop where gliders are tested and repaired. A porosity meter measures how quickly air can seep through the fabric. Strength testing of lines is done with a special scale and repairs are done with various types of sewing machines. There's more to it than meets the eye.

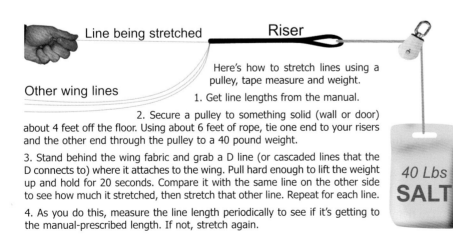

Here's how to stretch lines using a pulley, tape measure and weight.

1. Get line lengths from the manual.

2. Secure a pulley to something solid (wall or door) about 4 feet off the floor. Using about 6 feet of rope, tie one end to your risers and the other end through the pulley to a 40 pound weight.

3. Stand behind the wing fabric and grab a D line (or cascaded lines that the D connects to) where it attaches to the wing. Pull hard enough to lift the weight up and hold for 20 seconds. Compare it with the same line on the other side to see how much it stretched, then stretch that other line. Repeat for each line.

4. As you do this, measure the line length periodically to see if it's getting to the manual-prescribed length. If not, stretch again.

bear more load, they tend to stretch back to their proper length during flight leaving just the C's and D's shrunk.

Given that line length determines wing camber (curvature), they must be stretched back to their proper length as shown on the previous page. A wing that is getting hard to inflate may be suffering from line shrinkage and may benefit from stretching (also previous page).

If you cannot get the lines to be within a 1/4 inch of their specified length, or they stretch too far, the offending lines need to be replaced. In all likelihood, that's a sign that all the lines should be replaced.

After an Ocean Dunking

It is universally accepted that dunking a wing in salt water is bad—finely abrasive salt crystals remain after the water evaporates, shortening the glider's life (both lines and fabric). But if you remove the salt water right away by hosing it down with fresh water, the damage can be minimized.

To rinse a wing after immersion, clip it along the trailing edge to a strong clothesline. Hoist it up high enough to get the cell openings above ground.

Spray it thoroughly with fresh water to clean out any remaining brine. Get up inside each cell opening to get it completely soaked. That should drain away or at least dilute the briny badness to a safe level. Then leave it on the line, out of direct sunlight, to dry.

At least hose the wing down wherever it lays. This may be preferable to waiting but then go through the above method as soon as you can.

Whether fresh or salt water, take care when extricating a submersed wing—it becomes extremely heavy and will tear easily if lifted with water in the cells. Pull it out *slowly* by the trailing edge. One method is to stuff it in a wing bag while both are in the water.

Emergency Tool Kit

A lot can be fixed in the field with a few simple tools and parts that fit in your harness pouches. Mostly, you want to be able to tighten anything that can loosen, replace the belt (if applicable), adjust the carburetor and replace the spark plug.

- Allen wrenches. Almost all engines use metric sizes 3, 4, 5 and 6mm.

- Screw drivers. Make sure you can adjust the carburetor.

- Lightweight spark plug wrench. The type with just the round hex fitting and a hole is good—your screw driver can double as the leverage.

- Small knife, small locking pliers, and small socket set (3mm - 8mm sizes).

- Spark plug, wire ties, 2 feet of safety wire, and super glue (for the prop).

Multi-tools are convenient, but having a bunch of accessories that aren't useful just adds bulk and weight.

If you're flying enough distance to need this kind of kit, think about packing a very small container of 2-stroke oil—enough to mix up one full tank's worth.

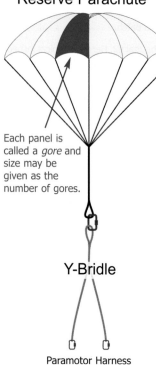

Reserve Parachute

Each panel is called a *gore* and size may be given as the number of gores.

Y-Bridle

Paramotor Harness Attach Points

Reserve

Reserves generally come from the factory ready to install and deploy; most come with containers that easily clip onto your motor frame and harness, but this *must* be done correctly. Installing it wrong may be worse than not having it at all.

There are several places where a reserve gets mounted: behind the head, on the side, in front of the pilot or under the seat. Each has advantages and disadvantages. A reserve on the side is reachable by only one hand. If it's in front, it's in the way of egress. If it's overhead, it can be difficult to grab in chaotic circumstances. Some motors come with a reserve mount in the seat bottom but that can make the seat stick out awkwardly on launch. For a machine to have the reserve mounted anywhere but on the side or in front, it generally must be *designed* for it.

Setup

Mounting must be done with an eye on easy reach and deployment. You need enough arm travel to pull it all the way out of the container and throw in a clear direction. Here are some considerations for reserve mounting:

- Mount it opposite the throttle. Some suggest this to be your dominant hand, but rehearsal can make either hand work. A front mount is acceptable but consider how the risers will pull on deployment. If your body gets between the risers and an inflating 'chute, it's you that will probably break.

- Change the throttle, if necessary, so you can mount it opposite the torque direction. If torque causes a left weight shift turn, mount the reserve on your right side.

- Consider a front mount where the reserve container clips in and its bridles go right to the carabiners. This is quick and easy.

- The reserve bridle should be routed along the harness or motor frame and remain clear of throttle cable, straps, speedbar, or anything else that would get in the way during deployment. Use Velcro or very small wire ties that break loose with about 20 pounds of pull. This will prevent nuisance breaks during normal handling but allow the reserve to pull free when needed.

- Go through a deployment in your mind. Think about where the reserve will come out, catch air, and pull as it extends fully with you hanging below.

- Do a deployment while hanging in a simulator then have someone pull the reserve bridles with enough force to peel them out of any retaining system (velcro or wire-ties). Make adjustments as necessary.

- Hook each reserve riser to a D-ring near or above your regular attachment. Hang from that point in a simulator to see what the landing would be like.

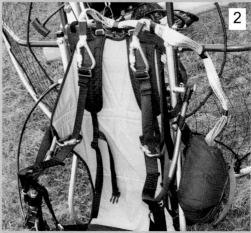

1. On this installation, the pilot had two loops to choose from for his reserve bridle. The top ones would have been preferable but they were in use by the main carabiners. So he routed the reserve through the main carabiners to the lower "D" rings. When the reserve deploys, it will immediately scrunch these two carabiners together (should be ok but is not ideal).

2. This installation is preferred; the reserve risers go to the highest point on the harness meaning the pilot would land mostly upright after a deployment.

The wire-ties/tape that keep the reserve risers/bridles together must be able to break with only about 20 pounds of pull.

Ensure the routing doesn't go through anything that would impede opening or cause injury.

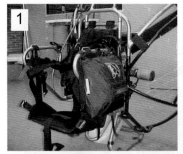

1. On units with a right-hand throttle the reserve is usually placed on left side or in front. The container must be secured both top and bottom so when the handle gets pulled, the whole container doesn't just rise up.

2. This paramotor can accomodate an overhead mount. The two small metal carabiners on either side of the letter "C" (above the mains) are made for a reserve hook-in.

> ⚠ **Caution!**
> Paraglider reserves differ from sport parachuting versions and must not be interchanged. Paraglider reserves open quickly which could be deadly to a skydiver while a skydiving reserve opens too slowly, if at all, under conditions likely in paramotor deployments.

Some instructors consider it beneficial to come down leaning back so the motor hits first. Most recommend being able to land on your feet for a parachute landing fall (PLF). If your harness comes equipped with reserve loops, use them—they will be designed for the opening shock.

Reserve Maintenance

Store the reserve as you would a paraglider—in a cool, dry place away from sunlight or chemicals. Of course, if it remains on your motor, be careful about where the motor goes. For example, getting the motor wet is no big deal, not so the reserve: it would need a repack.

Reserve Repacking

Have your reserve repacked once a year, or for those left in proper storage, every other year. Over time, fabric tightens into shapes that don't open quickly and rubber bands holding things together become brittle and break.

The preferable way to repack is sending it to the factory that made it since they'll know about any common problems. You can also send it off to an experienced rigger who is familiar with the design. They will inspect it and replace anything as needed. See FootFlyer.com "Resources" for a list.

You can do it yourself if you're certain about the procedure and have the requisite parts. Most reserves aren't difficult to repack, but the steps must be done correctly. Particular techniques make it much easier, and videos can help, but attending a repacking clinic is best because you'll have an expert there to help when questions arise. It's also a great time to rehearse tossing just before starting to repack.

Steerable reserves are more complicated so make sure the repacker/rigger is familiar.

Steerable Rogallo

NO! Pin is pulled *through* loop and would be stuck. **The reserve would not deploy.**

They should look like this.

Reserve bridles should connect high enough on the harness to land you upright and level under an open reserve. They can connect to your main carabiners but that offers no protection in a carabiner failure so, ideally, the harness allows for separate attachments.

As with any reserve, follow its user manual and consult with someone who is familiar with that model's installation and use, especially on motors.

Flying
Cross Country

13

Heading out on a cross country is strangely exciting. Exploring new directions, going for miles to nowhere in particular, poking about the landscape from barely above—it's a freedom that many have only dreamt about.

Obviously there are limits. Don't plan on commuting to work, although it's been done, and beware of small changes in weather that can lay waste to plans. Don't get out and *need* to get back—a pressure that clouds sound decision making. However, once armed with appropriate skills, gear, and weather knowledge, cross countries can be extremely rewarding. You launch from home, alight at some distant spot, relish the accomplishment, replenish, then head back or press on.

It sounds impressive: we flew across the whole country in one flight. But the country was Panama and it was only 40 miles across. Navigation was brainless too—follow the canal and don't land in Lake Gatun, it's full of caiman (South American alligators). Pictured is Jeff Hamann approaching the destination, Panama City.

Basic Tips

Whenever you fly farther than you're willing to walk, there are additional concerns. Some apply even to local flying but take on more importance with distance.

- Choose days with no weather changes anticipated near your flight times. You don't want to be away from your launch site when the weather turns sour.

- Let somebody know that you will be flying and take a cell phone if able.

- If the wind shifts, try changing altitudes to improve penetration (groundspeed into a headwind). Wind is normally stronger up high, but occasionally you can climb into a *weaker* wind. A GPS is invaluable for maximizing groundspeed—as you climb, just watch the groundspeed readout and note the best altitude.

- Avoid flying low, but if you must, do it while headed *into* the wind (see Chapter 16). Staying above 200 feet AGL is dramatically safer since you'll see or clear humanity's many protrusions (especially wires).

Road signs can be helpful to locate yourself but be careful, especially with wires being so hard to see. In this case the pilot found only the speed limit. *That* was useful!

Also, make sure there are no cars that could be distracted by your presence.

- Cross power lines at their supports (poles or towers), at least twice their height and at an angle. Judging wire height is surprisingly difficult unless you're over those supports. Crossing at an angle lets you turn away if the motor quits.

- Check the airspace if it's a new area.

- After takeoff, look back and see what the departure point looks like for your return. Find a prominent landmark since the sun angle or clouds may change appearances. It can be hard to recognize your home site the first time out.

- Take a map or GPS if the area is not familiar or you plan on a long trip. Its value comes as much from the groundspeed readout as the distance and direction.

- Don't ever let yourself get squeezed into night time. Besides being illegal, finding your way safely to the ground can be tough. On evening flights have a small flashlight or fully charged cell phone for its light. Even if you land before darkness settles, it would be handy to see what you're doing on the ground.

- Carry basic tools.

- Consider taking a small amount of two-stroke oil in case you wind up in someone's yard and they're willing to let you use their lawn mower gas.

As with all flying, stay within gliding distance of safe landing areas, favoring those that are downwind of you since they'll be easier to reach. Stay close to roads so egress is easier (unless you don't mind walking).

Summer Escape

A warm summer afternoon beckoned so I rushed home, loaded my gear, and slipped away before anyone could interfere: I had a mission. Fifteen miles south of my main launch was a new racetrack that I just had to check out. Plus, I wanted to fly to an airport just west of there. Quick calculations showed 3 hours of flight time—about my endurance—so I'd have to find thermals in order to loiter anywhere. True, it may not be a complete round trip, but landing sites were plentiful.

Off I went, running into the sky, climbing on course, taking detours to interesting targets along the way. When something cool came into view I just went down and checked it out. A motocross track appeared. Nobody was riding so I went down and carved out its hilly meanders, a few feet high, following the curves as best I could—*playing* on the ultimate off-road vehicle!

Then back up like a migrating bird, heading south towards a place I'd never been. Flight was so delicious. Earlier that day I was working, flying over that same area in a Boeing 737. I was now commanding 28 square meters of nylon, searching for lift, poking about the abundant thermals and their topping cumulus clouds. I circled in stronger updrafts, quickly passing 3000 feet. Brrr. Sitting in my chair, overlooking the speckled sprawl of civilization was incredible. Of course I've been that high thousands of times—three times just that day—but not suspended by fabric and sitting in a little seat listening to my favorite music.

Finding the racetrack was brainless from that high. Nobody was on it, so I went down for a closer look, first cruising its outer perimeter from 100 feet, then again from 10 feet. *This* is how to experience a NASCAR track. After scouring the course, I pressed onward, westward, exploring.

Landing at the Joliet airport let me really feel my new capability—actually *traveling*. Here I was, miles from home, having explored, gone to the heights, foot-dragged a speedway, and now stood at an airport, basking in the accomplishment. Checking my remaining fuel showed that it would be close—45 minutes of fuel for 45 minutes of distance. After a few minutes I relaunched but then a friend appeared below, waving wildly. It was flyin' buddy Nick—I *had* to stop. Of course that burned more fuel. Oh, but how I enjoyed being able to do that—coming back around, alighting, and chatting. After a few minutes, I launched and beelined it for home. Turning on the GPS showed bad news—with 15 miles to go, ground speed was only 12 MPH. Nope, that won't work. Oh well—press on to get closer.

Sure enough, the GPS was right and, even using thermals (slowing down in lift, speeding up in sink, circling in stronger lift) wasn't enough. Four miles shy of my starting point, Mr. Motor sputtered its last gasp and I went on glide. Good fortune let me slip into a field where I could stash the gear and grab a ride back. What an incredible treat!

Fuel & Range

When choosing a route, start off into the wind. It's no fun being airborne, trying to get back and fighting a headwind, especially when you're ready to be on the ground. Plus it makes fuel planning easier to go upwind for half of your endurance and then turn around. It's a conservative approach that is convenient and more fun. For one thing, when you've had enough, it's nice to get back more quickly.

If there is little or no wind, only fly 1/3 of your endurance before turning around just to leave some margin for error. If the route is a triangle, plan the flight's last leg to be going downwind.

Know how long you can fly before setting out. Also have an in-flight way to check fuel remaining such as a mirror.

If you're carrying oil, sometimes it's possible to land near a gas station and refuel. It does feel funny—walking up to the pump with your weird looking tank, filling it and knowing you'll be using it to run off into the sky. Strange, but amazing.

Getting Lost

In most areas of the country, getting lost is merely an inconvenience and is nearly impossible if you're carrying a GPS. It may be embarrassing when you land to ask for directions, but given the ability to land about anywhere, there is not much to worry about unless you're in the boondocks. But before getting to that dreadful state of affairs, there are ways to keep yourself oriented.

- After takeoff, look back towards your launch area. Do this first a mile out, then a few miles out. Remember what you saw, so on the way back you will better recognize it.

- Climb up higher. As long as airspace and clouds allow, you may get a better perspective.

- Use roads and other prominent landmarks. Think of major roads, rivers, or railroad tracks in your area and whether you've crossed them or not. For example, if a major highway runs northward and is west of your launch site, but you haven't yet crossed it, then you know you're east of it.

- Use road signs. Find a nice, landable field along a road with signs and scoot down to read it. Only with a PPG! Don't get below wire height though, and always maintain safe landing options. This could be quite risky if you're not careful or there aren't any good "outs."

Navigation

The following tools are not *necessary* to enjoy cross country flight but they can be fun to master. In fact, they are the basis for an entirely different skill set: *dead reckoning* and *pilotage*. These have been (and continue to be) used in regular airplane pilot training.

Dead reckoning is using a plotted course, calculated groundspeed, and heading to navigate and predict your future position. Using forecast winds, a map and a compass you can come up with the heading to fly that should keep you on course.

Is the airspace where you're going legal *today*?

Chicagoland pilots had this surprise one day when the President dropped into town. They closed airspace within 30 miles—including many popular PPG destinations.

When flying to or through new areas we must be especially vigilant about airspace issues.

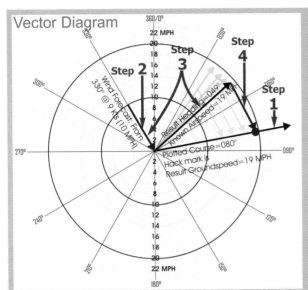

Vector Diagram

The latest blank version of this chart is provided at www.FootFlyer.com

Calculating Ground Track & Groundspeed

Once you know the desired ground track (plotted course) and your airspeed you can use this chart to derive heading and groundspeed:

Step 1. Draw your plotted course (080°) from the center outward.

Step 2. Draw your forecast wind (blue line above) as the direction the wind is forecast from and long enough to represent the windspeed with the arrow head touching center.

Step 3. You'll need two strips of paper. Mark one as a wind speed arrow (10 MPH) and the other as airspeed (19 MPH).

Step 4. Keep the wind arrow parallel with the wind direction while sliding its arrowhead along the plotted course. At the same time, have the airspeed piece go from the center and stay in contact with the wind arrow. When the tail of the wind arrow touches the airspeed's marking, you've got a wind triangle. The airspeed arrow points to the heading-to-fly and the wind arrow is pointing at the groundspeed.

The example shows a plotted course of 080° (true course, which has no magnetic correction). In this case, the quartering tailwind turns out not to have any effect on groundspeed—the usual benefit of a tailwind is celled out by the slowing effect of crosswind. The pilot will fly a 049° heading to maintain his 080° ground track.

Pilotage, covered later, is the process of reading the map in flight and adjusting heading to stay on the line. Manual navigation is a combination of these skills.

Even though we don't *need* all this, understanding it can be helpful. Mostly it can be a fun exercise—planning, then flying it accurately with just a map, compass, and watch. International competition pilots must get good at this since it makes up to 33% of their score.

The purpose of all navigation is to fly a desired track over the ground and arrive at the destination at an estimated time. Using the navigation log below, do the following (details on each step are provided below):

• Draw a line on the map representing your desired ground track. Mark the line at easily identifiable checkpoints along the way (2 - 7 below) and measure the distances between each mark. Enter these checkpoints on your PPG navlog.

• Measure the true course of each straight segment, then apply *variation* to come up with a magnetic course for that segment.

• Calculate the magnetic heading that corrects for wind and tells what the

Magnetism, Truth, & Courses

Aviation charts are laid out in grids of longitude and latitude with respect to true north. Compasses, however, point to magnetic north. The difference between true and magnetic north is shown on charts as lines of variation called Isogonic lines. For example, on this chart, the dashed line pointed to by #1 means that the difference is 14° east.

Magnetic course (MC) is derived by subtracting east ("east is least") variation and adding west variation to the true course (TC). So, in this case, the TC was 80°. After subtracting 14° of variation (use the closest isogonic line), you get a magnetic course of 66°. So if you used your compass to walk a 66° heading, you'd walk along the plotted line.

But air is usually moving, so we must account for wind drift. The result is magnetic heading (MH)—the compass heading you fly to stay on course.

Fig. 13.50

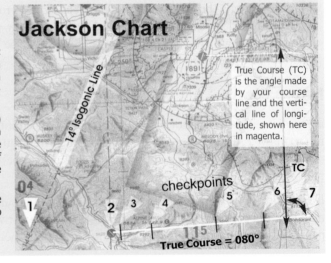

planned groundspeed will be (using the wind calculator described below)

• Build a navigation log to be used in flight or just for reference.

• Go fly the course using pilotage.

Plotting the Course and Heading

Draw your course line and determine true heading by the angle it makes to the lines of longitude (vertical lines). You get to use a protractor. Add or subtract the variation as shown on page 132, "Magnetism, Truth, & Courses." In this case there is 14° east variation.

Remember this saying: "West is best; east is least." That means west variation is added to true course and east variation is subtracted from it. So if you want to go *true* east, (090°), subtracting 14° from 90° gives a magnetic course (MC) of 076°. Flying 76° in no wind would yield a 090° ground track.

In Fig 13.50 the true course is 080°. With that in hand, add (for west) or subtract (for east) the variation to get a magnetic course. In this case, subtract the 14° east variation to get a magnetic course of 66°. That is the magnetic heading you would fly with no wind. We'll correct for wind next.

Choose checkpoints along the route that will be easy to identify and easy to get a time measurement on. The best ones will be usable even if you're off-course. Rivers, power lines, highways, or railroad tracks that cross perpendicular to your course are great. If they *angle* across your course, as in real life, it's more difficult—you must know more accurately that you're on the course line when hacking the time.

If you're writing out a navigation log, it can be filled in with the points, distances, and magnetic courses. After headings, these are the most useful bits. You're on a foot-launched craft, though, so writing on a log will be challenging. This is why competition pilots fly with clipboards Velcroed to their legs.

Wind Correction

Any wind will affect your groundspeed and track. Think of wind as a block of air in which you're drifting. When you're airborne, that motion is added to your own and must be accounted for to achieve a desired ground track. If you're trying to track due east and the wind is from the north (wind is given as the direction it's *from*) then you'll need to hold a heading to the left—what is called *crabbing*. With our slow speed, a little wind makes a lot of difference.

One way to figure this out is with a *vector diagram* as shown on the previous page—it represents speeds and directions visually. Vectors, in this case, are arrows, one for your in-flight speed and heading, and another for wind speed and direction. Follow the diagram's directions for "Calculating Ground Track & Groundspeed."

If you're flying a round trip that ends up back at your launch site, any wind will *increase* your total flying time. Also, direct crosswinds slow you down. If any wind is present, it must have some tailwind component to keep groundspeed equal to or better than airspeed.

Digging Deeper:

Earth's Moving Magnetic North

The Earth's magnetic north moves slowly over the years. In fact, the rate of drift is measurable and some charts show not only the current variation, but how fast it's drifting.

The Agonic Line shows where there's 0 variation between true and magnetic north (lucky compass users there). In the U.S. this line goes through Central Indiana—your compass heading is also your true heading.

The most significant difference between true and magnetic courses in the U.S. is on the northernmost coasts. Both east and west coasts have a difference of up to 20 degrees.

Competition pilots may find that filling this out while flying is helpful. The latest blank version of this log is provided at www.FootFlyer.com

Pilotage

Pilotage is flying a course using a map, log, and visual cues. It's particularly fun and pretty easy from a paramotor, given our awesome view.

Good planning provides ground track and initial heading to account for wind. It's only as good as the wind forecast.

After launch, take up the plan heading until you can find some of the checkpoints and see what kind of correction it *really* takes. The goal is to maintain a desired ground track: if there's a crosswind, don't just point at the next checkpoint when it comes into view—point upwind, *crabbing* into the wind enough to compensate. You want a straight line *over the ground*. It's not necessarily intuitive since you're pointing upwind of the target, so make sure it's your *ground track* that is heading towards the target. The pictures below give some insight.

Reading a map and associating ground features takes practice. Sectional charts work well for an airplane moving 100+ mph but, for us, topographic maps make more sense. They are far more detailed which is why they're used for competition.

Google Earth can help to visualization a route in 3D before flying. The illustrations below were made using it then we superimposed feet to show heading.

Even on detailed maps some things are nearly worthless—small roads and popu-

No Wind

Pick a point that's on your course, then pick a point *beyond* it. You'll use those two points to see whether you're drifting left or right.

As you approach the first point it becomes obvious whether you drifted left or right. In this case, there was no wind so simply pointing right at the points is called for.

In no wind: Desired course and heading are the same.

Point Beyond

First Point

1a

Oops: He's drifted to the right. Should have crabbed left into the wind.

WIND

2

Point Beyond

First Point

1b

3

Ahhh: Perfect. Crabbing left and staying on course. The points still line up.

WIND

Hdg

lated areas, for example, are similar to other small roads and populated areas unless they're next to some prominent feature. Once you identify town A, it's easy to see what the town just south of it is. Yellow areas on aeronautical charts try to indicate what they look like at night and have marginal semblance to what you'll see in daylight.

Obvious features, such as highways, railroad tracks, landmarks, and the like are best. Using a long, straight feature (like railroad tracks) requires some way to tell where you are along that feature.

Telling distances is tricky too; although it's easier in areas that are conveniently laid out in a N/S and E/W grid pattern. Early settlers were thinking of us. There is no such order to other areas, especially hilly ones.

The most useful tools on a navigation log are the mileage and estimated groundspeeds. You can either fill in the actual numbers or just use the log for reference. Some navlogs (or electronic calculators) have time in minutes; they must be converted to tenths— every 6 seconds is one tenth, so 8 minutes and 12 seconds is 8.2 minutes.

Calculating Groundspeed

With a stopwatch and a map, you can calculate groundspeed. Knowing that, you can predict your position at any future point and time. If you also know your heading and airspeed, you can even tell what the winds are although that's a bit much for someone piloting a paraglider.

Charts on the next page facilitate these calculations without any electronics. The charts can be taped to the same clipboard that you use for your navlog for easy reference. Competition is about the only time you would use these tools.

1. Wind is from the right, so he has to head into it a bit to keep on course.

2. Just because you *can* go direct doesn't mean you should. Besides safety, consider your retrieval options in case a landing becomes necessary. On this flight along the Panama Canal we could hear the chomping teeth of hungry caiman.

Altitudes

Choosing altitudes is critical for maximizing performance—climbing or descending can yield free additional groundspeed if more favorable winds are found. Start with the winds aloft information (see Chapter 7) to get an idea of what to expect, but improve your mental wind-image by trying different altitudes. Generally, the higher you go, the stronger the winds blow, but not always. Be quick to try different altitudes, especially if groundspeed dwindles appreciably.

Most airplanes cruise over 1000 feet AGL. Above 3000 feet they tend to fly in 500 foot increments with the eastbounders using odd altitudes (3000, 3500, 5000, 5500, etc.) and the westbounders using even altitudes (4000, 4500, 6000, 6500 etc.). Knowing that may help you know where to look out for them.

Lingering above 10,000 feet is a very bad idea since jets travel at their fastest speeds up there, but this is more of a concern within 60 miles or so of larger cities.

Using a GPS

Global Positioning System (GPS) provides reliable navigation from the remotest places on Earth using cheap *navigators* (see Chapter 2) Besides moving maps, the basic groundspeed and ground track values can be used to derive the winds aloft, which can help plan a different route.

If the GPS says you're tracking 120° (southeast) but you're pointed due east (090°) then you know the winds are out of the north or have a significant north component. If it says you're only going 15 mph and your normal airspeed is 25 mph, then you have a 10 mph headwind component. If your route has a northerly pointed segment coming up, you may end up with too much headwind. The vector diagram at left can help.

The GPS time-to-destination or time-at-arrival is valuable, but mostly on the last straight segment of a journey. On routes with course changes it's better to know the winds aloft. Then choose the best altitude to cruise. You'll also have an idea of what the wind will do to your overall groundspeed.

Estimate winds aloft using GPS by doing a slow 360. Note the slowest groundspeed and heading where it occured— that's the wind direction. Note the fastest groundspeed. The difference between slowest and fastest speeds, divided by 2, is the windspeed.

So if your slowest speed was 10 mph and your fastest speed was 30 mph, the wind is blowing 10 mph (30-10=20, 20/2=10).

A full-sized version is available from FootFlyer.com.

Loreto, Baja California Sur, Mexico

Once you know the wind at your altitude, a vector diagram can help calculate your groundspeed for an upcoming route segment. For example, you may be able to follow a road that goes due east in a northerly wind of 30 mph, but you'll make no headway trying to go due north.

Mixing Units: As with all charts in this chapter, different units can be used as long as speed and distance are compatible. For example, knots are nautical miles per hour. So if distance is in nautical miles, then speed must be in knots. If distance is in regular (statute) miles, then speed must be in regular miles per hour. U.S. air maps (*sectionals*) are marked in nautical miles so knots and nautical miles are a convenient combination.

Speed, Time & Distance Charts

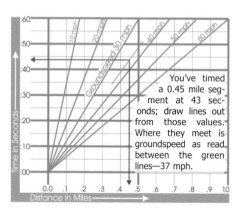

You've timed a 0.45 mile segment at 43 seconds; draw lines out from those values. Where they meet is groundspeed as read between the green lines—37 mph.

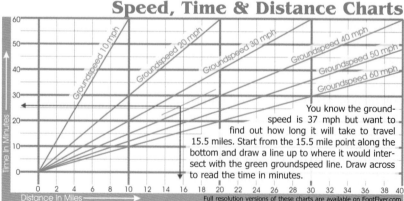

You know the groundspeed is 37 mph but want to find out how long it will take to travel 15.5 miles. Start from the 15.5 mile point along the bottom and draw a line up to where it would intersect with the green groundspeed line. Draw across to read the time in minutes.

Full resolution versions of these charts are available on FootFlyer.com.

Flying with Others

14

Eventually, most pilots seek out like-minded peers to share their passion with. It adds fun, education, and sometimes humor to the mix. But it can also complicate matters in unusual, possibly dangerous, ways; the more folks gather, the more complicated organization can get. Going to major events is the extreme case.

These pilots are keeping an eye on each other in a side-by-side formation over Northern Illinois.

Techniques for formation flying are covered in Chapter 16. This chapter concentrates on the basics of surviving, and getting along, while flying with others.

Courtesy

As with most issues of courtesy, common sense is key. But what is common? If an activity seems like it may be obnoxious, dangerous, or marginally safe—that's your better judgment whispering: "hmmm, maybe this isn't so bright." But since it's not always that clear-cut, here are some guidelines.

Where to Lay Out

If another pilot already has his wing laid out, avoid setting up in his way. Rather set up behind, or beside him. Even if you think you'll launch first, stay clear of his path in case you get delayed. It is bad form to lay your wing out in a way that requires another pilot to steer around it. If you think proximity is an issue, ask the affected pilot if it's OK or just move farther away. By the same token, you'll make no friends by leaving your wing laid out for a long time in a crowded field, taking up valuable space.

Look at where your run will take you and be sure that it's clear. Have a good climbout path that doesn't fly right over any spectators, campers, or other pilots. Besides being illegal, it's rude and dangerous. An inopportune motor failure would put others in danger. Even at official gatherings, be mindful of your noise during climbout; change locations, if necessary, to avoid getting too close to people.

0:00

Balloon (still on ground)

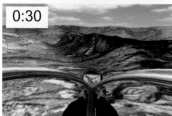

0:30

1:00

1:30

Flying with different types of aircraft adds complexity beyond what's obvious, even if they're slower than you. This animation, done for a real accident, shows how surprisingly insidious a balloon collision could be.

The PPG pilot was keeping track of a group of balloons to his left while a lone balloon, that had been on the ground for a while, launched without notice. Its relatively rapid ascent probably presented little relative motion and may have been partially obscured by the pilot's feet or trike frame.

When flying with others, be vigilant in all directions, including down, to keep track of other craft, especially with distractions such as photography.

A periodic turn of a few degrees will dramatically aid seeing another craft that may be coming up from below.

While airborne, avoid buzzing about the launch area, especially in light winds. Your wake may linger for several minutes, making it even more difficult for those trying to takeoff. Plus, pilots in challenging conditions may be waiting for just the right puff of breeze and won't appreciate your annoying presence when it comes. Climb up to at least 200 feet AGL after launch or go elsewhere so other pilots get a chance at clean air.

Prop Blast

Be mindful of your prop blast. Don't point it toward other people or their wings. Blowing someone's carefully positioned wing into a tangled mess will quickly sully your reputation. The same thing for fly-bys—be careful about where your prop blast goes. Even if nobody is preparing to launch, don't let wake or prop wash get to any laid-out wings. Flying near enough to roll up someone's wing is a sure sign of industrial grade ignorance.

Keep the plane of the propeller clear so that if a prop were to come apart, the shards would miss anyone in line with it.

Risks

We must manage additional risks when flying with others. First, be very vigilant about 1) your position, 2) the pattern, and 3) keeping an active scan for other traffic. If you do not know where your flying buddies are, carefully look around, including above and below. Do shallow turns to make sure they are not directly above you. Don't make sudden changes in altitude until you know it is clear in the desired altitude. Don't turn until satisfied there is nobody coming from that direction.

Follow the turning rule without fail: "Look, lean, turn." Besides weight shifting, the lean alerts other pilots of your impending turn. Even better is to **look**, start a **shallow** bank, look **up** and **down** in the turn direction, *then* start your **turn**.

Flying with one or two other pilots adds nearly as much risk as flying with a hundred because we tend to drop our guard. A moment of distraction may be all it takes if your buddy comes up on you unnoticed. Having a launching pilot climb into an already flying pilot is another too-common occurrence.

Collision

One valuable tool on sunny days is your shadow. Looking at your shadow to see if there are any other gliders nearby. The higher you are, the more blurry it is. So even if you *do* see the shadow of another wing near yours, use this technique to see if he's at your altitude. If you do not see any other wings near your shadow, you're alone. For now. If you see another wing shadow, and it's fuzzier than yours, then it's above you—descend while looking up towards the sun to find it.

Be leery of formation flying, especially with strangers but even with pilots you know (covered in Chapter 16).

Most collisions happen between two pilots **who know each other** and who are the **only ones flying**. And they frequently happen when one pilot takes off and climbs into the other. It only takes a few seconds of inattention to lose track of your flying buddy—pay particular attention when flying within a mile of another.

Wake

Flying through a paramotor wake can be rough. At best it will be startling; at worst it can fold part of your wing, especially if combined with other factors such as becoming unloaded (getting light in your seat). The motor, lines, and wing produce turbulence, but the swirling wing tip vortices are the strongest (see Chapter 22).

Wing wake settles, spreads out slowly, drifts with the wind, and is worse on heavier craft such as trikes, tandems, and even heavy pilots. The wake of any craft, including your own, is much worse if it's in a steep turn.

The powerful wake of heavier machines, like PPC's, must be given a wide berth, even more so in smooth conditions where it lingers longer.

Treat a wake encounter as you would any other turbulence—hold the brakes at pressure 2 or 3 and throttle for level flight. As always, if you feel the wing fall back, or misbehave, follow the mantra **"reduce power, reduce brakes, then steer."**

Fly *above* the path of preceding aircraft to avoid their wakes. Flying between the vortices is another bad idea—there is sinking air there. You may not have enough thrust to out-climb it if you're low.

Rescuing a Pilot

If you fly with other pilots long enough you'll probably be faced with the need to help extricate someone from one of trouble's many forms.

What a Drag

Kiting or flying in strong winds means that, eventually, somebody gets dragged along the ground. If you see this happening, don't lunge on the pilot or his motor—stop the *wing*. A wind-whipped wing can overpower even several burly helpers. Run around behind it so the wing drapes around your legs (see Chapter 3). Grabbing a wing tip and running it towards the pilot is also effective. Whatever you do, don't grab lines! They'll quickly leave painful burns.

Water

One of our biggest fears should be going in the water. Don't be fooled by stories of those who have survived—other pilots have not. And it doesn't take much water to be deadly, especially if it's moving. One pilot drowned after landing *beside* moving water—his wing went into a drainage culvert and dragged him under before he could unclip.

If faced with helping a pilot in the water, get flotation—*good* flotation. A boat is obviously best, but use whatever else can be found quickly, such as a surfboard, inflatable mattress, or life jacket. Don't jump in the water yourself since the lines may snag you when nearing the pilot's gear. The best response would be to give the pilot something to hold on to so he can unstrap and relax for a moment. If he is submersed, your options dwindle. Leaving your flotation could easily put you in the same tangled dilemma.

Power Lines

Voltage is to electricity what pressure is to water, and power lines have a *lot* of pressure—enought to push lethal current through paraglider lines. All it takes is for

1. Shadows know. The photographer is higher so his shadow is blurrier.

2. After crunching down through some branches, this lucky pilot was only a few feet above the helping hands of his rescuers. It's another example of why flying with others is a good idea.

3. Basic rules of courtesy apply when flying with others. Be aware of where your wake is going, don't prop blast others' wings, and help pilots setup after missing a launch (ask first).

Blurry shadow is higher than sharper shadow.

you to become a leak to ground (Earth)—a small one, to be sure, but the lowest voltage carried on poles is around 4000 volts and high-tension wires go up to half a million. While it may be current that kills, it's voltage that pushes it through our normally-resistant bodies and lines.

So if a pilot lands in power lines and does not fall to the ground, leave him hanging! Do not reach up for him—that could complete the circuit that kills you both. Rather contact the power company and wait until they shut the lines down.

Trapped by a Thrusting Motor

It can happen that a pilot's motor will unexpectedly go to full thrust, pinning him in the process. This is risky for the pilot but even more so for a rescuer. Before jumping into the fray, have a plan. Stay clear of the prop *and* make sure the pilot sees you coming so he doesn't swing the revving motor your way. Also, know how you're going to shut it off in case the regular kill switch has failed. Don't think this is so uncommon—a severed throttle cable usually disables the kill switch too.

Alternative shutoff methods are covered in Chapter 19. They include pulling the choke or covering the air intake. Pulling the spark plug off works but be prepared for a startling shock. Shutting off the master switch, if there is one, may not kill the motor—it primarily prevents inadvertent starter activation.

If you're flying with a buddy know how to shut off each other's motors.

Tim Kaiser (red), Phil Russman (blue) and Michael Purdy (yellow) pose in this formation flight just west of the Salton Sea in California.

A midair collision or entanglement would likely be catastrophic. There is more to formation flying than meets the eye, make sure you're up to the task. Two of these pilots had already worked together while taping parts of Risk & Reward before flying this close.

Communications

Flying with others gives added reason to have a radio (see Chapter 28), especially if it works through your helmet. Even if it doesn't, carry one so that if you go down, you can work out retrieval plans. Learn the *Bump Scale* (see Chapter 5) so you can communicate it to your flying friends.

Formation Flying

Formation flying requires precision handling (see Chapter 16) and should be avoided until you're experienced at precision flying. Specifically you should be able to actively keep the wing where you want it, even in turbulence, without really thinking about it. Until that point, avoid flying within 5 wing spans of other pilots and always keep your distance from someone who angles away when approached. They are obviously not comfortable with your proximity.

Never accept a visibly fast closure rate. It could quickly yield a collision or last-minute control inputs that cause you to spin or stall. If it looks like you're approaching someone quickly, turn away before it's too late.

Section III

Mastering the Sport

There's nothing wrong with having merely adequate skill. You can safely enjoy this sport without ever needing to go beyond basic launch, landing, and flying skills as long as you stay within your boundaries. Fly well-regarded, safe equipment from large enough fields and limit yourself to mellow weather. In fact, getting to a high level of mastery involves some extra risk since you must venture closer to control's edge in the process.

This section is for those who want to go beyond flight's pure joy, who want the thrill of surprisingly fine control—exploring the limits of what our craft can do. Because it can do a *lot*.

Section III is devoted to the pursuit of excellence. Here we will:

1. Show some of what's possible,

2. Explain the process to speed up learning,

3. Point out risks, where appropriate, and

4. Give methods to practice and to verify for yourself whether you've actually mastered the techniques involved.

Basic portions of this are helpful to any pilot, while other parts should be left to the more risk-tolerant. Find a mentor who also revels in fine control. Besides getting guidance, you may also find a kindred spirit.

$\mathcal{S}ection$ III

Mastering the Sport

"It's not how many flights you have;
It's what you've done with the flights you've had."

The Master Powered Paragliding video series, shown above, uses live action, animation, graphics, slow motion, and highly skilled pilots to make advanced topics crystal clear. They're intended for use with an experienced instructor who can coach you while reducing the likelihood of mishaps. This series will help anyone aspiring to mastery. Available from many schools and FootFlyer.com

By Mark MacWhirter

Advanced
Ground Handling

15

It's surprising what can be done with these wings when you know how. It's equally surprising how effortless the experts make it look, and how advancement can be so vexing! Fortunately, most skills can be practiced in the privacy of your own field.

Of course, if you see someone doing something that you want to learn, go talk to them about it; they'll almost certainly be happy to share. And the best pilots almost always have the best ground handling skills.

Build slowly! Master steady moderate winds before taking on anything that could lift you. Work with a coach: he'll reduce your chance of injury.

Upside Down Kiting to Clean out cells.

All manner of detritus gets into a wing, acting like sandpaper, abrading away the fabric's life. It must be removed. You *can*, of course, hold up the trailing edge and shake it out, but that's boring, so we'll kite the wing upside down.

Find a smooth, clean surface (preferably grass) with the wind blowing from 7 to 12 mph. You can do this in the sand, but until you're really good, it's tough to avoid re-scooping more sand. Gloves are nice because you'll be handling brake lines, not their toggles, which could cause line burns in a strong wind.

Before kiting, first shake the tips down since they don't have cell openings.

A harness makes it easier but you *can* use just the risers. It'll take good control to prevent the wing from slamming down onto its leading edge—potentially popping out cell stitching (yes, we've seen it happen). Hook into your kiting harness just like you were going to fly, then:

Getting The Wing Upside Down

Start from a regular reverse kiting position with the wing overhead. Or, build a wall and pull one tip A line just enough to get it turning over.

Keep pressure on the A line as the wing turns over. Walk with it until it turns but be prepared to pull on both brakes when it gets upside down.

As it comes over and down, pull on both brakes to cushion the touchdown. Do *not* let it whack down hard on the leading edge which can blow out stitching.

With the wing laid out upside down (or towards you, if flat on the ground), grab the brake lines above their pulleys to kite it upside down.

Here is another way to get debris out of your wing if you have two people. Lay it out on the ground with the leading edge downwind and the top up (line side down).

With one person on each end, pick up the trailing edge and, while walking it into the wind, shake vigorously in a coordinated fashion as shown. The leading edge openings must be facing downward for this to work.

- Get the wing lying on its back with the leading edge upwind. If there's not enough wind, walk it into position. You can also flip the wing over while kiting.

- Grab the brake line closest to each hand, above (beyond) the pulley as pictured in 4 above. Treat the brake lines like the A's of regular kiting. Pull them *just enough* to get the wing to come up while snatching your *body* backwards. Once up, pull the brake lines back and forth to shake stuff out. A satisfying show of falling debris indicates success. Let the wing down gently on its leading edge.

If you're doing this in sand, dump the debris as described then, just before the leading edge touches down, lean (or run) towards the wing so that its cell openings lay down, face-up, with*out* scooping up more sand. You can try to kite the glider back over when you get really good—but initially that will just net more sand. Instead, walk around it while holding the risers and bundle it up from downwind.

Kiting Without a Harness.

There are several reasons for learning this. It 1) is a great way to get some feel for the air, 2) spreads out the wing nicely, 3) lets you quickly check for tangles, 4) makes repositioning the wing easy, and 5) is fun. Plus it looks cool. Many techniques work and have advantages, but these seem to work especially well.

In stronger winds, more than about 7 mph, this is tiring. And it's dangerous *if* you let yourself get lifted without letting go right away. That sounds ridiculous, but pilots *have* been injured when they held on too long and dropped too far.

With any method you must move with the wing. If it goes left, go left with it. In fact, if you *want* it to go left, move right first, let the wing start falling left, then follow it. To stop a wing that's moving left or right, you must walk (run) *beyond* it. This works on all the kiting methods. As you build skill, you'll need to move less.

One Hand per Riser—Good for Higher Winds

The value of this technique is that, with each hand holding a riser, it spreads out the load, which is why it's the best technique for strong winds. Those who do summersaults while holding the risers use this method.

Face the wing and hold the risers as shown in Fig 15.13. Inflation may need to be done by first holding both the A's *and* B's in each hand. For most wings, hold the risers near where they split—the A's and B's towards you and the C's and D's (as equipped) going out the back of your hand. If the wing doesn't want to come up, move your grip so as to pull more A's. If it wants to frontal or overfly you, then move the grip back so as to pull less on the A's.

Holding firmly, lurch backward as you would with a harness. When the wing comes overhead, dampen it by decreasing the pull or "rocking" your hands back so as to pull the D's down. If it tries to overfly you, move backward while rocking your hands back. You have to be quick-footed to stay ahead of it. Primary steering is done by pulling down one riser and letting up on the other. To go left, pull your left hand down and vice-versa with the right hand. To force the wing more overhead, or prevent it from falling back, tilt your hands so the A's are pulled down more.

If the wing is rocketing up during inflation, meter it by moving *towards* it.

You can re-grip, but that's hard because of the wing's pull. If it is always trying to overfly you, let go of the risers briefly and grab them farther back. It's like letting go of a kite briefly while trying to catch its string in a different place.

There are several ways to bring the wing down: 1) walk towards it, steering it to the side so it falls over; 2) lett go of it (make a mess); 3) briefly letting go to re-grip back near the D riser; or 4) put both risers in one hand and, with the free hand, reach back to pull the brake lines or rear risers.

A's and Brakes

This method offers the best control in light winds. Leave the brakes in their holders and grab both A's with your left hand and the brake lines (not the toggles) with your right hand (Fig 15.11) beyond their pulleys. Then:

- Inflate by pulling both A's *and* brakes with just enough A-pull to keep it coming up. It's important to feel pull in both the A's and brakes or else the leading edge will want to tuck over (frontal) and it won't come up as quick, if at all. You want it to initially inflate like a sailboat's spinnaker sail, cupping the air.

- There is a lot of control because you can modulate the A's and brakes so widely. If it's jumping up quickly, pull more brakes with your right hand. If it's sluggish, walk backwards faster and let up on the brakes.

- Move left and right as necessary to keep under the wing. Steer with the brake hand, too—moving the hand right makes the wing fall left.

- If the wing wants to fall back, walk backwards faster and try one of these: 1) pull more A's up to a point, and 2) ease both hands downward. When the wind picks back up, let your hands go up. Modulating like this can absorb small changes in wind speed that might otherwise require more moving around.

- If the wind increases and the wing wants to continually overfly you, either pull more brakes or walk downwind to reduce the relative airflow.

While you always want to move around as necessary, the *goal* is to control it well enough to stand still. That, of course, requires a finesse born of much practice.

To deflate the wing in a stronger wind, get it to fly overhead, almost to the point of front tucking. As it does so, step towards it and aggressively pull full brakes to snap it down through the power band (angle of highest pull) quickly. If you try to bring the wing down while it's hanging back, it pulls much harder.

No Harness Kiting

15.11 Using the **A's & brakes** works very well in light winds. Pull just enough of *both* A's *and* brakes to hasten the initial inflation. Get the wing to billow first *then* add more A's.

Just being able to move your body in every direction while tweaking the brakes affords great control. If the wing wants to fall back, step backwards, lower the risers, and pull a bit more on the A's. This technique also allows your arms to absorb wind pulses by moving up and down.

15.12 & 15.13 **One hand per riser**: Exactly where to hold the risers varies by wing. Experiment, but make sure you can rock your hands back and forth to pull more or less A's.

In light winds you may need to start out by holding both risers in one hand as shown in 15.12 so you can pull the A's with one hand to help it up. Once overhead, switch to the grip shown in 15.13 (the swap takes some practice).

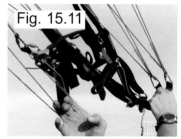
Fig. 15.11

Fig. 15.12

Fig. 15.13

A's and Rears

Using the A's and rears allows kiting with less lifting. But since the rear risers aren't as effective at steering, it's not as sensitive. Instead of holding the brake lines with your right hand, hold the rear risers. It's like what you learned in emergency handling when a brake line fails—the glider can be steered and slowed this way.

Loops and Brakes

This is where you hold the risers by the very ends (the loops) with one hand and reach behind to pull on one or both brakes with the other hand. The pilot at left demonstrates steering the wing by pulling the necessary brake line.

To inflate the wing, hold both risers at the loops with your left hand and the A's with your right hand. Pull primarily on the loops, but help it come up by pulling the A's as necessary. Once it nears the top, let go of the A's and be ready to go for one or both brakes with your right hand.

Loops & Brakes

Kiting with the loops requires holding both risers with one hand and using your free hand to control the brakes.

High Wind Techniques

This can hurt—be careful! Don't clip in until you're ready for a strong pull and wear a *good* helmet.

There must be nothing downwind that would hurt if you got blown into (or strained through it). Start learning these techniques in less than a 15 mph wind and, even then, only with someone else present in case you lose control of the glider. Brief them that, if you're being dragged, they should grab a wing tip and run it to you, or get behind the wing and let it drape around them. They should *not* tackle you—which may get you both dragged. Further, if you get lifted, they must not let themselves get lifted. Helpers have been seriously hurt by doing so.

Be prepared to deflate the wing as covered in Chapter 3 or later in this chapter.

Don't have the motor on—you are vulnerable to *turtling* onto the cage and getting dragged, spewing dollars, until you hit something. About the only way to stop the carnage is unbuckling from the harness (impossible while being dragged), jumping out, and running after the remnants of your bouncing gear. It's much cheaper to master these skills with*out* the motor, and in a harness with back protection.

Laying out & Clipping in

Don't stretch the wing all the way out. Either leave it in a partial ball or lay it out 90° to the wind as described later under "Smooth Surfaces." Only spread the wing out halfway with just the middle exposed.

Don't pull on the risers until you're ready to kite. Initially, lay both risers within 10 feet of the wing's trailing edge. Even a small riser tug can catch the wing and awaken the monster. Once that happens, it may spring to life with overwhelming power, dragging you along for the ride. So clip in close to the wing, risers loose, while getting ready to control it. Walk along with it if it starts drifting downwind.

Controlling the Wall

Be ready on the brakes when bringing your glider to "attention." Step back to tension the A's, giving them a small tug if necessary. As soon as it starts to inflate, pull on the brakes to hold it down; it may be necessary to pull them *way* back. But if

The Wall

1. Hold even brakes while pulling your body back against the wall to make it come up higher.

2. Step towards the wall to lower and reduce its tug.

3. With the wing too loose, or too much brake pulled, wind gets under the trailing edge which flails upwards. If the tips come up, reach out to the brake lines and pull them in. Keep the wall high enough to prevent this in the first place.

4. This is Section III, so you probably already know that this pilot needs to step right to bring down the high right side.

you pull too far, air *can* get under the trailing edge and may cause the wing to snake up out of control. With enough wind you may not need any A-pull at all—just step back and it will lurch to life. Be ready on the brakes to keep it down.

In stronger conditions, pulling brakes alone may not be enough to keep the tips down, especially with longer brake lines. If that's the case, reach to the rear risers and pull them back while keeping hold of the brakes. You can hold both brake lines in one hand, behind your back, to free up the other hand. Be careful wrapping the brake lines around your hand (taking wraps), which could cause line burns and cuts in strong winds.

Once you have a well-formed wall, it may be bucking up and down. As you've already learned, backing away from the wing will raise it while pulling the brakes more, or leaning towards the wall, will lower it. If you let the wall get too high, its pull may be overpowering. If you pull the brakes too hard, the trailing edge may flail up into the breeze; there is a balance.

Done correctly, you'll be standing there with *lots* of brake pulled, controlling the wall's height by leaning towards it to lower, or leaning back (away) to raise it.

If You Get Lifted off Your Feet

If you're hooked in reversed (as you should be) and get airborne, you'll tend to untwist until you're facing forward then get deposited downwind somewhere. The Alan method, described shortly, can prevent getting turned around—you'll come back down while still reversed and under control.

One thing: if you do get lifted, **don't pull the brakes!** Don't pull *any* brakes unless you're airborne and the wing is surging forward, and you know what you're doing. If you pull a bunch of brakes while facing forward, or with unsure footing, hang on for a whoopin'. The wing will go back with vigor, first lifting, then straining you through whatever is downwind. Even just tapping the brakes in a strong blow can start this carnage; less brake is best.

Inflation

On a normal inflation you lean back, away from the wing, and pull just enough A's to help it come up. In high winds that may be difficult—the minute you reach for the A's, you reduce brake pull which may allow the wing to start inflating. Many wings will inflate at the tips which then come up and inward, leaving a mess. If that wants to happen, here are some things to try.

• Pull the tips in. Start with the brake in your right hand, which is going across to the opposite tip—pull it way back. Then reach out with your other hand and

⚠ Caution!

High winds can be extremely dangerous with a paraglider. If it's blowing hard enough to use these techniques, then understand the increased risk and be ready to act the minute you clip in. First work with an instructor who is familiar with high winds and can handle getting lifted or dragged himself.

Climbing things is one fun way to put advanced ground handling skills to use. The risk depends on what can happen when you fall off, get blown downwind, or the wing collapses. Start low, build up slowly, and be careful!

High Winds

1. Don't take on strong winds until you're ready to get lifted and/or slide. Learn in moderate winds first, where you can run backwards and get airborne by pulling some brakes. Practice sliding on your feet during the inflation, too.

2. On higher performance wings, it's difficult to recover a dipping wing with brakes alone, especially if you can't move towards the low side. Try this: Let go of the dipping side's brake line and use some A's *and* brakes on the high side. Pull them at the same time while backing up to give the wing more airflow. Airspeed is life.

3. If you get lifted way up, go hands mostly up initially, then apply some brake pressure as you stop climbing. Look down and flare normally.

By Brad Powell

Pulling left brake and left A to get the wing to come back left.

By Tim Kaiser

By Eve Clarke

pull the tip in farther. Do the same for the other side so both tips are toward you. They may roll up a bit in the wind which is ok. Starting with the wing balled up, or horse-shoed slightly can prevent this from happening.

- Inflate the wing without pulling any A's at all. When ready, simultaneously reduce brake pull and step back. The wing will rocket upwards and pull you downwind—you'll need to run or slide towards it briefly. It can be tricky—the minute you let go of the brakes it will start coming up and want to yank you.

There is a balance in how much to resist the wing on its way up and how much to move with it. You must keep *some* resistance or it won't have any relative wind to work with. And you can't lock yourself in place (or try to) lest it shoot up and overfly you. That's why helpers, if used, must let you move with the wing some.

Sliding on your feet during inflation is perfect (and fun) albeit challenging. Done properly, you will slide (or run) about 5 to 10 feet then stop the wing overhead. When you apply brakes to stop the wing it may lift you—be ready. By walking (or sliding) towards it while it's rising, there will be less chance of getting lifted. Once it stops overhead you *must* let up on the brakes

The Alan Method

One way to inflate and kite in high winds is to use the brake lines *above* their pulleys (Fig. 15.30). Gloves are helpful since you'll be holding the brake *lines* (not the toggles) that could cause friction burns.

This gives deep control over the brake pull and, if you get lifted, allows you to remain reversed and in control which is hard while holding the brakes by their toggles. Once the risers start to un-cross, however, there is not enough leverage to prevent untwisting, so keep yourself a little more twisted than exactly reversed.

- Hook in reversed like you were going to fly but do not grab the brake toggles.

- Inflate the wing by stepping back with your body and pulling on the A's as necessary. As the wing nears overhead, let go of the A's, and reach back around the outside of the risers to grab the brakes as shown in Fig. 15.30. The challenge is getting to those brake lines quickly.

- Steering is no longer crossed. Watch the trailing edge to make it more obvious what's needed and what you're doing. Control surges and direction by modulating the brake lines.

- Keep the risers crossed and touching each other. That means you'll be turned slightly beyond 180° from facing forward. Doing so allows you to remain reversed if you get lifted off your feet.

- In stronger wind, lean way back to increase rotational inertia. That confers greater resistance to getting swung around if you get lifted off your feet.

If you do get lifted, keep yourself reversed by opposing the turn with the brake lines while maintaining wing direction. It's possible to actually fly this way but is confusing. Pulling with your left hand will turn the *wing* right. It's more clear by watching the trailing edge—pulling on a brake will slow that side down. This needs to be practiced *a lot* before letting yourself get very high.

During light conditions, when the wing falls back, you'll need to let go of the brakes, walk backwards, and pull on the A's to help it come back up. Quickly going

Fig. 15.30

from brakes to A's is the greatest challenge. Practice it during mellower conditions first since you'll need to be pretty fast-acting in stronger winds.

Once mastered, this technique has other benefits. With very light winds it's a way to go quickly from kiting with the A's to using brakes. That's handy when it's light *and* switchy.

Kiting Control

Minimize brake use in winds so strong you're getting lifted frequently. Move left/right instead or use weight shift—dip a hip towards the falling side. Lean way back so that getting lifted upwards a foot or so only angles your body up without losing traction. Keep knees bent to better absorb a gust without getting lifted or knocked off balance. Proper posture makes this much easier.

A good test of skills is to stand there kiting reversed while looking straight ahead at the horizon, past the "V" of your crossed risers. Practice this with a fairly steady wind of 8 mph or more. Use the risers and feel to know what the wing is doing.

Kiting while facing forward lets you learn a "feel" for the wing without looking at it. There is no magic, you'll feel it go left or right and see the risers on your periphery move subtly left/right and forward/backward. Getting used to handling the wing like this is useful.

Assisted Inflation with Motor

In strong winds, assisted motor launches are dangerous, mostly to the assistants, even if they're familiar with flying. They can and have suffered prop injuries from various causes. If you require assistance, it's probably too strong for your skill. Assistance makes some moves harder while adding risk to you *and* your helpers. It's only a bit safer if you have an electric start, but don't start until they're *well* clear.

If you feel compelled to get help, and your helpers are willing to donate body parts, make sure they know to let you slide (on your feet hopefully) during inflation. They can't hold you rigidly or the wing will rocket overhead and front tuck. They must move with you as it comes up, resisting your motion with 30 or so pounds of pull but letting you slide or move. That makes the inflation more manageable. Once your motion stops, then they can try holding you in one place while allowing left/right corrections as necessary. Instruct them that if you get lifted, they should walk downwind while holding you. Emphatically instruct them to let go if they feel themselves start to get lifted (for their safety).

To further reduce risk, have the assistants use short ropes (not long enough to get into moving parts) tied to a sturdy part of the frame. The assistants pull on those ropes which are easy to let go of. Assistance is most often used when a large wing makes initial inflation difficult.

The Alan Method and Flying Backwards

Kiting with the Alan Method (see text) allows far more control in strong winds than using the toggles. It also lets you oppose the untwisting force so as to remain facing the wing even after getting lifted.

Steering is easy, look at the trailing edge and imagine how the deflected brake will slow that side down causing a turn. Envision it that way and it will be obvious. Kiting practice will make it second nature.

Preventing the untwist isn't hard either. If the risers want to swing you left to face forward, use your hands on the brake lines to oppose it. Yes, you'll necessarily be pulling some brake pressure on both lines.

The hard part is combining steering and counter-twist inputs. It's a skill that highly experienced paraglider pilots learn for controlling launches in higher wind situations.

Once mastered, you'll also find it allows helps with kiting up vehicles, poles, etc. just for the fun of it.

By Tim Kaiser

Handling smooth surfaces

High winds on smooth surfaces like beaches are tough to manage. The minute you lay the wing out it wants to slide away. The solution is to minimize exposing its cell openings to the wind. Here are two methods.

1. If you normally stuff your wing, pull it out so that it's in a rosette but oriented properly to the wind. That's easier if you always stow it in the same way.

2. Lay the wing out parallel with the wind and have someone hold its upwind tip. If you're alone, lay something heavy on it that won't damage the fabric (image 3 left). Sand works but make sure it won't go in the cells during inflation.

3. A slight tug on the downwind A's will bring the wing to life, yanking it around into position. Use brakes or rear risers immediately to control the wall. You can also pull an A riser and brake on the downwind tip to bring it around.

Regardless of the method used, be ready to get dragged! Have a plan and be somewhere with nothing nasty downwind to get strained through. And be ready to fly (get lifted) since, once the wing comes to life, it may be difficult or impossible to unclip. Start with the rear risers pulled in, if possible, to have better control.

The smooth surface will make the wing quicker to "snake" above the ground so you must hold the wall in a very narrow height range using the techniques described earlier. More than likely, you'll have to inflate it without using the A's, which is hard on some wings.

Cart Reverse Launch

It is *possible* to do reverse inflations with a cart but requires high-end kiting skills; moderate, steady winds; and an appropriate cart. The one in "Cart Reverse Launch 2" (opposite page) is *not* ideal—its bars are in the way, it's too heavy to lift, and the nosewheel doesn't caster. The turn-around must be timed and steered to prevent flipping, which is especially challenging if there's much gusting.

Layout like a foot-launch reverse with the cart facing the wing and risers crossed for your turn. Hold yourself solidly by feet or wheel brakes (if equipped—few are). Bring the wing up, sliding/rolling towards it as necessary. Steer the wing slightly in the direction you'll turn then use *just* enough power to steer the cart around towards the wing then into the wind. Use minimal brake pressure. Don't linger while sideways to the wind—that's your most vulnerable time.

High Wind Landing

It's safer to leave the motor running if you'll be landing in strong wind because you have more options. True, in a fall there would be more damage, but with the motor

---

1. If you use a helper, tell him to let you move initially as the wing comes overhead so it doesn't overshoot you.

2. Only try this in a strong, steady wind with soft bailouts, and keep the wing loaded.

Approach the object from just below (a few inches), then add some brake to swing up to it. Control via braking, flexing the knees, and twisting the motor to redirect thrust opposite to an unwanted lean. Keep the power on and fly the wing while always maintaining some brake pressure. Master it first on level ground.

3. Sand is used to anchor the upwind tip. Clip in and start pulling the wing into a normal wall or inflate the downwind tip first, straight to overhead.

Piled sand for anchor

Cart Reverse Launch 1

running, it's easier to prevent a fall.

Two difficult steps after touchdown are: 1) getting turned around to face the wing, and 2) bringing it down.

To get turned around, it's helpful to unload the wing after landing. Keep enough power to stay in position and hold some brake—as much as you can without getting lifted. When you're ready to turn, let off the brakes and squat down so the wing surges forward. As it unloads, turn around while standing up straight.

Once turned around, bring the wing down (deflate it) using one of the methods described earlier. You can do the unloading trick again, then yank it hard through the power band. As it comes through, expect one brief, powerful yank. Run towards a wingtip and grab fabric.

Light Wind Techniques

Normally, if it's too light to kite the wing overhead, a forward launch is easier and safer. But if you're ready to reverse when the wind dies, these are nice tools to have.

It's easier with clutched motors because there's no opposing thrust. One way to help using any motor is to get some air flowing over the wing just before you inflate. While standing there ready, move towards the wing and turn around so idle thrust is just over the wing. Not too much—it blows by the wing too quickly. Then, in one fluid motion, let off the throttle, turn around, back up, and inflate.

Cross Armed Reverse

This method works in light winds by imparting energy to the wing as you turn around (see Fig 15.50 next page). With easy-inflating gliders and practice it can be done in no wind (see the video at www.FootFlyer.com.) Our description is for a pilot who turns *left* after inflating.

Clip in normally and grab the brakes as usual for a reverse. While holding the toggles, slide your right hand down the right riser to its A which will probably be to your left. Grab that A and continue left and up—that A should have a clear path to the wing (Fig. 15.50 #1). With your left hand, reach *over* the other A and grab it as shown in Fig. 15.50 #2; on some wings, it's easier to grab the quick links.

Pull your hands back towards you (arms are now crossed) to see that both A's are clear to the wing. When ready, lunge backwards with your body, pulling both A's as necessary. You can help a lagging side by pulling more A on that side. When the wing gets to about 60° overhead, turn to the left and throttle up. As you turn, your arms will uncross and move forward, which provides some pull to the A's during

Cart Reverse Launch 2

Single-Hold Reverse

Hold both A's with the hand opposite your throttle. You'll turn around in that direction, like the pilot shown above. He has the throttle in his right hand and A's in his left, so he turns to the left.

This allows holding/pulling the A's while turning nearly all the way around, even during the initial acceleration. That's helpful in light winds.

Another help with light wind reverses is to step towards the wing, turn around, and blow air over the wing at *just* above idle. Watch the lines, though. Throttle off, then immediately turn and start the inflation.

Light Wind, Single-Hold Reverse Launch

Non-throttle hand holding both A's

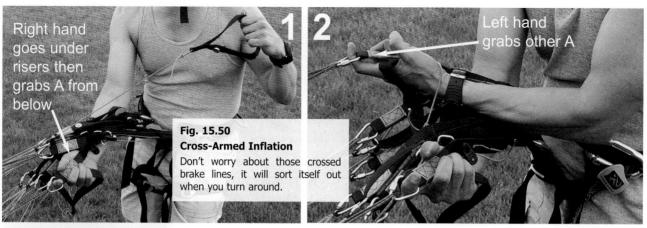

Right hand goes under risers then grabs A from below

1

2

Left hand grabs other A

Fig. 15.50
Cross-Armed Inflation
Don't worry about those crossed brake lines, it will sort itself out when you turn around.

A's

1

Left hand holding A's

Right Hand holding brakes **2**

1. Kiting with the A's works well with the "Alan Method" since you can quickly go from the A's to the brakes. In a strong wind, you'll want to walk towards the wing as it's coming up to reduce the relative wind and therefore the power of its pull.

2. Fixing a Wall: Your left hand holds the A line, and your right hand holds the brake line, to the wing's high side. part (high side). Get some air into the open cells so it blows out the mess to the left.

the turn—very helpful in light winds. This method doesn't work as well on wings that tend to front tuck easily.

Kiting with the A's

This technique allows kiting in light to moderate winds while keeping the wing only a few feet above the ground. It is almost useless by itself but the skill helps handle nearly all other inflations. It's handy, too, for kiting wars where the goal is to be the last one left kiting.

Set up for a regular reverse, but like the "Alan Method," do *not* grab the brake toggles. Grab the A risers beyond where they cross as shown in 1 at left.

Inflate the wing by stepping back and helping with the A's as usual. If the left side drops (as you're looking at it), pull more on that A while stepping back. If the right side drops, pull the right A while stepping back. You may have to walk left and right to keep yourself centered as gusts come through.

When the wing is low to the ground your left/right motion is just like when building a wall—step towards the high side. Once the wing arcs above 45°, go back to the normal movement of stepping towards the falling side. As always, the goal is to be able to kite with*out* having to move, but do move when it's necessary.

Inflation Issues

In a perfect world, launch runs are always downhill, into a steady breeze, and the sod farm entrance reads "**PARAMOTOR PILOTS WELCOME**." The following tips will help in *our* world.

Fixing a Wall

An even layout is always best, but sometimes the wing comes down in a heap after an abortive kiting effort. One side sits lifeless while the other has some form. Here's a way to rescue the mess quickly.

As long as some cells can get clear air, hold the A's going to those cells while holding their brake line in your other hand. Pull both sharply until they catch air. Done properly and with enough wind, it will billow out nicely. Too much A's will be ineffective. If a whole side is clear, use the riser to that side. Be careful when pulling only one or a few lines—it's easier to overstress the connection points or get line burns.

Salvaging Bad Inflations

In the beginning, an inflation that went this bad (above and right) had only two outcomes: Abort or crash. Aborting is always the safest option, but if you are intimately familiar with your wing and willing to take the extra risk, you can salvage many launches with these tips. Be forewarned that pushing too hard on launch risks feeding body parts, lines, or fabric to the ever-hungry prop.

- Keep forward motion. Speed is life. Powering up early, at least partially, makes it easier.

- Turn towards the wing and keep pressure on the low side's A riser. Get speed.

- Once you've got forward motion, use *just enough* brake pressure on the high side. The trick is using *just* enough—too much brake brings the entire wing back down.

- Like all launches, it's an inflation into a controlled run: do **not** accelerate or accept a liftoff until the wing is **fully under control**.

If things turn sour, be lightning fast to kill the motor.

Crooked Inflations

As learned in Section I, successful launches emerge from proper setups. Everything must be lined up, especially in light-wind forward inflations: lines clear, centered on the wing, and aligned straight into the wind. See Chapter 5 for troubleshooting launch problems because we're going to put some of them to use.

- Cause 1: The wing always tends to come up *into* the breeze. So a wind coming from its right will make the wing come up and turn to the right. The left cells catch the air more directly and come up first.

- Cause 2: Not running perpendicular to the wing will pull up the tip opposite to your run direction. So if you start your run facing slightly right of perpendicular, then the left cells get pulled up first. It doesn't take much before the wing is too crooked to recover. The left side shoots up first, and the wing arcs over sideways.

- Cause 3: If you're left or right of the wing's center when starting your run, the far side will come up first. So if you're off-centered to the right, the left side will come up first and fall over to the right before you knew what happened.

So if the wing "always comes up to the right," then point yourself slightly to the

This started off badly. The pilot looked left to see the wing leaning heavily. He kept up the forward motion and turned towards it—you can see the prop blast off centered. He also kept slight pressure on the low A-riser and applied the slightest brake on the high side.

Thankfully, it worked—this time!

Right Side

Left Side

No Wind

Light Wind

Turning slightly like this can counteract a natural tendency. If the wing always seems to come up to your right, angle yourself slightly left. The same is true for launching in a crosswind.

You can achieve the same result by slightly offsetting yourself from center. If the wing always seems to come up and go left, step a few inches to the right of centered.

left. Or step a few inches left after getting centered.

If you suspect there is a problem with the wing, try kiting it in a steady breeze or, better yet, have an experienced pilot kite it to check for unusual turns or other misbehaving. It may be that one brake is too short, the trimmers are not even, or lines have shrunk unevenly. If you can't figure it out, have it professionally inspected and/or repaired.

Handling Crosswinds

Normally you always launch into the wind, but at some sites, especially long narrow ones, you may be forced to accept a crosswind (see Chapter 17). Also, the wind may shift after setting up. That's pretty common when thermals are budding.

The key is to use the previously mentioned inflation problems to your advantage. Use them intentionally to counter the crosswind effect by running or setting up off-center.

Let's say, for example, that you've set up pointing into a 1-2 mph breeze. But just before launching, the wind shifts to be coming from your right. Simply driving hard may be enough, but the wing will want to come up to the right—into the breeze. So point your launch run about 3° to the *left*. Done correctly, the effects will cancel each other out.

Excelling at ground handling is well worth the effort, not only for success in launching, but for its own sake. The best ground handlers make the best launchers.

David Rogers brings his wing to life in a morning's light breeze; perfect for checking the wind, inspecting the wing, and reveling in your control of this amazing aircraft.

By Teri Johnson

Precision Flying

CHAPTER

16

Just *flying* a powered paraglider is all the enjoyment most pilots need. That can be enjoyed safely without ever becoming super precise—you just have to stay within your limits. Being skilled does prepare for the unexpected, but that advantage evaporates if it's spent taking on more challenging situations. Superior skill is easily overwhelmed by inferior judgement.

Start higher up then work your way into this, just one manifestation of precision flying.

For those who aspire to really *master* the craft, for whatever reason, this chapter is for you. Don't think our minimalist controls mean loose or imprecise control. Reality is so much more fun; in fact, *very* precise flight path control is available to those willing to own it.

Even in moderately bumpy air, a skilled pilot can stay within inches of his desired path. As you might imagine, such precision takes practice, especially since we hang so far below the wing. It requires anticipation and a sense for how long it takes your *body* to feel results from control inputs—both vertically and laterally. You must learn the feel of input and resultant motion. But, oh, how sweet it is once mastered!

Brakes—The *Feel* Position

A lot of precision flight is done using minimum brake pull—just enough pressure to affect minor corrections without giving up speed. This is the *feel* position—about a pound of brake, or brake position/pressure 1 on most wings. Hanging the weight of your arms is too much. That gives great control feel, but it also slows you down, sacrificing energy (speed) in the process. Find the feel position by pulling pressure without looking at the wing, until you just *start* to notice a course or speed change.

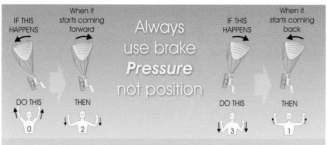

Wing *starts* moving back: hands up. Wing *starts* moving forward: pressure.

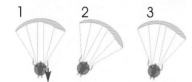

In a regular turn, you apply brake (1) and hold it. The wing banks out to a maximum (2), then levels back to a lesser amount of bank (3). It stays there as long as you hold the brake. The rate at which it goes out and back is the pendular rate for that motor and wing combination.

Coordinated Turn

The goal is to minimize diving and slipping, which is where the wing briefly moves sideways through the air. Do these steps about a half second apart until you get a feel for it.

1. Reduce power a bit, especially if turning against the motor's normal torque steer.

2. Weight shift (if able) to start the wing moving.

3. Brake towards the turn then,

4. just after the wing starts responding, prevent a dive by adding a bit of power and/or pulling slight outside brake. The resulting turn is smooth and level.

Pace it by speaking out loud at a conversational rate and doing the action: "Power back, weight shift, one, brake inside, two, throttle up/add outside brake."

Larger wings with their longer line lengths take longer to swing from side to side. Some gliders tend to have more level turns naturally.

Flying with *some* pressure is important for high precision, especially next to the ground. Of course you *can* fly with a lot more brake pressure but that requires even more finesse in another area: thrust control.

Straight Lines—Pendular Precision

Hanging below the wing means you swing—fore/aft and left/right. Like any pendulum, there is a natural frequency to that swing, its *period*. Controlling left/right oscillations is challenging because it's not intuitive—in fact, on a small scale, it is backwards from what the body feels. The fore/aft motion is easier to learn but has its own quirks.

Being able to stop oscillations precisely underpins nearly every other aspect of fine control; it's what gives us rule over the inches. A telling test of whether you have this skill is being able to fly a straight line, within 3 to 6 inches, both vertically and laterally. Of course the only place to even recognize such precision is while flying a few feet above the ground. Features such as corn rows, tracks in the sand, or lines in a field are good for this. Gradual curves are fine, too.

Crop boundaries are perfect, especially tall corn next to something short like beans. Fly a track just over the corn row. If you hit sink, throttle up and turn towards the beans for an instant extra 5 feet of clearance.

Only do this into the wind with heightened vigilance.

Pendular Precision: Roll Recovery

You can feel the pendular action of a PPG by letting up quickly on the brakes from a stable turn. It will recover past level, swinging back and forth at its natural pendular rate, in decreasing amounts, until you are flying level again.

To fly precisely, these oscillations must be dampened.

From an established right turn, let off the inside (right) brake. You will swing back to level and beyond. Just as you *start* to swing left, pull a quarter left brake in the direction you're about to swing. Hold it for *one* second then ease up. Done correctly, you will reach zero brake input just as the wing levels.

This works both for preventing oscillations and for damping them once begun. If you have already started a swing (by a gust or your own action), let it crest, then, as soon as your body reverses direction, pull brake in that direction for a second then release.

Timing is crucial—if turbulence swings you right, let it finish swinging, then just as it *starts* swinging to the left, pull a quarter *left* brake for a second and release. It may feel backwards at first—you start swinging left and have to pull left brake immediately. Don't hold it for too long or you'll make it worse. The amount of correction should be proportional to the swing's intensity. It may feel unnatural at first but will become automatic with practice. And practice you must.

The best way to rehearse this is by doing mild wingovers (see Chapter 18) and practicing returning to level flight with the least amount of oscillation. Fortunately, this skill can be mastered in the safety of altitude.

Pendular Precision: Roll Prevention

Being able to closely follow a line on the ground requires mastery of the pendular tendency—you must catch it *before* getting swung. The previous explanation primarily covered how to stop it after it started—this is how to stop it before it even starts.

This takes practice. Lots of practice. You must feel the slight motions and modulate brake pull accordingly—stronger swing, more brake. Your reaction must be quick—any delay will only make it worse. The key to *preventing* oscillations is to apply brake in the direction of your body's movement *as soon as that movement starts*. Hold for one second then let off.

For example, you're flying along a line (like a corn row) and feel your body start swinging left (body left, wing right). You must *immediately* pull left brake, the moment you feel it, for about a second, then let it up. As long as you catch it *before* you've moved more than a few inches, you will dampen the oscillation before it has a chance to get going. If you wait too long, you'll make the swing bigger.

Don't try this until you've mastered *Pendular Precision: Roll Recovery*.

Fore/Aft (Surge Control)

The wing always wants to maintain an equilibrium known as *trim speed*—20 mph in the illustration below. If you release brakes from a stable, slowed condition, you'll cause a slight dive with acceleration back to the no-brakes trim speed. Pulling trimmers sets a new, slower trim speed equilibrium.

A sudden increase of headwind immediately increases your *air*speed—you'll swing forward, climb and lose forward momentum (groundspeed). With no further wind change, the glider settles back to its trim speed. You're moving slower over the ground and a few feet higher.

A sudden decrease in headwind (or increase in tailwind) does the opposite: airspeed drops, the wing dives a bit, and you accelerate over the ground. Once it stabilizes, you'll be at trim airspeed but going faster over the ground and a bit lower.

A brief gust is worse than a one-time change because it's really two changes. In a headwind gust, for example, the wing surges back and you climb as it seeks trim

Digging Deeper

Pendular dampening *seems* backwards because we are not exactly pendulums. When the wing goes left, your body goes slightly right. Since we control the *wing,* we must translate that kinetic feel into what *it's* doing.

Feel the body go right? *Immediately* add some right brake then let up. When you felt rightward motion, the *wing* was going left and, if you reacted quickly enough, that stopped it.

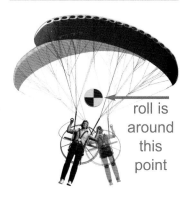

roll is around this point

Constant Power
Headwind Increase
Holding brakes 2
Reduce brakes when pitched back.
Back to brakes 2
20
20
25
23
20
20
20
20
20
18
15
15
Calm
Wind Increase
Headwind

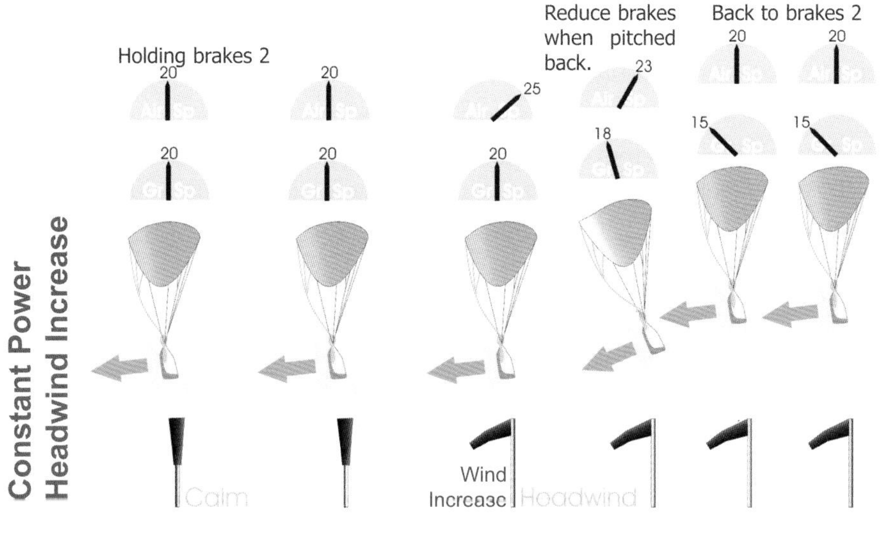

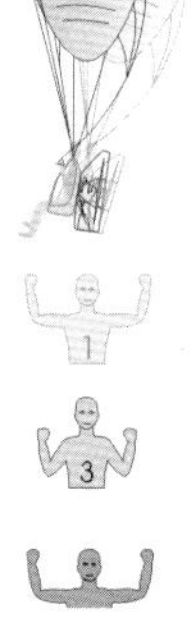

You're flying along with brakes 1 when the wing suddenly surges forward.

Quickly pull to pressure 3 for a second, then back to pressure 1. As you gain experience, you'll do this naturally with good timing.

It's just like the left/right pendulum: Give the input just as the wing *starts* to change direction. So if it goes forward, just as it *starts* to come back, let up on the pressure.

Controlling with pressure, not position, is critical in turbulence. Brake pressure 3 may happen at position 4 or more under some circumstances. Go to the pressure, not the position.

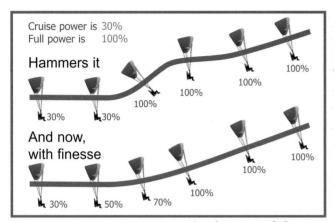

Cruise power is 30%
Full power is 100%

Hammers it

30%   30%   350%   100%   100%   100%   100%

And now, with finesse

30%   50%   70%   100%   100%   100%

speed. Groundspeed (momentum) decreases too. Then, when the gust subsides, the wing suddenly feels less airflow (less airspeed) and dives to get back to trim speed. This can be dramatic and cause large pitch changes where your body (and wing) angles upward or downward.

You can minimize all this with the brakes and power, keeping the wing overhead as much as possible—an essential skill to safely maintaining altitude within a few inches of the ground. It's part of *active flying* covered later.

In the case of the wing surging forward, it will make you want to dive at the ground—you must quickly pull some brake to stop its surge. The moment you sense the wing *start* forward, you must immediately dampen it with brakes. Pull for a second, then let up as it starts coming back.

In turbulence, hold brake pressure 2 to 3 while being mindful of keeping up forward speed. Airspeed means brake authority, especially in case you must stop a drop. You'll be modulating thrust, too. So if you get lifted and tilted back, do this: simultaneously reduce brakes and throttle. Then, as *soon* as the wing starts coming forward, come in with enough throttle and brake to stay level and maintain speed.

You must build skill through practice to really master the necessary reactions. This chapter may explain the principle but its greatest contribution is describing what to practice and what to expect when you do.

Start off in fairly smooth conditions, flying 10 feet over landable terrain, as always. Sod farms, beaches or smooth desert floor are perfect. Try to hold altitude precisely. As you improve, go later in the morning (or earlier in the evening) when bumps appear but are not severe. You will build skill faster if practicing with *some* level of turbulence.

Finessing the Climb

Going from level flight into a climb can be graceful (see graphic above).

If you just hammer the throttle, you'll swing out into a brief, steep climb, then shallow out and settle into a stable climb. It works, of course, but it doesn't look good and, if the motor quits just after that initial strong swing out, the wing's forward surge will be dramatic.

Let's do it with finesse. From cruise power, throttle halfway to 100%; let it swing forward. As you feel yourself *about* to start swinging back, *smoothly* add full power. This is similar to how a go-around (aka balked landing) should be done.

Balance of Power

In normal flight, you've learned that power controls altitude—power up to climb, power back to descend. But throttle changes take a second or two to act. To effect an *immediate* climb or descent use brakes. It's a limited and fleeting effect, but if you're cruising along at a few inches, that immediacy is key. You'll need to adjust the power soon afterwards to maintain your energy state.

Energy State

Energy state is a term, fancied by fighter pilots, that describes the trade-off between speed and altitude. It's like a roller coaster that accelerates going downhill, trading height (potential energy) for speed (kinetic energy). Climbing the next hill trades speed for height. Friction makes the cars gradually slow down (losing energy), but power overcomes it. A paraglider is no different. If you're going fast, you have energy available to trade for height (briefly anyway) which is what a quick pull of brakes do. Reducing brakes will trade some height for increased airspeed. Increasing thrust increases total energy.

When flying level, a few feet above the ground (or any altitude), use reduced brake pressure. That leaves some brake authority for an immediate climb. If you start to sink, pull brakes to arrest it; then, before slowing down too far, add power to regain the lost speed (energy). So if you hit sinking air again, you can use the brakes.

Slow Flight

Slow flight puts you close to stalling or spinning. If you feel the wing start to slow unexpectedly, or a brake gets mushy, reduce brake pressure *immediately*.

To get into level slow flight, reduce power then pull enough brakes to prevent descending. Once the speed starts decreasing, you will need to add power to hold altitude, eventually requiring more power than before. You must be 100% sure where the wing will stall and what that feels like. Don't go beyond brake position/pressure 4.

In slow flight, the roles of brake pressure and power reverse. Since brakes are already pulled, you must control altitude almost exclusively with power. The good news is that, with so much brake applied, the wing responds quickly to increased power. And since you'll be carrying plenty of power, the motor should respond quickly to throttle changes. Flying at *minimum* speed requires holding the wing near stall while controlling height with power. Practice this either up very high (and with a reserve) or within a few inches of the ground.

The least amount of power is required when flying at the glider's minimum sink configuration: usually slight brake pressure, trimmers slow, and speedbar off.

Turns

Turns require more power to prevent altitude loss since some of the wing's lift is spent turning. More bank requires more thrust. Competition pilots doing steep low turns are almost always at full power as they swing around pylons then completely off the power as they start to level out. They may even use speedbar to convert the turn energy into level speed.

When entering a turn, it can be helpful to reduce power briefly, start the turn, then come back in with power. That reduces the chance for spinning or stalling, especially if the turn is opposite your motor's natural torque turn direction.

Low Flying

For some, low flying is the single biggest appeal of PPG—the ability to cruise at any altitude while exploring a three dimensional realm. Unfortunately, it's also where most of the risk lurks.

Eric Dufour picks up three cones in Albuquerque, NM.

⚠ Caution!

Doing steep maneuvers down low is incredibly dangerous. Don't do anything down low that you haven't mastered up high, and don't ever let any kind of vertical velocity develop. Competition pilots minimize their risk because the rules discourage maneuvers with a big vertical component (big dives, for example).

Flying low and downwind sacrifices the inherent slow speed safety advantage of our craft. Higher speed makes it harder to detect/avoid an obstacle while increasing the consequence of a collision.

As always, stay within reach of a safe landing spot, climbing if necessary when unsavory terrain is traversed. Flying 3 feet over grass has minimal risk; flying 3 feet over craggily rocks is tempting fate with ice cream.

Start out by flying relatively high, at least 10 feet, doing gentle maneuvers. Remember that any turn loses altitude, and steep turns lose a *lot*. You must build up to getting lower or to turning steeper. Never let yourself get deep in the brakes—they are your only control, and once pulled, there is nothing left to maneuver with. Like foot dragging (covered shortly), if you notice that you're pulling high brake pressure, add power and ease your hands back up to recover back to cruise speed.

Foot Dragging

1. Before trying this, remind yourself to be extra vigilant about your surroundings—numerous pilots have hit their cages while trying this or lost track of nearby wires when concentrating on such tasks.

2. Foot draggin' Christy Damon squeezes the throttle and pulls brakes after settling too much. But the motor takes a second to spin up, and if there's not enough energy (speed) in the wing, it may not be enough.

It's an amazing accomplishment to be flying with your feet on the ground, especially in mildly bumpy air (no more than 2 on the bump scale). You must first master precise control of altitude, within a few inches, while also minding power, ground track and speed.

Always do this into the wind until you're extremely proficient—then doing it crosswind is possible. Crosswind foot-dragging is riskier since you'll be sliding somewhat sideways and be more susceptible to falling.

The safest stance for a foot-drag is with one foot out in front of the other so that you can be ready to run if necessary. Don't put much weight on the foot—drag can slow you down, forcing a run or fall. Modulate the brakes and power to keep your cage from touching the ground. On wet, smooth ground you *can* get away with sliding the cage but it risks damage.

Use brakes to control altitude, and throttle to keep the speed up. If you drop, immediately pull some brake to prevent sinking, then add power to accelerate back to speed. Brakes can arrest a drop far quicker than throttle. Cruise at about brake pressure 1 so you'll have both up and down control. If you get gusted upwards you can immediately reduce brake pressure to avoid climbing then pull more brakes if you get dropped.

If you find yourself getting heavy in the brakes, airspeed is slowing down—get on the power immediately!

Picking up Ground Objects

Start this slowly—first be able to do foot drags and control altitude within a few inches. Get down nearly level with the object so you're not descending on it. Otherwise, you're likely to hit the ground while concentrating on the object and not powering up in time.

Be flying level with no more than a quarter brake so that when you close your feet to grab the object, a handful of brake will give an immediate climb. The moment you've got it, pull brake and add power. On approach, be stable so that you can concentrate on finesse and plan the snatch.

The best objects for this are medium-sized exercise balls with low pressure or orange traffic cones. Hard or heavy items can be all but impossible to grasp with your feet. And be careful with anything you're unsure of. One pilot almost broke his foot when the kickball he was nabbing turned out to be a bowing ball. Ouch.

Having a Motor Failure

A motor failure while flying low leaves little time to react. The wing surges forward into a dive, which must be checked immediately (see page 46) with brake.

If it happens below about 10 feet, pull immediately to pressure 2 and hold until flaring fully at 2 to 3 feet. It may be firm since there's less flare authority. If you were turning, level out before touchdown.

Catching Suspended Targets

Trying to hit or grab something floating, falling, or flying through the air is a fun challenge. One way to practice is with partially deflated helium balloons since they're neutrally buoyant. Tie it to your front harness webbing for launch. Get to a safe altitude, hold the balloon out to the side, throttle off, then let it go.

As you approach the object, try to put it on the horizon so that it's at your altitude. Head straight for it—if there is no relative motion of the object, then you are dead-on. Make *small* adjustments as necessary.

Formation

It's fun to fly in formation but there are important details to make it safer. Have radios, a plan that everybody knows, and avoid having more than one inexperienced pilot in any formation. Build slowly, starting with loose formations, then tighten up only if desired. Here are some other suggestions:

1. Never, ever accept a high closure rate. If one becomes apparent, break it off and re-form. This can happen weirdly and surprisingly quickly.

2. If you're closing on a pilot who doesn't know you're there, allow room for escape by either pilot. Approach slowly and clearly, staying 5 wingspans away until he's aware of you. If he turns away, leave him be.

3. Keep both hands in the brakes. If taking pictures, be holding the brake that would steer you clear.

4. The lead pilot needs only to fly smoothly and avoid abrupt maneuvering unless it's highly rehearsed. More skilled formation flyers should be followers with the

Tucker Gott launched and caught this paper airplane in flight.

Flying a loose vertical slant formation into Oshkosh. Keep looking around, above, beside, below, especially during impromptu groups.

Lead→

Formation By Relative Position

Flying a tight formation requires precision flying and discipline, mostly to safely maintain long periods of concentration while holding relative position. It's like driving 3 feet behind a truck at highway speed—you gotta be attentive the entire time.

Some positions are easier than others to make look good. The one illustrated at left is easy by keeping the preceding glider on the horizon and staying behind a particular row of line cascades (red circle) for further precision. Most positions can be maintained like this, using two points on the preceding glider—most of your attention goes there. If this example was your view, you'd need to come forward until all the pilots are lined up (dashed line).

The bottom pilot is lead; the 2nd position is most critical because it largely sets the shape for everybody else. Numbers 3, 4, and so on can also use relative position by looking down the other pilots (dashed red lines) but should focus only on the preceding glider. You just have to trust whoever is following you. Each pilot should maintain a set, identifiable distance back from their lead. A coach on radio is indispensable for this.

Be aware of wake with its lift and sink (gray arrows). Level formations are toughest for this. A noticeable decrease in power can be had by putting your wing in the rising portion of a preceding pilots's tip vortice.

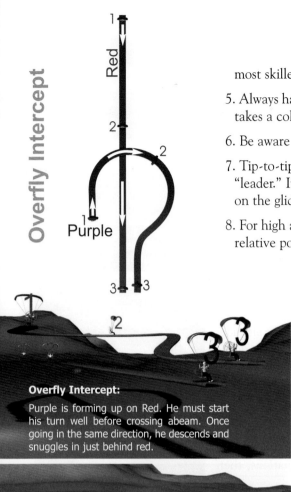

Overfly Intercept

Overfly Intercept:

Purple is forming up on Red. He must start his turn well before crossing abeam. Once going in the same direction, he descends and snuggles in just behind red.

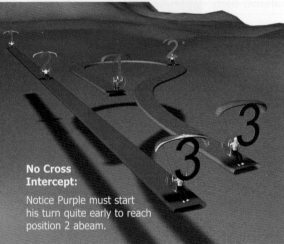

No Cross Intercept:

Notice Purple must start his turn quite early to reach position 2 abeam.

Head-On Intercepts

Forming up, or *intercepting*, another pilot head-on is more challenging. The no-cross path is safer than the overfly since paths don't cross. In both cases the interceptor must start his turn *well* before passing the interceptee. It's better to start your turn early rather than late. If you get ahead of the interceptee, do S-turns to get back in position. If you get behind, it will take time to catch up.

Having the Interceptee fly a steady, shallow turn will let others join up on the inside of the turn.

Consider starting above the interceptee then descending down to his level once you're laterally in position. That way misjudgement can't cause a collision and it avoids wake. When in position, descend into the desired formation.

most skilled in the #2 position(s) behind lead.

5. Always have an out. Plan an escape in case someone maneuvers unexpectedly, takes a collapse, or has a motor failure.

6. Be aware of wake and stay clear or manage appropriately.

7. Tip-to-tip formations are harder. Like any, each pilot must concentrate on his "leader." If lead is the leftmost glider then everybody would be concentrating on the glider immediately to their left.

8. For high accuracy, pick two points on your lead and keep them aligned. Using relative position of other pilots is useful but should be secondary.

Intercepting

Joining up to fly alongside another pilot requires care and anticipation since speed is minimally adjustable. The most common error is not leading the intercept enough—you start turning to follow too late and wind up lagging far behind. It's easy to join someone going basically the same way so we show two ways (left) to do it from head-on (left).

Turning

While turning in formation, the outside pilot must go faster than the inside pilot which may be impossible. A solution is for following pilots to climb up and get just *behind* and above the inside pilot. When leveling out, move back to the outside. Timed right, it looks good.

Other Considerations

"Walking" on another pilot's wing has ended poorly. The walker can get tangled or disrupt the lower pilot's wing enough to collapse it. A reserve may not even help with the resulting carnage.

Active Flying in Turbulence

Active flying is using the least amount of control necessary to keep the wing essentially overhead. Passive flying is just holding pressure while letting the wing move around. The challenge is dampening oscillations (left-right) and surges (fore-aft) with correct input quickly with*out* overdoing it. And if you feel airspeed decay, reduce bakes and power then add power as necessary to fly level.

Use what's necessary, and in a big surge that can be several *feet* of brake pull, but use the *least* amount necessary—letting the wing wander a bit rather than jabbing at every little twitch. As you improve, you'll be able to make very small corrections before the wing gets very far out of position. Until then, it's better to let the wing wander within a range while mostly holding pressure.

For most gliders, the best configuration in turbulence is: no speedbar, trimmers slow, brake pressure 2 or 3, and enough thrust to fly level. Lighter pilots on larger wings must be especially vigilant about parachutal stall (see Chapter 4) and be quick to reduce brake pressure and power at the first sign of slowing airspeed.

Becoming effective at active flying will take at least 50 flights and then only if you really work at it, such as flying exactly straight lines within 100 feet of the ground in mildly bumpy air. While practicing, keep looking forward; use your kinetic sense to detect motion, then provide control inputs.

If at any time you start to "lose it" (not sure what to do), reduce brake pressure, reduce power for 5 seconds, let things settle down, *then* re-engage your corrections.

You must learn to interpret the small angular changes that get transferred to your harness as the wing moves around overhead. That takes practice. You'll apply techniques covered earlier regarding pendular control: if your body swings left, apply left brake *as soon* as the swing starts then let up. It's not intuitive—the skill must be practiced, and must be automatic to be counted on.

With repetition this becomes automatic. Don't try damping oscillations for landing until it is automatic since your attention is so focused on the flare that your steering inputs will likely devolve into pilot-induced oscillations (PIO's).

The Perfect Touchdown

Landing can be remarkably graceful. And consistent. These tips will help achieve finessed touchdowns. The *slider* is good for fast touchdowns on smooth surfaces while the *one step* helps to minimize run-out when terrain is rough. *Getting* to the target (spot landing) is covered in Chapter 17.

Sliding In—the *Swoop* Landing

Sliding in for a landing works better on smaller and/or higher performance wings (high glide ratio)—those that allow coming in for a power-off landing that have lots of flare authority in the brakes. You have such a wing if, on a power-off landing, you can flare and climb back up a few feet.

For a basic slider landing, also known as a *swoop* landing, start from a nearly hands-up glide at 50 feet. Reaching about 8 - 10 feet, higher on smaller wings, pull enough brakes (position/pressure 1 - 2) to get your body swinging forward, then ease up on the brakes briefly. That initial pull gets your body swinging forward which pitches the wing up, nearly stopping your descent. Time it so the level-off happens right as your feet reach the ground. Practice will reveal how much pull, how high to start, and how long to hold it. As you level off, speed will quickly start bleeding off—apply more brakes to keep weight off your feet as long as possible. Done properly, you'll skid to a stop with full brakes.

This is useful when ground speed is high on landing and the surface is smooth. Even if you don't

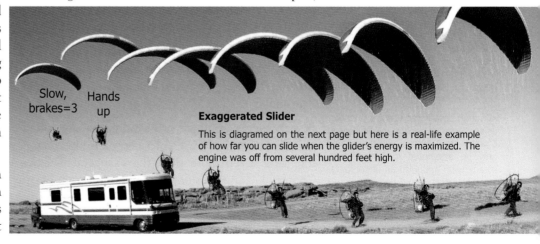

Slow, brakes=3

Hands up

Exaggerated Slider

This is diagramed on the next page but here is a real-life example of how far you can slide when the glider's energy is maximized. The engine was off from several hundred feet high.

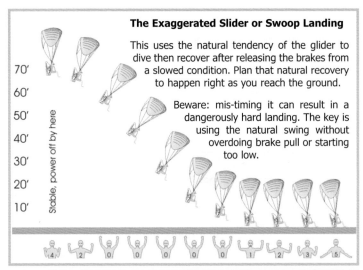

The Exaggerated Slider or Swoop Landing

This uses the natural tendency of the glider to dive then recover after releasing the brakes from a slowed condition. Plan that natural recovery to happen right as you reach the ground.

Beware: mis-timing it can result in a dangerously hard landing. The key is using the natural swing without overdoing brake pull or starting too low.

Power-On Landing

Landing with power can make you look good. Plus, in turbulent conditions, it gives you more options in the event of getting dumped.

One good technique for power-on landing is to come in like any other approach, but during the last 30 feet or so, throttle up enough to shallow the descent rate by half. That enables better timing of the flare since you'll have more time to finesse out any errors.

Another technique that's fun and looks good, is to turn a foot-drag into a landing. While foot dragging, be prepared to bear all the weight in case of a gust—it's easy to fall if you're not ready for it.

One Step with Power

This shows one technique for landing on an elevated spot (motorhome here). Come in slightly below the top, pull some brakes to swing up and touch down, then reduce brakes as necessary to keep kiting the wing. Use power to avoid getting pulled back. Not quite one step, but close.

Although power was used, the idea of using the swing applies as you'll see in Chapter 17. A landing like this should only be attempted in a moderate, steady wind and with an understanding that errors would be most unforgiving!

skid to a stop, the slide bleeds off a lot of speed that you don't have to run off.

The *exaggerated* slider (see diagram) is a more aggressive swoop that's fun but with little practical value. Practice it up high to get a feel for how much dive you get by letting off the brakes. If you start it too high on landing, you'll level out too high on the recovery. If you start it too late (low), you'll hit the ground while still diving before it has a chance to recover. *Be careful!*

Even with high-altitude practice, start it slowly, doing only a little dive at first then increasing it as you gain familiarity.

You can exaggerate the slide even more by doing it from a bank. This dangerous maneuver is hard to judge and has very little margin for error. It's unforgiving, too. Many sky divers have met their demise in an extreme version called the *hook turn*. Start with shallow banks and know that risk rises with steepness. Also, rolling out of an excessively steep bank means reaching the ground with too much speed—you'll climb back up. You must bleed off the speed by remaining in a turn (while skimming the ground) then leveling off as speed dissipates. It takes lots of practice and adds significant risk.

The One-Step

This is probably the most challenging type of landing to nail and the easiest one to get hurt on.

Everything is normal down to the last 50 feet. Hold minimum brake pressure, making steering inputs as necessary. Then at 4 to 8 feet (depending on wing), pull and hold some brake to start the swing, enough to swing out a bit in front of the glider; climb slightly then drop the last foot or so. As the swing completes be adding brake, going to full just before touchdown.

Your starting speed must be such that you don't climb up more than a couple feet. That would hurt. Timing must be right on, too—start the final brake pull so as to exhaust all speed just as you touchdown. Some wings will require starting this from a no-brake position and maybe even swooping a bit to climb at the end.

Be extremely careful—if you wind up having pulled all the brake too early, you'll plummet those last few feet to a *very* hard landing. A good place to practice this is soft sand. Even more than the exaggerated slider, errors are unforgiving. See Chapter 17 for power-on spot landing over an obstruction.

Challenging Sites

17

The fact that we *can* launch from so many places is incredible. But some of them, under some conditions and for some pilots, are really dangerous. Sites should match your skills, and these tools will help. Nearly a important, they will help recognize when to just say no.

What makes this tight are trees and water. A quick right turn keeps the pilot over terra firma, weaving between trees that are *just* far enough apart.

The Horror of Hot, High, and Humid

The effect of high elevation on performance is dramatic. Flying gear that easily blasts you aloft at sea level may be downright doggy at 5000 feet MSL. If a machine is weak at sea level it may not even get you airborne that high—it takes more thrust to launch than to simply fly.

Everything works against success at high elevations. Thinner air decreases thrust, you get winded quicker, and have to run faster for the same lift. All told, launching from high elevations can be tricky, especially with no wind. Add in high temperatures and/or a weak motor and you will be in for some exercise.

Go to a high-altitude fly-in and you'll witness (or fall victim to) the struggle with still air—sometimes pilots simply can't get airborne. More thrust would be handy at those times, but it can also cause a faceplant without appropriate skills. Here are some other possibilities.

- You may actually have a slight tailwind at 15 feet AGL, up where the wing feels it but you don't. Try extending a telltale (small, very sensitive wind indicator) up high or just attempt launching the other way.

- The motor is not putting out full thrust for that altitude. A quick check of max RPM will confirm it. Thrust will, of course, be diminished, but the RPM should be close to its sea-level value if everything is set up correctly. Chapter 27 has a chart that equates sea-level thrust with what you'll get at higher altitudes.

Tim Kaiser launching from near Kingman, Arizona. Moderately high elevation, nil winds and rough terrain made this a tough launch. The wing must come up straight and the pilot must be able to steer his run.

Hot & High: Density Altitude

Density altitude is elevation adjusted for atmospheric pressure and temperature. It's how high we and our equipment *feel* like we're operating.

Humidity has a small effect on performance but a larger effect on our bodies. Hot, humid air makes it harder to cool off—we sweat, but it doesn't evaporate. The effect can make us feel like we're wearing concrete shoes. High humidity also reduces thrust.

Atmospheric pressure has a small effect—100 feet per 0.1 inches of mercury (Hg). So a real high pressure area will lower the density altitude by a few hundred feet.

The big bugaboo is temperature. As a rule of thumb, every 10°F warmer than standard (59°F at sea level) increases density altitude by about 600 feet.

In a standard atmosphere (see Chapter 24), it gets colder as you go up. At 5000 feet the standard temp is only 42°F. So a 72°F day (30° warmer than standard) at 5000 foot elevation is 6800 foot density altitude. You'll feel like you're launching at 6800 feet.

The effect is significant. At higher density altitudes you'll need to run faster and your motor won't push as hard.

Leg Drag

A more insidious cause of launch woe is our landing gear. When carrying all that weight, legs can only push up to a few mph. They're great for initial inflation, but beyond about 4 mph, legs slow us down—thrust must do all the work. This *leg drag* can prevent launch and is aggravated by:

- High density altitudes (see margin) which require more ground speed.

- No wind (requires more groundspeed).

- Seatboard bottom sticking out, hitting your legs.

- Limited thrust.

- Angled-back motor styles. Adjust the motor so that the propeller plane is more vertical in flight rather than leaned-back. If you're leaning back as the wing lifts a bit, you'll actually be pushing slightly *against* your run. Being vertical reduces this. It won't be as comfortable while airborne, but at least you'll *get* airborne.

- Rough or soft surface.

- Short steps instead of long strides as the wing lifts. Also, make sure the seat board is flat so it doesn't interfere with your upper leg's running motion.

You must accelerate to get lift from the wing which then reduces leg drag. But if you can't accelerate enough to get that lift, takeoff may be impossible. You may just have to wait for some wind. One way to increase wing lift is with brakes, but pulling too much, or too early, can be worse. It's a fine line that requires experimentation while running.

Hot and High Solutions

These tips may help with high density altitude launches.

1. Start with the smoothest surface available, downhill if possible. In a very light wind, it may be better to launch crosswind from a smooth, firm surface than upwind through a soft or rutted surface. For example, soft sand can be impossible in still air whereas the nearby road, even if it's slightly crosswind, might be manageable. Never accept any *down*wind component.

2. If you have a choice of wings, pick the slowest one; usually that means the largest size. It must also be easy enough to inflate.

3. If you have a choice of motors or propellers, go big; be pushy.

4. If you don't need all the fuel, tools, spare parts, spare oil, bug spray, camera gear, and food, leave them behind. Lighter is better.

And when you're ready to launch:

1. Do a power forward inflation, keeping pressure on the A's until the wing is nicely overhead and you're moving briskly.

2. Once you've got speed and are no longer worried about the wing falling back, concentrate on staying upright and running as fast as you can with your hands mostly up. Use the smallest steering inputs possible—you'll barely feel any feedback.

3. On soft surfaces, or if you've reached maximum speed, add enough brake pressure to get the wing lifting. That should relieve some weight from your legs. Don't add too much, though, and be ready to back off if you slow down. Add brake slowly to find the happy balance of wing lift and leg drag.

4. Steer yourself to the smoothest, hardest surface possible or into the wind if you're not already.

If all goes well, this run will give way to long strides, then to slapping the ground with your feet and finally, to flight. Once airborne, ease up the brakes *slowly* to avoid settling back down. Best climb rate requires no (or very little) brake pressure.

If you do settle back down, be prepared to run and start the process again.

Tight Spaces

Make no mistake, shoehorning yourself into sub-optimal spaces is risky. However, with skill, the right conditions and appropriate equipment, you *can* fly from surprisingly small areas.

Besides having sufficient room for running, a site must provide a clear path for climbout and departure. Make sure that if the motor quits at any point, you can either land safely along the departure or be high enough to circle back.

High and Dry

I was just outside New Mexico's Sky City, a 6000 foot elevation, with my underpowered motor (for that altitude) on a rutted surface. There was nary a whiff of wind. But I wasn't about to let that deter me.

Or so I thought.

After two tries, running my little legs off, I was exhausted. I simply could not generate enough speed in those ruts for the wing to lift the motor so that I could accelerate—leg drag held me back. I begged off to wait for a puff of headwind.

Finally I felt it, and a smoke source agreed, the lightest little headwind oozed in, maybe 1 mph, so I stood up and went for it.

The wing came up sluggishly as I lurched over deepish ruts. Thankfully it came up straight. Running my hardest with hands up and motor screaming, I slowly gathered speed. Finally, it felt fast enough to apply some brakes—too much, it seems—since I slowed down. I reduced brakes and concentrated on speed. By now I had reached a smoother surface which made a huge difference and pulling some brakes added enough lift to unload my legs to accelerate further. The pace quickened. More lift. More speed. Longer strides. And then finally—the magic smoothness of flight. I was skimming just inches high as I eased off the brakes, accelerated and settled into a *very* shallow climb. Oh sweet rise!

Trials like these create an appreciation for *low* elevation launches. Admittedly, with more power and a bigger wing, it would have been easier but the challenge sure made success taste

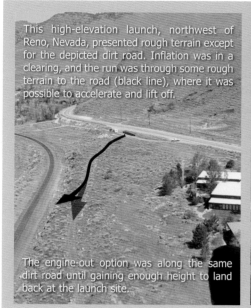

This high-elevation launch, northwest of Reno, Nevada, presented rough terrain except for the depicted dirt road. Inflation was in a clearing, and the run was through some rough terrain to the road (black line), where it was possible to accelerate and lift off.

The engine-out option was along the same dirt road until gaining enough height to land back at the launch site.

An engine failure immediately after launch would have meant a swim. After launching, he circled up to gain altitude while maintaining the launch field as a landing option. Shallow water near shore would have allowed landing but that's still not ideal—it's hard to stay upright, even in shallow water.

Wally Hines is seen on approach, staying between the two buildings.

Any site that doesn't allow inflating into the wind will be tougher (like roads), but it can be managed. The skills described in Chapter 15 will be helpful. Be leery of wind shadow—if the site is surrounded by high obstructions you'll be hard pressed to tell what the winds are doing up higher, and powerful turbulence may lurk in the transition.

Steering the Launch

Being able to steer while running or walking with the wing overhead is key to success in tight locations. It allows launch from places that require a turn before liftoff, such as an L shaped or obstructed field. This is useful elsewhere, too. You can avoid obstacles, like another flyer or his gear, without having to abort. It can let you inflate into the wind, then turn, then finish the takeoff in a better direction like a crosswind runway.

Steering with the wing overhead is easy to practice. Go out on a mildly breezy day and start to launch but don't actually take off. You'll be powering forward while keeping the wing overhead and walking briskly (or slowly in a stronger wind). The goal is learning how to steer the wing without looking up at it. Get it going where you want, then follow it. If it's gusty your walking speed represents a steady wind component so don't dawdle.

Remember, the wing has momentum, too. If you and the wing are angling to the right and *you* stop, the wing will keep going right. You must lead it—while walking right, pull left brake to stop the wing; take a few more steps, then *you* can stop and the wing will drift overhead. Obviously getting the brake input and movements down for that to happen will take practice.

While facing forward, learn to *feel* where the wing is without looking. Only look at it when necessary, especially while figuring out the feel. Walk forward enough to keep sufficient airspeed—you should feel the lines tugging just a bit. When the glider drifts off to one side, use just enough brake to bring it back overhead.

Here's another example about leading with the wing. To go left, get the wing going

⚠ Caution!

Never choose a site that requires the motor's continued operation to clear obstacles. Always ensure that if it quits at any point, you can land safely.

left first, then follow it. You and the wing are now going left. When you want to stop going left, pull right brake while still walking left. When the wing gets slightly to your right, but is still barely moving left, stop—momentum will carry it a few more feet, drifting to be overhead.

The goal is to steer *primarily* with the brakes. Move left or right if needed to keep the wing up, but strive to use *only* the brakes. This will improve success in areas where you don't have much room to move around.

Another skill that improves feel is controlling the wing with *only* your body (no brakes). It's difficult but will help gain understanding for how the wing reacts to being offset. Walk left to get it going right, then follow it. You'll quickly learn to use small motions, and how much to *lead* the wing with your movements.

As wind gets lighter, these exercises get harder, but are certainly doable. You can even practice in no wind but it's too tiring to last—it takes a lot of running to keep the wing up with enough feel to be helpful.

Climbing Out

The climbout should always allow a return to the field until you're high enough to circle back. If the field is surrounded by obstructions, climb out on the inside edge so that if the motor quits you can turn towards landable surface. Avoid high climb angles for the first 30 feet or so lest a motor failure swing you into the ground.

If possible, plan turns in the motor's normal torque-turn direction.

Landing Pattern

Tight spaces sometimes require different landing patterns. Fly it as standard as possible but realize that odd field shapes can dictate odd patterns. Plan it into the wind and away from rotor as much as possible.

An obstacle-lined field will require your final descent to follow the contour of obstacles. In the tree-lined field shown lower right, you would plan your descent to be just inside the trees, ending with a short final into the wind. Be careful not to snag a wingtip in the trees—a surprisingly easy, potentially lethal mistake.

Dealing with Winds—Using Power

In turbulent conditions it is beneficial to keep the power on. Even if you need to get into a tight space, the value of having thrust available outweighs the chance of breaking a prop on landing. And it's not just to enable a go around—it can salvage what would otherwise be a very hard arrival.

Providing there is room, come up slightly on the power just before touchdown to shallow the descent. In a tight space, wait until you're within 10 feet of the ground or so. This will also "spool up" the motor enough to have instant throttle response if necessary. That will leave you better prepared for a downward gust while landing.

If everything goes well and you do *not* get dumped, then do a nor-

Water is bad; every launch should be planned so as to stay dry if the engine fails.

This launch, from a private park in Florida, shows how the pilot kept his options open. The numbered paths are where he would have gone after an engine-out.

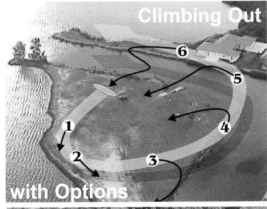

This is obviously an emergency landing. Plan your approach to touch down as far as possible from rotor-causing obstacles. You'll have to hug the edge of the field but don't get too close—hitting a tree up high is far worse than hitting rotor turbulence down low.

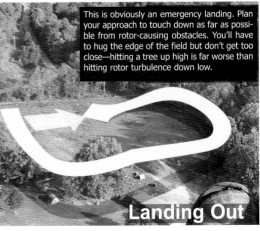

Effect of Brakes on Glide

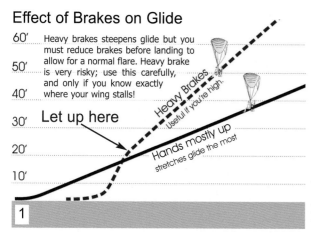

60'
50'
40'
30' Let up here
20'
10'

Heavy brakes steepens glide but you must reduce brakes before landing to allow for a normal flare. Heavy brake is very risky; use this carefully, and only if you know exactly where your wing stalls!

Heavy Brakes. Useful if you're high.

Hands mostly up stretches glide the most

1

Effect of Wind Gradient on Glide

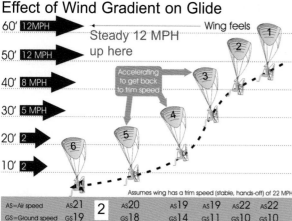

60' 12MPH   Wing feels   1
50' 12MPH   Steady 12 MPH   2
                  up here
40' 8MPH   3
       Accelerating
       to get back
       to trim speed
30' 5MPH   4
20' 2   5
10' 2   6

Assumes wing has a trim speed (stable, hands-off) of 22 MPH

| AS=Air speed | AS21 | 2 | AS20 | AS19 | AS19 | AS22 | AS22 |
| GS=Ground speed | GS19 | | GS18 | GS14 | GS11 | GS10 | GS10 |

1. Pulling brakes can steepen glide if you get too high but don't stall.

2. Chapter 5 introduced wind gradient effects during landing. To understand them better, this shows what would happen if no brake was applied. You can see why it's even more important to be hands nearly up by 50 feet so you have flare authority.

When dropping into a decreasing headwind, airspeed slows, causing a dive as the wing seeks to regain trim speed. A high (200 foot or more), gradual gradient improves glide, but a small, strong gradient will dump you early, and possibly hard, as the wing dives aggressively.

mal flare and landing. In strong conditions, be quick to turn around and get the wing down while killing the motor.

This is something to practice long before it's needed. Become adept at making flawless power-on landings during smooth conditions, then practice them when it's a bit rougher.

Without power, a gust that swings you forward (and possibly up) will sap your airspeed followed by a drop and possibly hard landing. As *soon* as you feel the wing start going back, let up the brakes while preparing to dampen a forward surge. You may still have less flare authority so consider a squirt of power to regain lost speed and preserve brake authority for flare.

Spot Landing

Next to steering the launch, spot landing skill is what makes tight spaces manageable—consistently touching down within 25 feet of your target. Practice and master it from a large area where there is no consequence to missing. Don't do it for real until you're consistently nailing the spot with and without wind.

Come in with the motor idling but do *not* plan on using it. And don't fly over anything where a power loss would be a crash. Use turns if necessary to keep landable terrain available.

Fly a normal, but slightly tighter landing pattern to stay oriented and aware of altitudes. Vary the pattern as necessary to maintain safe landing options. Your goal is hitting a 75 to 100 foot final approach where you can accurately judge the crucial final glide. Use S-turns on final, if necessary, to bleed off excess altitude but be level by about 50 feet—less as you gain skill.

If the touchdown area is small and obstructed, consider using heavier brake application to slow down and steepen the glide (see Figure 1 upper left). Be *extremely* careful though—you'll be closer to a stall and have very little extra speed to maneuver with. Once the wing is slowed there is nothing more you can do with those brakes; it's too close to stall or spin. Practice this where a spot landing is *not* required and the surface is forgiving. Avoid turbulence. Be ready to recover from an incipient (beginning) stall or spin by immediately reducing brake followed by powering up to half. Recover at the first feel of limp brakes or airspeed decrease.

Judging glide is an important skill that must be mastered. Practice this judgment (or envision it) during your next approach in smooth air. Put a foot up so that it visually touches where you think your touchdown point will be. If your foot starts to pass over the spot then you're high; lift it up a bit to reflect the better glide. If your foot sinks below the spot then you're low and would land short. Move your foot down to reflect the steeper descent. Once the spot is no longer moving up or down, that is your aim line; it is where you'll touch down if nothing changes.

With any headwind at all, glide is extended by letting the brakes up and steepened by pulling more brakes. As the wind gets stronger you'll need to plan a steeper approach. Be ever mindful of pulling too much brake—pilots have been seriously hurt when they were high and stalled or spun after pulling too much brake.

Once below about 30-50 feet (lower as skill allows), avoid turns. Manage the aim line (glide angle) so that it stays on the target. Fortunately you can change your glide angle but only so much.

Until you gain experience, forget the spot below about 30 feet and concentrate on touchdown quality, not location. Increase your speed (hands mostly up) to allow for a full flare. You'll briefly dive as the wing accelerates. Improving skill will let you concentrate longer on making the spot—staying on the brakes longer when necessary. That will, however, sacrifice flare authority and must be timed *very* precisely. Flaring from more than half-brake (pressure 3) is almost useless; you will just whack hard. There must be enough brake authority to cause *some* forward swing which is what actually slows your descent.

More headwind means worse glide—speed up to go farther (penetrate). Above 100 feet, go trimmers fast, pause, then push smoothly on the speedbar. You'll drop initially then glide will improve. Avoid pressing speedbar at the same time you let off the brakes which makes a front tuck more likely.

Holding a lot of brake (don't stall it) steepens glide after you initially apply the brakes. Leave enough altitude to re-build airspeed for the flare—a landing from this slowed condition is less predictable and may be painfully hard.

Flapping is another technique for descending steeply without stalling. The pilot repeatedly snatches heavy brakes, then releases them in a "flapping" motion. It doesn't *prevent* a stall, it just insures that the wing sees some time without brake input while creating enormous drag. Regardless of technique, pulling heavy brakes like this adds extra risk for a stall or spin.

Spot Landing Pattern

The pattern is flown tighter to reduce the effect of changing winds and thermals.

Go to brake position/pressure 3 after turning base leg. That way you can extend glide by reducing brakes. By 20 feet you must be concentrating on the flare, regardless of the spot. Land wing level even if you're not going right into the wind.

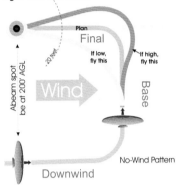

Spot Landing Last 100'

This technique is for hitting an exact spot such as a frisbee—it's riskier than a normal landing so be careful. To make it safer, allow more room for error and avoid brake extremes.

If it's bumpy, don't use any more than brake pressure 3 or you'll risk hitting sink and having too little brake authority to arrest the drop.

The basic steps are:

1. Use a normal power-off landing pattern that is slightly high.

2. S-Turn on final to bleed off any excess height, but start the final glide with brakes around pressure 3.

3. Hands up to extend the glide if you get low; brakes to pressure 4 if you get high.

4. At about 30 feet, forget the spot and reduce brake pressure to regain speed for a normal flare and touchdown.

Spot Landing
The Last Hundred Feet

100'
90'
80' Don't expect to land and stop unless there
70' is some wind.
60'
50'
40'
30'
20'
10'

Aim Line

Energy Build

Slow/Steep Phase   Decelerate   Setup Phase

Level Off

Flare (Energy Loss)

Caution: *This technique carries extreme risk for stalling the wing or misjudging the level off. Either one would result in injuries at best. You must be very familiar with your wing's handling at large brake inputs before attempting this.*

1. Don't launch where you'll cross a road (or railroad) unless you have someone looking for traffic. In the heat of launch it would be easy to miss a vehicle from the side.

2. This beautiful slice of New Mexico sits over 6000 feet high, giving these para-campers a challenging launch. Off the road, scrub brush and general roughness make it difficult.

A small crosswind on a smooth surface may beat into-the-wind through difficult terrain.

Power-On Spot Landing over an Obstruction

If you're trying to make it into a really confined area, like the boxing ring below, here's how. Come in with power, be level or slightly below the obstruction (ropes), holding moderate brake pressure (about 3). A second or two before crossing the obstruction, pull more brake to swing your body forward and slightly up. Coming over the obstruction, throttle off and increase brake pressure to keep the wing behind you as you plunk down onto the target.

The approach is moderately slow, using a combination of power and brakes to hold altitude just a few feet high while keeping *some* brake authority to stop a drop and to flare. The reason for braking just before the obstruction is to swing your body out front, then, after crossing the obstruction, further braking keeps the wing behind you, slowing to touchdown.

Mis-timing this would be painful, so practice with imaginary fences on soft targets. Beaches are perfect. Be proficient before trying it somewhere hard or important. A motor with rapid response time is helpful since, with all that brake pulled, you'll need throttle to control height.

Choose the slowest wing possible to improve your odds, and be careful!

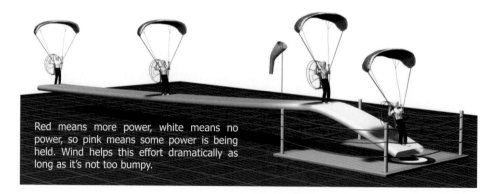

Red means more power, white means no power, so pink means some power is being held. Wind helps this effort dramatically as long as it's not too bumpy.

by Ryan Shaw

Advanced Maneuvers

Maneuvers serve various purposes: losing altitude, changing flight path, skill enhancement, demonstration, and just plain fun. But danger abounds; the more extreme, the more risk. Before doing anything steep, we strongly recommend a special *maneuvers clinic*, sometimes called an *SIV* course (Simulation d'Incident en Vol - simulated incidence in flight). Don't try them on your own since they may become un-recoverable. You can do the course as soon as you're comfortable with basic launching and landing skills, but it's more meaningful if you have at least 100 flights. Courses teach the latest methods for recovering from unusual situations and, more importantly, let you practice them in a safer, more controlled environment.

Techniques do change with technology. What you read here, or even learn in a clinic may become dated as knowledge and gear improve. Experts acknowledge that they are always learning better methods to fly and train. Ask instructors and respected pilots about the latest wrinkles.

Inducing wing malfunctions outside of a clinic is risky. Whenever going steeper than normal flight or flying in turbulence, make sure you have a suitable reserve and know how to use it (see Chapter 12, 4).

Aerobatics such as loops, rolls, helicopters, SAT's, and such are maneuvers intended for show. Only the most risk-tolerant souls should consider attempting them and then only with the highest level of training—be ready for reserve rides!

Advanced maneuvers are best learned in a free flight harness first to reduce the chance of getting tangled in the cage. Plus, the paramotor complicates matters by adding twisting mass (possibly causing severe riser twists). If the extreme risk of a motor is to be accepted, at least have the propeller stopped before trying anything.

by Carl McCall

> ⚠ **Caution!**
>
> The Department of Obvious Risk warns: seek proper guidance from a qualified, experienced instructor before attempting any steep maneuver! Limbs, life, and significant others will thank you.

1. It's in the hips. This is a low hook-in machine with pivoting arms. Weight shift comes from some whole-unit tilt and some pivoting bar action.

2. Machines with high hook-ins like this are weight-shifted mostly by lowering one leg on the turn side. That pulls the harness webbing down, which lowers the attached riser.

Weight Shift Turns

This isn't an advanced maneuver but is included here because it's not intuitive on all machines. Weight shift steering is helpful in precision flying but is not necessary.

Weight shift is where you move in the harness so that one riser goes up while the other goes down, starting a small turn towards the lowered riser. It gets the wing moving in the desired direction so brake input can be more effective. The whole goal is riser shift. Body contorting and leg swinging may look cool, but if the risers don't shift, the wing will not be impressed.

Use weight shift to begin a turn, *then* apply brake. As the bank increases, pull slight outside brake pressure to reduce diving tendency and prevent collapse of the outside tip. This *coordinated turn* allows faster entry into banks since less total brake is required (more valuable if you're soaring or competing). Combining weight shift with medium brakes will induce a turn as quickly as heavy brakes alone but with less risk for spinning.

High Hook-Ins

High hook-in models have less weight shift than low but it can be significantly improved with a moving bar or sliding straps in front of the J-bar. Fixed, over-the-shoulder J-bars have the least amount.

Pilot technique varies but the effect must be the same: differential riser shift.

On high hook-in systems, the pilot pushes one leg down to push that side of the seat down which lowers its attached webbing and riser—right leg down to turn right. On units with ground handling (shoulder) straps even more weight shift may be possible by pushing your shoulder against the strap while pushing down the leg. Experiment to find what works best on your unit.

The harness's chest strap and anti-torque strap (if equipped) should be fairly loose for best weight shift. Tighten them back up, as needed, before landing.

Low Hook-Ins

Low hook-in models generally have the best weight shift. A very few models require tilting the entire machine left or right, more like a free flight harness. Pivoting bars provide about half the riser movement, tilting does the rest. On these machines, you lean, shift your hips, and throw your weight over to one side. This is made easier because the center of gravity is so close to the attachment points, although most machines now incorporate geometry that raises the pivot point through S-arms or something similar.

Machines with low hook-ins but no moving arms will likely have less weight shift, especially if the center of mass is below the hook-in point. Even just a few inches lower sacrifices weight shift ability. Check with the maker or an experienced pilot who knows the model.

Some pilots of low hook-in motors cross their legs when turning, putting the high-side leg over which makes it easier to hold for a longer time, but it doesn't improve the turn. It can also serve as a signal to nearby pilots that you are about to turn which adds value to the "lean" in "look, lean, then turn."

Speedbar Usage

Our craft isn't known for speed but we can hasten it up with the speed system, especially on reflex wings. Be careful, though: non-reflexed models are more susceptible to a front collapse and reflexed models must be flown a certain way. Apply speedbar slowly while adding power at the same rate to fly level. If combining speedbar with trimmers; let out the trimmers first, wait a second, then apply speedbar. And keep your hands on the brakes while accelerating, ready for action.

Most maneuvers have more severe consequences if things go wrong while accelerated (trimmers fast, speedbar engaged). Adding speedbar to sporty handling, highly loaded wings can have eye-popping results. On non-reflex wings, avoid speedbar use in bumpy air or less than about 100 feet AGL. On most reflex wings, speedbar should only be used while trimmed fast and without using the main brakes.

It takes significant leg-push to keep the speedbar engaged. That's good on standard gliders because it can be released quickly, restoring the wing to normal flight if rough air is encountered. Trimmers, however, take longer to reach and require that your hands release brake pressure—not good in turbulence.

More advanced wings may come with a Speedbar/Trimmer Interconnect (STI – see Chapter 20, 26) aka PK System. When hooked up, it puts both trimmer control and speedbar at your toe tips. Use it gingerly, especially in any maneuver that involves feeling light in the seat.

Maneuvers Course

Well-coached maneuvers clinics help rehearse extreme situations and how your wing behaves in them. Flights are almost always done over water, in good air, after getting towed up a couple thousand feet by boat. The tow operator and helpers must be extremely competent. Take this very seriously, a water impact at high speed can be fatal. Clinics won't make you an expert—they merely give you some tools. Pilots have died after going home, then trying the maneuvers on their own, over land and without coaching. Weather conditions play a big part too; a recovery learned in smooth air may go much differently in turbulence.

Proper and rapid recovery from many maladies requires correct, decisive reactions

1. Getting ready to engage the speedbar from its retracted position.

The green line shows a better pulley position and routing. Line tension should be aligned with the risers as much as possible, not pulling them forward. The line should be routed closer to your hips to avoid squeezing the seat upwards when pushing the speedbar.

2. Fully accelerated. It also shows another possible pulley arrangement that may be more comfortable (green line and pulleys).

3. Pilot's-eye view of extended speedbar.

Speedbar *setup* is in Chapter 12

Having the pulley closer to your hips and secured to the frame will likely be more comfortable.

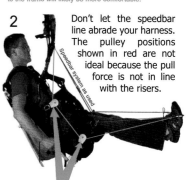

Don't let the speedbar line abrade your harness. The pulley positions shown in red are not ideal because the pull force is not in line with the risers.

TWO Pulleys will help keep pull force more in line with the risers but they will want to squeeze together.

that, if done at the wrong time, can make matters worse. Keep in mind that accident reports show most control-related mishaps in paramotors result from *too much brake*. If in doubt, reduce brake input; then steer. Certified gliders are designed to return to normal flight with *no* input from the pilot in most cases, spiral dives being an important exception. More on that shortly.

Descent Techniques

As with all maneuvers, do these under the guidance of an instructor first!

Start the following descent methods with trimmers neutral, usually full slow, unless told otherwise. Power should be off with the propeller stopped or windmilling. Build up gradually, starting out shallow and increasing very, very slowly.

This adds stress to individual sets of lines. If done repeatedly, your glider may wear out faster and should be inspected more frequently (at least once per year).

Big Ears

Big Ears is a fairly benign technique that roughly doubles your normal descent rate. Combining Big Ears with speedbar (pull ears first, though), adds about 25% to that rate. Steer using weight shift, if available, and avoid adding power or brakes which increase the chance of entering parachutal stall. Stress increases on the center lines, which must support everything once the tips are pulled down. Forward speed stays about the same because while wing area is reduced, drag is increased.

Descent rate: Up to 800 FPM (4 m/s).

Entry: Reach up with palms facing outward (thumbs down) and pull the outermost A lines down. Twist the hand inward so that your palm faces you. It is easier if the wing is equipped with split A's like the one shown below.

Recovery: Let go of the A lines and do not pull any brake—see if the tips open on their own. Higher aspect ratio wings tend to recover slower and may even need a brief brake pull to pressure 1 or 2.

Spiral Dives, covered shortly, can be one of the more dangerous descent methods. An *Asymmetric Spiral*, where the pilot shallows out each revolution, is safer.

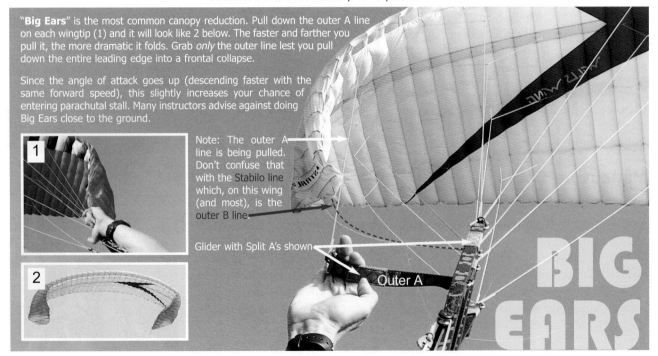

"**Big Ears**" is the most common canopy reduction. Pull down the outer A line on each wingtip (1) and it will look like 2 below. The faster and farther you pull it, the more dramatic it folds. Grab *only* the outer line lest you pull down the entire leading edge into a frontal collapse.

Since the angle of attack goes up (descending faster with the same forward speed), this slightly increases your chance of entering parachutal stall. Many instructors advise against doing Big Ears close to the ground.

Note: The outer A line is being pulled. Don't confuse that with the Stabilo line which, on this wing (and most), is the outer B line.

Glider with Split A's shown

Outer A

BIG EARS

B-Line Stall

A B-Line stall (fig. 1, next page) stops the wing's forward motion while leaving it fully inflated and descending vertically. Air spills equally around the leading and trailing edges. It stresses the B line attachment points so use it sparingly, especially if heavily loaded. And it's far more dramatic than Big Ears with more complications. For example, excessive pull may cause a front horseshoe and cravat on exit.

Descent rate: Up to 1600 FPM (8 m/s).

Entry: Reach up high on the B lines (quick links if possible) and pull them down to your shoulders with forearms upright. It will initially take a lot of force which decreases once established. The wing falls back abruptly (you swing forward), then settles overhead in a vertical descent. How far you pull the B's down depends on the wing and where you grabbed them.

More pull gives more descent but too much pull may cause a front horseshoe where the tips fly forward into a U shape. If that happens, immediately let your hands up slightly.

Recovery: Let up on the B lines *quickly* and *evenly,* but don't just let go. Some instructors recommend letting up slowly, but that may cause a parachutal stall and letting up unevenly may cause a spin. Also, let the wing get fully flying before applying any brakes—it will typically surge less than 45°.

Steep Turns

Pull one brake to pressure 2 and hold it. The glider banks some then shallows out a bit, remaining in the turn as long as you hold that pressure. Small or sporty gliders may keep getting steeper with that amount of brake, but we'll address the norm.

Pull more brake and it does that again—banking more, then mellowing back a bit. At some point, if you pull harder the bank *continues to steepen* (not coming back towards level). You're entering a steep turn. Once you feel pressed into the seat, those are G-forces building as the bank increases. Brake responsiveness and pressure increase. Reduce brake pressure to avoid going steeper and don't let it devolve into a spiral dive, the dangerous sibling of steep turns. Start out slowly.

Any turn causes more altitude loss (or requires more power) at steeper angles. A 60° bank is pretty steep—imparting 2 times the pull of gravity (2 G's) and requiring probably half-again more thrust. Much steeper than that is considered a spiral dive.

Descent rate: Up to 2000 FPM (10 m/s).

Entry: Initiate a turn and hold enough brake so that it gradually steepens to about 60°, then modulate the brakes to hold it there. It looks about like frame 2 at right. Enter into the turn gradually to avoid pulling the wing into a spin.

Recovery: Enormous energy builds up during a steep turn and must be managed. Remove the turn input and the bank should start leveling out. Once it *starts* doing so, be ready to re-apply a bit of inside brake to slow the recovery. Much of the risk comes during this level-out—your body and motor are travelling far faster than the wing and want to swing up into a steep climb, possibly followed by the lines going slack. That could result in severe collapses, cravats, or lines wrapping around the cage.

Spiral Dive (Symmetrical)

Spiral Dives are just steeper turns that result in a rapid descent (steeper than frame 2 at right). Beyond a certain point, many wings, including beginner models, will become "locked in" to an essentially vertical spiral. It can take strong opposite brake pressure to start the recovery (possibly two hands).

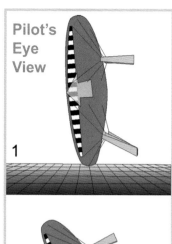

Pilot's Eye View

1

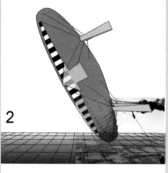

2

3

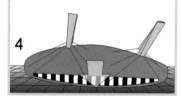

4

Banks 1 & 2 are steep turns, 3 would be considered a spiral dive. By the time a bank reaches 4, it may not be possible to recover. This "over-the-nose" spiral may inflict G-forces that prevent the pilot from even getting to his reserve.

⚠ **Caution!**
When initiating a turn, if pulling more brake does not cause more turn, don't pull more brake—you may spin the glider. Also, once you start coming out of a steep turn, don't try to go back into it; let it fully recover first.

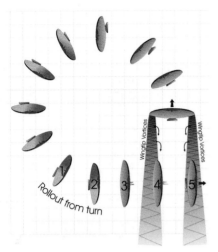

Once established, the heavily loaded wing is hyper-sensitive to brake input. You'll quickly get to 4 G's—enough to possibly black out. It has happened numerous times where a pilot blacks out and spirals into an unforgiving Earth. Vertigo, where the pilot gets disoriented to the point of not knowing what brake to pull, is also a possibility. Think about recovery *before* starting the dive.

In rare situations, these can become unrecoverable. For one, this *over-the-nose* spiral is enormously disorienting. Besides vertigo, your body is going to the left and the wing is rocketing right (or vice-versa), possibly confusing which brake to pull. Plus, high G's can prevent deploying a reserve.

Descent rate: Up to 5000 FPM (25 m/s).

Entry: Note the direction. Weight shift (if able), then pull enough brake to keep the bank increasing. You may have to start with a wingover the other way first. Build slowly, taking an entire 360° turn to get into the spiral—too much brake can cause a spin.

Recovery: Remove any weight shift, put both hands up and let it start rolling out. If it doesn't start right away, pull both brakes some then opposite brake. As soon as it *starts* recovering, let up. If it's leveling off quickly, ease in some inside brake (in the direction you're turning) to dampen recovery.

The steepest spirals may require weight shift and *heavy* opposite brake to start the recovery.

Think about the spiral in advance. With your body whistling earthward and G's building, the recovery direction may not be obvious. In a right spiral, for example, your body is swinging left while the wing races rightward. Remember that you used right brake to enter, little or no brake to stay in it, and will need left brake to initiate the recovery (if just going hands up doesn't work). Then use right brake to slow the rollout.

An **Asymmetric Spiral** is a spiral that's shallowed out a bit on each revolution. It's safer because the chance of "locking in" is lessened. G-load decreases in the shallow portion but high-G's on the steep part makes it very sensitive to inputs and the pilot can quickly get slack lines on the shallow part if not careful. Solid active flying skills or competent coaching are a must.

Recovery is just like a regular spiral but less extreme. Like all these maneuvers, there's a lot more than this can cover.

Level Steep Turns

Steep, level turns produce a powerful wake due to high wing loading when banked. If you roll out just before hitting it, the wing wants to go back, then surge overhead, unloading a bit. That's when you're vulnerable to a collapse.

These steps will help prevent that.

1) Initiate rollout by reducing left brake. Once it starts leveling out, reduce power and reapply some left brake pressure to slow the rollout.

2) There will still be some climb, topping out at about point 4. As the wing surges forward into a descent, add some brakes and power. They must be added when the glider *starts* surging forward.

During the rollout always keep some pressure (2 to 3) on both brakes in anticipation of going through the wake.

Staying in the bank is another way to keep the wing more heavily loaded and therefore collapse resistant. Consider climbing to avoid the wake altogether.

During a symmetrical, steep, level turn, the wing vortices should remain outside your flight path.

B-Line Stall

Full Stall

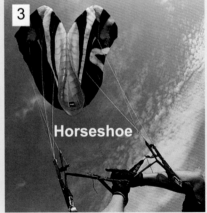
Horseshoe

Wing Malfunctions

Bad stuff happens, especially to those who push the limits of weather, skills, or both. Maneuvers clinics are good, but avoiding nasty conditions is even better. Inducing these on your own can prove fatal, especially without proper training.

Parachutal Stall is covered in Chapter 4 under Emergencies.

The standard response to unknown situations is: smoothly "**reduce brakes, reduce power, then steer**." If you're near terrain use *just* enough brake to steer away. Look up at the wing to see what has happened; then look back at the horizon to stay oriented. Again, *too much* brake causes more problems for motor pilots than not enough. For sure do what it takes, but be mindful of over controlling.

Turbulence can play havoc on recovery so even if you've practiced, don't expect it to always go the same way in rough air.

Cravat

Chapter 4 covered small, milder cravats—large ones can be way worse. A 60% clean wing fold is quite manageable, whereas a mere 30% fold, when tucked against the lines in a cravat, can be deadly. The same is true if a wing half folds down against the lines but doesn't get stuck. It presents a huge resistance, pushing that side of the wing into an abrupt, plunging, spiral dive. Reserve or not, this is bad.

Cravats are frequently complications of collapses from turbulence or botched maneuvers. Once you are in the spiral, G-forces build rapidly, making recovery difficult or impossible. Tossing your reserve may be all that's left—but do it quickly, especially down low. Otherwise do what you can to stop the spiral. If you can find the stabilo line, pull it hard, hand over hand if necessary. If you can't find it, use whatever opposite brake it takes.

Spin

Spins are another malady caused by excessive brake pull. If it's uneven pull, especially against the motor's torque, part of the wing stalls while the rest keeps flying. The glider slows then rotates nearly overhead as you descend. A riser twist is possible as the pilot tries to catch up to the spinning wing, potentially locking the brakes in place and preventing recovery.

If you feel any unusual slowing or turning, reduce power and brakes immediately! Most pilots won't detect the spin until it's already spun half way around; that's why prevention is so important.

Descent rate: Around 1200 FPM (6 m/s).

Cause: Uneven heavy braking, especially in turbulence or against the torque. If you're pulling both brakes heavily, like on a spot landing, and let up on *one* brake, it can cause a spin in the other direction since that slows down the other side slightly.

Recovery: Reduce power, reduce brakes immediately, and prepare to dampen the surge. If you get a riser twist, and you're in

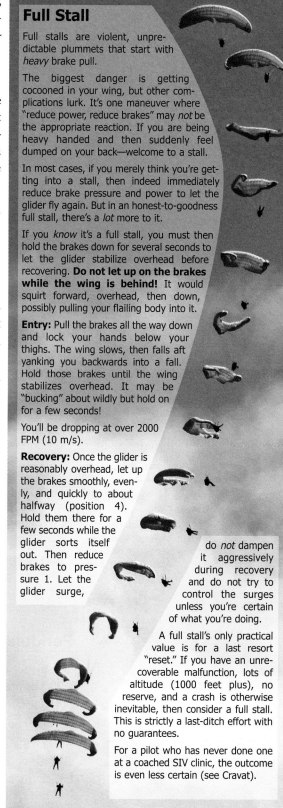

Full Stall

Full stalls are violent, unpredictable plummets that start with *heavy* brake pull.

The biggest danger is getting cocooned in your wing, but other complications lurk. It's one maneuver where "reduce power, reduce brakes" may *not* be the appropriate reaction. If you are being heavy handed and then suddenly feel dumped on your back—welcome to a stall.

In most cases, if you merely think you're getting into a stall, then indeed immediately reduce brake pressure and power to let the glider fly again. But in an honest-to-goodness full stall, there's a *lot* more to it.

If you *know* it's a full stall, you must then hold the brakes down for several seconds to let the glider stabilize overhead before recovering. **Do not let up on the brakes while the wing is behind!** It would squirt forward, overhead, then down, possibly pulling your flailing body into it.

Entry: Pull the brakes all the way down and lock your hands below your thighs. The wing slows, then falls aft yanking you backwards into a fall. Hold those brakes until the wing stabilizes overhead. It may be "bucking" about wildly but hold on for a few seconds!

You'll be dropping at over 2000 FPM (10 m/s).

Recovery: Once the glider is reasonably overhead, let up the brakes smoothly, evenly, and quickly to about halfway (position 4). Hold them there for a few seconds while the glider sorts itself out. Then reduce brakes to pressure 1. Let the glider surge, do *not* dampen it aggressively during recovery and do not try to control the surges unless you're certain of what you're doing.

A full stall's only practical value is for a last resort "reset." If you have an unrecoverable malfunction, lots of altitude (1000 feet plus), no reserve, and a crash is otherwise inevitable, then consider a full stall. This is strictly a last-ditch effort with no guarantees.

For a pilot who has never done one at a coached SIV clinic, the outcome is even less certain (see Cravat).

1. Pulling the right A riser down hard caused this 60% collapse. Even with that, it's completely controllable:

- Pull just enough left brake (the inflated side) and weight shift left to keep it flying straight.

- Don't pull too hard lest it spin or stall. You'll normally be at position/pressure 3 or less to go straight. In this case, the right hand will be limp; let it go down until it feels about pressure 1.

- Long pumps of the deflated side may help after you have *some* speed and a safe heading.

2. Pulling down all the A's caused this frontal.

A downward gust of wind has the same effect but will be less predictable. On beginner wings recovery is usually quick, even with no pilot input.

a low hook-in machine, you may be able to reach *above* the twist and pull outward to help untwist yourself. Be aware of altitude and know where the reserve is.

Asymmetric Collapse

Remember that what nature doles out can be far worse than what you induce. A big asymmetric collapse may cause a violent bank, dropping you towards the collapsed side as it erupts into a diving turn (more collapse, more turn). Don't just start yanking on things, but carefully do what it takes to prevent a spiral.

Descent rate: From 600 FPM (3 m/s) to 1000 FPM (5 m/s).

Cause: Turbulence. It can be simulated by reaching up high on one A riser (or both parts of a split A) and pulling down slowly. A faster (harder) pull will collapse more wing—be careful, a fast pull can cause a big (70%+) fold.

This has also happened to students who inadvertently grabbed a riser while trying to get in the seat.

Recovery: If possible, steer using weight shift and *careful* brake pressure on the open side. As always, too much brake risks a stall or spin. The deflated side will probably be limp, but as soon as pressure builds (the collapse starts coming out), let that hand come up while keeping some pressure (about pressure 2). Consider "pumping" the deflated side by using long brake pulls. "Accelerate briefly, steer, *then* clear" (by pumping) the collapse.

Pilots usually make matters worse by pulling too much brakes; be careful.

Frontal Collapse

A *frontal*, or *front tuck*, results from the leading edge being forced downward, closing off the cells. You drop and the wing falls back, normally followed by a quick recovery with no pilot input.

Descent rate: Up to 1000 FPM (5 m/s).

Cause: A sudden and strong forward surge of the wing, like from a bad maneuver recovery or turbulence, especially a strong downward gust.

Aggressively applying speedbar while at fast trim *and* letting off the throttle can also cause the wing to rocket forward enough to frontal. It is more likely when trimmed fast.

Using main brakes while in reflex mode on most reflex wings can also cause a frontal, especially in turbulence.

Recovery: Release the speedbar, if engaged, and "tap" the brakes if needed (to about pressure 2). Let it surge forward to get the glider flying before adding more brake which could cause a parachutal stall (also called constant stall). If *that* happens, reduce power, reduce brakes, then steer and recover as described in Chapter 4.

Pendular Control

Wingovers and surges are foundational maneuvers for anyone wanting to move into acro but are extremely risky when pushed too hard. Start off gently and without power. Rehearse the reserve deployment sequence in your mind just in case things go awry.

Stay up high and never get so steep that the wing unloads (you feel light in the seat). Also, keep *some* brake pressure on to reduce the likelihood of a front tuck or collapse. Once you've really mastered this level of control, it will help you handle turbulence too. As always, fly by brake pressure, not position. Let the brakes "float" at a given pressure instead of holding them rigidly. Your hands may move a fair amount (lots of brake *travel*) even though the pressure is relatively low.

Wingovers

Wingovers are sequential turns done at the glider's natural pendular rate. Start with left turn input (weight shift if able, then brake to pressure two) and hold for one second, then let up. As your body crests and *starts* coming back, apply right turn input, holding it for two seconds, then release. Smaller wings require less time due to their shorter lines. Adjust the timing for maximum effect.

Just like a swing set, you don't need *much* input, it just has to be at the right *time*. Controls get more responsive at the bottom of each swing due to increased G load. At 2 G's, a 200 pound pilot/paramotor feels like 400 pounds at the wing.

Use some outside brake at the end of each swing and be prepared for the wing to twist you slightly outward too. This is a great exercise to learn pendular control but build slowly; it can get too steep quickly.

Recover to level by using the opposite actions.

Finesse requires using both brakes at times to prevent the tips from curling up or collapsing. If the tips *are* folding in periodically, you're probably not using enough outside brake. Always keep some brake pressure throughout, especially on the ends when you're less loaded. And don't let the glider get too far ahead.

Fore/Aft Pendulums (Surge and Retreats)

Add power and pull brakes to pressure 2 for two seconds then let off. You'll swing out forward as the wing falls back. Then you'll swing back under the wing. When your body starts swinging forward again, gingerly add power and brake for a second, then let off. Like on a swing set, you'll gradually get steeper and steeper. *Build slowly!* Practice stopping the maneuver quickly. Like the swing, you want to build instinct for how to dampen these pendular actions.

Big wingovers tend to look like figure eights with the ends raised. Heading changes a lot while continually adjusting the turn using fine inputs.

Another characteristic of wingovers is a little twist at the steepest bank. The wing turns quicker than you because of your rotational inertia and propeller forces. Heavy motors or carts make this more noticeable.

Wing briefly turns faster than you do here.

At this steepness a mistake is very unforgiving. Twists, collapses and line tangles are possible.

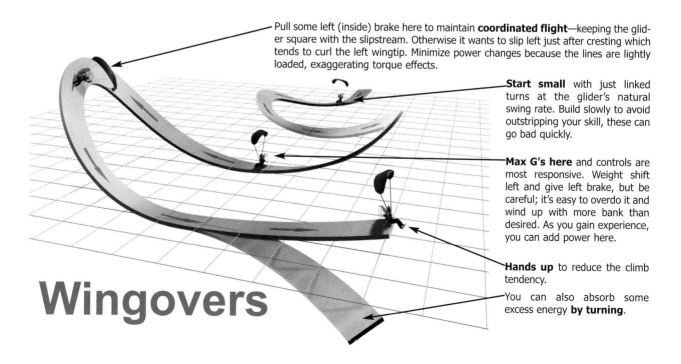

Pull some left (inside) brake here to maintain **coordinated flight**—keeping the glider square with the slipstream. Otherwise it wants to slip left just after cresting which tends to curl the left wingtip. Minimize power changes because the lines are lightly loaded, exaggerating torque effects.

Start small with just linked turns at the glider's natural swing rate. Build slowly to avoid outstripping your skill, these can go bad quickly.

Max G's here and controls are most responsive. Weight shift left and give left brake, but be careful; it's easy to overdo it and wind up with more bank than desired. As you gain experience, you can add power here.

Hands up to reduce the climb tendency.

You can also absorb some excess energy **by turning**.

Wingovers

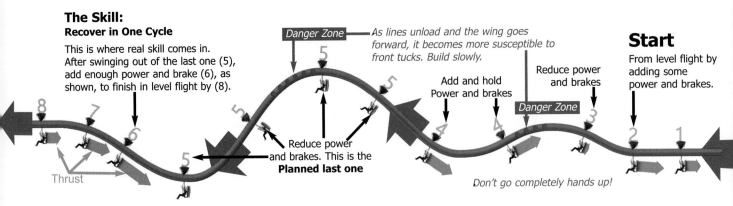

The Skill:
Recover in One Cycle

This is where real skill comes in. After swinging out of the last one (5), add enough power and brake (6), as shown, to finish in level flight by (8).

Danger Zone — As lines unload and the wing goes forward, it becomes more susceptible to front tucks. Build slowly.

Start
From level flight by adding some power and brakes.

Add and hold Power and brakes

Reduce power and brakes

Danger Zone

Reduce power and brakes. This is the **Planned last one**

Thrust

Don't go completely hands up!

Surge & Retreat

Like any maneuver, as the wing surges farther forward, it gets closer to front tucking, possibly only one side. To reduce this possibility, be mellow and always keep *some* pressure on the brakes to ensure there is fore/aft tension on the wing fabric.

Also, never get so steep that you feel near weightless in your seat. That puts you perilously close to unloading the lines and taking a major collapse. Also, avoid using both power *and* brakes until you're very experienced.

Tip Line (Stabilo) Line Pull

The stabilo line is the outermost B or C line that goes to the tip and is often a different color. Its importance lies in clearing cravats, discussed earlier.

While kiting, practice finding the stabilo line after inducing a tip collapse—it can be hard to locate with other lines draped around it. Then do the same in flight by pulling an outer A line down slowly (makes one "big ear") and watching what happens with the stabilo line, so you'll know where it is when you need to use it.

Tip Line (Stabilo)

1. This moderately steep wingover shows why it's so important to use brake *pressure,* not position. The wing is unloaded and surging forward. Heavy trailing edge deflection shows lots of brake *travel,* a necessity here, but not much *pressure.* Without this input, the wing would likely take a collapse (frontal or asymmetric).

As soon as the wing starts loading up, the brakes will want to come back up. Let them! Keep the brake pressure on, and your hands will return to a nearly full-up position. Holding them against an increasing pressure may lead to a stall or spin.

2. A *frontal collapse* is induced by pulling down both A's. Recovery is normally quick when the A's are released. Most wings come out on their own, but some may require a tug (position/pressure 2) on the brakes. On some wings this can result in a front horseshoe where the wing tips come forward.

Risk
Management

19

We're fortunate that most mistakes in paramotoring have already been made. And even more fortunate that we know how to prevent them.

A lot can be learned from the airlines which have achieved remarkable safety by analyzing accidents to develop better hardware and procedures. Success has turned an inherently dangerous operation (flying jet airplanes at ridiculous speeds) into the safest form of transportation ever devised. This chapter and, in fact, much of the book, aims to do the same for powered paragliding.

The familiar saying, "It's as safe as you make it," is especially true for us since nearly all risk comes from pilot action, not equipment failures or other peoples' actions. Enormous risk can be avoided through behavior changes and an intelligent application of knowledge. It's sad enough when tragedy hits known risk takers, but seems so unnecessary when it's from ignorance.

Probability and Severity

Some behaviors increase the *probability* of an accident and some increase the *severity*. For example, foregoing maintenance on your gear, using really old fuel, or ignoring fuel quantity, all increase the *probability* of a motor failure. Flying beyond the reach of a safe landing site increases the *severity* if it does happen. Each probability has a related severity which changes throughout a flight.

Another good example is flying without a helmet. The probability of a mishap is no higher but the severity sure is. Just like seat belts in a car — they don't prevent the accident, they just lessen its horrific consequence.

Some actions increase both probability and severity. Doing foot drags in deep water

Low over water, steep and with no helmet? He *has* built up to this very slowly, and has flotation, but the risk meters (next page) are still high.

Everybody has a different idea of what it takes to have fun. Some ideas are vastly more dangerous than others but it's more about margins. This maneuver is risky no matter what but, for a new pilot, it would verge on suicidal.

Unlike other segments of microlight aviation, a catastrophic equipment failure is incredibly rare, far less than even general aviation. Pilot behavior and questionable weather conditions are where most risk comes from.

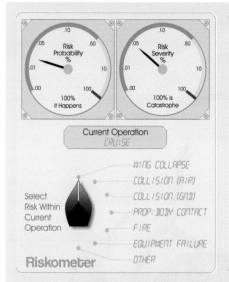 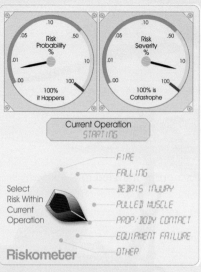

Gauging Probability & Severity

If we had risk gauges they might look like these—one for probability and another for severity. They would know the current operation (starting, takeoff, climb, cruise, etc.) and let you select the risk type for that operation then display its severity.

For example, the probability of a mishap while cruising along at 2000 feet AGL is minuscule. Select FIRE and the probability gauge would be near zero but with a high severity. Fire is extremely unlikely but it would be severe given the longish descent time.

Sitting next to your paramotor, the current operation would read PREFLIGHT and both needles would be 0. Starting the motor while standing in front of it moves both probability and severity needles way up since that has proven so risky. Once the motor is running and strapped on your back, both needles go back down to near zero—almost nobody gets hurt at this point.

Doing foot drags is interesting. Of course bad things can happen but the pilot doesn't have very far to fall. So, while the probability of a mishap is high (falling), the severity is low as long as the terrain is smooth and they're done into the wind. The probability goes way down for pilots experienced at foot dragging.

Both needles would frequently move in unison. For example, flying downwind, in the mechanical turbulence of large buildings or mountains increases both the probability and severity of a mishap. More wind, more risk.

Flying out of a tight field with surrounding corn yields a high probability of hitting the corn, but with low severity. While flying out of a tight tree-lined field is another matter given the severity of hitting a tree. Flying over water, beyond gliding range of land does not increase the probability of an engine failure, but its severity skyrockets (drowning) if you don't have flotation.

One common practice is to keep the severity reading low while letting the probability fluctuate. Maneuvers clinics (SIV courses) are this way. You'll induce serious things (like wing collapses) to learn proper reactions but, through careful preparation (rescue boat, pilot flotation, radio instructions, etc.) organizers keep the severity reasonably low. Frontal collapses, spins, asymmetric collapses and so forth are all induced over water, with a boat and safeguards in place to handle worst case scenarios.

is a good example—the chance of a motor failure increases due to water spray fouling the ignition and the severity increases due to the likelihood of drowning. Shallow water (less than 6 inches) carries the same increased probability but without the severity.

Energy and Injury

Our sport's overall safety comes mostly from its very low speed. Increasing the speed dramatically increases the injury potential, especially considering how exposed we are. Energy dissipated in a collision increases by the square of the speed, so doubling the speed quadruples the energy (and injury). For example, hitting something at 30 mph has four times the energy as hitting it at 15 mph, making it potentially lethal.

Anything that puts you in a high-energy state, especially near Earth's many protrusions, ramps up severity. That's why flying low and downwind or doing steep, low turns are so treacherous.

Getting Away With It

Why do I need to use a helmet anyway? Personal choice is a valued freedom but *know* your risk. Standard aviation safety practices—helmets, patterns, footgear, preflights, reserves, checklists, and so on, are layers of protection. Never accept the argument "such and such has never happened to me or anyone I know," that's a fallacy of small sample sizes.

Take helmets. They reduce injury from impacts to the cage, ground, and exploding props. How often does it happen? Not often, but it *does* happen and sometimes with fatal results. Quality footwear reduces the chance of injury from rough ground or prop strikes; at least one pilot avoided a prop-mangled foot because of his stout boots.

This sport is replete with examples of those who ignored common safety practices and it caught up with them. New people come in, forego collective wisdom or never learn it, succeed for a time and then consider the risk acceptable. Then it gets them. The worst thing we can do is assume that past success will continue in the face of bad practice. Fortunately, accidents are rare, but when they do happen it's usually to those taking chances most often. Relish our freedom but wield it knowingly.

Where the Risk Is

Here is where our highest risk lurks and some ways to minimize it. Always evaluate whether a planned activity is worth the possible consequence. What is the likelihood? How bad would it hurt, and is the reward worth it?

The top fatality risks are: 1) drowning, 2) training, 3) steep maneuvering low to the ground, especially spiral dives and extreme wingovers, and 4) weather-related wing folds/collapses. It's not the gear we should fear, it's ourselves.

Starting and Handling the Motor

Propellers are the most dangerous part of our sport for injures—especially during starting. Serious and permanent disabilities have disfigured those who lost sight of this fact.

It happens, even to conscientious pilots who, in a brief moment of inattentiveness, let the motor get away from them. Then whack! "Body contact with spinning propeller," as it's called by USPPA.org. These are rarely forgiving.

> *Always* inspect the throttle linkage before starting. *Do it every time*, insuring that the carburetor is at idle and throttle can't be increased accidentally.

Training

Training is already a risky time but poor or inadequate training ramps it up dramatically. Sadly, some won't even know it because they didn't read this.

Even *with good* training, the early stages are risky. Improve your odds by going tandem in *something before* soloing. The closer to a paramotor the better. Also, make sure your school uses a benign handling beginner wing to start and has you practice emergencies in a brake-equipped simulator (having full risers is better).

Towing (if used) is also risky but can be made much safer with a good instructor who uses appropriate precautions. Overall, instruction risk is reduced with the use

1. Good training with appropriate training aids, such as this riser-equipped simulator, helps prepare for both normal flight and in-flight emergencies. In the hands of a good instructor, it's invaluable.

2. Just because you've succeeded at a risky endeavor before doesn't make it safe. For example, you may fly low over wires all the time. But if a problem, such as misjudgment or motor failure does happen, it will have potentially dire consequences.

Nobody launches expecting to crash. Analyze the operation: is it late in the morning? Is there questionable weather? Has someone suggested not flying? Am I going to fly low? Am I wearing appropriate safety gear?

Testing New Gear

Trying or testing new equipment is risky; here are some ways to make it less so. Before flying, review the gear while hanging from a simulator with the owner or instructor present.

1. Note the attachment points. Low hook-ins will have a lower average brake position than higher hook-ins, possibly by a lot.

2. Find out where the harness adjustments are and how they should be set for takeoff, cruise and landing. Having this wrong could render an otherwise fine machine unsafe.

3. Operate the throttle, starter, and kill switch, especially if the throttle is in a different hand than you're used to. Locate the master switch and think of other ways to shut off the motor.

4. Prepare for the torque effect which may differ in both amount and direction. Belt driven machines twist left, causing a right bank, gear driven machines twist right, causing a left bank.

5. Learn any special instructions for getting into the seat. On some low attachment machines, brake toggles can get in the prop if released, especially while you're still hanging in the harness.

6. Find out what the wing's trimmer settings are for cruising, turbulence, launch and landing. Learn what special handling or procedures apply to the wing, especially if you plan to use the speed system.

This is the single most likely time to be seriously injured with a paramotor. See Chapter 4.

What Is The Risk?

Foot or cart launching a PPG is about the same risk as moderately aggressive skiing. You may get a twisted ankle, or its equivalent, but won't likely get a toe tag. Fatality rates appear to be similar to motorcycle riding based on the number of participant hours in both activities and the number of fatalities.

Unlike motorcycles though, we control more of our own risk. Good choices can make paramotoring much safer whereas motorcyclists depend more on the actions of others.

of a thorough, standardized syllabus, simulator work, a methodical approach, and appropriate location. Simulator rehearsal of emergency procedures helps you be prepared (see Chapter 4).

Intermediate Syndrome

Guard against Intermediate Syndrome, a common haunt of moderately experienced pilots. As skills improve they start taking on challenges beyond their ability.

Excelling at anything *will* put your skills to the test, but choose situations where failure isn't fatal. For example, take on higher winds to improve your skills, but choose places where getting dragged won't hurt.

Inappropriate Gear

Inappropriate gear or improper technique for that gear adds risk. Most equipment trade-offs are covered in Section VI but here are some common risks related to having inappropriate equipment.

• Excessive power for your weight increases the risk of riser twist and, to a lesser degree, makes falling more likely due to weight and torque. It can also increase the chance for a "face-plant."

• Insufficient power increases your risk of tripping during the extended run and will not allow a quick climb over surprise obstructions. Plus, the slow climb adds vulnerability to even small downdrafts after takeoff.

• Flying an advanced wing without a mastery of active piloting increases risk, especially if flown in conditions other than calm.

• Unduly small wings increase speed, lengthen the takeoff run, and make handling much more reactive, possibly leading to loss of control.

• Unduly large wings increase the chance for parachutal stall, collapse and slow speed may prevent penetration into a strong wind.

• Poor design (structurally weak, dangerous attributes, etc.) is always inappropriate. Seek out models that embrace safety features over those using older, less-safe technology. It's always a tradeoff—sometimes safety features get traded for other attributes. Talk to respected, experienced pilots who are familiar with various models and see "A Better Paramotor" in Chapter 27.

Steep Maneuvering & Aerobatics

Steep maneuvers at low altitude, especially those with a vertical component, have proven particularly lethal. Second only to drowning, they represent a quarter of all our fatalities.

It starts slowly, too. After gaining some experience pilots get braver, trying maneuvers beyond their skill and without instruction. Little banks graduate to steeper banks that become spiral dives. Little pendulums morph into wingovers, etc. Given the need for our soft wing to always be loaded, these maneuvers can go bad quickly. Plus, when the wing is heavily loaded (as in a steep turn), the controls become extremely sensitive—surprising pilots who get into large excursions following small inputs. Steep maneuvering also adds enormous speed, too. Remember energy and injury?

Becoming nearly weightless is *really* asking for it. Consider what happens when lines have no pressure with which to hold the glider into its gliderly shape. Worse yet, those loose lines can now find things to wrap around (including pilot parts) only to reload with a bang.

If done without instruction, and/or low to the ground, aerobatics are a terrible risk. Low-level maneuvering has been the final ingredient in a dangerous cocktail of risk for pilots who pushed too hard.

Low Flying

You can't hit something if you're above it. Almost all the airborne injuries happen while cruising or maneuvering down low. Not only is mechanical turbulence more likely, but there is less time to recover. Staying above 200 feet eliminates most risk.

Simple misjudgment of turns is aggravated by low flying. The distraction of nearby ground objects contributes to this, especially with any downwind component.

Wire strikes, even at slow speeds, are a big risk, with most injuries coming from the ensuing fall. Electrocution and burns have also happened. In most cases, the pilot was in a familiar area but just forgot about the wires, and didn't see them in time. At some angles they're essentially invisible.

If you can't resist flying low, these tips will help mitigate *some* of the risk:

- Avoid flying *downwind* down low. Higher ground speed makes any miscalculation, unexpected obstruction, motor failure, or collision far worse. There's less time to notice and react to obstructions.

- Fly into an area above 200 feet AGL and scout for obstructions before descending into the danger zone. Look for poles or their shadows and be suspicious of any straight lines (road edges, field edges, etc.) but, as the picture below shows, this is still no guarantee.

- As always, stay over landable terrain. This is even more important when flying down low because you won't have time to maneuver after a power failure.

- Respect power lines and other obstructions. Don't ever plan to climb over something if a power loss would leave you without options.

Approach wires at an angle so that you can quickly veer away if the motor quits or you get surprised by sinking air. Fly over the poles since the wires are difficult to judge height over. Be at least twice their height.

Wires don't stand out like they do from the ground where they're contrasted against a plain sky. From above, they can blend completely into the background, especially with a bit of haze. This was taken just before the pilot nearly wrapped himself up some cleverly hidden wires.

by Travis Burns

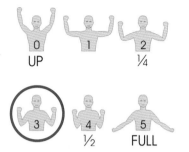

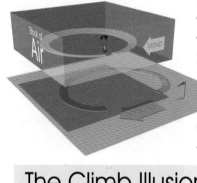

During climb, especially down low where these illusions are so powerful, avoid using brakes beyond pressure 3.

Think of 0 and 1 as the "Green zone," 2 and 3 as the "Yellow caution zone," and position 4 or more as the "Red danger Zone."

Downwind Operations, The "Demon"

To the paraglider itself, flying downwind is no different than flying upwind. The same for turning from upwind to downwind—it's no different. But talk to enough pilots and you'll eventually hear of the dreaded "downwind demon," a myth incorrectly suggesting that, when turning downwind, the air "hits the back of the wing, causing it to sink." It simply isn't so. Like a boat in a wide river, our craft operates in a fluid-like environment (the air) that is moving along over the ground. The best evidence is to go up high and do your turn. You'll see there is no difference whatsoever; in fact, it's hard to even know what the wind is doing up high. Look at the wake of a boat doing a nice, round 360° turn in the middle of a river—the whole circle is moving downstream but no part of the turn feels different to the boat driver.

There are, however, some powerful *illusions*, and one real effect, that happen when turning from upwind to downwind—and they can easily fool us into **pulling too much brake**. Those are the real "downwind demons." And they only happen down low.

Much of this is because pulling brakes affects a fleeting sacrifice of speed for altitude, training the subconscious mind—incorrectly—that you "pull brakes to climb."

The Climb Illusion: Take off into a 10 mph headwind, flying 20 mph and climb at 200 fpm. Groundspeed is only 10 mph so that climb looks impressively steep. Now turn downwind. The *angle* decreases a lot even though the *rate* of climb remains unchanged. Earth is zinging by at 30 mph while you continue climbing at 200 fpm. The subconscious inclination is to pull more brake so that the climb looks the same as before, relative to the ground below.

Wind Gradient: This effect is no illusion. If you climb into an increasing headwind (wind gradient), the wing "sees" a bigger headwind and really does climb better as it seeks its trim airspeed. Groundspeed is slowing down in the process.

The reverse is true when climbing downwind through that gradient. You'll encounter an increasing tailwind that reduces climb as you must *accelerate* to maintain trim airspeed. The stronger the gradient, the stronger the effect and it is usually most dramatic down low. Climbing upwind for the first 200 feet usually gets you above the gradient.

The Turn Illusion is usually a mild effect that, like most, *can* become overpowering in stronger winds and lower altitudes.

That's because the *rate* of turn depends only on bank angle and *air*speed. If it takes you 2 minutes to turn all the way around when it's calm, it will take you 2 minutes to go all the way around

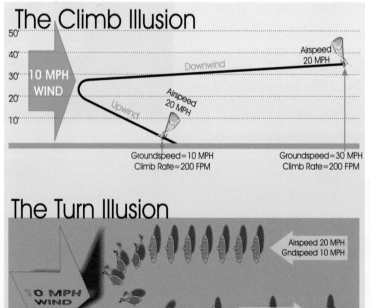

in a strong wind. And the rate of turn is exactly the same whether going upwind or downwind. However, if you're looking at the *ground* track (fig. 1), the upwind portion describes a tight arc while the downwind portion has a shallow arc. If you're low, that shallow arc can *feel* like you're hardly turning.

A pilot in the throes of this illusion will subconsciously add more inside brake to steepen the turn so it looks the same as a no-wind or upwind turn. Bank angle can steepen dangerously before the pilot realizes it. Once banked up, the pilot dives into the ground, usually at high speed because it happens during the downwind portion.

You can avoid all these effects by climbing *into* the wind to 200 feet before turning.

Distractions

Taking pictures, flying formation, and listening to or fiddling with music are among the many distractions that increase risk. They divert attention from the primary task of maintaining a safe flight path. Additionally, items can easily slip from your grasp and head for the prop.

Stuff hung around your neck holds the potential to slide back and catch on a moving motor part—not necessarily the propeller. Straps can get pulled into the motor, bringing whatever they're connected to along. One pilot almost got decapitated when his camera strap went into the pull-start mechanism. Fortunately, the strap broke before his neck did.

Cinch neck straps so they cannot slide backwards into the motor area.

Formation

Flying near others adds a serious risk of collision or wing collapse due to wake turbulence. There are many nuances to formation flying (see Chapter 16) that should be learned gradually and first learned with large margins.

Before flying close formation, both pilots should be skilled with active flying and understand the severity of any mishap. What carnage remains after two wings get tangled up may not even allow tossing a reserve.

Watch This!

An interesting observation is how many serious accidents have spectators watching or cameras rolling. The term "Kodak Courage" is an apt epitaph for many pilots who crash in front of a crowd and its cameras.

Professional airshow pilots practice routines methodically at high altitudes to perfect them. Over and over. Then when they perform they do exactly what was practiced without exceeding their usual limits. "Show-Offs," however, tend to *exceed* their limits in front of eyes or lenses. Be like the pros and stick to what you know.

Terrain

Flying from flat land, with its more benign weather patterns and forgiving sites, adds safety. We cede a lot of margin in mountainous terrain, or by flying from confined sites. Other risky terrain features include water and congestion.

Mountains serve up serious weather complications, too. Local knowledge can be a valuable antidote.

Tip:

Remember, our wing flies in reference to the air, not the ground. All "downwind demon" illusions happen when pilots look at the ground while maneuvering down low. It causes them to pull too much brake in certain situations. Use minimum brake and practice ignoring the illusions.

You can avoid *all* the "downwind demon" risk by climbing up to 200 feet, into the wind, before turning.

Mid-air collisions are rare but disastrous. Formation flight requires extreme care. Collisions happen quickly and with surprisingly few people in the air at once. In fact, having just a few people aloft can foster a deadly complacency. Mind your mates.

When flying with others, use the admonition to "look, shallow, up, down, turn". That is **Look** in the planned direction, start a **shallow** bank, look **up** and **down** then begin your **turn**. Another variant is "Look, Lean, Up/Down, Turn" for those who use weight shift to initiate a bank.

Planned formations, like the one above, should only be done by experienced pilots with a plan and good communications to minimize risk.

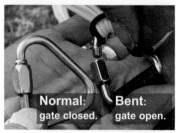

Normal: gate closed. **Bent:** gate open.

By Mark MacWhirter

You don't expect new equipment to have problems but it can—brand new gear still deserves a close inspection. The above quick link on the right was discovered *after* the pilot landed from a high G flight. It was the glider's first time out of its bag.

Quick links should look like the left one.

This wing arrived from the factory like that—all the screw gates were open, cutting their strength by more than half.

Equipment Condition

Wings get porous, lines break, motors wear out, things loosen, harnesses weaken, carabiners get scratched and other critical components degrade with time and use. These must be maintained properly and inspected regularly, especially the wing.

Carabiners represent a single-point whose failure would be catastrophic. They must not be bent, have scratches or malfunctioning gates. Steel is preferred.

The wing should command most of our attention; its degradation is most likely to cause problems. Having porous fabric, shortened, or stretched lines dramatically increases the possibility of parachutal stall. Add some other factor such as being too lightly loaded, or flying in turbulence, and a stall may be inevitable.

Don't neglect the motor—some failure modes involve the prop coming off and slic-ing into the fuel tank. An engine failure, while usually benign, can be unsavory depending on where it happens.

Disintegrating props can send shards flying in all directions. Most of the time this happens when a piece of machine vibrates loose and goes through the prop. Anything that can work loose should have lock nuts, safety wire, or other means to prevent ejection. Bad prop repairs, especially on composites, are more suscepti-ble to failure even with no prop strike.

Weather

A large accident category is weather related—pilots ignore weather warnings and fly anyway. It's an easy deception: you get away with something several times and now falsely think that the risk is small.

For example, and this is one of many, most thunderstorms don't actually cause problems until they're fairly close. But *occasionally* they do, causing horrendous winds from some distance—a gust front—and there's no warning.

Competition

Competition involves low-level maneuvering, high speed, and flying at the pilot and equipment's limits. Add distracting goals and the scene is set. Yeah, it's obvi-ously riskier than regular flying.

Some risk is mitigated by keeping pilots from getting high enough to develop dan-gerous *vertical* speed. They may fly low and fast but are rarely pointed at the ground. That has probably helped with the lack of fatalities in competition itself.

The best way to minimize competition's higher risk is to fly within your skill level. If conditions deteriorate too far, man up and decline to fly. You may save someone else by your example. Crashing is bad for both body and score. In practice, improve *gradually,* then don't do anything in competition that you have not mastered—a middling performer who finishes safely will beat the aggressive pilot who crashes in pursuit of perfection.

Unloading The Wing

Minimize low G conditions, like the top of a roller coaster, where you unload the wing, even partially. It leaves you far more vulnerable to wing collapse from even small downward gusts, especially if the wing is allowed to surge past overhead.

Turbulence or pilot action that rocks you back and causes a momentary climb can

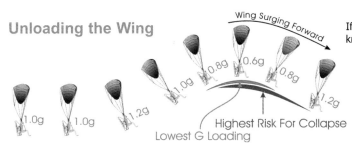

Unloading the Wing

Wing Surging Forward

1.0g 1.0g 1.2g 1.0g 0.8g 0.6g 0.8g 1.2g 1.1g 1.0g 1.0g

Highest Risk For Collapse

Lowest G Loading

If you get into this situation, where the wing has shot back and you know it's about to surge forward, be prepared to pull a bunch of brake. But not yet—this is a risky moment where the wing gets unloaded and timing is critical. Add brake pressure and power at the *beginning* of the green band—as the wing starts surging—and remember it takes a second for the motor spool up. These actions reduce unloading and prevent the wing from getting too far ahead.

cause unloading. Improper recovery from a steep maneuver is another common culprit, especially if you fly through your own wake made stronger by a steep turn.

Adding Safety Equipment

Our choice of safety equipment depends on flying style and locale. If you fly over forests, a tree extraction kit is essential. If you fly over water then flotation would be prudent (see Chapter 28). Certain items will help regardless of locale and style—a cell phone and hook knife are good examples.

Some safety gear reduces the *odds* of a mishap while some reduce its severity. Some, like tree rescue kits and flotation, help in the aftermath.

Reserve parachutes are severity reducers. They won't decrease the probability of a malfunction but may improve its outcome. Flying in rowdy air makes a reserve that much more beneficial. Of course, it must be installed properly (*see Chapter 12*) and its use rehearsed (*see Chapter 4*). There is some risk of accidental deployment (*covered later in this Chapter*).

Gloves are important for operating in windy conditions since ground handling the glider is where you're most likely to get line burns.

Boots can prevent ankle injuries and other foot-related maladies. Rough or rocky surfaces make boots even more valuable.

A helmet is probably the single most important safety element because, although unlikely, head injuries are so dire. Helmets are essential for ground handling in strong conditions, too. Remember: "Helmet on before hooking in."

Combining Risks

Combining risks can increase the chance of a mishap exponentially—way more than just adding them together. A perfect example is doing steep maneuvers down low. Both the *odds* of calamity and *severity of its outcome* skyrocket.

Another example is doing just about anything in rowdy air. The overall probability of an accident increases, especially during takeoff or landing.

Knowing what risk is involved in what operation lets you carefully choose only those operations that are worth it. Such knowledge can also direct extra attention (skill building or learning) to where it is needed most. This book was largely motivated by a desire to expose *where* risks are so pilots could make informed choices.

Some safety equipment will only help after the fact. See chapter 28 for tree self-rescue kits.

Courtesy TowMeUp.com

Gusted

After a week of lousy, unflyable weather I was anxious to get airborne. The receding rumble of thunderstorms left a quiet calm.

Hmm...maybe flyable?

A mellow sky beckoned and I gathered my gear, heading out to the nicely open field nearby. After getting there, I could see to the horizon and noticed darkness in the distance.

Hmm...

I waited 5 minutes and, sure enough, through the silence of that calm I could make out a muted rumble. More storms growled in the distance. Deciding this wasn't such a good idea, I packed up and headed home.

Shortly after settling into my project du jour, I heard it. Even before thunder signaled the storm's arrival was the unmistakable howl of a gust front. Within minutes, a destructive wind blew that would have been disastrous to anyone flying *anything*, let alone a 15 pound wing.

It was good to be inside.

Handling Situational Emergencies

Dangerous situations may arise with time to make choices. These cannot be rehearsed in a simulator but rather require a cool, thinking head. Most are incredibly unlikely, especially during early training where the instructor keeps closer tabs on you. And yes, they can mostly be avoided, but we're all human.

Situations may have several options, not necessarily covered here, that must be considered with your particular skills and situation. What's appropriate for one pilot, in one situation, may be disastrous for another. Weigh your choices and pick the least objectionable.

Be wary of absolutes and analyze your options before acting. Sometimes the first action that pops into your head isn't the best one. Having thought about options in advance (like reading this) can be helpful, but anything that requires a quick response must be rehearsed. The airlines have learned that reactionary physical skills, if not rehearsed, cannot be counted on.

Landing In Water (Ditching)

Your life really does depend on this, especially if you don't have flotation. Hopefully you have time to:

1. Undo your leg, chest, sternum, anti-torque, and reserve straps. That obviously means you can't get out of the seat yet.
2. Don't jump! Pilots have died after misjudging height and jumping early. Telling height over water can be weirdly deceptive.
3. Lighten up. Time permitting, dispose of anything hanging on your body (camera, radio, etc.), remove shoes (if practical), and prepare to jump out of the seat on contact.
4. Grab and extract your hook knife or at least practice reaching for it.

Options Trading

If water is your only power-off landing option, the outcome is far from guaranteed. Pilots have drowned even after doing all the right things. These suggestions merely improve your odds.

Flotation

If you must tempt wet fate, an auto-inflating device, such as the Agama (2), may save your life. It mounts to the paramotor and inflates upon immersion, keeping the paramotor afloat. But *you'll* enjoy flotation, too. Consider a ski-type life vest as pictured in (1) to help after leaving the paramotor (see Chapter 28).

At least one pilot, a strong swimmer, drowned after landing in a pond. He successfully got away from the motor but became exhausted while swimming with clothing on.

Inflates after submersion

Bobbin — Quick-dissolving paper — Body — Firing Pin — Plunger — **Inflation Initiator**

Auto Inflation Device

Approach with about brake 2 and don't flare unless you're absolutely certain of your height—that can be deceptively difficult. In a light wind, less than about 5 mph, consider landing downwind so the wing goes in leading edge first, trapping air in the cells. In a stronger wind, land into the wind with a firm pull at touchdown to ensure the wing, and its tangly lines, stay well behind.

Take a full breath of air just before impact. As soon as your feet touch the water, exit and swim away from the gear unless your motor has flotation. Otherwise the motor, especially carts, may sink quickly. Also, carts may flip forward, leaving you upside down.

Once clear of the gear, do not swim back to get it, especially in moving water. Entanglement is likely. The wing will probably float but the motor will sink once its cavities fill. The wing may hold the motor up for some time. Only go back for your gear with a boat.

If you start getting entangled in lines, *immediately* start cutting them with your hook knife as much as necessary to swim away.

If you end up on land but your wing goes into active surf, or a stream, *immediately* unclip. If a riser is taut, walk briskly toward the wing while unclipping. If it *does* start pulling, you won't likely be able to unclip and may have to start cutting with a hook knife. Seconds matter. Pilots have landed on dry ground then drowned after their wing fell into moving water. It may seem benign, but can quickly become life threatening.

If landing in very shallow water (less than 3 feet) you obviously don't need, or want, to jump out. Unclip as described above but consider landing seated, with one or both legs forward, especially if there is no wind (high groundspeed). This will prevent you from "face planting" since it is impossible to run out a landing in even a few inches of water.

Gust Front and Landing Backwards

Gust fronts occur on many scales, the worst being thunderstorms. Cold air plummets earthward, spreading rapidly at the surface in a deadly cauldron of swirling nastiness. It may be preceded by virga, dust, or debris, but not always. Your first indication may be nasty bumps or negative groundspeed—you are flying into the wind but moving backwards over the ground.

To ease your exodus from a machine with old style buckles (normally done like 1), fasten them as shown in picture 2. Simply pulling on the end will release it immediately.

If you get caught in such a front, expect a wild ride with occasional collapses and extreme oscillations. Follow the turbulence penetration guidance in Chapter 4. Here are some other considerations:

- If you can, land before it hits but only if you *know* it won't catch up with you during landing.

- If you don't think you can land before it reaches you, make a downwind dash to get as far from the source as possible. Even if you can't outrun it, getting farther away may let the front expend itself into a weaker state. Consider going crosswind if that will keep you out of an advancing storm.

After the gust front passes and you're in a strong wind, consider these options:

- If you are over a lake consider landing on the downwind shore, even if it's farther than the nearest shore, before exhausting your fuel.

- If you suspect the wind will worsen, power off and land immediately. Accept a backward landing even if it means that you may get dragged. Aim for an area offering the most forgiving blowback zone and least mechanical turbulence (which will be wicked).

- Some gust fronts are short lived. If you can safely control the wing and expect the wind to subside quickly (i.e., it's not associated with major weather such as an approaching thunderstorm) you may be better off waiting it out. The same is true if landing options are unsatisfactory—consider riding it out.

- Typically, there is a gradient where winds diminish close to the ground. Going lower may allow upwind penetration but, be careful, it will also be more turbulent, possibly too much. Don't ever put yourself behind an obstruction that could cause severe rotor. Also consider that gust fronts can be limited, low-level affairs and climbing may help.

If you become committed to a high wind landing while drifting backward here are some ideas:

- Be thankful you thought to wear gloves!

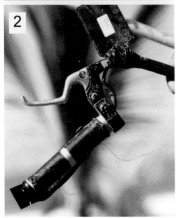

1. After landing in a strong and increasing wind, the pilot got lifted, dragged, and turtled but got it under control with the help of some fellow pilots.

2. This throttle got damaged by the prop. The most common cause of a stuck throttle is either debris in the cable or damage when the cable gets hit by the prop. That usually happens when reaching down to get into the seat using your throttle-holding hand.

- If it's smooth enough that you can momentarily let go of a brake or maybe hold both brakes in one hand, unclip from all but one leg strap to enable a rapid exit after landing. That may avoid getting dragged without being able to exit the harness. Mentally rehearse going for that remaining buckle.

- Locate your hook knife and be prepared to use it.

- While still airborne, find the rear risers and prepare to pull them hard at touchdown. Even if you fall, keep pulling until you are able to get up and run around the wing. Unclip as soon as you're able.

- Kill the wing using one of the methods in Chapter 3. If you are getting dragged and risk getting dragged through something harmful, use the hook knife to cut through the A risers or lines.

Consider finding a site where getting dragged back will be less injurious. Landing in front of a solid tree line, for example, will stop the wing when you get dragged to the trees. Be leery of small ridge-shaped obstructions, though, as the wing can pull you right up over the top.

Motor Stuck at Full or Partial Power

The most likely cause of this is having the throttle cable, and enclosed kill wire, go into the prop. One option is just running out of gas. Pulling Big Ears then going fast or doing asymmetric spirals will help prevent a climb. *Don't* do B-Line stalls since the recovery may not be possible with the motor at power and don't do round spirals. See Chapter 18 for information on these maneuvers.

If you decide to reach back and kill the motor, understand the risk—hopefully you've rehearsed it in a simulator. On most units, you *can* get your hand into the prop so favor whatever requires the least reach. For example, if the air vent is by your head, plugging it may be safer than reaching farther back for the spark plug.

After making sure you're over landable terrain, here are some ways to shut off the motor. Pick the easiest, most accessible one:

- If you have an alternate kill switch, relish your forethought and use it.

- If there's enough of the throttle left, try to work it down to idle.

- If you have a remote choke, or can reach the choke, pull it.

- If you can reach the fuel line, pinch it hard until it quits (may take 20 seconds).

- If you can reach the air intake easily, cover it—it takes about 5 seconds for the motor to run so rich it quits.

- If you have a primer bulb (or knob), squeeze it to flood out the motor.

- If you can yank the plug wire out or pry the spark plug cap off without touching it (you'll get shocked) then do so.

- If you can plug the fuel vent, do so. It may take several minutes though.

- If you cannot kill the motor safely, you'll have to run it out of gas.

Landing in a Tree

Trees only look soft from above. If there is no better option and you're going to wind up in a tree, go for its middle near the top and, as always, land into the wind. Grazing the branches may simply collapse the wing, sending you free-falling to the ground. Do a normal flare and keep your feet together, in front, with knees bent. Once motion stops, your ride may not be over. Grab a stout branch and hang on.

Getting Out of a Tree

If you fly where tree landings are a possibility then carry a tree rescue kit (see Chapter 28). It includes a roll of dental floss (or similar) and a fishing weight. The weighted line is lowered down to a rescuer so that a strong rope can be pulled up.

Most injuries come from falling out of the tree afterward so remain in your harness while waiting for help. The wing may be all that's preventing a fall. If help is not likely or your status is precarious, try using the wing's lines to secure your harness to a solid part of the tree. Do that before trying to climb down.

If help comes with an adequate rope, lower a line to the rescuer. Pull the rope up and loop it over a strong branch. Secure the rope around your waist and have the rescuer wrap the rope around a strong, low branch for friction so he can lower you gently to the ground. If you're 50 feet up, you'll need probably 110 feet of rope.

If you have no rescue kit and time is critical (impending cold, weather, darkness, etc.), consider using your reserve or glider lines to help lower yourself.

Getting Out of Power Lines

Paraglider lines can conduct current from even low voltage power lines, most of which are at least 4000 Volts. High tension lines have over 100,000 Volts. Do not allow yourself or rescuers to touch any part of the gear *and* the ground—they have been electrocuted just by getting close to a hung-up glider. Wait until the power company has removed power. They will also have equipment that can reach up to allow for easy retrieval.

If you're low enough, jumping is an option but it's easy to misjudge height and get hurt. Awaiting rescue may still the best bet.

Cloud Suck

Cumulus clouds over about 500 ft thick can have powerful lift just below the bases. This *cloud suck* can be dramatic in bigger clouds, with violent updrafts and downdrafts exceeding 3000 feet per minute (fpm). Pilots have died from hypothermia and/or hypoxia after being sucked up by these behemoths.

If you start getting lifted, act quickly, using one of the descent techniques in Chapter 18. Realize that Big Ears, while benign, will not likely be enough.

A quick spiral may work if done right away but do *not* use it after being enveloped in cloud—you risk vertigo or blacking out from G-forces. B-line stalls are reasonably effective but can have exit problems. The full stall, which plummets nicely, is even more risky in recovery unless you're experienced with them. Do *not* toss your reserve since that would eliminate all control of descent rate.

You can see why the ounce of prevention is so valuable, given how problematic the pound of cure can be.

Motor Failure and Outlanding

The specifics of spot landings are covered in Chapter 17, but when the motor quits away from your field, there are some other considerations.

If the motor is just running poorly, try to find a throttle range that works ("milking

1. Obviously, staying out of the wires is best. But if this happens, don't let yourself or anyone else touch the ground and gear simultaneously until you know the power is off. High voltage has a way of finding ground and both humans and lines work just fine if given the chance.

Also, after a hit like this, have your wing inspected. This wing was flown later, without an inspection, and had a cascade failure of several A lines.

Chapter 14 addresses power lines for rescuers.

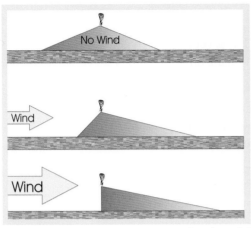

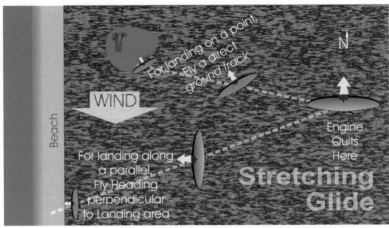

Cone of Range

With no wind, your glide options are the same in all directions. With wind, you have more options downwind than upwind.

The bottom frame illustrates a wind that's blowing as fast as you're flying. Groundspeed is 0 if you're pointed directly into this wind meaning that *all* your options are downwind.

Extending Glide & Spot Landing

If forced to land at a spot far away, make your ground track straight towards it, using every means available. Pick a spot where you can arrive with some altitude to spare in case of unplanned headwind or sink, and to inspect and fine tune the landing location.

When it's obvious you've made it, plan at least an abbreviated pattern with base leg and final as shown here. It improves your odds of nailing the spot. Never turn completely away from the target unless you're *really* high—instead, make all turns *toward* the spot.

the throttle"). You may be able to hobble back or make it to a better landing site.

An unusual vibration usually means that something bad is about to get worse and landing is normally best. Continuing may cause carnage: motor separation, prop shards through the wing, or other calamity involving damage and dollar signs.

Once an outlanding (off your airfield) is inevitable, here are some priorities. There is no hard and fast rule—choose the best option.

- If you were stretching glide downwind, be into the wind by touchdown.

- *Land into the wind, level, and flare!* All things being equal, it's almost hard to get hurt if you follow this rule. Land crosswind or downwind only if it's a much better option. Avoiding rocks or power lines, for example, might be such a justification. See "Landing Priorities."

- Favor rotor-free spots with no upslope. Avoid landing in a wind shadow or rotor.

- When presented with multiple safe, landing options, consider retrieval difficulty or whether you can re-launch.

- Scout for wires on the way down. Any straight-line features or poles should raise suspicions that wires may be present. Plan your approach accordingly.

- Look for animals. A single cow in a field may be a bull.

- Consider where the wing will go if landing near water. Avoid moving water, including surf. If a water landing is inevitable, prepare as covered earlier.

Here are ways to **stretch** your **glide** depending on the situation. When flying upwind (penetrating), fly faster. More headwind, more speed. Anything over about a 12 mph headwind will call for maximum speed on most gliders, but only do that if it's fairly smooth or your glider is stable while flying fast.

With a tailwind, fly near minimum sink speed for best glide. That's trimmers slow and brake pressure 1 or 2 on most gliders.

Regardless of wind, maximize glide by minimizing drag. Lift your legs and bring your arms in to present the smallest frontal area possible. Do turns using weight shift, stabilos, or tip steering instead of brakes, if possible.

Fogged In

Besides being illegal, it's extremely dangerous to fly without ground reference. Even though the craft is stable, fog conceals wires or other surprises. So if you see fog forming or rolling in, *land while there is still enough visibility*, even if away from your launch site. Failing that, climb up above it, but do *not* put yourself in busy airspace. A PPG should be landed in the fog before risking heavy airplane traffic. If you can fly to a fog-free location, do so.

Here are some things to think about if landing in fog:

• Note or recall the wind direction; you may need that later.

• Having a GPS in this situation is obviously helpful. Hopefully you've stored your launch site as a waypoint. If not, mark your current location and stay nearby. On many units you may be able to follow a plotted ground track back to your site.

• Consider circling above and waiting if you think the fog may move through or burn off. Use this option only if you're certain that wind drift won't take you somewhere undesirable.

If you must land in the fog, use whatever means are available (compass, GPS, sunlight) to stay pointed into the wind. Keep some power on to reduce the descent rate for an easy go-around in case something unpleasant emerges from the murk. There is, however, some benefit to having the prop stopped in case you hit an unseen piece of planet.

On final descent, go to quarter brake (pressure 2) and be ready for impact. Keep your feet angled down and forward, knees together, bent, and ready to absorb the energy of a collision or to run. Even in thick fog you should have enough visibility to flare—but beware of illusions that could spur an inappropriate reactionary pull on the brakes.

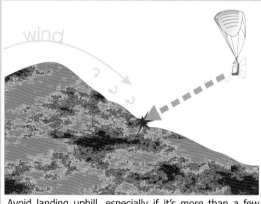

Avoid landing uphill, especially if it's more than a few degrees steep. Besides the possibility of rotor, upslope touchdowns can be *very* firm—the descending glide and rising terrain make it like hitting a wall with your feet.

Impending Aerial Collision

If you see a threatening aircraft, watch it for *just* long enough to know that it's really on a collision course, and then act decisively. If it's stationary relative to the horizon (not moving left/right/up/down) then it's on a collision course. For example, an airplane may be just above you but descending quickly. An aggressive descending spiral could put you in its path whereas doing nothing may let it pass.

If you're sure a collision is imminent, quickly enter as steep a spiral as you're comfortable with. Since you're so slow, this makes you more visible while also getting out of the way quickly. If the other pilot suddenly sees you he will also see your downward

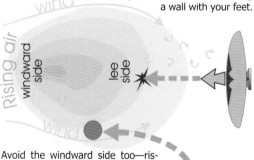

Avoid the windward side too—rising air may make it difficult to get down in your desired spot. Go for the hillside (green spot) parallel to the wind flow. In a calm wind, land parallel to the slope.

motion and should pull up in response. Don't yank the glider into a spin and create another emergency.

Failure of Wing, Line, Riser, or Connection

Be thankful you carry a reserve as this would not likely be survivable. You'll probably be thrust into a spiral with only a few seconds to get the reserve out before rapidly building G-forces prevent it. With no reserve, you'll be riding half the wing down in a high-speed spiral. Pulling brake may only worsen the spiral since most brakes act more towards the tip. The brake on the failed side will probably have ripped out of your hand but, if not, hold onto it as long as you're able.

Consider reaching up (if able) and trying to pull the inside rear riser line to oppose the turn direction. Pull just one line. Given the angle that you'll be dangling from, reaching it would be a long shot, actually pulling it even longer.

Quality carabiners and a back-up strap that goes from your harness webbing into the riser loop nearly eliminates the dreadful results of this extremely rare failure.

Accidental Reserve Deployment

Shut off the motor. Realistically, that's all you'll probably have time for. As long as the reserve comes out properly, ride it down as described in Chapter 4. Only if it looks like you'll be set down somewhere that's lethally unpleasant, *and your wing is still inflated*, consider cutting away the reserve bridles with your hook knife or disabling it with your hands by pulling in some reserve lines (extremely difficult).

Grabbing the reserve on its way out is probably only possible if it gets snagged or malfunctions. Even then, having a hand full of reserve lines when its fabric catches air may cause severe line burns as it snaps open.

Fire

Fire is extremely rare and even more rare in flight. There's little to do besides shut off the motor and land immediately. It's so rare that no established procedure has come forward but here are some recommendations:

- Spiral down to minimize your time aloft. Consider leaning forward to keep your body farther from the fire and twisting to reduce the swirl of wind around your back.
- If the motor has an ejection feature, this is the time to use it! Grab those tabs and pull outward just like you've rehearsed.
- Unclip from all but one leg strap and be ready to get away from the machine quickly. Rehearse going for that remaining strap.
- Consider landing next to, or in, shallow water so you can immerse yourself after getting free of the machine. Only land *in* water you know is very shallow.
- Roll in dirt, a blanket, tarp, or water as available to put out any remaining fire.
- Approach the motor with great caution. Although it's unlikely, certain failure modes can allow the tank to burst, spewing flaming fuel.

Reading this chapter is like reading a medical book—lots of maladies, but they're mercifully rare. The sport has proven safer than appearances would indicate but, being aviation, it needs constant vigilance to keep that way.

Risk To Others

Your most important obligation is not risking others. The three primary ways you do so is threatening them with your flight path, departing pieces of your machine, or having someone help you, especially while the motor is running.

While launching and flying avoid "directing energy" at people. That is, don't allow a situation where loss of control would result in hitting them.

While starting or running up your motor, avoid the scenario where people are within 20 feet or so of the prop plane (shown at right). Metal pieces from the cage of an exploding prop have embedded themselves in the ground over 50 feet away.

Kite Lines

The Jolly Roger was reduced to this after flying through a $4 kite line near Daytona Beach. They're not as benign as they look and their line is nearly invisible.

If you're up fairly high and do contact a line, consider circling down to a landing so the string is not able to cut all the way through your wing. Once the kite is de-tensioned from its mooring (the child below), the damage may be reduced.

by Adriana Lukačova

Competition

20

Weaving the course at a World Pylon Championship in Poland.

It is human nature to see what we're capable of. Like all competition, with the right attitude, it's a healthy motivator to excellence.

To be sure, competing is riskier than just flying around, primarily the low-level tasks. It's mitigated somewhat by 1) minimizing tasks where pilots dive towards the ground, 2) minimum experience requirements, and (3) rules that penalize dangerous maneuvers. Still, you're putting a lot on the line.

Those steep and low turns flown by competition pilots are not as dangerous as they seem, at least for the reasons people frequently cite, like engine failure. As long as the pilot knows how to keep his turns level (no diving), even touching the ground doesn't guarantee damage or injury. Of course it does mean zero points. A common question is "what happens if the motor quits during those turns?" Surprisingly, for an experienced pilot, the answer is nothing. There's enough energy for a skilled pilot to level off and land on his feet—it has occurred a number of times.

Rules for competition can be arcane but their goal is to: 1) recognize skill in a fair manner, 2) minimize risk, 3) limit arbitrary factors, and 4) keep the event flowing. Rarely is the simplest solution the most fair. Rules must be understood, too— knowing how a task is scored can be just as important as being talented. More than one loser's last words were "I didn't know you could do that!"

Different sanctioning bodies have different flavors of the same basic tasks, so check the rules closely. The Fédération Aéronautique Internationale (FAI) is the worldwide governing body for all competition and their International Microlight Commission (CIMA) handles microlight activities, including PPG. Most countries have national organizations that govern national competition and work with the FAI. Some countries have national organizations whose competition is run independently.

Equipment Selection

Low-level precision tasks benefit from powerful motors and small, fast wings. Cross country tasks like efficiency. That's why 4-stroke, and small 2-stroke motors are popular at navigation-heavy competitions. When both types of tasks are flown it's tougher to choose. If you're really good at precision tasks, favor more thrust. If you excel at navigation tasks, lean towards efficiency. Most comps require the same equipment for an entire event so choose wisely.

Reflex wings are good for competition because of their larger speed *range* which is helpful for both cross country and precision tasks. That speed range must be employed carefully since using center (main) brakes while fully accelerated can be risky. Check with the wing's maker about how best to steer in different combinations of speedbar and trimmer settings.

Animation extracts used here are from The Master Powered Paragliding Video series. These put precision flying techniques in motion with both live action and animated explanations. They are available at footflyer.com (QR code points there) and other paramotor retailers.

1. Rodriguez touched his Excitor tire and wingtip and tire while rounding a corner.

2. It's not whether or not you hit the target, it's whether the judges *think* you hit the target.

by Adriana Lukačová

⚠ **Caution!** Using speedbar may increase vulnerability to collapse, especially while flying through your own wake.

How Good Do I Need To Be?

Everybody has to start somewhere. If you have 50+ flights, can reliably launch and land within 50 feet of a target, then you have the bare minimum to compete. Other minimums may be imposed by organizers. Being *competitive* is, of course, another matter but simply entering these events will improve and focus your skills.

If you've been honing finesse, even just for the fun of it, then you're probably ready. To win, you must indeed be a master of the craft, able to control your path within inches on a calm day and within a few feet in level 2 turbulence (see Chapter 5 for the Bump Scale). You should be able to prevent swings and generally keep yourself locked under the wing even with some bumps. Having the skills as described in Chapter 16 (Precision Flying) may earn a top 25% ranking.

Whether you're new to competition or a veteran, be ever mindful of personal limitations; it's easy to get carried away and damage yourself or your gear. Many pilots have done well by consistently just *finishing* each task, even with average points.

A common pitfall is a good pilot pushing too hard and hitting the ground, zeroing his points for a task. That really hurts in a close contest. Plus, the damage may prevent scoring on the next few tasks while repairs are affected.

Ground Precision

For many pilots, ground precision is the fun stuff. It can be intimidating, though—the key is to stay within your ability and build skill slowly.

The Cloverleaf

This is the mother of all precision flying tasks. It mixes several skills: turning, power management, speed control, spatial orientation, adjusting constantly for the wind, and planning ahead. Don't minimize spatial orientation—it's not as obvious as it seems. When you're down low, cornering hard and looking to the center, telling position can be confusing, leading to wrong turns especially in wind.

It's typically only flown with winds less than 10 mph, to avoid fast, downwind ground speeds.

Here are some practice tips:

- Be able to kick the center stick. You cannot win without doing this *every time*. So go out, find some small bush or other safe target, and practice kicking it from

The Cloverleaf

an approach in all directions. Set up 2 meter sticks if possible.

- Practice level, steep turns that require modulating power and speedbar as you roll in and out. Pick a distant spot on the horizon and practice rolling out towards it without climbing.

- Make sure you know the order. Fly it first from a couple hundred feet while looking down on it. Then do it at 50 feet, then at 30 feet, etc. Don't worry about time until direction is nailed.

- Before starting, mentally go over it. Look at the center, then the left-far stick (1st one), look back to the center, then across to the opposite stick, etc., until visualizing the last stick and finishing kick. Good pilots have lost because of turning the wrong direction or even not finishing all four corners.

- Only after the above skills are mastered, work on time. Being fast on the wing helps but you must minimize distance. On some courses, only your body must pass the corners. If there are pylons don't get too close, a potentially fatal mistake that also zeroes your score. In the same vein, always plan your turns to finish with the least distance to the center *and* next stick.

Power management is crucial—as you go into each turn, throttle up enough to prevent settling (red in the illustration above). Steep banks may require full power. As soon as you *start* rolling out from the turn, relax the power—from a steep bank you will go completely to idle and still climb a bit. If you're using a speedbar, start applying it as you level out while adding power to keep from settling. Be careful using a speedbar on this task, it is difficult and makes it harder to kick the center stick since your feet are on the speedbar (or stirrup).

Being fast is good, to a point. Some pilots will add fuel and ballast but don't be so heavy as to blow a launch. Setting the trimmers fast may be beneficial, especially if there's much wind. Having a speedbar/trimmer interconnect (see Chapter 26) helps because it puts the wing's full speed range at your feet.

Wind changes how the cloverleaf is flown quite a bit (see diagram at right). With wind, the basic idea is to always go upwind of the upwind sticks before turning. That minimizes the turn required to get back to the center and aim for the next stick. When flying downwind, anticipate the need to start turning earlier. Finish all turns with a crab into the wind to further minimize distance flown.

Collapse risk is high because every trip through the center involves flying through your wake at maximum speed—a vulnerable time. Know your wing, know its steering, know its limitations, and learn these things up high or over water. Mishaps while doing these over land has caused many injuries—be careful.

Foot Drag

Once you've mastered the foot-drag basics described in Chapter 16, you can apply them to competition. Mostly you must learn how to do it fast (trimmers out), with some crosswind, and how to turn while dragging.

The course is a simple slalom of three gates where the center gate is offset. You

Cloverleaf At Home

Make your own course by planting 5 sticks as shown above. The center should be springy enough to be easily kicked without getting in the prop. Put foam material on top like pool "noodles" for better visibility, and ribbons on the center stick for wind direction.

Time runs from first center kick to last, but some contests may begin timing when the pilot is told to launch.

In the above illustration, dark red equates to max power and white equates to idle power. It assumes you use moderately steep banks in the turns. Do only what you're comfortable with, though, since crashing scores no points.

Cloverleaf With Wind

In general, if there's some wind, you must move your flight track to be some amount upwind of the sticks. More wind, more change.

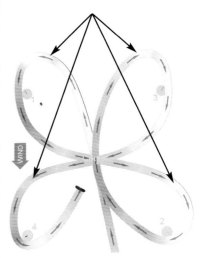

Foot Drag Course

On reflex wings pilots will fly trimmed fast and primarily use tip steering but must still be able to use some main brake.

1. The *slow* course requires lots of brakes, power, finesse, and hopefully smooth air. Don't go *too* slow since you can't just pop up with the brakes which are already pulled, and adding power may take too much time.

Here, the author is braked heavily "hanging on the prop" during a Florida competition. Don't touch that cage!

2. Going fast makes it hard to stay low and enough to kick the sticks since, at speed, it's easy to get popped up.

Tim Kaiser on speedbar in a Chicago area competition.

drag at least one foot the whole distance through each of the gates. Faster is better and speed counts heavily. Passing all the gates with a foot on the ground is most important because lifting a foot or running reduces points significantly. Don't try too hard, though, falling scores a 0.

The best stance is one foot out in front of the other so that you can be ready to run if necessary. Don't put much weight on your foot—drag will slow you down and leaves you vulnerable to a point-sapping run. But do run, if necessary, to avoid losing so much speed that the wing falls back—that's another 0.

Minimizing brake use is good for both points and options: If you slow down too much, the brakes will no longer be effective at quickly adding lift. If you wind up heavy in the brakes it means your airspeed is slowing down—add power immediately!

To be competitive, you'll need to fly with the trimmers out (fast) but only if you're willing to be dumped going fast. Dumping happens whenever you get a sudden tailwind or downward gust, thus losing lift and forcing a run or possibly a fall. Using the speedbar is nearly impossible and, since touching any frame part on the ground zeros all points, wouldn't likely be worth the risk. Tying off the speed system to its accelerated condition seriously risks frontal collapse since the wing gets partially unloaded during the foot drag.

Slow/Fast

This simple task is surprisingly difficult to do well. You fly a straight course as slow as possible then do it again as fast as possible. To be competitive, though, you must be comfortable trimmed fast and on full speedbar while only a few feet high. In a calm wind, that's fast! Contestants must stay in a 5-meter wide lane or kick three 2-meter tall sticks in a row.

Reflex wings are all but required to be competitive because it's about speed *range*. One common method is using tip steering for directional control and speedbar for height. That's tough, though—if you drop, you must *immediately* let up on the speedbar then get back on it as you climb, a reaction that must be automatic.

The slow part requires heavy brake pressure which leaves you vulnerable to getting dumped by sink or lifted too high. Altitude is controlled mostly by power since the brakes are already pulled about as far as they can go—adding more brake will just stall the wing.

Spot Landing

Power-off spot landings are covered in Chapter 17 but here are some tips for competition. Normally, you climb to 300 feet or so, power off, then glide down to land on a Frisbee-sized target *and stop*. Where you first touch counts most.

It's a great task to master given that every flight ends with a landing. But it's risky, especially if you're high and pulling fistfuls of brake to steepen glide. That can easily lead to stalling and falling—a painful, expensive way to score zero points. Some pilots prefer *flapping* (see Chapter 17) to steepen their glide. But let up in time to accelerate and flare so you don't fall or touch the cage which may be disqualifying (a rule that discourages trying too hard).

With practice, many pilots can touch the spot nearly every time, but arriving with minimum speed is another matter. Some tasks reward energy management (the USPPA's, for example) by also scoring how far you travel after touchdown. Less is better. Regardless of scoring, though, it's most important to hit the target: don't miss or fall because you're worrying about traveled distance.

If the scoring does *not* incorporate stopping distance then the *swoop* landing (Chapter 16), where you come in fast and just touch the spot, is best.

One way to minimize excessive run-out is to use moderate brakes (pressure 2 - 3) nearly all the way down. Have just enough speed to flare hard and swing forward slightly, stopping just as you touch. Be careful, with too-little flare authority, this technique risks a point-sapping cage-touch or fall.

Another variation is where there are 5 cones lined up 10 feet apart. Your goal is to kick cone 1, then kick as many of the other cones as you can before touching down. It's tougher because you must land along the cones regardless of wind. Small wings excel. They allow a bigger dive and higher speed during the bottom swoop.

On all spot landings, especially in windy conditions, faster trim is generally better since it allows greater control over energy management.

Japanese Slalom

Kick sticks 1, 2, 3; come back to slalom around 1, 2, 3, then come back to kick 1, 4, 3. Time is from the first to the last kick.

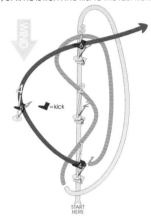

The Japanese Slalom requires the same basic skills as a Cloverleaf but reduces low altitude wake turbulence penetrations. It also takes less room to set up.

Flight Precision (Navigation)

These tasks challenge a completely different type of piloting skill. You must be adept at planning, reading maps, pilotage and know your machine's fuel burn characteristics. Scoring involves flying with a covered GPS (so it can't be used for navigation) that will later be read by a computer to see what points you actually flew over and at what time. Other methods can be used for scoring where the pilot is given photographs that are used to identify (and write in a log) locations on the ground.

Competition directors will provide maps, pictures (if used) and instructions after which, pilots are given some time to do planning. This is where competition organizers spend a lot of time, getting all these things together. For the competitors, though, it can provide many hours of enjoyable flying. It is, in many ways, the relaxing part of competition. Of course that depends on your intensity—there is always *something* that motivated flyers can do to improve their odds or awareness—verifying position, studying the map for coming waypoints, determining wind, checking fuel, strategizing, etc.

Finding Points on a Map

One key skill is being able to correlate what is on the map or photograph with what you see on the ground—not necessarily an easy task. Some of the tasks require familiarity with your machine's fuel burn in various configurations.

Fly with a speedbar since some of the tasks are almost pure speed. There's no fuel limit but you have limited time to go find as many map points as possible.

Planning

You must have some idea of the winds aloft and apply that to your planning (see Chapter 13) for flights. Understand the effect of wind gradient and try to maximize it. For example, if the winds at 1000 feet are south at 15 mph but at 500 feet they

The author, scouring Indiana for clues during one of the few full U.S. competitions, put on by the U.S. Ultralight Association (USUA). A GPS is covered up and sealed to make it unusable in flight. The camaraderie of pilots in these events is a powerful benefit.

Road Rally in the Air

European style competitions involve a wide variety of navigation tasks. An amusing, fun example is the *Circle and Two Lines*.

The pilot gets a map with a circle drawn on it and a bunch of pictures. His mission is to fly the circle and put a hack mark each time he identifies one of the pictured points. Once all four marks have been made, the pilot draws two lines that intersect those points. Where those two lines cross is the new destination. A judge awaits at that location for those who figure this out (while flying, I might add.)

It doesn't have to be a circle either—the same task is flown with other shapes using the same concept. If a possibility for ambiguity exists, the instructions will indicate the outlanding site's general direction.

Since it would be possible to fly the circle, miss only one point and therefore not be able to complete the task, an option is given. Just before takeoff, each pilot is given a sealed envelope. It contains the out landing site plotted on a map, just open the envelope and go find it. Of course, opening the envelope entails an enormous penalty but it's still better than not finding the site at all.

The FAI "Circle and Two Lines" navigation task is a fun challenge. Don't miss a point though, it forces you to open your sealed pre-launch envelope containing the destination.

are west at 12 mph, plan accordingly.

Don't count on trying to do much writing in flight; organize the map and pictures to minimize moving things around. Some contestants have a larger map board that is several pages wide so they don't have to flip pages.

Fuel Limited Tasks

A variety of fuel-limited tasks require optimization based on conditions. You must cover the most amount of ground with the least amount of fuel. In no wind, fly at your glider's most efficient speed. Fly faster in a headwind and slower in a tailwind but never below minimum sink speed (see Chapter 22).

When flying between thermals, speed up in sink and slow down (or circle) in lift. That feels counter-intuitive since, in sink, you're already plummeting and speeding up makes it worse—but more importantly, speeding up gets you out of the sink faster and you'll end up higher than if you stayed slow. Depending on how the scoring is weighted, it may be beneficial to circle in thermals when going downwind and slow down in thermals when going upwind. The more important time is, the less circling you want to do.

Endurance

Endurance, also called *economy*, is a fuel-limited task that rewards those with soaring skills and efficient gear (motor and wing). It is normally flown just as thermals start heating up or later on when they're diminishing, but still present. Cloudy days, with little thermal action, primarily rewards the lightest pilots flying the smallest motors on the most efficient wings.

Pilots meet in a common area to ensure that tanks are empty (motors run out) and each one gets the same amount of fuel. They all must launch within a given time window and the longest one up, in minutes, wins. Another fueling option is where pilots are weighed with a highly accurate scale before launch and after landing. Their fuel burn is calculated from the difference and scored by a formula.

One proven method is to climb to a couple hundred feet then throttle back just enough to hold altitude or climb slowly. Keep that power until you find a thermal then reduce power to about half of what it took to fly level. Circle in the thermal's lift, building a mental picture of where the strongest updraft is and trying to center on that. If lift is strong you may be able to shut off the motor (providing you can reliably restart it in flight). In weak lift, use *some* power to help you stay in the thermal.

Kiting

This simple competition is unique to the U.S.—a colorful spectator favorite, too, judging from the many images that make it to social media and publications.

Competitors start off in the field, arrayed evenly within a boundary. When the judge calls "GO," theeveryone has a few seconds to bring their wings up and begin to battle. Kiters must stay within the designated area and keep their wing up for at least 2 minutes to score anything. They are allowed to maneuver so as to bring other wings down but cannot touch other competitors with their bodies. The last 3 wings up get 1st, 2nd and 3rd place according to who stays up the longest.

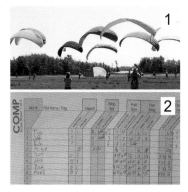

Tactically, the best way to bring down someone else's wing is to block their airflow with your wing. Advanced kiting skills are obviously a must, especially kiting with the A's, but even then it's difficult. If a couple of wings get upwind of yours, it might be impossible to stay up, especially if your route to clear air is blocked.

In really light winds the challenge is simply keeping the wing up for longer than everyone else, and staying in bounds. Kiting without a harness is the best strategy if you're comfortable doing so.

Here are some other points of strategy.

- Pick the right location if choosing is an option. In a stronger wind, be as upwind as possible. In a really light wind, where simply keeping the wing up will be difficult, start downwind.

- Avoid battles if possible, but when one becomes inevitable, try to always stay upwind. You can turn and run forward but mind the boundaries—it's easy to go out. Strategy changes when you're one of only two remaining and you *must* get in front.

- If your wing gets down low, grab the A's to kite it just above the ground.

- If rules allow grabbing other pilots' lines, use that more as a threat since it tends to pull their wing into yours, taking both of you out.

This task is worth only a few points but can make a difference in a close match.

As with all tasks, you must use the same wing you started with but are allowed to choose any kiting harness or no harness.

1. This physically demanding task is a lot of effort for the few points it's worth.

2. Knowing the rules and clearly completing a task properly is critical. After all, it's not whether or not you did a task correctly, its whether or not the judges *recorded it!* Be obvious.

Each organization has a process to help ensure fairness. They know it must be fair but also recognize that nobody is perfect and sometimes bad calls get made. Don't take it out on the volunteer judges, it probably won't do you any good, and will make finding these valuable volunteers harder.

Pilots preparing for the real deal at a pylon competition in Poland. For safety, these tasks are normally run over water.

by Adriana Lukáčová

Tucker Gott captured this Canyon scene during his winning run at the Icarus Race, an unsupported 1000 mile run through some gorgeous, but treacherous, U.S. countryside.

Tent

by Shane Denherder

Refueling the paramotor

by Tucker Gott

Refueling Tucker Gott

Unsupported Races

A challenging, fun, and rewarding competition is the unsupported race. Pilots fly a long cross country without having anyone to provide transportation, maintenance or fuel. Different events allow different levels of support, but most all require at least one overnight and multiple refuelings.

It takes grit. Successful pilots will be able to reliably launch a fast wing while hefting serious kit. In the least supported races, pilots may carry a lightweight tent and 2-stroke oil although there are places that sell both fuel and oil. Success is significantly about planning first but then being flexible enough to draw benefit from changing situations. Tenacity and a willingness to endure discomfort seem to be winning elements, too.

Risk goes up mostly because pilots are motivated to fly in conditions they would normally avoid. But then that's true of all competition.

Demonstration Competitions

A hybrid type of competition is where the organizer chooses sufficiently skilled pilots to fly tasks that are intended for an audience. It's a show. They are indeed competing but, more importantly, they are entertaining. Emphasis is placed on being fun to watch and not having mishaps so pilots don't push quite as hard in the traditional sense.

Tasks and timing are chosen for their crowd appeal and ability to be performed in a small area. Pylons, water slides, balls, and other "toys" add to the effect. Tasks are brief and easy to see when someone is doing well, usually by watching a huge clock with the pilot's time. There is no need for arcane scoring methods.

These are not part of the normal sanctioning system because pilot selection is based on criteria other than just ranking.

A "Parabatix" competition and demonstration course.

Free Flight Transition

21

Free flight paragliding is an adventure worthy of its own pursuit, an enjoyable use of many skills that have already been learned. Both variations deserve respect; adding a powerful motor to the mix, and taking on conditions strong enough to keep you up.

Many free flyers find that power opens a gratifying addition to their sport. Be ready to learn, though, it's a lot more than just adding another launch skill.

When launching a free flight harness you lean forward with your hands back. When launching with a motor you must stand up straight to let the motor push.

Transition to Thrust: Becoming a Power Pilot

Power expands your opportunities, allowing exploration of new launches, soaring sites and lift bands that were beyond reach. For example, rising air that coalesces well above its source becomes accessible, offering power-off soaring for hours. You can climb *through* the air to better understand it, or use partial thrust to mimic high performance gliders. But what so captivates most motor pilots is the ability to go almost anywhere in the smoothness of morning and afternoon.

Exploring terrain becomes a purpose unto its own. Portability and launch flexibility find their ultimate expression in this craft.

It's a completely different challenge, of course. Where soaring pilots strategize to fleece air of its precious lift, motor pilots may seek precision control of flight path; control that is measured in inches. Of course you don't *have* to go that far, but it's possible, and the best motor pilots do it effortlessly. A pilot can be excellent at soaring without needing such precision, just as a skilled motor pilot can be masterfully precise without a clue about coring thermals. Fortunately, the endeavors go wonderfully hand in hand.

1. Eric Dufour sets up for the typical power reverse with one hand on the A's and the other hand holding a throttle.

2. Starting a reverse inflation the wing comes up crooked. You can manage that by giving it the finger.

3. Jose Casaudoumecq leans back into the power during a forward launch.

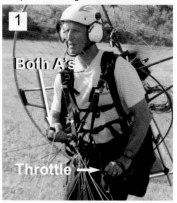

Throttle hand finger pulling brake since the other hand is holding both A's.

Throttle In Right Hand

If you're an accomplished paraglider pilot who is willing to adapt, then motor flying will come quickly. A very few points must be minded, but then the transition will be easy. You will want to pay attention to reflex wing differences, and thrust adds some potentially dangerous differences, but they're easy to understand.

Seek out an experienced, certified paramotor instructor. His best service will be to set up your equipment properly and instruct you on its nuances and launching.

Launch Differences

Hefting the motor will seem awkward at first. A lightweight motor, adjusted properly, speeds the process.

Reverse Inflation: Getting ready will be quite different. A common method in paragliding is to hook in while facing forward then turn around as you pass one riser overhead. That doesn't work well with a cage so you'll learn a different technique. You may find the alternate hook-in method described in Chapter 3 to be easier. You stand next to the risers facing forward.

Walking backwards is harder, especially if the paramotor cage hits your legs. Avoid doing reverses in winds too light to kite the wing.

Another difference is the riser hold (refer to fig. 1). You'll have the correct brake in each hand, as usual, with the risers crossed, both A's in one hand (right shown) and the other hand holding the throttle.

If the wing comes up crooked such that you would need to pull brake with your A-holding hand, instead, use a finger on your throttle hand to pull the brake *above* its pulley (Fig. 2).

Be ready to throttle up as soon as you turn around or even while turning around. Turn and *move forward* with some power, then, when everything looks good, add power into a run, check the wing, and go for launch. While learning, it's better to abandon a crooked inflation and try again.

Forward Inflation: Hook-in is the same, but the launch itself has one glaring difference: As the power comes up, you *must* stand up straight and lean back against the motor's push—no "torpedo" here. **Don't stay leaned forward like a free flight forward.** The initial inflation is mostly the same, lean forward, but not as much as you would free flying. Dig into it with your hands back, pressing upwards on the A's, but once you start applying thrust, stand up straight. You must not throttle up while leaned over or it will thrust you into the ground. Some pilots struggle with this. There's even a name for it: face plant. Remember: "Stand up at throttle up."

The *partial power forward*, shown in Chapter 5, where you throttle up some then start running, gives the most consistent low-wind success, but starting without power has the least equipment damage. The most common cause of failed motor launches by free-flight pilots is leaning forward. Thankfully, that's easy to fix.

All Launches: Learn to be quick on the kill button; if a launch goes bad you must act fast to prevent parablending. If the wing gets nearly all the way up but you need to abort, quickly turn around to face it. Step backwards, if needed, to make sure the wing comes down away from the prop.

Some motors make it hard to see the wing because your helmet hits the cage. Get used to looking left or right to tell what the wing is doing.

Be mindful to stay on the power after lifting off—free flyers tend to throttle back and settle to the ground.

Climbout

Torque will be your next surprise: the more power, the more torque—a surprising array of forces that conspire to cause a turn (see Chapter 23). These can be dramatically reduced by proper setup (see Chapter 12) which is why a capable motor instructor will quickly earn his keep.

Depending on your motor model, the turning tendency can be so powerful that trying to counteract it with brakes alone can cause a spin. If it wants to turn mildly, let it. If it's still turning too much, or in a bad direction, ease back on the power *then* correct the flight path. It is entirely possible for a powerful machine to spin you around into a riser twist. Reduce power *smoothly*.

Maneuvering Differences

By virtue of adding weight and pushing so far below the wing, motor thrust tends to reduce the chance for collapses (slightly). And when they do happen they're typically shorter lived. However, there is potential to get lines wrapped around the motor or prop in wild air—a good reason to avoid such air while powered. Plus, the motor adds twisting mass and offers less weight shift (very little on many units) so recovery from malfunctions can be more difficult.

Also, be sensitive to the wing falling back. Thrust can hold a glider into parachutal stall which is almost unheard of in free-flight but *far* more common in motoring. It frequently ends in a spin.

If you do feel the wing go back, or your speed suddenly slows, *immediately* reduce power, reduce brake pull and be prepared to dampen the surge. Rehearse that action in normal flight so that it's automatic. Of course, if it feels like a full stall (*very* unlikely unless you were holding heavy brakes) then react accordingly.

Landing

Once you're experienced at landing with the motor (power off), it can be helpful to land power-on in turbulent conditions. Having some thrust (maybe 10% power) reduces your descent rate and may prevent an otherwise firm arrival if you hit sink just before touchdown. You must be quick to add throttle when needed—if you get that sinking feeling, quickly squeeze on some thrust to regain airspeed for the flare. If things look really bad, go around and try again. New pilots (including recently transitioned free-flyers) should land power-off since the chance of falling is higher with the motor's extra weight and complexity.

Be ready for the extra weight after landing. Have your knees slightly bent, one foot forward, and be ready to run. A fast, smooth arrival can be slid out. Most motors will allow sliding on the cage bottom (curved base skids) but that risks damage, it's always best to try landing on your feet.

Kiting

A good kiter will do well, but there are some differences, especially since you can't lean forward as easily (lines go awkwardly around the cage hoop). The only way to kite safely while facing forward is with the motor pushing you. Trying to kite forward with*out* the motor's thrust is a bad idea—a gust can pull you back into the

Torque and its twisted sisters can quickly derail the best launch. Be prepared to reduce throttle if you feel yourself twisting. You can easily go all the way around, a decidedly bad "turn" of events. See Chapter 23 for more on torque. The mantra "reduce power, reduce brakes, then steer" works well.

Gear reduction drive motors twist right, pushing the pilot right and the wing left.

Tip: Handling The Unknown

If something unusual is happening, remember: **Reduce power, reduce brakes, then steer**. Prepare to dampen a surge if the wing is back. A skilled pilot may get better results by actively controlling the wing, but experience shows that too much brake is more often the culprit rather than not enough. Also, be smooth on power changes—abruptness makes matters worse.

turtle position (on your back with arms and legs flailing).

Reverse kiting is tougher on units with high hook-in points—you use back muscles instead of body weight which is quickly tiring. Plus, if you get lifted in a strong gust, the motor's inertia can make getting turned back forward difficult at best. If that happens, remember to keep flying the wing!

New Capabilities

The motor offers more options—keep them in mind as you fly. Primarily, if the wind picks up you may be able to reach a more favorable landing site, maybe even your original site. Consider going higher or lower to find less wind—normally it's weaker near the ground but expect more mechanical turbulence. At least there's no reason to let yourself get blown into a bad rotor situation.

Landing in turbulence is easier with a motor. Once you're accustomed to the throttle and how it interacts with surges, you can essentially make every landing far more predictable. However, as a beginner, it's better to land power off until you gain skill at managing power.

If you're doing power-off soaring with the ability to restart in the air, you can let yourself get out of gliding distance from launch but always stay in range of a safe landing option. This is a great way to explore an area's thermalscape—you can launch from nearly anywhere and land back there when you're ready.

Added Vulnerabilities

It's easy to get complacent about motor failure. Resist. If you fly long enough, it *will* fail! Always be mindful of available options for when it does, including while you're at full power right after takeoff. Be leery of steep climbouts. Having said that, be aware that an even bigger risk for newly transitioned free flyers is letting off the power abruptly just after takeoff and swinging into the ground. Until you're experienced, and as long as you're not twisting under the risers, keep nearly full power until you've reached at least 100 feet. Then, as always, reduce it *gradually*.

You can soar with the motor but glide performance suffers by up to 20% due to the frame's drag. Below, Thad Spencer powers up to cross a low spot on the ridge; weak lift would have otherwise dumped him to the beach.

Spinning propellers represent the sport's single most common cause of severe injuries. Most of them happen while starting or running up the motor when it is *not* on your back. A few have also resulted from pilots reaching back during launch or in flight. Bare feet have been sliced. Respect the prop anytime it's powered.

Wires and obstructions become greater risks now that you can spend more time down low. Flying low *and* downwind is dreadful because of increased ground speed—illusions cause misjudgment, escape time plummets, and results worsen.

Soaring

You lose efficiency with the motor, a full point or more off your glide ratio, but you can still soar. The windmilling prop of a clutched unit creates more drag than a stopped prop. Prop protection is draggy but obviously well worth it. Going cageless is nearly suicidal—pilots have been permanently disfigured and nearly beheaded when trying such folly.

Soaring with the motor running at some constant thrust lets you simulate a high performance glider. Just pick a throttle setting that yields some lowered sink rate.

Quiet beauty brings many pilots into free-flight. There is also the challenge to match wits with nature, to stay aloft, and even go cross country. Eric Rys is pictured here enjoying smooth, easy ridge lift off the Pacific Ocean in Baja California, Mexico. Lift contin-ued well past sunset—he stayed airborne into evening with no worry whatsoever.

Noise

Possibly the biggest drawback to motoring is noise. The quickest way to lose sites, or gain the ire of authorities, is to buzz around the same locale. If people complain, you will get noticed. People complain the loudest about noise. Altitude is a won-derful buffer and distance is even better. Climb up and get away—adopt the phi-losophy "launch and leave." When returning, do so with minimal power.

Transition to Free Flight: Goin' Soaring

Free flight is a quiet realm that warrants preserving. Sites are limited with some teetering on extinction—they must be avoided with motors to keep the area quiet for both free flyers and the surrounding property owners. Always respect the local's requests regarding where motoring is to be avoided.

The view alone from many launch sites is invigorating; it can be intimidating too. Running into the air from cliffs and mountains can be a thrill in its own right.

Your wing handling, especially in high winds, and flying skills will serve you well; a talented motor pilot will do fine flying a paraglider—the challenge will be soaring. Additionally, there are some skills that must be learned to handle potentially per-ilous sites that are far from flat and grassy. And thermal flying means conquering the turbulent air that comes with stronger conditions. Your early flights should be in relatively still air with less emphasis on soaring and more emphasis on getting used to the differences in feel and technique.

Free-flying adds risk in some areas while reducing it in others; most soaring risk comes from strong conditions and challenging sites. Even ridge soaring, which looks benign, requires significant skills and knowledge to do *safely*.

The best money you'll ever spend is to take a course from a free-flight instructor that offers transition training. Seek out material on paragliding since what's cov-ered here only scratches the surface. Dennis Pagen's "The Art of Paragliding" cov-ers this subject in depth.

Free-flying in mellow mornings and evenings is not much different than motoring other than the requisite power-off landing. Conversely, flying in air buoyant enough to remain aloft requires far more attention. You must have, or develop,

Basic Right-Of-Way

Free flight, especially on a ridge with limited lift, can concentrate traffic in a small area. So a few simple rules have been adopted to minimize conflict.

First and foremost is see and avoid. Use the rules below in conjunction with common sense. When turning, remember "Look, lean then brake."

For **thermalling** it's pretty easy—if there's already a pilot circling, go in the same direction. If another glider is below you, give way to him—he can't see you as well.

On the **ridge**:

1. Always turn away from the ridge. Always. This is a survival rule.

2. Overtake other gliders between them and the ridge. This allows them to turn away from you and be turning away from the ridge.

3. When head-on, the pilot with the ridge to his right has the right of way. "Ridge on your right, you're alright, stay in tight." If not head-on, give way to whoever is closer to the ridge.

So if you're flying along with the ridge on your left, move away from it to let oncoming traffic pass (the ridge is on their right). Exceptions to 3 are:

a. With the ridge on your left, when you turn around it could be confusing. Do what makes sense.

b. A lower pilot has the right of way—he's probably trying to "scratch" back up and needs to stay close to the ridge.

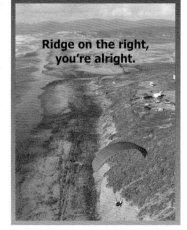

Ridge on the right, you're alright.

active flying skills (see Chapter 16) that let you keep the wing overhead without thinking about it. The adage "less brake and let it fly" applies here too. Just like in motoring, more pilots get into trouble by pulling too much brake rather than not enough. However, active flying is a far more important skill than in motoring. If you haven't mastered how to keep the wing overhead in rough air, avoid excessively turbulent conditions (thermally or gusty) like the plague.

An experienced motor pilot should devote from 1 to 3 full days of free-flight instruction before going on his own. Plus, many sites require ratings (such as those from the USHPA in the U.S.) and, in some countries, licenses to fly.

Weather at the typical mountain site is often unique; even rated pilots should seek local expertise before flying a new site. Locals will have knowledge gained from sometimes bad experience—it's worth not repeating the experience.

Equipment

You'll love the harness. After being so much more upright, the laid-back position of a soaring rig will feel downright dreamy. Almost all harnesses come with a reserve mount, speedbar accommodations and low hook-in points for comfort and weight shift authority.

Most harnesses include some form of back protection—learn how that protection works because it may require proper setup. Airbag harnesses, for example, *must* be zipped a certain way (using the correct compartment) to have any effectiveness. Other styles have their own specifics.

Your motor helmet would work, but since you don't need the ear protection, a lightweight model is far more comfortable. Many free-flight sites use 2-meter FM (in the U.S.). They have special frequencies officially dedicated to their use.

Your motoring wing should work just fine as long as you follow the common practice of being heavy on the wing while motoring. If the wing was specifically made for motoring, then it may not be as efficient as those specifically made for soaring. A wing that takes a lot of power to fly level will take a lot of lift to stay up.

You'll want a reserve parachute even more than with a motor. They have scored many saves for free-flyers who ran afoul of mean-spirited air. Good boots are helpful, too, especially in the mountains or other challenging terrain.

Launch Differences

Being able to deal with rough surfaces and a brisk wind is part and parcel of paragliding. Whether thermals are cranking up the hillside or stiff winds are making a ridge lifty, it is quite common to be launching in winds over 12 mph.

Learn the high-wind techniques of Chapter 15 and practice them in safe areas. You'll quickly warm up to kiting with a

1. When kiting on a slope the wing wants to overfly and front tuck, or pluck you off the hillside. Consider kiting with the rear risers instead of the brakes, especially while reversed.

2. Never give up. It was blowing hard so he started lower on the hill to take advantage of weaker wind due to compression. He still got lifted and twisted awkwardly but kept working it, garnering enough control to end up triumphantly on top. Never give up.

3. Most free flight harnesses have excellent back protection and some, like this one, are made to reduce wind resistance.

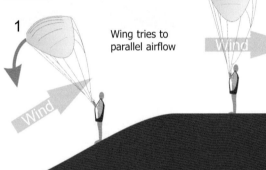

1

Wing tries to
parallel airflow

Wind

Wind

2

3

by Karen Hadley

light-weight free-flight harness. Since lift is required to stay aloft, pilots frequently seek out wind blowing up hills. Although thermals thrive in low-wind conditions, they get good starts when forced up a mountain or some other land perturbation. The vast majority of sites are found atop ridges or mountains, facing the prevailing wind. Expect to deal with small obstructions (plants, rocks, etc.) that are there to snag wings and lines. They're usually good at it.

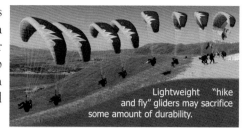

Lightweight "hike and fly" gliders may sacrifice some amount of durability.

As for technique, the main difference on launch is that, once committed, you must lean forward to run since there is no motor pushing. Whether the initial inflation was reversed or forward, once facing forward, lean over while putting your hands back and up to avoid the risers, prevent engaging the brakes, and keep your feet from yanking out forward near liftoff. Then run hard until you get lifted off the hill. The leaned-forward free-flight stance is called a torpedo.

Doing no-wind forward launches is easier in some ways since the downward slope helps with your run and getting the wing to come overhead. Be quick to dampen it though, it will probably want to overfly you.

One situation that commands respect is launching from a cliff. Air carries great momentum and a vertical cliff will direct it up right in front of launch, leaving you in a difficult rotor. You may have to move back away from the edge just to get your wing in clear enough air.

The risers are usually farther apart in free flight harnesses to improve weight shift in turns. Plus with low hang points, the pilot is essentially tilting on the balance point.

Be mindful of the preflight check—forgetting to hook up properly is usually fatal when launching from a hill. There is a way to get into your harness in such a case, but you better have practiced it beforehand. The technique, covered in Dennis Pagen's "The Art of Paragliding," requires some physical dexterity, too. For starters, *never* unhook your leg straps without also unhooking the chest strap too. That will help prevent launching without at least one leg strap hooked up. Modern harnesses incorporate buckle systems that reduce this possibility—buy one of those, if able.

Maneuvering Differences

The brakes behave the same, of course, but free flight harnesses add significant weight-shift capability. That becomes more important for several reasons:

• It's way more effective—the typical harness allows over 12 inches of up and down riser travel.

• It is more efficient than using brakes alone. When soaring, the goal is to minimize drag while staying in lift. That means flying near the minimum sink speed of the glider—usually only a few inches of brake pull, any more hurts sink rate.

• Recoveries from asymmetric wing malfunctions or spirals are enhanced.

Weight shifting is done differently in paragliding than some motors. Instead of shifting the whole motor or moving the thigh and shoulder, you use your hips. It's not what you do with your body, it's in the hips. Lower your right hip to turn right and left hip to turn left. Some pilots cross the high leg over the low one but do whatever it takes to maximize riser movement. Use the same coordinated turn technique as described in Chapter 16.

Alpine Harness

1. A group of pilots paramotored over to this beach and set up camp. They pulled out alpine soaring harnesses and proceeded to soar all day long.

2. Phil Russman is helping Alan Chuculate launch a tandem during strong conditions on the western Baja peninsula of Mexico.

If you get recruited as a helper: Never let yourself get lifted all the way off the ground while hanging on—let go *immediately.*

Big ears are easier to pull since the risers, and thus their A lines, are easier to reach. Plus, with better weight shift authority you can steer more effectively while holding big ears.

Free flying means you're usually seeking out lifty conditions and it's entirely possible to get into so much lift (on a mountain or ridge, especially) that you cannot come down at a desired location. Big Ears is one way to do that, but there are other, more effective ways to consider (see Chapter 18).

Kiting

There is little difference in basic kiting although, absent the motor, you can get lifted easier. Plus, many mountain sites will be steep and bringing a wing up in strong, mountain conditions must only be done if you're ready to fly. Learning, and becoming proficient, at one of the advanced methods mentioned in Chapter 15 will be invaluable since you will stay reversed and maintain better control if you do get lifted.

New Capabilities

The best new capability is to fly soaring locations where motors are not allowed (soaring sites that are sensitive to noise). These treasured spots are gained by and maintained by dedicated volunteers and should be respected.

To realize these capabilities, most sites require free-flight ratings to ensure some minimum skill level. Working towards these ratings will further advance your skills and is fun to boot.

Added Vulnerabilities

Without the motor there are some new concerns to deal with. The obvious lack of go-around capability must keep you even more focused on your landing options. Plus, unless you're willing to land away from your landing zone (and the ride home), you must keep getting closer to it as you descend. Pilots do frequently head out on cross-country adventures but they usually have a ride arranged.

You're far more likely to need to do a spot landing somewhere strange. Make sure your skills are up to par.

You will be inclined to fly in more turbulent conditions since, by nature, you need thermals or ridge lift to stay up. Most of the increased risk in free flying comes from this fact. Thermal turbulence in some areas, at some times of the day, and some locations can be disastrously strong, especially for pilots not adept at active piloting.

The wing is slightly more susceptible to collapse since it will be loaded lighter. It should also be less violent in the recovery but be ready to handle it or avoid stronger conditions altogether. You'll want to use more brakes in turbulence, about position/pressure 3.

For those who plan on venturing into the "biggest" (most turbulent) air, a maneuvers clinic is highly recommended (see Chapter 18). You will learn recovery and descent techniques that may be extremely beneficial, if not life-saving.

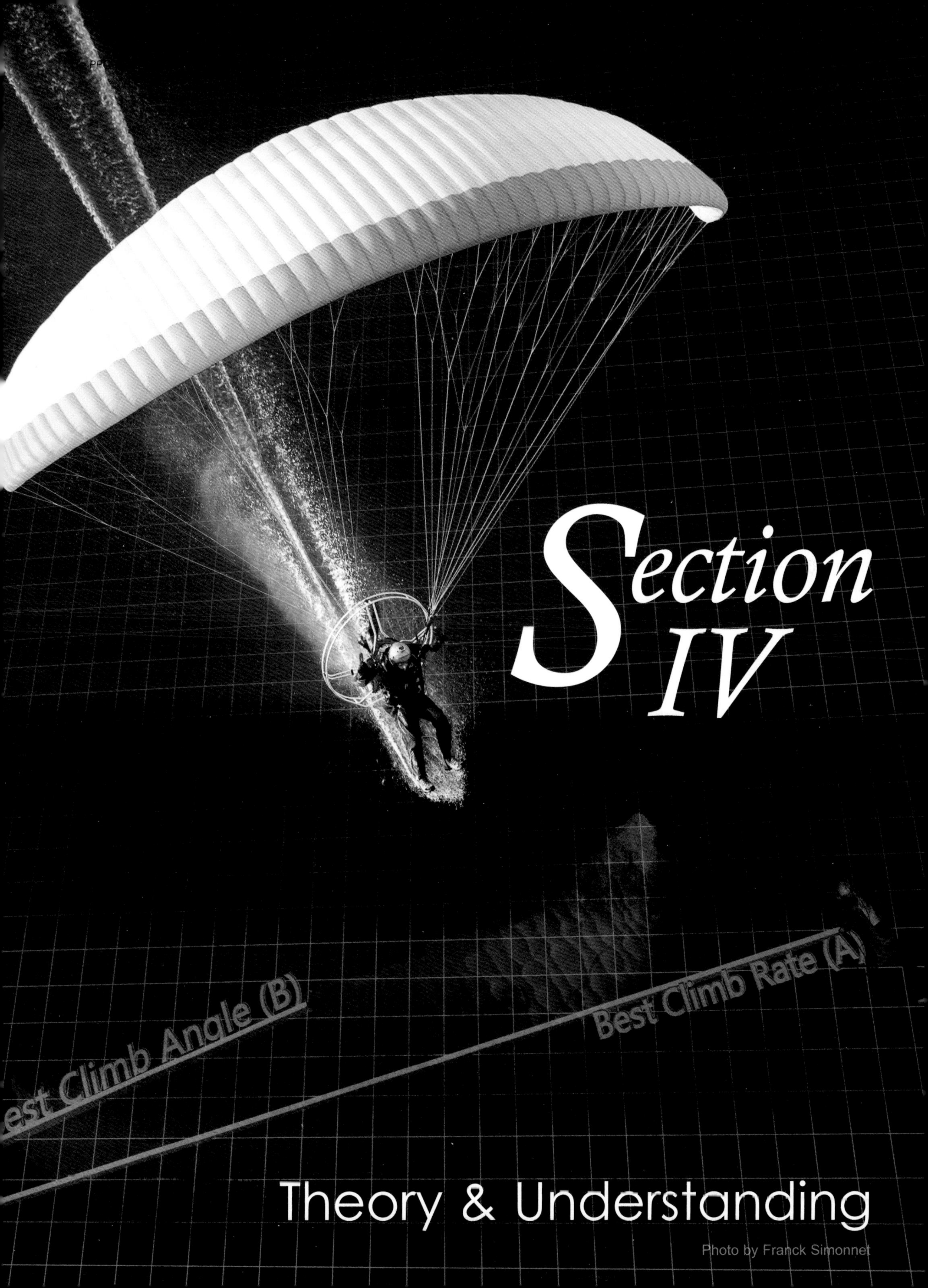
Best Climb Angle (B)
Best Climb Rate (A)

Section IV

Theory & Understanding

Photo by Franck Simonnet

Section IV

Theory & Understanding

Section IV erects an important foundation of *understanding*—knowledge that can improve decision making and possibly lead to being a safer pilot. Mostly it's for the curious—for those who enjoy the simple pleasure of knowing how things work, and for future designers of our next generation of gear. The humble paramotor turns out to be far more involved than a first glance would suggest.

This material is best digested gradually by reading, asking questions, and learning through experience. After gaining some flight time, you'll probably get more out of it. There's nothing like time aloft to grease the gears of understanding.

The PPG Bible: A Complete Guide and Reference

The PPG Bible: A Complete Guide and Reference

Section IV

Theory & Understanding

Section IV erects an important foundation of *understanding*—knowledge that can improve decision making and possibly lead to being a safer pilot. Mostly it's for the curious—for those who enjoy the simple pleasure of knowing how things work, and for future designers of our next generation of gear. The humble paramotor turns out to be far more involved than a first glance would suggest.

This material is best digested gradually by reading, asking questions, and learning through experience. After gaining some flight time, you'll probably get more out of it. There's nothing like time aloft to grease the gears of understanding.

Section IV

Theory & Understanding

Section IV erects an important foundation of *understanding*—knowledge that can improve decision making and possibly lead to being a safer pilot. Mostly it's for the curious—for those who enjoy the simple pleasure of knowing how things work, and for future designers of our next generation of gear. The humble paramotor turns out to be far more involved than a first glance would suggest.

This material is best digested gradually by reading, asking questions, and learning through experience. After gaining some flight time, you'll probably get more out of it. There's nothing like time aloft to grease the gears of understanding.

Aerodynamics

22

Flight is a fine dance of forces that must remain in step for you to stay aloft and in control. We follow the same aerodynamic rules as our fixed-wing brethren, but with a few important differences.

- Thrust, weight, and drag all hang well below the wing. That gives great stability but imparts some different behavior, too.

- There is no tail which means very limited control of pitch and yaw (covered later).

- The soft wing and lines must always be under tension so weightlessness or negative G (like the top of a really big roller coaster) maneuvering is *verboten*.

Balance of Forces

You can learn most of what you need to know by sticking your hand out the window of a moving car. Keep it flat with the air stream (or *relative wind*) and there is no lift, but it still gets pushed back a bit (drag). Angle it up slightly (increase the *angle of attack*), and it generates lift like "A" to the right. Angle it up more and it gets more lift while pushing backwards more too—more drag like "B." Angle it up too much and the lift stops altogether while drag skyrockets—that's a *stall* like "C." At a given angle, driving faster increases both lift and drag.

Some dynamics of our pilot-on-a-string craft can be understood by imagining a small rock tied to a foot-long string hanging from your finger. Push the rock out and let go. That's like goosing the throttle and letting off. Turbulence is like moving your finger (the wing) around.

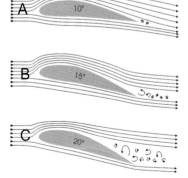

The air can only "stick" so much. Beyond a certain angle (the *critical angle of attack*), it separates, killing lift and adding immense amounts of drag: a stall.

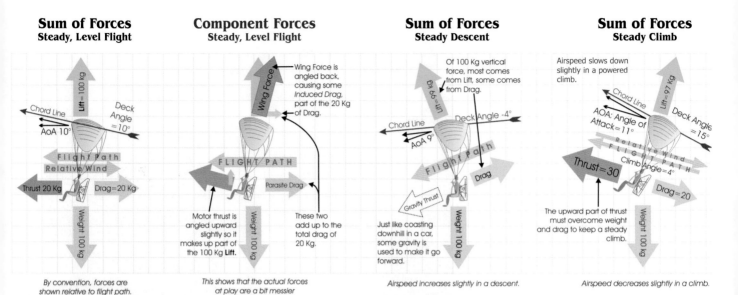

Sum of Forces
Steady, Level Flight

By convention, forces are shown relative to flight path. Relative wind is opposite flight path.

Component Forces
Steady, Level Flight

This shows that the actual forces at play are a bit messier

Sum of Forces
Steady Descent

Airspeed increases slightly in a descent.

Sum of Forces
Steady Climb

Airspeed decreases slightly in a climb.

The 4 forces are described relative to flight path but it's actually kind of messy. For example, since thrust is angled upwards, it contributes slightly to lift (green). Wing force is tilted back, adding *induced drag* (defined below) to parasitic drag. Each force is represented as an arrow (vector) with direction and magnitude. In steady (unaccelerated) flight, they must all balance each other out as shown in the **Sum of Forces**.

Throttling up changes everything. After swinging forward then settling back into a steady climb, the flight path tilts up and the angle of attack (AoA) increases slightly. Wing force decreases slightly as engine thrust lifts some weight. Speed slows down slightly and induced drag goes up a bit. Since weight is always pulling down to earth, thrust must maintain speed *and* overcome gravity (just like going uphill).

Climb = thrust in excess of what's required to maintain level flight.

Forces are in kg (think kgf). Feel free to multiply the numbers by 9.8 to get Newtons and maintain balance in the Force.

G Loads

Flying along in level flight, you feel your body weight in the seat; that's 1 G (force of gravity). In a bank, as you swing around, it forces you against the seat and makes you feel heavier. When you steepen the bank to 60° it feels like you weigh twice your weight—2 G's.

Just like swinging a rock around on a string, the faster you swing it, the higher the G's.

Lift

There is no magic here; we fly by spending money. Aerodynamically, though, it's all about redirecting air downward—just like your angled hand out the car window. A wing's curved surface just does it more efficiently. Motor thrust provides forward speed while the wing redirects air downward. It's a bit of Bernoulli and a lot of Newton: redirect enough air downward and up we go.

A plywood board will generate lift but curving it helps keep air sticking to the top which increases efficiency. The board's sharp angles would make airflow separate quickly from the top into useless, draggy eddies, leaving only lift from the bottom and boatloads of drag from the top. Lift is our superhero; drag is the villain.

Drag

PPG's, with all those lines, frame, and a distinctly un-aerodynamic pilot, have lots of drag. Shape has a lot to do with it—round tubes are terrible while the familiar teardrop shape is pretty clean (less drag).

Drag comes in two forms: parasitic (aka *form* drag) and induced. Parasitic drag is basic air resistance. Induced drag is a result of the wing's lifting force angling backwards from the flight path—a by-product of lift. Wingtip vortices contribute to induced drag, too; *something* has to generate all that swirling air, and it isn't lift.

Put a symmetrical wing (curved the same on top and bottom) parallel with the slipstream and it produces no lift, only parasitic or *form* drag. Angle it up, like your hand out the car window, and it comes to life with lift. Induced drag goes up too since you had to angle it back slightly, so part of the total wing lift is rearward.

The *Center of Drag* is where drag appears to act—for our craft, it falls about a third of the way from the pilot to the wing.

Speeding up increases drag dramatically; a doubling of speed quadruples the parasitic drag. That's why our abundant drag is less of a problem—we go so slow.

Thrust

Thrust overcomes drag. Whenever thrust exceeds drag, we get acceleration. In our case, having the thrust hang so low also causes the pilot and motor to swing out in front of the wing. That pitches the wing up, angling flight path upwards and slightly increasing angle of attack. Thrust imparts a pitch torque on the wing.

In level flight these forces are balanced; just enough lift counteracts the total weight, and just enough thrust overcomes the total drag. Climbing flight obviously requires more thrust since the motor must overcome gravity *and* keep the airspeed.

Thrust is vectored—it will always push in the direction it's pointed which is not necessarily the same as the flight path. Serious problems can occur when the thrust line gets too far off kilter. If thrust pushes the pilot left, for example, the wing goes right.

Weight

Weight is what lift overcomes—gravity pulling down on a mass. The center of mass is where an object theoretically balances—for a PPG, that's near the pilot's neck since there is so little mass (in spite of all the area up there) in the wing.

Stability

Stability is resistance to upset and the tendency to return to a previous steady state. By virtue of having the center of gravity (CG) so far below the center of lift our craft is inherently very stable. Unlike almost any other type of aircraft, if the pilot does nothing, it will tend to fly straight and at its *trim* speed (see below).

Sometimes *stability* is erroneously invoked to describe collapse resistance. More accurately, it describes a wing/pilot that resists fore/aft movements and returns quickly to steady flight. For example, if a gust makes the wing surge forward, it will then go back and forth in decreasing amounts. A stable wing will not surge as far forward, will not fall as far back, and will settle into a steady state more quickly.

Motor units that mask wing movements to the pilot are frequently called "stable." This is another misnomer because they do not affect stability, but rather the *sensation* of stability. Having hook-in points well above the CG means that wing motion does not get transferred as much to the motor unit. A motor with *low* hook-in points, closer to the CG, responds actively to wing motion. It only *feels* less stable but the wing is moving around the same amount.

Axis of Motion

There's a roll axis, a pitch axis, and a yaw axis. Motion occurs around these various axes as shown below.

Pulling both brakes makes you pitch around the lower (motor) latitudinal axis. Changing power makes you pitch around the upper (wing) latitudinal axis. Yaw is left-right twisting around the vertical axis and happens initially when pulling one brake. Roll happens around the longitudinal axis whenever you enter a bank.

Pulling one brake does attempt to cause some opposite roll due to increased lift on that side, but it's overwhelmed by the pendular stability of a low-slung pilot and motor.

Stability is like the hanging rock example mentioned earlier. Move the finger once and the rock swings in diminishing amounts until it's still again. Dynamic stability is that the oscillations tend to decrease in amplitude.

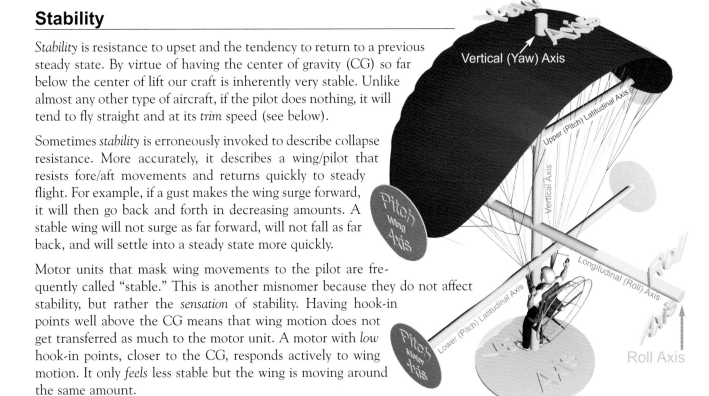

You need to have a GPS and variometer. An altimeter and watch works in place of the variometer.

Set up the GPS to display speed (it only measures groundspeed). Climb 1000' up into smooth air and align yourself into the wind, watching the ground for left/right drift and correcting until you're flying exactly upwind.

Throttle off. Once in a stable descent, watch the ground speed while staying into the wind. Note the sink rate (or calculate).

Do that for a half minute; then climb back up to 1000' and turn exactly downwind. Throttle off and again watch the ground speed and sink rate. Average the two groundspeeds and sink rates. A 10 mph upwind speed and 30 mph downwind speed means your zero-wind groundspeed would be 20 mph. Sink rate should be the same both ways.

Convert sink rate in feet per minute (fpm) to miles per hour (fpm x 0.011) and divide the zero-wind groundspeed by sink rate to get glide ratio.

Note: a windmilling prop, and in some cases, an idling prop (depending on how fast it's idling), will worsen glide performance.

Glide & Drag

Without power we glide, going downhill at a steepness defined by our *glide ratio*—the forward distance divided by the vertical distance. This primary measure of efficiency is also known as the Lift/Drag (L/D) ratio—how much lift versus how much drag is produced at any given speed. Reducing drag (friction) is the best way to improve glide since the wing planform and shape is fixed. Changes to the wing, such as using brakes, trimmers, speedbar, or Big Ears, change the glide ratio.

A 6 to 1 glide ratio (or L/D) is just stated as 6. That means it will go 6 feet forward for every foot dropped, so higher numbers are better. From a given altitude, an 8 to 1 (8:1) wing will go farther than a 6 to 1 wing.

Glide ratio varies with speed and configuration. Each wing and motor combination will have a speed at which it is most efficient: its *best L/D speed.* Going faster *or* slower will steepen the glide (worsen it). For most wings, in no wind, the speed for best glide occurs at *trim speed,* which is usually hands up, no speedbar, and trimmers neutral (as marked), but as always, check the manual.

Adding drag always hurts glide. Hanging a flag from your wing lines, for example, adds a lot of drag. In this case, speed stays the same while sink rate increases. Going faster than *best L/D speed* with the extra drag dramatically increases sink rate.

Wing manufacturers advertise their glide ratio with*out* a motor to get the best number possible. They shoehorn a skinny pilot into a minimal free-flight harness with his hands and feet tucked in. But a paramotor with its hoop, netting, frame, and normal sized pilot make that number but a distant dream.

Windmilling props have more drag than stationary ones. That's because the spinning keeps the blade's angle of a attack low enough for air to stick to the back. A stopped prop, on the other hand, only represents the drag of its frontal area. A gyrocopter is a good example—it creates lift by having the air flow past its spinning rotors. Stop the rotors and the area represented by the blades is woefully inadequate to stop its plummet. Expect a 10-20% decrease in glide performance with a windmilling prop.

Good glide performance comes from:

• Large span wings. They reduce inefficiencies due to the tendency of air to flow spanwise around the tips rather than back and downward. The reason that soaring wings are long and skinny is to keep the total area the same but reduce these tip losses.

• Fewer and skinnier lines to reduce drag. Higher performance wings take this further—leaving off the protective sheath from lines to reduce their radius. They'll also have fewer lines by employing more cascades, where one line goes up then splits into two which then splits and so on.

• A flatter profile—longer lines allow a flatter wing which improves efficiency but at the expense of increased line drag.

• More cells. More ribs mean a more precise airfoil shape. Closer spacing prevents each cell from billowing so far out of shape.

Interestingly, increasing weight doesn't change the glide performance, it just increases the speed at which it occurs. *Sink Rate* will be higher, but the maximum glide ratio stays the same. This effect can be useful and, in fact, competition soaring pilots sometimes carry ballast to increase their cross country speeds. For example: A 150 pound pilot on an 8:1 glider may have a best glide speed of 20 mph. With a 200 pound pilot, that same glider still has a maximum 8:1 glide ratio but it will occur at 22 mph and will sink proportionally faster, too.

Wind has a strong effect on glide ratio over the ground. See page 60 for an illustration of the effect.

See page 60 for an illustration of the effect.

Center of Lift and Drag

The center of lift is a point on the wing where lift is said to act. The entire wing provides some, lift but it is concentrated in the first 30% of the chord (front to back measurement) and the inside 60% of span. If you could attach a rope to this point the glider/pilot combination would balance from it.

The center of drag is the point where drag is said to act. It will be somewhere between the pilot and wing. If you could attach a towline to the glider/pilot from this point it would have no tendency to pitch or twist due to drag.

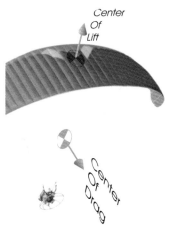

In level flight, deck angle is the same as angle of attack. Powering up will only push the pilot into a climb, not increase speed.

Sink Rate

How fast you descend is *sink rate*, commonly measured in meters per second (m/s) or feet per minute (fpm). Minimum sink rate is the lowest descent rate the glider is capable of. Minimum sink *speed* is how fast you must fly to get that minimum rate. Going faster or slower than this speed will always increase descent rate. Unlike glide ratio, increasing weight *will* increase sink rate.

Wing area, usually measured in square meters, is hugely important. More wing area means a better (lower) sink rate but at a slower speed. A small wing will be faster and cover ground faster than a larger glider of the same efficiency but will sink faster.

The *Polar Curve* (at the end of this chapter) shows these relationships. At each weight there is a speed that produces the minimum sink. For most gliders, that speed comes trimmed slow with about brake pressure 2 (one quarter).

Speed

Adding power does not add speed—it causes a climb along with a slight slow down. If you could move the motor thrust up to the center of drag, then throttling up would indeed make you go faster.

There *are* other ways to go faster, and they *do* always require more power. Anytime the speed goes up, more thrust is required to overcome the increased drag—and these craft have *lots* of drag. Here are some ways to go faster with a PPG:

1. Design. Some wings are made for speed. Reflex wings, in particular,

Level Flight
Deck Angle = Angle of Attack

Digging Deeper: Angle of Attack (AoA)

Confusion can arise about what happens when adding power regarding AoA and flight path.

Experiments have shown that adding power mostly affects the flight path, but also *does* increase the Angle of Attack a small amount.

Parachutal stall has proven nettlesome for powered flyers far more than non-powered flyers. It usually happens at higher power. Thrust can help keep the wing stalled once it hits critical AoA. Without power, most wings recover immediately on their own.

effectively decrease wing area with trims full up (fast).

2. Higher weight or a smaller wing. You'll take more space to launch and will, of course, require more thrust.

3. Trimmers can increase speed by about 15% (more on reflex models.)

4. Speedbar activation increases speed by about 25%. It also increases the possibility of frontal collapse in turbulence. Reflex wings sometimes advertise better collapse resistance while accelerated. If a speedbar/trimmer interconnect (STI) or *PK system* is installed (mostly on competition reflex wings), then the speedbar and trimmers can be activated using just the speedbar.

5. Angling the thrust line upward (thrust vector downward) is like adding weight. You're leaning forward and down, which isn't terribly comfortable, but it slightly increases the speed just like adding weight does.

Digging Deeper: Ground Effect

Ground Effect doesn't affect us much since it happens when a wing gets within about a half wingspan of the ground. Lift increases and drag decreases because the tip vortices are reduced. Air is prevented from circling around the wing tip.

Paraglider wings are too far above the ground to benefit. Plus, paragliders by design of their anhedral tips (downward curved), reduce the amount of lift lost to tip vortices.

Efficiency Under Power

Thrust results from the propeller accelerating a mass of air from some speed to some faster speed—pushing us in the opposite direction. How much thrust depends on how much air and how quickly it's accelerated. We can either accelerate a little bit of air a lot, or a lot of air a little. Jet engines burn copious amounts of fuel to accelerate a little bit of air (relatively) a lot. That's great for going hundreds of mph but not very efficient for going dozens of mph. It's noisy too. For slow craft—and we're about as slow as it gets—higher efficiency comes from accelerating a lot of air a little; i.e. using a big prop. That is, fortunately, also the quietest arrangement.

Efficiency can be spent either on improved fuel consumption or more thrust. In general, the larger the prop, the quieter and more "thrusty" the machine. Even jet engine makers have taken the large mass route, designing *high bypass* motors with huge fans that are quieter and more powerful.

Wing

The airfoil shape is chosen by designers to optimize performance. Although, in principle, airfoil design is identical to rigid wings, softness dictates some special requirements.

Anhedral Curvature

That graceful arc carved by the wing's drooping tips is *anhedral curvature*, a concession to a support structure that can only pull. It must keep perpendicular pressure on the lines. Without that 90 degree pull angle, the fabric would deform. Higher performance wings minimize the curvature using longer lines at some expense in drag.

Tip Tornadoes

Tip vortices are a pair of surprisingly strong airflow spirals attached to the tips of any lifting wing. They

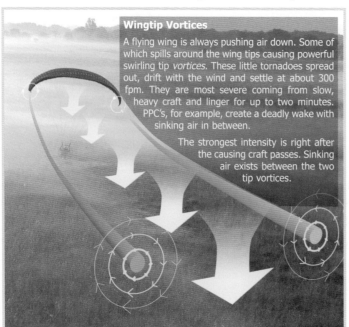

Wingtip Vortices

A flying wing is always pushing air down. Some of which spills around the wing tips causing powerful swirling tip *vortices*. These little tornadoes spread out, drift with the wind and settle at about 300 fpm. They are most severe coming from slow, heavy craft and linger for up to two minutes. PPC's, for example, create a deadly wake with sinking air in between.

The strongest intensity is right after the causing craft passes. Sinking air exists between the two tip vortices.

represent the most dangerous element of wake turbulence which is left by an aircraft, like a boat leaves a wake in water. Prop blast also stirs up the air but that is just turbulence and doesn't linger for long.

Wake turbulence is worse when it's generated by craft that are heavy, slow and clean. Powered paraglider tandems and powered parachutes, for example, meet two of the criteria and can make vicious turbulence that must be avoided for at least 2 minutes.

Tighter turns load the wing more which generates commensurately more powerful wake turbulence. If you pull a 2-G turn, the wake turbulence will behave like it came from a craft weighing twice as much.

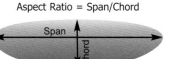

Aspect Ratio = Span/Chord

Aspect Ratio

Aspect ratio is wingspan divided by the chord (see illustration at right.) A 32 foot wingspan with an 8 foot average chord means the aspect ratio is 4:1. Without knowing the average chord, you can also derive the aspect ratio using $Span^2$ divided by Area. Flat aspect ratio is measured with the wing laying flat, while inflated (aka *projected*) aspect ratio is measured from an inflated wing's shadow.

Long, skinny wings are more efficient (better L/D) than short fat ones because they minimize tip vortices, but there are trade-offs. On a paraglider, the only way to have long, skinny wings is to put them on long lines which increases line drag. Long, skinny wings (high aspect ratio) also tend to have some unsavory behaviors (see Chapter 26), which is why beginner wings have lower aspect ratios.

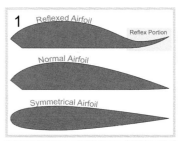

Airfoil Shape and Bernoulli

A plank will create lift, but shaping it like an airfoil will do so with far less drag. Bernoulli's law, which describes conservation of energy in a fluid medium, helps explain how air behaves around airfoils. It doesn't explain lift in the way old textbooks say it does, but that's only because the law was misused.

Our soft wings give up some performance due to their puffed-up cells. Builders employ many tricks to minimize this through line cascades, internal bracing, and different types of reinforcement, but losses are unavoidable. Higher performance wings typically reduce the effect by having more cells and fewer lines. This reduces the need for magic dust.

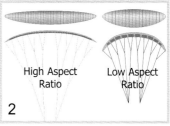

Shapes have trade-offs too. Some sacrifice stability or collapse resistance for performance and vice-versa.

Angle of the Dangle

Air flowing past the pilot/wing combination is called the relative wind or slipstream. Angle of attack (AoA) is the angle between the wing chord line and this relative wind. The climb or descent angle is the angle that your flight path makes to the ground. *Angle of incidence* (AoI) is the angle the chord line makes to the B lines, or more accurately, a perpendicular line to the B lines.

Deck angle is the angle made between the chord line and Earth.

Increasing the angle of attack increases lift up to a point. That point is called the *critical angle of attack* beyond which airflow breaks off from the wing's top, causing lift to plummet while drag soars—an aerodynamic *stall*.

1. *Reflex* airfoils have an upward tilt near the trailing edge that makes them more collapse resistant at higher speed. This is mostly because the center of lift moves forward. See Chapter 26 for more on reflex wings.

A normal paraglider airfoil has more curve on top than the bottom, while a *symmetrical* airfoil has the same curve on top and bottom. Symmetricals are never used on paragliders since they're primarily to allow aerobatic aircraft to fly upside down. That wouldn't go well for us.

2. High aspect ratios are commonly found on high performance soaring wings. Beginner models usually have a lower aspect ratio.

A lot happens when you throttle up. This pilot went to full power starting at 2; here's the result:

Angle of Attack (AoA) increases as your body swings forward, increasing lift and accelerating you upwards into a steep climb briefly. The AoA peaks (4). Then the wing surges forward, causing AoA to decrease as the wing catches up (6).

Finally, you settle into a steady state climb (7) with the AoA only slightly higher than when you started. You'll keep this condition as long as the power lasts.

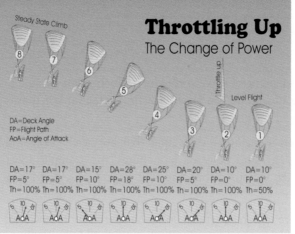

Throttling Up
The Change of Power

DA=Deck Angle
FP=Flight Path
AoA=Angle of Attack

DA=17°	DA=17°	DA=15°	DA=28°	DA=25°	DA=20°	DA=10°	DA=10°
FP=5°	FP=5°	FP=10°	FP=18°	FP=10°	FP=5°	FP=0°	FP=0°
Th=100%	Th=100%	Th=100%	Th=100%	Th=100%	Th=100%	Th=100%	Th=50%

Adding power increases AoA which increases lift, drag, and causes a climb (or decreases descent) with a very slight airspeed decrease.

Angle of Incidence (AoI)

Figure 22.60 shows AoI and how it relates to the same value on an airplane. Our "fuselage" is us, so we use a perpendicular line off of the B-lines.

Pressing speedbar reduces AoI. So does letting the trimmers out. Speedbar action primarily lowers the leading edge while trimmer action primarily raises the trailing edge, but each one *may* deform the wing also. Trimmers on reflex wings frequently deform the wing in a way to reduce effective wing area.

Different manufacturers use speedbar and trimmers differently in how much they change the airfoil (profile) as opposed to how much they change the AoI.

Changing Angle of Attack (AoA)

Lift of a given wing varies by speed and Angle of Attack (AoA). More speed, more lift. More AoA, more lift—up to a point. So changing the AoA will have a big effect. Adding or subtracting power imparts a small change to AoA. It feels like more because the flight path also changes.

Pulling brakes increases the AoA by lowering the trailing edge which immediately tilts the chord line. That also adds drag by making the airfoil shape less efficient.

Reflex Airfoils

Reflex airfoils have been used for many years on tailless aircraft to increase pitch stability. On paragliders they allow greater speed while increasing collapse resistance; whereas non-reflex paragliders are *more* prone to collapse at their higher speeds.

By raising the aft portion of the airfoil (fast trimmer setting), the center of pressure moves forward and tuck (collapse) resistance improves. You can see this when kiting a reflex wing by pulling down hard on the A lines—regular gliders front tuck, while highly reflexed gliders tend to maintain shape. This comes at some small penalty in efficiency—the more reflex is employed, the less efficient the airfoil is.

Pulling brakes while trimmed fast is particularly bad because it moves the center of pressure aft and makes the wing far more susceptible to front tuck, which is why tip steering is almost always included on highly reflexed wings.

Turning

When you pull one brake, the trailing edge deflects downward, increasing lift and drag on that side. You might think the wing would bank opposite to brake pull since there is more lift on the braked side—much like how airplanes bank their wings with a downward deflected aileron. But, due to pendular stability, a paraglider acts more on the drag, slowing down that side and causing a turn. As the wing changes direction, you swing outward, causing a bank. That bank is what actually does the work by redirecting the wing's overall lift to pull you around the turn.

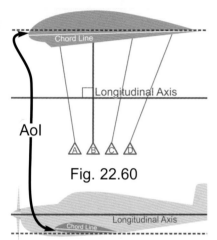

Fig. 22.60

Angle of Incidence (AoI)

Angle of Incidence is the angle between the longitudinal axis and chord line.

This shows how AoI is fixed to the wing lines in the same way an airplane's AoI is fixed to its fuselage (body). On paragliders we say it's perpendicular to the B-lines. You could use a line drawn across the quick links, but that varies based on speedbar and trimmer position. A 10 degree angle change at the quick link line would only be a few degrees at the wing's chord line.

Notice on the paraglider that AoI is slightly negative, while on the airplane it's slightly positive. Gravity, and the pilot hanging below, forces paragliders to have some amount of negative AoI.

Don't confuse this with (AoA) which is the angle between the wing's chord line and the *slipstream* (relative wind).

On many designs, each brake also pulls the wing sideways a bit, which improves handling. Any brake input slows down the overall airspeed, which will either require more power or, if gliding, will worsen glide performance.

A turn always increases sink rate since some of the wing's lift is now being spent pulling you around the turn.

Thrust Vectoring

Normally the thrust should be nearly perpendicular to the C line of the wing, pushing nearly straight backwards while in flight.

If the thrust line is angled upwards (thrust vector pushing you down slightly) then increasing power will increase down force on the wing, increasing speed slightly. If the thrust line is pointed downward (motor tilted back) it will have the opposite effect. This small effect can generally be ignored.

If the thrust line is offset relative to the risers' center, you'll twist which will cause a bank in the opposite direction. A motor pushing your body left will cause a bank to the right.

In very few cases, the wing and motor can interact in a way that causes a "wallowing" action back and forth while under power. This is due to *loaded riser twist*: as the wing reaches a bank limit and starts coming back, uneven riser load causes the motor to twist the pilot slightly, redirecting thrust which pushes him in the other direction. It's more pronounced on smaller wings.

How a Wing Collapses

A *collapse*, or *deflation*, occurs when part of the wing folds under (it can't fold upwards) after getting pushed down by a vertical or horizontal gust. Usually it recovers before the pilot even knows it happened. A frontal collapse is where the leading edge tucks under while the rest of the wing remains mostly inflated or forms a "horseshoe" shape. There are two basic causes, **atmospheric turbulence** and **pilot inducement** (see chapter 18).

Atmospheric turbulence is what most pilots fear—getting swatted out of the sky—and it is surprisingly rare, unless you seek out lively air. Usually it comes from flying through a vortex or swirl that hits the wing, blowing it down and out of shape. The slipstream pushes the now-loose fabric (with probably closed cells) back for a few seconds until internal pressure and line geometry sort things out. Pressure to stay inflated (or "open") comes both from the leading edge openings and from the exterior surface tensioning its lines.

One way to get a turbulence-induced collapse is to fly into a rapidly changing wind such as a thermal. If you fly into a horizontal shear, it can "curl up" a tip as air tries to push the fabric in a different direction. Low G's, such as from a wingover where you feel light in the seat (unloading), makes a collapse far more likely.

Stalling

A wing stalls when airflow over the top separates into a turbulent, random flow. That happens when the *critical angle of attack* is exceeded, and although technically not related to speed, high angles of attack result from

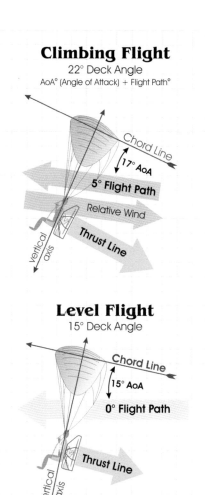

Climbing Flight
22° Deck Angle
AoA° (Angle of Attack) + Flight Path°

Chord Line
17° AoA
5° Flight Path
Relative Wind
Thrust Line
vertical axis

Level Flight
15° Deck Angle

Chord Line
15° AoA
0° Flight Path
Thrust Line
vertical axis

Ground (Deck)

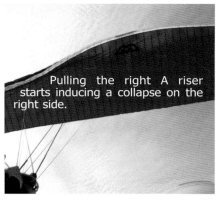

Pulling the right A riser starts inducing a collapse on the right side.

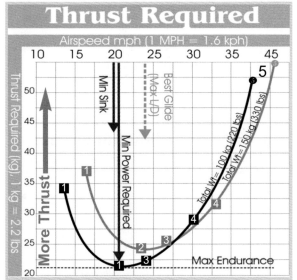

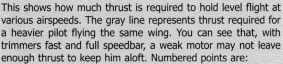

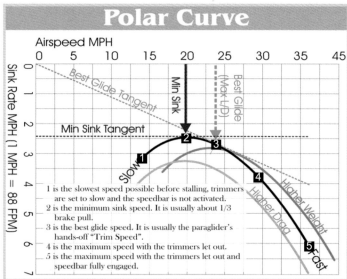

Thrust Required

This shows how much thrust is required to hold level flight at various airspeeds. The gray line represents thrust required for a heavier pilot flying the same wing. You can see that, with trimmers fast and full speedbar, a weak motor may not leave enough thrust to keep him aloft. Numbered points are:

1: The slowest speed possible before stalling. Trimmers are set to slow and the speedbar is not activated.

2: Minimum thrust required. On most wings it is the slowest trimmer setting and about brake pressure 1.

3: Trimmers slow (or neutral) and no brakes, which is normally very close to the best L/D speed.

4: Trimmers fast but no speedbar.

Polar Curve

Polar curves (shown above) graph a glider's sink rate and flying speed. It is a great way to understand many relationships between control settings, speed, sink rate, glide ratio and endurance. The next chapter has a discussion of power vs. thrust but know that *power* must take into account airspeed.

The polar curve shows sink rate as speed changes. At your slowest speed, just before stalling, the sink rate is quite high. As you speed up, the sink rate improves until reaching the "Min Sink" speed. Then sink rate increases again as you speed up. The tangent line to the curve from 0,0 is the best L/D (glide). Where it touches the curve is the speed, and its slope is the best glide ratio itself. Being heavy doesn't worsen the glide *ratio*; it just increases the speed and descent rate where it occurs. Sadly, paraglider wing manufacturers don't go to the trouble of producing these charts.

heavy brakes and flying slow. If you're already flying slowly, it doesn't take much of a gust to cause a stall. A spin happens when only half of the wing stalls and the other half keeps flying, causing a rotation around the vertical axis.

What is frequently called a full stall, when the pilot stuffs the brakes below his seat, is really more of an aerodynamic aberration than a stall—and far more violent, too. The wing does indeed whip through the stall AoA but then essentially becomes a luffing sail—flapping wildly in a hurricane force wind as you plummet. Raising the brakes lets it re-inflate, returning normal aerodynamics with an unpredictable bang and surge (*see Chapter 18*).

Maximum Range speed, the speed that results in the most distance for a given fuel burn, is close to best glide speed in no wind. In a headwind, it's some higher airspeed, and in a tailwind, it's some lower speed, down to minimum sink speed. That's an approximation since maximum range speed is affected by fuel consumption at each speed.

Combining aerodynamics with shenanigans, Phil Russman surfs Glamis Dunes' sea of sand in California.

By Robert Kittilä

Motor & Propeller

Thrust comes from pushing air. Rockets would work, but the fuel is hard to come by and smells bad. Jet engines are thrusty but thirsty, plus they're expensive and loud. Electric motors await improved batteries, and fuel cells await affordability. Four strokes are quiet, clean and efficient but are heavy for their power, at least on back-packs.

So that leaves the venerable 2-stroke, powerplant of choice for chain sawmen, go-cart racers and nearly all foot-launch powered paraglider pilots. Wheeled craft have more 4-stroke options since wheels do the heavy lifting.

Thrust & Horsepower

The only measure of power that we really care about is thrust—how hard will it push. The industry has never settled on a thrust testing standard, and claims are frequently exaggerated, so independent tests are valuable. Even more so if they use the same tester, under similar conditions, and with stakeholders mothering over the process. Tests are sometimes done at fly-ins. Ignore *absolute* thrust values, which vary due to conditions, but value the *comparison*. It's cheating if a motor is tested without the harness.

Horsepower (HP) is commonly used to measure power, but it's only marginally useful to us. A 30 HP motor is powerful for PPG, but mated to the wrong prop, it's worthless—you might as well be spinning a plank. Horsepower only suggests what a motor can do given the right propeller and reduction ratio. It has some value since manufacturers will always try to extract the most thrust and therefore end up with similar efficiencies. Still, thrust is what we're ultimately after.

Expect a lot of variability. One motor that tests at 100 lbs on one day may do 105

Torque is interesting, but we're more interested in horsepower—the result of torque applied at RPM. You can have a lot of torque, but if nothing spins, no power is delivered.

We're even *more* interested in thrust, which comes from a propeller harnessing horsepower. More on that later.

Charted below is the relationship between an engine's torque, RPM, and the resulting hp.

Torque & Power

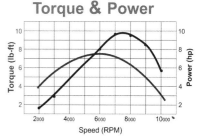

This Bailey 4-stroke motor is one of few to make it commercially as a paramotor powerplant. Although it is heavier for the power, its efficiency allows carrying less fuel which partially offsets the extra weight.

lbs on the next day, even using the same tester. Plus, there are surprising variations within brand and propeller. Manufacturing vagaries can incur a 10% difference from the same model of paramotor and prop. Wooden props can account for rpm differences up to 5%. Molded props, usually carbon fiber, are more consistent.

2 And 4-Stroke Motors

"**Suck, squeeze, bang, and blow**" is the mantra of all internal combustion engines. The term "2-Cycle" (or "2-Stroke") means that a complete cycle of the piston takes only 2 strokes, up and down. It fires every time the piston reaches the top whereas a four stroke motor fires every *other* time. That's why 2-stroke motors get more power per pound than 4-strokes and why they run hotter.

Four-stroke motors have valves and cams so they require better lubrication, ergo crankcase oil, whereas two-stroke engines get lubricated from a gas/oil mix.

Four Strokes

The four-cycle (4-stroke) motor, common in cars, lawnmowers, snow blowers, etc., is more complicated. It has intake and exhaust valves in each cylinder's head (the uppermost part) that open and close in conjunction with the piston's travel. They control how fuel/air flows and exhaust gases flow in four distinct strokes or *cycles*.

The valves, piston, camshaft, oil pump and other moving parts add weight and complexity. Some small 4-strokes get by with just splashing the crankcase oil to needy parts.

Understanding the 2-Stroke

Two stroke motors have come a long way in 60 years ago. Accumulated tweaks, like reed valves and tuned pipes, are the big improvements, but geometrics, electronics and materials have helped as well.

During one crankshaft revolution, the piston is being pushed down by burning fuel on top while compressing the next crankcase full of fuel/air below.

A *tuned pipe*, common on modern 2-strokes, optimizes performance but only works through a narrow rpm range called the *power band*. The improved efficiency can be spent on either reduced fuel consumption or more power.

With a two-stroke motor, all the interesting stuff happens during the piston's bottom half of travel; and a lot is happening.

- As the piston rises, it sucks a new fuel/air charge through the carburetor and reed valve, into the crankcase below (**suck**).

- Above the rising piston, a fuel/air charge is being compressed (**squeeze**).

- When the piston nears its peak a spark ignites the mixture, powering the piston downward (**bang**).

- On its way down, the piston's bottom compresses a new fuel/air charge in the crankcase (**minor squeeze**).

- About halfway down the exhaust port is exposed, squirting the burned, high pressure gas out (**blow**). Some of the incoming fuel/air charge can escape out the exhaust, too, but a tuned pipe uses pressure waves to push it back in.

• As the piston continues down, a transfer port is exposed allowing the newly compressed crankcase fuel/air charge to rush up around the piston and into the cylinder starting a new cycle.

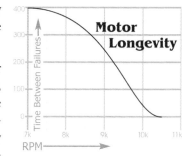

Motor Longevity

As you would expect, a good motor motto is: "run hard, fix more."

Wear increases in proportion to heat and high RPM. Operating near a motor's limits can dramatically reduce its lifespan.

Besides producing power, the piston doubles as intake and exhaust valves. Fewer moving parts on a two-cycle makes it lighter and helps reliability. Unfortunately, minimal lubrication and heat (twice as many power strokes as a 4-stroke) sap some reliability which is why they need more attention than four-strokes. Plus, lubrication relies on the proper type and amount of oil being mixed in with the fuel. Any malady that increases heat or decreases cooling can cause piston seizure, an unwelcome welding of piston to cylinder wall.

Carburetors

Carburetors feed an appropriate mix of fuel and air to the motor according to throttle setting. Piston action is always sucking air through the carburetor during intake pulses.

The primary structure of a carburetor is some sort of throttle valve that operates in a venturi, a constriction that lowers pressure to help suck fuel in as a fine mist, atomizing it. As the throttle valve is opened, more air gets sucked in, thus pulling in more fuel that gets mixed in to speed up the motor. Nearly all carbs have various adjustments and/or interchangeable parts designed to optimize operation based on elevation and temperature.

Engine Cutaway
Vitorazzi 185 cc

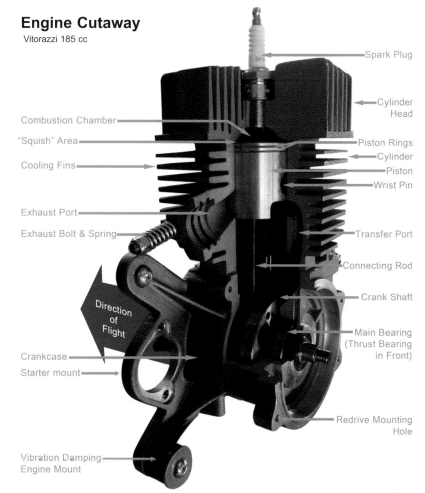

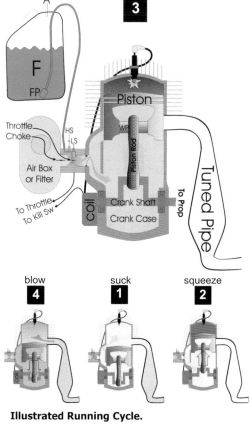

Illustrated Running Cycle.

Suck, squeeze, bang, and blow, starting with a bang above. The devil is in the details.

1. The drive side of a Top 80 reveals some common features on reduction drive machines. The clutch, in this case, has 3 *shoes* (in red) that move out to engage the clutch bell as engine rpm increases. The prop is attached, through gears, to the clutch bell.

2: The motor's other side reveals some basic parts of a fan-cooled motor with the cooling shroud removed. The fan wheel blows air upwards where the cooling shroud redirects it over the motor's cooling fins. If the fan breaks, the motor will overheat in just a few minutes.

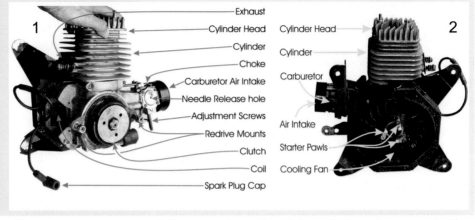

1 — Exhaust
Cylinder Head
Cylinder
Choke
Carburetor Air Intake
Needle Release hole
Adjustment Screws
Redrive Mounts
Clutch
Coil
Spark Plug Cap

2 — Cylinder Head
Cylinder
Carburetor
Air Intake
Starter Pawls
Cooling Fan

1. This pull starter assembly is what the starter pawls (see motor above) engage when you pull it. Springs hold them against the teeth, then, when it starts, they ride over the back side of the teeth. At idle rpm, centrifugal force* pulls the pawls outward so they don't wear out riding on the teeth.

*Centrifugal force: the common term for an inertial effect on spinning objects that behaves *like* a force.

2. **Flash Starters** make it more practical for larger motors to have clutches. On belted machines the prop acts as a flywheel, making it easier to get past the compression stroke during start. On clutch units the prop is free-wheeling until the clutch engages, so it can't act as a flywheel.

The heart of a flash starter is its powerful main spring that gets wound up as you pull. At a set tension it releases, spinning the crank shaft and (hopefully) starting the motor.

by Nayot Kurukitkoson

Two types are common, differing on how they deliver fuel to the venturi: *Float bowls* and *diaphragms*, each with advantages and disadvantages.

Float bowl carbs use a bowl and float like in float bowl toilets. Fuel is delivered into the bowl through a valve. As the bowl fills up, a float inside rises to shut off incoming fuel and maintain a constant level. That means constant pressure at the pickup near the bowl's bottom. A higher float level makes for a slightly richer mixture.

Fuel is sucked up from the bowl's bottom through the *main jet* (an orifice) into the venturi past a tapered needle. How far that needle goes into the jet determines how much fuel flows. The needle is attached to a *slider* that opens up the air passageway, exposing more of the venturi opening. Opening the throttle opens the air passage and, by lifting the needle, increases fuel flow. Ergo, more power.

Once properly set up, float bowl carburetors generally provide a somewhat smoother throttle response with fewer adjustments. The drawback is that large changes in average mixture require installing different jets. Thankfully that's a painless job. Higher elevations may require smaller jets since less fuel is needed to mix with the thinner air. Other minor adjustments can be available either by raising or lowering the needle position or changing fixed air inlets for idle.

Float bowl carbs must be oriented right side up, relative to the frame, and be under positive G-Loading. Given that the paraglider needs positive G's, too, that isn't much of a problem. Lines can't push, fuel doesn't flow uphill.

Membrane (or Diaphragm) carburetors work by filling a small expandable *metering chamber* with fuel then pulsing it into the venturi. This process uses changing crankcase pressure and one-way valves within the carb. Fuel runs into the chamber when crankcase pressure builds above a certain point, pushing against a needle valve held closed by spring pressure. See illustration on page 232.

They were originally intended for power tools to work in any orientation. The membrane expands as fuel comes in through the inlet needle so it matters little whether the carburetor is right side up or sideways. They can be finicky, though. Small particles have myriad nooks to lodge in and the membranes, springs and other small parts can get worn, become brittle, or damaged without looking bad.

Most of these carbs include a *high speed* and a *low speed needle* valve to allow fine mixture adjustments for their respective realm. These needle valves alter how much fuel passes by—unscrew the needle and it opens up for a richer mixture. Some adjustments, though, affect *air* flow—always consult the engine's manual.

Tuning a Membrane Carburetor

A user manual, if you have it, is your best source, but absent that, this advice may help. If your motor strays too far from the recommended initial settings, there's probably a problem that tuning won't help. Consult the troubleshooting chart in chapter 12.

This guide applies primarily to motors with membrane-type carbs having a low and a high mixture screw. The high screw primarily affects mixture at high rpm while the low screw primarily affects the mixture at low rpm although they each have some affect throughout the throttle range.

First, a note about tuning. When a two-stroke motor is rich, it runs rough and sometimes fires every other stroke, that's called *4-cycling.* As you lean the mixture, it runs smoother and faster, eventually peaking then decreasing while remaining smooth. Further leaning makes it die. Whenever a needle valve controls fuel (as most do), screwing it in (turning clockwise) makes the fuel/air mixture leaner (less fuel) and unscrewing makes it richer.

Set the motor to its initial factory settings, strap it to something solid (tree, stout fence, stout friend, rack, etc.) and start it. *Remember, more serious injuries occur from prop strikes than from flying.* When cold, they tend to be lean then get richer during warmup. After a minute or so, you're ready to begin the adjustments. Use increments of about an 1/8th of a turn when making changes.

Start by adjusting the low screw. Adjust it so the rpm peaks, then unscrew it (richen) slowly until the rpm drops a bit. It should remain smooth. If the motor quits when throttle is applied, richen the low screw further. If it coughs or runs rough when throttle is applied, then lean it a bit.

Now to the high screw. Throttle up to full power. Just like before—you want to adjust the high screw until the rpm peaks, then back off (richen) a bit, about 50 rpm. This is called being slightly "rich of peak." It sacrifices higher fuel flow for cooler running—a good trade since a lean mixture frequently overheats and seizes the motor. An excessively rich mixture makes carbon deposits on the cylinder head and spark plug. Unlike human health, motors are better rich than lean.

With the high screw adjusted we need to recheck throttle response. Try adding power quickly—if it runs rough, lean the high screw just a bit. If it dies, richen the high screw slightly. You may need to repeat this whole process once or twice.

Higher elevations, above 3000 feet MSL, require leaning the mixtures. Once set, however, you should not have to adjust it until changing elevations again. Be especially careful to re-adjust after going to a *lower* elevation—the mixture will be lean which risks overheating.

When a problem is elusive, consider replacing the whole carburetor. They are inexpensive, install easily, and can save many, many hours of headache. If that's not the problem, then you've got a spare carburetor on hand.

Float Bowl Carb

The float-bowl carburetor doesn't need much tuning. But when you go to a significantly different altitude, you may have to screw in a different *jet,* an orifice that the needle (inset) slides into. A bigger jet lets in more fuel which richens the overall mixture. At higher altitudes, a smaller jet is required.

On this carb, the barrel slides up and down which also regulates the amount of air that flows through. The tapered needle, which is attached to the barrel, lets more fuel in as the barrel lets more air through. This generally gives a smoother throttle response since it provides a gradual but immediate increase in both fuel and air as the throttle opens. Besides changing jets, the only adjustments are for idle—a large screw (1) sets the idle stop up or down and a small screw (2) can change the amount of air let in; screwing it in decreases airflow, making the mixture richer.

Fuel comes up from the bowl that stays about 3/4 full to provide constant pressure to the orifice. A float valve keeps the level just like a float-bowl toilet keeps the tank at a constant level.

Inset courtesy SouthernSkies.net

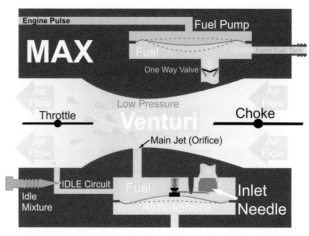

CARBURETOR *membrane*

IDLE

Engine Pulse | Fuel Pump
Fuel | From Fuel Tank
One Way Valve

Choke Closed

Throttle — Low Pressure

Very Little Airflow with Throttle Closed — Choke

Air Flow

Main Jet (Orifice) | From Air Filter

IDLE Circuit | Fuel | Atmosphere | Inlet Needle
Idle Mixture

MAX

Engine Pulse | Fuel Pump
Fuel | From Fuel Tank
One Way Valve

Air Flow

Throttle | Low Pressure Venturi | Choke

Air Flow

Main Jet (Orifice)

IDLE Circuit | Fuel | Atmosphere | Inlet Needle
Idle Mixture

Throttle closed means there's little airflow and low suction, so almost no fuel is sucked out of the main jet. Instead, fuel comes through the idle circuit. The choke stays open except for starting where it's closed which causes vacuum, sucking lots of fuel out of the jets and into the engine. The inlet needle is popped off its seat by fuel pressure.

Throttle Open allows full airflow which sucks maximum fuel out of the Main Jet and a little bit out of the idle circuit. The inlet needle's purpose is to keep fuel in the chamber and prevent it from leaking out when the engine is off. Remember, these carbs are made for power tools that may get used upside down.

Membrane carburetors (carbs) are the most common type found on paramotors. They're lightweight and cheap.

Besides the main venturi and fuel outlet, most models have two circuits that influence mixture for high and low power. But this one only trims idle (1). Screwing it in leans the idle mixture. The other rod (2) controls how far open the throttle is at idle. Screwing it in increases idle rpm.

Reed valves are one-way valves that open every time the piston draws in a new fuel/air charge. Like a heart valve, goo squirts through, then it closes so nothing comes back out.

The curved metal parts are strain relief—they make the reeds open around the curve thus preventing extra stress at the attachment points.

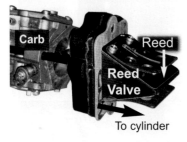

Carb | Reed | Reed Valve | To cylinder

Pop-off Pressure and Other Membrane Carburetor Issues

The membrane carb's metering chamber is like a float bowl. An inlet needle reacts to incoming fuel pressure and vacuum in the venturi to keep the chamber nearly full of fuel, ready to deliver it to the various throttle circuits. Atmosphere air is on the membrane's other side. When fuel pressure pushes the needle off its seat, fuel flows into the "bowl." That's the *Pop off pressure*.

If the inlet needle can't unseat easily enough, fuel doesn't fill the chamber and the mixture will be too lean. If the spring is weak and the needle pops off too easily, excess fuel makes the motor run rich. Cutting the inlet needle's spring a bit shorter decreases pop-off pressure and stretching it increases pop-off pressure. Only do this if you know exactly what you're doing, though.

Other little details can muck up the works too. Have a good fuel filter to keep unwanted debris from gumming things up. Carburetor rebuild kits are cheap and relatively easy to install. They usually replace the spring that determines pop-off pressure although that's rarely the problem. They also replace the fuel pump membrane and a miscellany of gaskets and springs.

Reed Valves

Most modern two stroke motors employ reed valves (pictured left) to increase efficiency. These stout one-way valves mount between the carburetor and motor. As the piston moves to compress the fuel/air mixture, the reed valve prevents it from going back into the carburetor. They do eventually wear out but are easy to replace.

Compression Release

Some motors come with a *compression release* (decompression) valve that makes pull starting easier. It works by venting the cylinder during compression. As soon as the motor fires, the valve closes. Manual versions must be reset after each start but are less prone to sticking open which renders the motor unable to start. Some motors use just a small internal hole that goes from the cylinder head to the crankcase—these must be cleaned out about every 10 to 20 hours of use.

Propeller & Reduction Drives

A propeller is a rotating wing, pitched steeply at the center and flattening out to a skinny tip. Since the tip is moving very fast, it has a shallow angle to the air. Strangely, the most efficient propeller would have only one blade since that blade would have the least amount of interference from the other blade's wake. The extreme imbalance would be a bit problematic.

Propeller choice dramatically affects a motor's performance—it's a case study in compromise. Matching the right prop to a particular motor is critical for harnessing the motor's full potential. Here are some of the trade-offs:

- Long, skinny blades are better for thrust but are harder to make strong. Plus the tips must not be allowed to go near supersonic due to noise and drag.

- Lighter is better for rpm acceleration but doesn't wear well in the presence of abrasives (beach sand and gravel roadways are good examples).

- Fewer blades are more efficient but more blades allow bigger motors to have a smaller prop diameter.

Tip Speed, Noise and Performance

The only things that move fast on a paramotor are its propeller tips—and they move over 350 mph. That's more than half the speed of sound, or Mach 0.5, where Mach 1.0 is the speed of sound. Any faster and loud, thrust-robbing supersonic shock waves start to form. Above Mach 0.6, (60% the speed of sound), noise and drag increase dramatically with Mach 0.8 being a practical limit.

High rpm is doubly bad for noise since, besides creating stronger sound waves, their high pitch is more annoying. Given the same tip speed, a small prop at high rpm will sound louder than a large prop at low rpm.

The quietest combination for any motor is to spin the largest possible diameter prop (45 inches or more) at the slowest possible rpm. The large prop disk helps by having more clean air since it extends outward farther beyond the pilot's body.

Getting the RPM Right

Most two stroke motors get their best power at high rpm. A reduction drive lets designers to use that high rpm while keeping the prop at a more desirable (lower) rpm. Using gears or pulleys, a reduction drive lowers the output rpm by some ratio. If the input gear has three times as many teeth as the output gear then the ratio is 3:1 (three to one). The motor spins the small gear at 9000 rpm which drives the propeller gear at 3000 rpm. The extra weight and complexity of a reduction drive is *well* worth it.

Direct drive motors, where the prop is bolted to the crankshaft, don't balance the slower rpm needs of the prop with higher rpm needs of the motor. Plus they're noisy.

Since larger pistons typically get their horsepower at lower rpm, larger displacement motors have a better chance of working as direct drives but still give up enormous thrust potential. Larger pistons are heavier,

Propeller Efficiency

Propeller efficiency is how much of the motor's power gets converted into propulsive thrust. It varies based on airspeed and propeller design. Most props are designed to be more efficient while in flight rather than at 0 airspeed.

Reduction Drives

Reduction drives come in many ratios. The same housing is frequently used with different gears to give the user a choice. A larger ratio means the motor's high rpm will be converted to a lower prop rpm. The lower the prop rpm, the larger the prop can be.

The gears bathe continuously in gear oil or grease. The prop is connected to the large gear in a ratio determined by the relative tooth count of each gear. This reduction drive utilizes four bearings, two for each gear, to keep things running smoothly.

Prop is attached to this gear

Motor spins this gear

Calculating Tip Speed

If you're considering a different sized prop then you must take into account the ideal rpm and tip speed with respect to the speed of sound. Besides being loud, a lot of power is given up at high tip speeds.

Mach 1 is the speed of sound. It varies only by temperature and is faster in warmer air. At the standard temperature of 15°C (59°F) it is 761 mph.

To calculate tip speed as a mach number, use the following formula:

Tip Speed Mach = Prop rpm x prop diameter (in inches) / 256000. So a 48 inch prop spinning at 3000 rpm would have a tip speed of 0.56 Mach (56% the speed of sound).

Most thrust comes from the outer portion of a propeller.

though, so most engines use a small piston and spin it *really* fast (high rpm).

For example, the legacy Solo 210, a relatively large displacement motor (210 cc's), gets its peak HP near 6500 rpm. The Top 80, a small displacement motor (80 cc's), hits peak power over 9500 rpm. The lighter weight Top 80 generates about 90% of the Solo's HP. But the Top 80 could definitely not work as a direct drive.

Even for the slower spinning Solo 210, which *was* used on direct drive machines, it didn't work well. If a 48 inch prop were attached directly to the Solo, it would need an impossibly fast tip speed of Mach 1.2 to get into the motor's power band. So a smaller prop is used. Even with a tiny 30 inch prop, the motor only achieves 5500 rpm—a noisy Mach .65 (noisy at that high an rpm) and it only gets about 75 pounds of thrust. That same motor, spinning a big prop through a reduction drive, puts out a much-quieter 100+ pounds of thrust.

One major prop maker recommends that wooden PPG propeller tips never exceed Mach 0.75 and should remain under Mach 0.6 for quietness. Mach 0.6 at 3000 rpm will sound quieter than Mach 0.6 at 5000 rpm (smaller prop). And the quietest motors spin large props (48 inches or more) with tip speeds of less than Mach 0.5. On those machines the prop will likely be quieter than the motor, intake, redrive, or exhaust.

Where the Thrust Is

Most thrust comes from the prop's outer third (shown at left) which is faster moving and has the cleanest air. Blades get thinner near their tips which allows forward flexing and some twist. This doesn't affect thrust but could allow flexing into the cage. A long prop may flex up to 2 inches at full power. Twisting can reduce thrust and, if one blade twists more than the other, cause vibration since it will be pushing differently than the other blade(s).

Pitch – A Bite of Air

A higher pitch equates to a higher angle of attack on the blades. Pitch is commonly described as how far the propeller would travel forward during one revolution in a frictionless fluid. Propellers may give two dimensions—length and pitch. So "48 by 23" means a prop that is 48 inches long and would travel 23 inches forward during one revolution in that magic fluid. Since the outer portions of the propeller travel a greater distance, the blade angle steadily decreases outward but the *pitch* is the same. For various reasons, props are made with pitch that varies along the blade, but it's commonly measured 3/4 of the way towards the tip.

Like a wing, more pitch means more lift (thrust) *up to a point*. Beyond that point it produces less thrust since the airflow separates early. But if the propeller is moving quickly forward, like on a fast airplane, then the angle of attack decreases. Some airplanes use *cruise* propellers which are good for high speed flight but sacrifice slow speed thrust. For most of us, the difference between static thrust (no forward airspeed) and cruise thrust is small.

For going fast this may matter since cruise props have more thrust at 40 mph than at 0 mph. In practice our props are designed to maximize static thrust, especially since that's what thrust comparisons measure.

Some props have special hubs with pilot-settable pitch. It allows finding the best prop pitch for a particular motor and redrive combo. Internal mechanisms ensure each blade gets the same angle.

Like wings, long skinny prop blades are more efficient but require more strength. That's why more-expensive composite props enjoy some thrust advantage—they can be made skinnier while maintaining sufficient strength.

Designing For Thrust and Quietness

When designing a paramotor there is a lot to propeller and redrive selection. **Low noise** means low tip speed and low rpm. **Maximum thrust** means the most powerful motor you're willing to lift and the largest prop you can fit without having the tips exceed about Mach 0.75. That's still noisy but doesn't have too much sonic drag (from shock waves that form near the speed of sound). Excessive pitch is less efficient. If you have more power than your maximum-radius two-blade prop can handle without over revving then you'll need more blades or fatter blades. More blades *can* be quieter since the smaller diameter means lower tip speeds.

Let's say, for example, that your motor turns out 25 hp at 8000 rpm and you can fit a 48 inch propeller. For maximum thrust, you want the prop rpm to get the blade tips to hit Mach 0.75. Calculations (download the spreadsheet from www.FootFlyer.com | Educational) show that the prop should spin at 3900 rpm which requires a reduction drive of about 2. At these tip speeds, it will be an absolute screamer. Next you need to find a prop whose pitch allows the motor to accelerate to 8000. Too much pitch or too much prop area will bog down the motor without ever hitting 8000—this is called *over-propped*. Too little pitch would make it *overrev*, probably causing internal engine damage. If you find that the pitch must be over about 26 inches, then you'll want more or bigger blades. Two-blade props are more efficient than 3 bladers which are more efficient than 4 but more blades are better than having too much pitch.

Fatter, thicker blades can increase the effective push of a prop, and it may be quieter, but there's some cost in efficiency. You can see this gets complicated.

Tip shape affects noise—curves are quieter. Even the flat end should be rounded. Makers of higher speed props sometimes angle back (rake) the tips to reduce noise. Our props aren't fast enough to benefit from the technique.

A spinner can increase thrust up to 5% and coolness by 10%.

There is a small weight penalty and it does sit at the worst place—far back.

1. These are getting ready for their final treatment by hand. Wood is well suited to this application although it has more variation in shape and strength than carbon fiber props.

2. Lightweight props spin up quicker—weight towards the tips should be minimized the most.

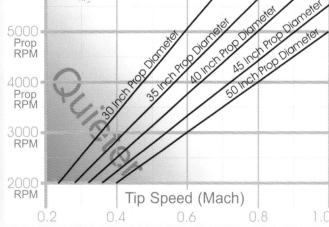

Courtesy Sensenich Props

Horsepower Revisited

Your motor's horsepower turns torque into propulsion through the prop. In level flight, the resulting push can itself be measured as horsepower using the airspeed. HP = Thrust (lbs) x Airspeed (mph) / 375.

For example, cruising at 30 mph with your motor pushing out 100 pounds of thrust, is 8 HP. The motor is probably putting 14 HP into the prop to achieve that. The difference is due to propeller inefficiency. Normally, cruise thrust is far lower but, with the trimmers out and speedbar engaged, it could easily require that much push.

Center of Gravity (CG) is the center of mass for the motor and pilot combined. Additionally, the motor pivots fore/aft around its hang points. If thrust acts above those hang points then you will tilt forward.

Although thrust always acts forward, you'll sometimes hear that "your thrust line is angled down" meaning that the air is blowing downward some amount.

High Hook-In

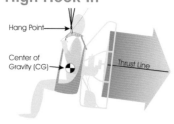

Low Hook-In

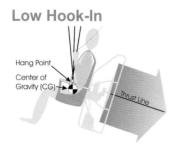

Materials: Rigidity and Strength

Propellers should be lightweight while being strong enough to handle normal loads. That means they break easily when striking something other than air such as poorly designed cages or careless human parts; it's far better to sacrifice the propeller. That is why most PPG props are made of lightweight wood or carbon fiber material that shatters relatively easily. Although damage will *still* be severe, it will be *less* than if the prop were made of super strong, heavy material.

Frangible props also help prevent motor damage since they impart less impact energy to the crankshaft and other rotating parts. In certified aircraft, a prop strike frequently requires an engine teardown and inspection.

Being lightweight also helps the prop spin up faster, especially if weight is concentrated close to the hub. Rotational inertia is based on both weight and its distance from the center. Five pounds, centrally concentrated, will accelerate quicker than the same weight spread out near the tips.

Balance & Paramotor Geometry

A lot of paramotor behavior hinges on geometry—especially where the pivot points are relative to thrust line and center of gravity (CG). Geometry can also eliminate twisting forces which we cover shortly.

CG, Hang Point and Thrust Line

The pilot/motor CG is the balance point. It largely determines how far it leans back in level flight. Machines with a heavy engine, set far aft, will have an aft CG that tends to tilt the pilot/motor back. A heavy pilot will tend to lean back less.

Hang point is where the carabiners, or their extensions, connect to the harness (see Center of Gravity at left) or motor frame. It is also the point around which fore/aft motor swings occur—the *Pivot Point*. A thrust line above that point will mean that throttling up causes a forward tilt. Ideally, the thrust line will be on or below the pivot point. With the CG well below the pivot point there will be less swinging around in turbulence. Hang point has no effect on *wing* stability, it just affects how "busy" the ride feels.

On low hook-in machines with pivoting arms, best results come from having the thrust go nearly through their pivot points, shown in red. That reduces forward tilting due to thrust.

If either pivot point is too low, pilots will feel pronounced forward tilt with thrust application. Most modern low hook-in machines avoid that with various methods including a vertical metal piece mounted on the swing arm, but the S-arm is most common. It moves the pivot point to a place where the pilot's arm would normally be while the S shape gives arm clearance.

Low Hook-In with pivoting S arms

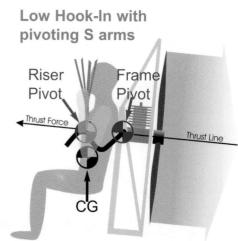

Twisting Forces At Work

Twisting on takeoff is a scourge that fells many pilots. It has many causes with cures covered in Chapter 12 but, operationally, the best one is decreasing power.

Effects of Torque

Spin a prop one way and the attached motor/pilot tries to spin the other way. It's just like drilling into wood where your hand/drill is the pilot/motor and the prop is the drill bit. This basic torque effect causes one riser to lower and the other to rise which induces a weight-shift type turn force towards the lowered riser. But there are other, more significant, twisting forces at work while under power.

Effects are more pronounced with more thrust. This incontrovertible physical relationship is one reason why more power is not always better. Two forces act around two axes: weight shift effects act around the propeller axis and riser twist forces act around the vertical axis, also known as yawing.

The next page has a summary reference to the twisting forces that most affect us; below is an overview.

Weight shift turn. This would more accurately be called riser shift and is relatively benign. Even a full weight-shift effect due to power will move the risers less than 2 inches (4 inch differential). That's easily countered with opposite medium brake. This force does *not* try to twist the pilot left/right (yaw) in the risers.

Vertical axis twist is any force that tries to yaw the pilot's heading left or right. Offset thrust is one pronounced cause and, although not a product of torque directly, it happens when the motor's thrust line slides into an offset position, pushing on a shoulder.

Any twisting will redirect thrust which now pushes sideways, decreasing climb and causing a bank. The cure is to reduce thrust—very unintuitive at low altitude with failing climb. We've seen pilots twist all the way around while clinging tightly to full throttle, inevitably ending with an expensive, painful crunch.

The most common torque related accident comes from vertical axis twist. The pilot launches and starts twisting to the left (to the right on geared redrives). Sideways thrust pushes him left, putting the wing in a right bank. The flummoxed pilot is confused because his body is pointing left and the wing is going right. He doesn't want to go right and pulls more left brake. Climb suffers and he either reduces power to recover, lucks out and doesn't splat, or twists all the way around and piles in. The only cure for this, once in flight, is to reduce power and, if necessary, land.

Horizontal Component of Torque, called "lean back twist" in the summary, is the part of propeller torque we care most about. It contributes to vertical axis twist, especially on motors that are leaned back a lot.

Imagine the motor leaned all the way back where the thrust line is pointing straight down. Throttling up in that scenario would create an immediate and powerful twisting (yaw) in the risers. Tilt it up partway. The effect would be there but not as powerful. It goes away as the propeller plain approaches vertical.

Angled Thrust. If the motor hangs off the harness angled left or right then it will push sideways. This is very minor, enough that it's not on the summary.

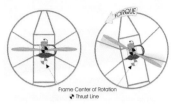

Torque Causing Offset Thrust

Frame Center of Rotation
↓ Thrust Line

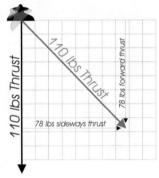

Off-Center Thrust

110 lbs Thrust

110 lbs Thrust

78 lbs forward thrust

78 lbs sideways thrust

1. Torque can twist the motor into an offset position. It then pushes on your shoulder, causing you to twist in the risers and re-direct the thrust line.

2. Once twisted, the thrust is no longer helping but rather spends itself pushing sideways into an ever increasing bank. The only immediate cure is reducing power. This is one of the strongest and most common causes of power-related crashes. Chapter 12 covers adjustments that can nearly eliminate the problem.

Torque's most obvious effect is the prop spinning in one direction trying to twist you in the other direction. A far more insidious effect is how it also causes a yaw (heading change). Riser tension is what opposes that. As you get into a steep climb, line tension decreases and you become more susceptible to riser twist. The only solution is immediately reducing power.

Many other factors, including wing selection, play a part in allowing torque to cause problems. In almost all cases, an experienced pilot or instructor can adjust out most twisting tendencies.

Twisted

All illustrations assume **belt drive machines.**
More power means more twisting!

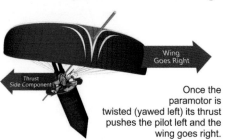

Once the paramotor is twisted (yawed left) its thrust pushes the pilot left and the wing goes right.

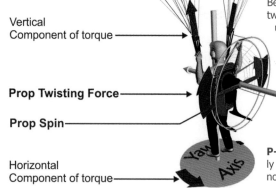

Vertical Component of torque

Prop Twisting Force

Prop Spin

Horizontal Component of torque

Thrust Axis

Below are the most prevalent twisting forces at work while under power. **Rotational Mass Acceleration** is not included since it only happens *during* throttle up.

P-Factor (next page) actually OPPOSES these forces so is not a factor for our craft.

Lean Back Twist: The more the paramotor leans back, the bigger the twist around the vertical (yaw) axis.

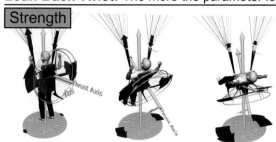

Strength

Effect: Pilot yaws around the vertical axis. On belt drives this left yaw redirects thrust to push the pilot left and the wing right. Also called the *horizontal component of torque*, it is the most powerful torque effect.

It's more pronounced with the prop plane tilted back. Imagine being tilted all the way back like in the diagram.

Counter: *1) Reduce motor tilt back, 2) On belt drives, move the risers right or the thrust line left, 3) have the right riser clip in forward of the left riser, 4) have cage vanes that redirect airflow to counter prop spin to reduce total torque effect.*

Loaded Riser Twist: When the wing goes to one side, the paramotor yaws around the vertical (yaw) axis.

Strength

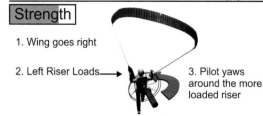

1. Wing goes right

2. Left Riser Loads

3. Pilot yaws around the more loaded riser

Effect: Pilot yaws around the more loaded riser. When the wing goes right, the pilot yaws left. It's most pronounced at liftoff because the pilot is upright and, when the wing goes right, it loads the left riser and vice versa if the wing goes left. It's also proportional to thrust.

Counter: *On belt drive machines, lift off with the wing either directly overhead or slightly left.*

Gyroscopic Precession: Yaw & roll force while changing the propeller disk angle.

Strength

only happens during tilt *changes*

1. Force applied here

2. Acts here

Effect: On belt drive units, it yaws the pilot left as he goes from tilted forward to leaning back at liftoff. It aggravates the other left-yawing forces. This fleeting effect *only* happens during *changes* in tilt, most notably during takeoff when going from upright to leaning back.

Counter: *1) Less lean back on the motor, 2) lower prop mass, 3) less prop radius, 4) lower RPM.*

Riser Shift: Twist along the thrust axis tries to impart a "weight shift" force, lowering one riser.

Strength

Wing tends to bank towards lowered riser

Effect: One riser goes up and the other goes down in opposition to prop spin. On belt drives that means the right riser goes down and the left riser goes up. It slightly aggravates the other twisting forces by making the wing want to bank more. Also called the *vertical component of torque*. It's slightly more pronounced on low hook-in machines.

Counter: *1) Aerodynamic airflow re-direction (see next page) on cage, 2) Anti-torque strap to reduce riser movement (reduces weight shift). On belt drives, it goes from the harness upper forward left, angling down to the right side. 3) Have more weight (like a reserve) on the raised side.*

Thrust Line Offset: Thrust is not centered on the risers' midpoint, causing yaw.

Strength

From a little to a LOT

Midpoint between Risers

Effect: Thrust pushes left or right of the center causing a yaw, like pushing on your right shoulder. It can be used to counter other yawing forces.

Counter: *Insure the thrust line is centered. To oppose other forces on belt drive machines, move the motor left and/or the risers right.*

Gyroscopic Precession

This force isn't a big factor for us but it does happen at the worst time during takeoff. Try this sometime: with the motor on your back, run it up while leaned forward then quickly stand up straight. On a belt-drive machine, you'll feel a momentary left twist (right twist on a gear drive). Once you're erect, the force stops. It's very fleeting.

Rotational Mass Acceleration

If you've felt your car tilt when stomping on the gas then you've noticed rotational mass acceleration. Any motor has a rotating mass—the crankshaft, flywheel, belts, propeller, etc. When that mass is accelerated, it wants to twist whatever is causing the acceleration in the opposite direction.

Precession Experiment

Gyroscopic precession is the same force that keeps toy gyros from toppling over. As the gyro tries to fall over, the force keeps acting 90° off so it doesn't actually fall over. This experiment (if you can find a vinyl record) shows the force in action. A bicycle tire works well, too.

Countering Thrust Line Offset

Hang Points

(Red) Other torque forces causing some left twist.

Thrust Line

Hang Points

Offset thrust aggravating the existing torque turn tendency.

Thrust Line

Torque induced Offset Thrust

Hang Points

Offset thrust (green) cancelling out existing torque turn tendency.

Thrust Line

This illustrates one method to counteract offset thrust. Adjust your harness so the motor is pushing on the *other* shoulder. If you always twist to the left, move your motor so that it's trying to twist you right. The two tendencies will cancel each other out to some degree.

However, the effect is fleeting, vanishing once the motor is up to speed. It's only present during rpm *acceleration*, that's why it's not on the "Twisted" summary.

You may hear that geared reduction drives reduce torque because the prop and engine's rotating mass are opposite. Not so. There is a difference, but *only* during prop spin-up. Otherwise torque is *identical* in strength, and opposite in direction.

Transverse Flow or Uneven Thrust

Having some airflow blocked by the pilot/motor may induce a slight force left or right at the prop (up or down too but that would be less likely). The farther the prop disk is away from the hang points, the more pronounced the effect. Gyroscopic precession can aggravate this force by making thrust at the top act on the side, causing a twisting force.

It's too weak to include in the summary.

Wing-Enabled Riser Twist

This isn't a force but is important. Wing shape and lines play a large part in allowing or preventing riser twist. While the motor always *causes* the twisting force, the wing and lines work to prevent it. Short fat wings (lower aspect ratio) are less prone to riser twist than long skinny ones.

It's simple: angle the lines away from the pilot more and the wing will be more resistant to riser twist. Skinny wings (high aspect ratio) and long lines aggravate the problem. That leaves high-performance wings most susceptible since they are usually long and skinny with longer lines.

Loaded Riser Twist

On launch, when the wing goes right, the left riser loads up, making the motor try to push you around to the left. While flying, this left yaw increases a right bank.

On belt drive machines it aggravates other left yawing forces and may be enough to spin the pilot all the way around. So avoid lifting off with the wing to your right. *After* liftoff, a shallow right turn is fine, even preferable.

P-Factor: An Irrelevant Effect

P-Factor, also called *Asymmetric Blade Thrust,* is what happens whenever the propeller disk is not hitting the air head-on. It results from one blade having more relative wind than the other. With the motor angled back (as is normal), the descending blade has more relative wind so it pulls slightly harder. Picture the prop disc angled all the way, as shown below, until it's flat. Now the "descending" blade experiences a headwind while the "ascending" blade has a tailwind. More airflow at the same angle of attack means more lift.

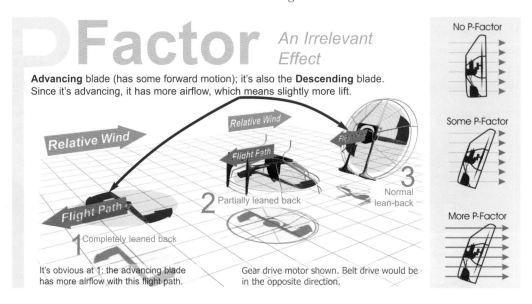

Not only is the effect minor, since it depends on the difference between forward airspeed and blade rpm, but it's *opposite* to the other twisting forces. We're just too slow to notice.

Stopping Torque At The Source: Aerodynamic Airflow Redirection

The prop spins right, the pilot/motor tries to spin left. But what if we could oppose the force at its source? That's what some manufacturers have done, including one who developed an aftermarket torque mitigation using *lamels*—thin plates mounted to the cage's netting. In our tests these all worked. Thrust loss is kept to a minimum by virtue of the redirecting elements being on, or replacing, otherwise draggy cage parts.

The best effect is gained when deflection is concentrated nearer the prop tips.

Torque Mitigation

Cage spokes (radial arms) have been cleverly repurposed as anti-torque vanes. More thrust means more torque but it also makes these vanes work better.

Airflow is strongest in the prop's outer third so redirection is most effective there.

www.FootFlyer.com

Weather & Wind

24

You don't have to be a meteorologist to manage a useful understanding of weather. Grasping *micro*meteorology, however, is quite helpful and that is our focus. Entire books are devoted to atmospheric lore, a complicated puzzle that academia is piecing together. This chapter covers what's more useful to a paramotor pilot.

Most weather predictions revolve around the "big picture," stuff that can be left for the pros—frontal passage, strong winds, precipitation, etc. We're not interested in taking on such violence with our uniquely susceptible wings. However, on days where basically benign weather is forecast, knowledge of the little stuff will be invaluable. Some basics on the big stuff are provided for completeness. Dennis Pagen's "Understanding the Sky" covers this topic in far more detail.

Using Forecasts

You've learned the basics in Chapter 7 and should know how to get the forecasts and make basic decisions on when it's appropriate to fly. These extra details will help you interpret them and better understand what's going on. We can now delve deeper into the details: what happens around this one cumulus cloud? How does air behave in the presence of hills? What happens from the surface up to 100 feet, and so on. Use professional weather people for the big picture, and this knowledge for applying it to our smaller scale.

A forecast can be trusted more if what they expected earlier is becoming reality *right now*. That shows the weather service grasps what's going on atmospherically. If the current weather doesn't match what was forecast to be the current weather, their model is no longer valid—watch out. Did they expect a south wind and it's actually from the northwest? If so, be suspicious of their remaining predictions.

While out west one time, I was motoring along a 20 foot ridge that ran parallel to, and below, a bigger mountain. I saw a chance to experiment; to see if my understanding was accurate.

Waning sunlight meant the ground was cooling, which in turn was cooling the adjacent air. Indeed, the bottom few feet was now 4° to 5°F cooler than at 50 feet. The ridge had channels carved out where water drained to the lower level. I wondered— shouldn't the cool air try to drain down those channels, too, and spill out at the bottom of the ridge? It was otherwise calm, so I decided to find out.

I flew parallel along the ridge's bottom where the culverts drained and, sure enough, as I passed along each culvert, I felt a noticeable spill of air. It worked just as published!

Principles

Peeling back the onion of atmospheric understanding can water the eyes. Deep physics underpin the rules but here are some fundamentals to help understand our most important micrometeorology.

- Hot air rises, cool air sinks and then flows downhill to the lowest point, just like water seeks its lowest point.

- Air gets thinner with altitude and its pressure drops about 1 inch of mercury per 1000 foot increase. Sea level is the deepest reach in an ocean of air where, just like in deep water, pressure is greatest.

- *Radiant cooling* is where the earth loses heat into space just like a radiant heater can make your hands warm without warming the air. Solar heating is the warming part, where sunlight heats the land.

- *Conduction* is when terrain warms (or cools) the overlying air and *convection* is when heat is transferred by warm air moving into an area of cold air (or vice versa).

- The earth is always radiating heat, day and night; more with clear skies since clouds reflect infrared energy back down. During the day, sunlight adds more heat than radiant cooling subtracts. Heating starts at sunrise and quickly (in about a half hour) overcomes radiant cooling. Sun-facing hills or dark, dry spots warm up first.

- In a standard atmosphere (see below), air at higher altitudes is colder than at lower altitudes. The rate that it gets cooler is the *lapse rate*.

- If you expand a parcel of air (increase its volume), without adding or removing heat, its pressure and temperature drops. That's called *adiabatic* cooling because there's no external exchange of heat. The reverse happens when you compress air such as when it descends. So, rising air cools at the *Adiabatic Lapse Rate*. Moisture complicates matters. The condensing process releases heat so air, rising as clouds, will be condensing out its moisture and releasing heat. That slows the rate at which the parcel cools as it rises. It's the *Wet Adiabatic Lapse Rate*.

- Warm air can hold more water vapor (an invisible gas) than cold air. Cooling the air beyond what it can hold forces its load of water vapor to change state (condense) into very fine droplets (liquid) better known as clouds or fog. The temperature where this occurs is the *dew point*.

Standard Atmosphere

A standard atmosphere is meteorology's common point of reference. It is also used by aircraft makers (and others) to base performance numbers on.

The International Standard Atmosphere (ISA) is 0% humidity, 59°F (15°C) and has a pressure of 29.92 inches of mercury (Hg) at sea level. For every 1000 feet of height, the temperature decreases by 3.5°F (2°C) which is the standard *lapse rate*, and the pressure falls by about 1 inch of mercury (Hg). So at 3000 feet, you would expect the pressure to be 26.92 inches Hg and the temperature to be 10.5°F cooler or 48.5°F.

Daily Cycles

Depending on your local terrain, there is an underlying daily cycle that represents the norm. Experienced local pilots know it best which is why they can provide such valuable input. This cycle can be as powerful as it is predictable. Some locations have very specific places and times when flying is very dangerous owing to these daily cycles.

Since the cycle is driven by sunlight, clouds usually reduce its intensity. But clouds and pressure systems may point to some greater atmospheric change that will overpower the daily cycle. Be extra leery at such times.

Radiation Cycle

Overnight, the ground radiates heat into space, cooling off the land. The land in turn, cools the air just above. That increasingly chilled (and therefore heavier) air tries to sink, finding its way into low spots. The cooling ground is like an ice cube—it just keeps cooling the air nearby. If the air cools enough, some of its water vapor condenses into fog or onto the cold surfaces as dew. This is why low spots get foggy first—cool air flows downhill. All this cooling inverts the normal atmospheric temperature gradient. Instead of being cooler aloft, a cooler layer along the ground forms, so by morning the coldest air is at the surface. At some point up higher (maybe only a few hundred feet) there is a significant increase in temperature called an *inversion*. Above that, the normal temperature gradient of cooling with higher altitude resumes.

Sunrise is typically a very stable time—cool air sits in low places, with no desire to go anywhere. The sun starts heating the land right away while heat loss from radiant cooling continues. Soon, around a half-hour past sunrise, the sun's heating wins out and temperatures begin to rise. Dry, dark spots heat up first and the air above them tries to rise. Hills that face sunward will heat up even more in the direct rays. Soon these warmer areas become the day's nascent thermals. They are joined by many others as the day wears on, mixing and warming the atmosphere.

At sunrise, there is typically an inversion—warmer air sits above cool surface air. Sunrise starts warming the ground which starts warming the air just above. Morning thermals start rising but stop when they hit the inversion air.

As the sun continues heating up the surface, thermals get hotter until they are warmer than even the overlying inversion air.

By mid-day, a more normal lapse rate exists: warm at the surface, cooling with altitude. If enough moisture is present, cumulus clouds will form atop thermals as the rising air cools to its dewpoint.

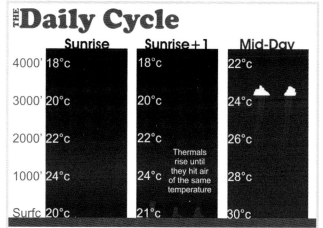

As air rises, it expands and cools. As long as it stays warmer than the surrounding air, it will rise. Eventually the cooling due to expansion exceeds the atmosphere's normal lapse rate and the upward movement stops. With enough moisture present, it will form clouds when cooled to the dew point.

As the day wears on, thermals get stronger and go higher. Cloud bases go up, too. Solar heating peaks at noon but this process peaks a couple hours later. Late afternoon's decreasing sun angle finally takes its toll and the process wanes although cloud bases keep rising. Thermal strength can easily be dangerous up to within a couple hours of sunset depending on location.

These are mid-day summer cumulus clouds that top many thermals. Smoke from field fires show how erratic airflow is in the afternoon cauldron.

Flatland

In flat areas there is little beyond the daily cycle and large scale changes. Afternoons can be dangerously turbulent during periods of instability so stick with the first and last 3 hours of sunlight, especially in the summer.

Typical days start out smooth with nearly calm winds in the morning. These can be wonderful times to fly—smooth and pristine. The "dog days of summer" describe the flatlander's heyday—calm mornings and evenings with sultry afternoons of light breezes.

If the wind aloft is very strong, expect it to get bumpy quickly. Wind and thermals don't mix well. You'll know soon after launch what the wind is doing. In fact, it's not difficult to climb up into a perfectly smooth wind that matches or exceeds your airspeed. You wind up parked over one location (or moving backwards) while facing into the wind. It's strange and can happen pretty low. This is a wind gradient and the smoothness will be short lived once sunlight churns up the air.

courtesy Wikipedia.com, Argon Ice

Digging Deeper: State Change

A significant impact on weather is the *state* change of water—going from ice to liquid to gas. Its lowest energy level is ice. If you add heat (energy) to ice it will warm up at a constant rate until it gets to the melting point (32°F). It will remain at that temperature while absorbing the heat until changing to the new state at which point it continues warming.

For example, put a 10°F block of ice in a 300°F oven and stick a thermometer in the ice. The ice will warm gradually until it hits the melting point (32°F) where it momentarily stops warming as it changes from ice to water. The difference in energy between the two states is called *latent heat*. So immediately after changing from 32°F ice to 32°F water it is said to have gained some latent heat energy. The water will now continue warming at a steady rate until it reaches the boiling point (212°F) where it will again stop warming to change state from a liquid to a gas. Then the water vapor will continue warming.

Sublimation is where water vapor comes directly from ice. Evaporation is where liquid water changes to gas even though it's below the boiling point. As it evaporates, it cools the surface from which it evaporated. All evaporative coolant systems rely on this principle. The higher the temperatures, the more sublimation or evaporation happens.

The reverse happens during cooling. As water vapor cools, it does so evenly until becoming a liquid, like cloud. Cloud is made up of liquid water particles that have condensed from invisible water vapor onto particulate matter like polution. As it makes the change, it resists further cooling for a period of time until the state has fully changed.

These physics drive the formation of severe weather—giving teeth to a process that would otherwise peter out, allowing thunderstorms to reach momentous heights and powering hurricanes. If lifted air is cooled quickly, it would soon become the same temperature as the surrounding air and lose its buoyancy. The process would die out. But water vapor will hold its temperature while rising because it needs to make that state change—staying buoyant as it slowly changes state from vapor to liquid. This phenomenon happens on smaller scales, too, and pilots call it *cloud suck*, where the cloud formation itself is driving the lift instead of the original thermal. Air mixing with the cooler surrounding air is what prevents it from shooting out of control.

Hilly

Surprisingly intense micro meteorology happens when air interacts with hills—even before the sun comes up. That's why flying in mountainous areas warrants so much attention. As air cools it tries to flow downhill, sometimes becoming a torrent. Like an avalanche, it gathers speed, causing rapid wind changes, intensifying in mountain passes or other constrictions. It's just like a wide, mellow river that narrows to rapids in tight places.

Hills also interfere with larger scale movements and mask winds. If the air is forced to go up or around a geographic protrusion you can expect turbulence in the lee (downwind of it). Be careful if launching in a valley with calm air but a known wind aloft—up near the level of the mountain tops could be a wild ride. And that turbulence *can* come down well below the peak's height.

Coastal

The beauty of a beach is in its smooth predictability. Usually by 11 AM the warming land is sucking air in a steady *sea breeze* (on shore) that makes launching painless. Free of thermal turbulence, this airflow from the water is usually very smooth. Most of the time the wind continues well past sunset. The cycle reverses at night when the land cools and a *land breeze* (off-shore) sets in with wind blowing out to sea.

One risk is when a prevailing off-shore wind gets overcome by the sea breeze. A few miles inland the wind is blowing out to sea but on the beach it's coming on shore. Somewhere in the middle, these two airflows meet in a confused *convergence zone*. Besides turbulence, if you're flying beachside when the prevailing off-shore breeze wins the pushing contest, you could be blown out to sea.

Desert

Deserts are beautiful in their own dry, rugged way. And they spawn the strongest, meanest thermals in the country—making for a wild daily cycle that can be much more dramatic than in wetter areas. It happens because the sun's rays don't get used up in evaporation—they go right into heating the ground.

One indicator of thermal strength is the difference in temperature from morning low to afternoon high—something deserts have to an extreme.

These factors combine to make mid-day desert flying a spin of the roulette wheel.

Dust devils are the visible manifestation of a violent phenomenon that causes a rapid swirl of air as thermals surge upwards. These little tornadoes may also be occurring up high but would be invisible.

Flying the desert is beautiful in the mornings and evenings, but deserves great respect during mid-day.

Yearly Cycle

Many yearly cycles overlay daily temperature swings: The monsoons of Tucson and Phoenix, the dry period of Portland, hurricane season, Santa Ana winds, etc. Some of these involve winds erupting with little warning. Long term local knowledge can be a life saver—if you don't know a local pilot, seek one out from the nearest airport. Most are happy to answer such questions as "I'm gonna be flying an ultralight in the local area, is there any significant seasonal weather I should know about?"

The most prevalent and relevant cycle, though, is thermal intensity. It follows the length of day where thermals are strongest in summer and weakest in winter. That makes sense—their driving force is sunshine, and summer's mid-day packs many more heating hours, at a more direct angle than winter's.

The difference can be a dramatic. Long hours of direct sunlight heat up the ground, boiling its atmospheric soup into a sporty cauldron. The short days of winter get only a few hours of low-angle light leaving many smooth days to fly even in the desert.

All About Thermals

A lot has been written on this topic but anyone who has watched a 1970's lava lamp (pictured at right) knows the process: sun-warmed patches of ground heat the air immediately above, making it want to rise. At some point this warm air blob punches through the overlying cooler air to begin ascending. Air rushes in below to fill the vacated, rising mass. Free flyers ride these updrafts to sometimes great heights. Most motor pilots avoid them and their related turbulence. Some motor pilots use them for soaring and simply accept the increased risk of collapses.

Thriving thermals need the right type of atmosphere. Primarily that means a steady decrease in temperature with altitude (lapse rate), direct sunlight and a heatable surface. An overcast douses the process which is why you can frequently fly all day long on cloudy days (as long as no rain is expected), even in the middle of summer.

Telling Thermal Intensity from the Ground

A good way to predict thermal turbulence from the ground is by wind gusts. Stand in one place or just be observant while setting up. Calm conditions on the ground portend calm air above while gusty conditions suggest lumpy air aloft. Sharp gusts,

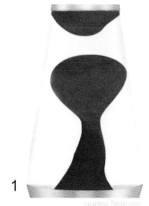

1

courtesy Target.com

2

If a dust devil is present, don't even be hooked into your glider.

1. If you see this coming your way, unclip! Then pack up. If you're airborne, stay well away but land when your LZ is clear. Free flyers avoid landing during the worst part of thermally days and the most aggressive of them use dust devils to mark thermal bottoms.

2. A Lava Lamp demonstrates thermal action nicely.

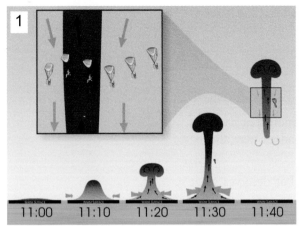

1. Here is a fairly typical thermal and what it can do when a paraglider flies through it. As the pilot exits, downward moving air makes him susceptible to a frontal collapse (see Chapter 18).

2. This illustrates the distribution of thermals on a bright, sunny day, especially in the summer. Yellow represents moderate thermals, red represents strong ones, and the skull represents dangerous-to-us versions. How many of these strong thermals exist depends on many factors, but ultimately, missing that killer thermal is a matter of luck on strong days.

Summer afternoon's invisible fury should not to be treated lightly.

where the wind speed or direction changes rapidly, indicate sharper, more dangerous thermals.

Flying on a day with rapid gusts from 5-12 mph could be deadly whereas soft changes of the same magnitude might be manageable. Wind direction must be watched too—if it goes from east at 12 mph (the wind is coming *from* the east) and suddenly switches to west at 5—that's bad.

Thermals and strong winds don't mix. Gusts from mechanical turbulence add to energetic thermals to make potentially dangerous air.

Dust devils show that, even away from the swirl itself, the atmosphere is particularly turbulent. Any day brewing sufficiently vigorous turbulence to trigger dust devils is brewing nasty conditions.

Where Thermals Thrive

Cross country soaring pilots know where to find the "biggest air"—a description for powerful thermals that can carry pilots skyward at well over a 1000 fpm. Associated turbulence can play havoc on a paraglider, causing collapses. The immediate spiral that spurts from such a collapse may require immediate and correct action or a reserve toss. Every year, it seems, at least one experienced free flyer succumbs to an unpleasant fate in "big air."

Dryer air breeds more dramatic thermals. Arid regions consistently give soaring pilots the highest altitude gains and longest soaring flights.

The *lifted index* is an atmospheric measurement that tells whether a parcel of lifted air will be warmer or colder than its surroundings after reaching a certain height. Negative numbers mean the parcel is warmer—it wants to accelerate upwards. That's unstable. It has to do with the atmosphere's lapse rate and moisture content. In an atmosphere that gets cold quickly as you climb, a lifted parcel of air would tend to remain warmer and therefore keep rising. Moist air rises more readily because water vapor is lighter than dry air. Lifted index charts can be found on the Internet although you'll need additional study to really know how to use them.

Clouds

The highest clouds, *cirrus* (or *cirriform*), are wispy affairs comprised of ice crystals. They form above 25,000 feet and can sometimes spread out from jet contrails. Mid-level clouds live between about 8000 and 25,000 feet. They're usually prefaced with the word *alto* (e.g. *altocumulus* and *altostratus*) and mostly only concern our micro view for their value in blocking out thermal-producing sunshine.

Stratiform

Stratus clouds are the flat, boring, frequently drizzly, clouds that form mostly on weekends. Their flat, gray appearance generally indicates stable conditions with little vertical movement. When they drop rain, they're called nimbostratus.

Smooth and frequently layered, stratus clouds are usually associated with fairly benign weather although they *can* conceal significant ugliness. They frequently follow fronts and occupy large swaths of low pressure areas. The two worst worries of flying under stratus clouds are rain and imbedded thunderstorms. However, if neither is forecast, then all-day flying may be possible. By blocking the sun's most direct heating rays, they block most of the thermal-induced turbulence, leaving good, but bleak, motoring conditions (and lousy soaring conditions).

Stratus clouds must not be ignored when the forecast includes rain showers. It's hard to tell where the rain showers are and, with thicker clouds, it's easy to get rained on by surprise. If you see a darkening in the sky, then it's most likely because of embedded cumulus clouds which indicate coming trouble.

Stratus clouds that form around severe weather are particularly dangerous in that they conceal where the really bad weather is. That is why it's important to know the forecast and only fly on forecasted dry days.

Cumuliform

When vertical development gets involved, the term *cumulo* (having a heaped on appearance) gets appended or prepended to cloud names. Cumulus clouds that form mostly on nice summer afternoons cap thermals and indicate bumpy conditions. Any cloud with more than about 3000 feet of vertical development can produce rain. Once a cloud produces rain it earns the *nimbus* moniker: Cumulonimbus is the most violent example and is what thunderstorms come from.

The wispy beginnings of cumulus clouds typically form about 3 hours after sunrise and a few thousand feet high. If a steady breeze has picked up within a couple hours of sunrise *and* cumulus start popping, expect sporty air. Dry air could be just as sporty but without the cumulus clouds.

Stratiform clouds usually indicate benign conditions. Be sure you can see everything though, they sometimes hide cumulus clouds.

Christine Doughty is flying over a low scattered to broken layer in smooth air. She had good ground contact, good visibility and was able to stay clear of clouds. Had she been above 1200' AGL, she would have needed more cloud clearance (see Chapter 9 for all the airspace details).

Pay close attention to cumuliform clouds. What goes up must come down, and big cumulus clouds (aka cumies) can bring air down as strong downdrafts that spread out from where they hit. These are *gust fronts* (see below). Little ones are felt all the time, both from popping thermals sucking in air, and from sinking air spreading out. But bigger cumulus clouds or, even worse, lines of them, can cause gust fronts tens of miles away. Technically gust fronts are associated with thunderstorms but they happen on all scales.

Be leery of wandering too close to large cumulus clouds. The cloud formation process itself generates extra lift which increases as you near the base. This *cloud suck* can easily overpower a paraglider pilot's ability to descend. Getting caught in such lift is a chilling experience that some pilots have not survived. Depending on the cloud's size, it can easily take you to heights where the temperature is well below freezing and the air is too thin to keep you conscious. But at least it's extremely violent.

Thunderstorms

Nature's fury is unleashed in the majestic and deadly thunderstorm. These mammoth storms,

"It's better to be on the ground wishing you were in the air, than in the air wishing you were on the ground."

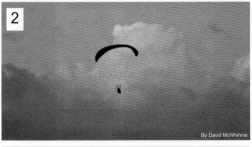

By David McWhinnie

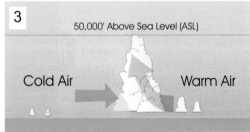

50,000' Above Sea Level (ASL)

Cold Air   Warm Air

1. An old but appropriate axiom.

2. The zoom makes this menacing storm appear much closer than it actually is. However, thunderstorm wrath can extend tens of miles beyond the cloud itself.

3. A cold front spawning thunderstorms.

covered in Chapter 7, play havoc with winds over a broad area.

They come in two types: Air mass and frontal. Air mass thunderstorms are usually scattered buildups on otherwise nice but muggy summer afternoons. They are typically not as severe. Normally air-mass storms germinate in aging high pressure areas with lots of moisture and some instability in the air.

Frontal storms come in lines and are associated with fronts, usually cold fronts. They produce the worst weather including tornadoes.

When an atmosphere is unstable enough to produce thunderstorms, it's no place for a paramotor. In most cases, two hours after a storm passes is enough to consider flying as long as there are no more storms (or cumulonimbus clouds) anticipated. First, find out what the weather is doing elsewhere before taking off.

Gust fronts are probably the thunderstorm's most dangerous fallout. Rain pulls cold air downward until it hits the ground and spreads out in a fast-moving, turbulent boil that can extend many miles from the storm. Although technically related only to thunderstorms, gust fronts happen in different degrees from other causes, too.

Fronts

These really belong to *macrometeorology* which we don't cover in great detail. Fronts are the boundaries between air masses of different temperatures. They get moved around by high level winds, frequently swirling around low pressure areas. Low pressure areas arise from many causes including high level winds, called *jet streams*, which can suck air upwards under some conditions. Low-level air tries to flow inward to fill the low pressure and gets turned by Coriolis effect (the result of a spinning world)—thus the low spins, dragging fronts along with it.

Cold fronts are the most violent. Cold air wedges under a warm air mass, lifting it quickly and creating lines of cumulo-nastiness. These fronts spawn the worst of all thunderstorms because they combine several powerful forces. Fortunately, they are usually fast moving—doing their damage and moving on.

Warm fronts ride over retreating cooler air and are more typically wet and mellow. Be careful; they sometimes do harbor thunderstorms in the stratiform mass of clouds. Unfortunately, they tend to linger and can muck up the weather for quite some time.

Lots of bad weather happens near fronts. If there is a forecast for frontal passage, even if no rain or clouds are present, be very wary of flying. Check out the wind forecast—there can easily be a dangerous wind shift forecast that you should avoid. If you're out on the field, unusual, especially sudden, temperature changes should lead to suspicion. For example, a day that gets to 80°F by noon but then forecasts a temperature drop to 70°F by afternoon would likely have a wind shift. That is a dry cold front—you would want to avoid flying until after the wind shifted since it could easily be violent.

Getting Weather Info

Chapter 7 covers acquiring weather through Flight Service. But a good way to improve your awareness of what's happening aloft is to get the weather at locations around your site, especially upwind of it. It's not foolproof, and it doesn't work as well in mountainous regions, but it's a good start.

Be aware that the surface wind is not a good indication of where the weather is coming from. Look at the clouds and see which way they're moving. Different cloud layers may well be moving different directions; you're most interested in the low to mid-level layers (between 3000 and 10,000 feet).

TV is a reasonable source for weather information but phone apps and the internet are better; you can customize what you're looking for and probably get more detail on your particular area. Sites come and go but you can find links to good ones on www.FootFlyer.com.

Turbulence from Wind

There are some important differences in what pilots frequently lump into the term *rotor*. Knowing what those differences are could be a life-saver.

Mechanical turbulence is the general bumpiness that extends downwind from anything that sticks up into a wind, up to 20 times the obstacle's height. The resultant eddies drift with the wind and spread upward above the height of the causing obstacle. Turbulence extends further downstream as wind speed picks up. So, too, does intensity and quite dramatically—a 15 mph wind will have over double the intensity of a 10 mph wind.

Rotor itself is a stationary swirl of air that spins immediately downwind of the causing obstruction. It can be very powerful and produce incredibly strong shear since it's so well organized. Rotors don't always form—it depends on the obstruction's shape, wind speed and wind gradients.

Wind shadow is the calm that exists just downwind, and usually at the bottom, of an obstruction. It's what you feel when seeking shelter from the wind behind a building (or other obstruction). It extends about to the height of the obstruction. Picture your paraglider moving from that stillness out into the free airstream. That would be bumpy.

In a light wind, less than about 5 mph, mechanical turbulence and rotor are almost nonexistent—flying next to obstructions poses little problem.

Mountain Waves

When strong wind blows perpendicular to a mountain range, there may be mountain waves and severe turbulence downwind of the range. It can extend many thousands of feet above the mountain, but our real concern is what happens below the wave action—rotor.

1. A localized front near Phoenix, AZ. Fortunately, the dust makes it quite visible. These happen on various scales from a few miles to over a hundred miles and the results are always dangerous.

2. Another type of localized front that was spawned by a line of cumulus clouds. Virga (rain that evaporates before reaching the ground) was an early indication of dangerous gusts that were soon to hit the ground.

Also, avoid dark bottomed clouds, they indicate there's a lot of vertical development above with potential turbulence.

Can't Get Down

The worst flight of my life, in *anything*, was after making a bad decision to fly in the lee of a small mountain. I had already begged off the flight but a local pilot told me that this condition was common and shouldn't be a problem. It was in another country, on an unfamiliar coast, and I figured he should know. Turns out, weather knows no boundaries and doesn't care what locals think.

When we got near our destination, downwind of the mountain, it started. Turbulence and extreme updrafts—so much that we couldn't get down. Three of us took three different approaches, including one who went well out to sea. It took the last pilot over an hour, in sometimes severe turbulence, to finally land safely.

Besides the main rotor, powerful eddies cause turbulence that even sailplanes try to avoid. It's no place for a paraglider. Rotor extends from just below the mountain's crest down to a few hundred feet AGL, sometimes to the surface.

There are also *standing mountain waves*, with smooth lift and sink, that reach into the stratosphere. Glider pilots use these for record altitude gains.

Terrain and Flow

Whenever air is squeezed between two hills, its speed will pick up just like where a river narrows and the water speeds up. In a craft as slow as ours, that could stop all forward motion. Fortunately for power pilots, we can throttle up and climb away from this *venturi effect*.

When air is forced up over obstructions it causes lift just upwind of the obstruction. Ridge lift, as its called, remains fairly smooth as long as there are no thermals in it and the pilot stays upwind or over the causing obstruction. The obstruction's shape determines the strength of the lift—a smooth, steep rise in the face of a steady wind creates the most lift. Terrain can also act like an airfoil where the air goes over the top then back down the back side, sticking to the surface and creating sink. For example, flying just downwind of a tree line can create enough sink to make climbing difficult or impossible.

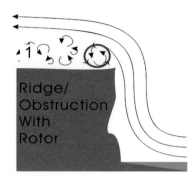

Ridge/ Obstruction With Rotor

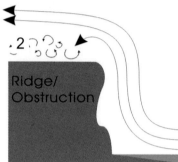

Ridge/ Obstruction

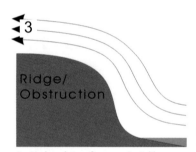

Ridge/ Obstruction

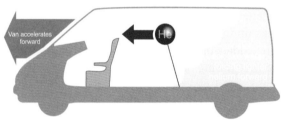

Van accelerates forward

Visualizing air motion

Try this in your car to see air's mass in motion. With a helium balloon on a string, drive around and watch how the balloon moves opposite to the air "sloshing" around like water.

1. Air has lots of mass. Just like over an airfoil, it won't make sharp bends. So when you envision the airflow past obstructions, expect turbulence and dramatic changes in the area of those bends. This shows that the air cannot stick and creates a standing rotor.

2. The lip of this ridge is sharp enough to create turbulence but not enough to create a standing rotor.

3. This smooth ridge would be perfect for soaring. If you stand near the lip of a sharp edge, you'll feel very little wind on your face. Setting up to launch there would be difficult at best. But on a curvy ridge, like #3, the wind flows steadily along the smoother surface—a much easier launch proposition.

Digging Deeper: Highs And Lows

Areas of high and low pressure resemble swells on the ocean but on a very, very large scale, spanning hundreds of miles. The troughs are low pressure and the peaks are high pressure. Air moves, in some ways, like a big Slinky; piling up both vertically and horizontally. For example, it's possible to have air pile up high in the atmosphere. It will, of course, start falling but air has a lot of mass and that will take time.

Other forces act to lift air and pile it up in different ways. For example, the jet stream has influence. It can start moving air upwards into the jet, creating a low pressure area.

A hurricane is a good example of another force that forms a low pressure area. Warm water feeds a group of thunderstorms that create enormous lifting force. They're like a bunch of vacuum cleaners, accelerating air upwards and spitting it out the top. Air flows into this continuous low pressure and gets turned by the Coriolis effect (like the marble that you roll inward on a rotating record). Rotation keeps pressure low because the air can't fill in the center low. That's why hurricanes cannot form on the equator—there's nothing that causes them to rotate. You get low pressure areas at the equator, but air is able to fill them in fairly quickly since it's not deflected into a spin.

Why do lows get the bad rap? Almost by definition, the air in a low is being sucked (or lifted) upwards, frequently by jetstream action. The motion is too slow to feel from the ground or even in flight, but is enough to cool the air which tends to form clouds. Air in a low pressure area gets concentrated since it's flowing inward and upward. Conservation of energy means that when the air is deflected inward, toward the low, it wants to speed up, like a ballerina tucking her limbs in to speed up. But air in a high pressure system is generally *descending* and heading outward—like a ballerina spreading out and slowing down.

Courtesy Didier Eymin

Roots:
Our History

25

It's a short history. Powered paragliding grew from paragliding which itself started in the early 1980's. Paramotors have several other interesting roots, not all contributing to the same tree, but rather growing in an underbrush of ultralight flying that prospered simultaneously.

Parasailing

You will soon tire of hearing your sport called parasailing. After all, you *ride* under a parasail; you *pilot* a PPG. Not that there's anything wrong with parasailing; it's a fun activity to be sure, but it's essentially a brainless amusement for the parasailor. A stable platform leaves the rider with no control, enabling operators to whisk unsuspecting tourists up in reasonable safety. Don't try that with a paramotor!

Our sport has no origins in parasailing, a sport that branched off from the round canopies of sport parachuting. They still use modified rounds for stability's sake.

Hang Gliding & Ultralighting

Development of hang gliders started in earnest during the mid-1970's after a few enterprising individuals adopted Francis Rogallo's 1948 design. Rogallo was scheming to safely return spacecraft through the atmosphere while enterprising 1970's earthmen were applying his designs to create bamboo gliders. Eventually, professional manufacturers entered the fray with real soaring craft. Efficiency and safety drove improvements into fixed wing variants that eventually included propulsion. Strangely (and fortunately), the FAA did little about any of this since the pilots stayed mostly out of everyone's way and risked only themselves. They remained, literally and figuratively, "below the radar."

Frenchman Didier Eymin has done photo work using a paramotor all over the world. He is pictured here taking off with one of his first machines in the early 1990's.

Below: Phil Russman takes wing on one of the earliest hang gliders, before motors were being added.

As weight increased, wheels were added and Ultralighting was born. Flex wing Rogallos got longer, skinnier wings and became capable soaring craft. The proliferating rigid wing configurations all but took over the powered segment.

Sport Parachuting

Pilots first used cloth to soften their intentional falls in the late 1700's when balloons and buildings were the only way up. But until 1961 there was no control of the canopy—it just broke the fall and sometimes the legs. Then the *Paracommander* came along with holes in the back that streamed enough air backwards to gain minimal forward speed. At last the parachutist could influence his destiny. At about the same time, a Rogallo shaped parachute was devised but never really explored.

The big development came in 1964 with the square Ram-Air parachute. This design formed the underpinnings of modern paragliding.

These sport parachutists could fly almost like a glider but with very limited glide performance. French mountain climbers learned to launch their canopies from the slopes, a much quicker way down from the scaled heights. Others saw an opportunity and began to improve the wings, getting the sport well established in Europe by 1986. Modern paragliding came to Joe Public when manufacturers actually started producing wings for the masses by about 1988.

Efficiency gains earned it the name paragliding and enterprising European pilots started adding power. Large motors were required to overcome the drag penalty of early wings. These had necessarily high hang points to balance the heavy motors.

As wings became more efficient, the motors got smaller and lighter, requiring less thrust. By 1989 the Pagojet, using a 3-cylinder radial engine, became the first production unit available to the public. Not that the masses flocked to it, but at least they had the opportunity. By 1991 a number of European manufacturers were building machines and the US market was soon to follow.

Lost Lineage

An evolutionary aside to the paraglider story is that of David Barish; an airline pilot turned aeronautical engineer turned parachute designer. Like Rogallo, he was thinking about space as humans raced moonward in 1965. He and Rogallo only met once at NASA but their re-entry designs both shared some commonality— both sported about a 4 to 1 glide ratio and both were abandoned by the space agency.

But Barish, an avid and accomplished skier, took his single-surface paraglider to the slopes – scooting/flying down the hills at no more than about 30 feet high. He toured the country's finest ski sites in the summer of 1966, demonstrating his newfangled version of "downhill" with an apparently cool reception; it seems the public just wasn't ready yet.

He even tried using a motor with his creation but must not have found an adequate power system that he could lift; there is no record of any motorized flights with his wing. That's not surprising—at least one manufacturer had started producing single surface gliders, but they would have needed lots of thrust.

Alan Chuculate is braving the -20°F Alaskan air to try his 11-cell Harley. It was an English parascending canopy built in about 1987 to carry two people.

Efficiency has come a long way; it took Alan 500 feet of altitude loss to do one 360° turn.

The shape was not very distant from its sport parachuting origins although it did have unsheathed lines that are now common on competition wings. But it had a *lot* of lines, far more than on modern gliders.

Photos courtesy Geoff Soden

Mike Byrne about to launch on a 5 minute flight with his home-grown, Konig-powered early paramotor in 1980. He could only fly for 5 minutes because the 100-pound motor hung from him, not the harness. That got uncomfortable in a hurry!

The rightmost picture was him flying the same wing but with wheels.

Powering Up

Englishman Mike Byrne made the first recorded paramotor flight in the fall of 1979 and, by the summer of 1980, was intriguing airshow and television audiences around England. The 95-pound home-built unit used a 3-cylinder Konig motor and hung from his back. It had no seat and probably limited appeal. Flights only lasted about 5 minutes since the motor's weight hung from his back and he hung from the harness. Ouch. He was also probably the first to name the craft, along with his brother Johnny, calling it a paramotor.

It obviously didn't catch on and Mike moved to bigger, faster craft, mostly with wheels or skids (helicopters). No more hanging from a harness: the family jewels could only stand so much.

Barndt Bartig was another pioneer, foot launching from level ground in 1981. But he kept it secret until the German-built *PagoJet* became the first commercial paramotor for sale in 1987. It too had a 3-cylinder Konig engine.

Digging Deeper: Fan Man

By Pat Lynn

James Miller had a passion for both flight and for freedom—paragliding gave his desire wings. He took to it quickly, learning from a friend before instruction was widely available. Residents of Juneau, Alaska spotted him frequently flying from Mt. Roberts near his home. He knew the value of training, though, and sought out advanced instruction in flying and towing, from Alan Chuculate, one of the sport's early instructors and certainly one of very few in Alaska.

Alan noted that besides "Having a lot of energy," James was enthusiastic, motivated, and his previous experience made him an easy student. James earned his USHPA (then USHGA) P2 paraglider and tow ratings in the fall of 1990 but he wanted to add the additional freedom that power provides. For that he would have to leave Alaska.

James' date with fate and fame was set when he traveled to Las Vegas in 1992. He hooked up with Patrick Sugrue who had recently started importing the LaMouette paramotor. After a few days of instruction he set out on his own flying with power.

Having flown for some time in Alaska, he found the desert conditions quite different. The dry, high-powered thermals caused frequent wing collapses and other maladies. Alan remembers getting a call from James with two questions: "How do I recover from collapses?" and "How do I thermal to stay up?"

The night before his famous flight, James called his brother Eric: "I'm going to do something big tomorrow," he said. Sure enough, on Nov 6, 1993, two minutes into round 7 of the Evander Holyfield-Riddick Bowe heavyweight championship, James Miller landed in history by landing his PPG in the ring. It cost him a beating to unconsciousness by the crowd, 4 days in jail and a $4000 fine. A year later he made headlines again by landing on the roof of Buckingham Palace, naked.

His irreverence and free spirit bubbled up in English court just before being deported. On hearing the judge banned him permanently from England, he asked "How about my ashes, can they come back?" She said no.

He eventually gave his life back to the mountains he loved so much. Health problems made the strapping 37 year old James Jarrett Miller unable to care for himself; in 2002 he took his own life in a wilderness area near his home.

Thanks to Mike Coppock of the Anchorage Press for information used in this story.

Right behind him was Jet Pocket (also known as Air Plum), the first French company to manufacture and commercialize a foot launched paramotor starting in 1988, quickly followed by the Propulsar whose owner then joined up with Guy Leon Dufour of Adventure. There are several pilots in Italy who also started making personal units as early as 1987, including the past owner of Vitorazzi and Diego of Miniplane.

The U.S. saw its first paramotor when Patrick Sugrue flew one in 1988. He imported the LaMouette brand and his most notorious customer was James Miller (see previous page) who really brought the sport, if briefly, into American minds.

Performance Improvements over time

Most of the technology has matured quite a bit, slowing the rate of improvement in both wings and motors. Gear does get better, knowledge improves, and training generally gets more available—all good progressions.

Advances come in spurts when some new development lifts the entire sector. Hopefully electric motors will be next. Manufactures employ various innovations and the good ones propagate. Copying is rampant because of the sport's small size which makes patent efforts unduly expensive and difficult to enforce.

Motor technology mostly comes from go-cart racing and motor scooters although purpose built motors have started to evolve. Economies of scale mean that developments in other areas is more likely to drive innovation in our sport since paramotor production runs are way too small compared to the thousands built for larger industries. A few manufacturers do specialize in paramotors but improvements are incremental. Power to weight ratio, which measures power per pound, is the best measure of a new motor's performance.

It's hard for a company to invest heavily in an endeavor with so little payoff. Fortunately, enthusiasts come along periodically and pour themselves into a project without need for large profits. We all benefit from their vision.

Our future is bright, with weight coming down, performance improving, and, even more importantly, with knowledge increasing. We have a lot to look forward to.

1. Powered parachutes (PPCs) came first although we share a common ancestor in the square parachute of sky diving.

Early wings were glorified air-plows and required relatively heavy, powerful motors and the wheels to heft them. As wings grew more efficient, resourceful pilots strapped on relatively tiny engines. The paramotor was born.

The sometimes blurry difference between PPC's and PPG's is mostly weight and control method. If the engine is commonly used for foot launching, and the craft uses hand controls, it is more PPG trike than PPC.

Anything over about 120 pounds (trike and motor) was probably designed from the outset to be wheel launched and would be considered a PPC.

Most PPC's are *way* heavier (over 200 lbs) and have proportionally more power.

2. The Electric PPG will be an ideal solution when batteries and/or fuel cells get better. Fortunately, improvements continue apace. Electric cars and solar solutions are driving battery technology in both performance and price, eventually trickling their benefits down to us.

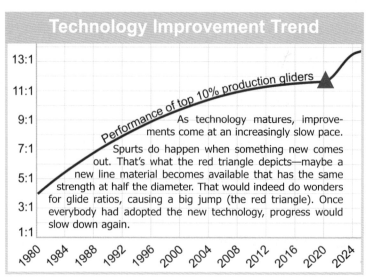

Technology Improvement Trend

Performance of top 10% production gliders

As technology matures, improvements come at an increasingly slow pace. Spurts do happen when something new comes out. That's what the red triangle depicts—maybe a new line material becomes available that has the same strength at half the diameter. That would indeed do wonders for glide ratios, causing a big jump (the red triangle). Once everybody had adopted the new technology, progress would slow down again.

Section V

Choosing Gear

*S*ection V

Choosing Gear

By Eric Sansli

Other Ultralight Types

Weight Shift / Hang Glider Trike

Powered Parachute

3-Axis Control

If you're just starting out, review Chapter 1 to help choose an instructor—a choice that will have far more influence on your success than gear. A good instructor will help select the right equipment. This section is meant for *after* training.

Who to Talk To

The fact that you're reading this book is a great sign; you want to be informed. Hopefully these words get to you before some shady salesman does. The Internet is rife with them.

Your best resource is a trusted, appropriately certified instructor or, absent that, experienced pilots who have nothing to sell. Seek out pilots who have flown a variety of wings and motors. A great approach is going to a fly-in to see what's out there. Not only will you *see* the various offerings, but you'll also see what people like and find out why. There will be a broad group of folks to talk with and pilots love talking about their gear. Visit www.USPPA.org for the events calendar.

Sales pitches are just that, pitches, and a few of them are out in left field. There is no perfect machine, or wing, but there are many trade-offs.

Appearances

We all want stuff that looks good, but remember that your life depends on your choice—prioritize accordingly. The best looking gear on the ground pales next to the ugly duckling that will get you airborne. If you can't fly it, looks won't count for much.

Cost

No, it's not cheap. While this is one of the least expensive ways into the air, it's still aviation. Requirements for lightweight reliability drive up the cost as does low sales volume. It's necessary that sellers and instructors make profits; their success is good for all of us and for the sport in general.

Cost will certainly be a factor for most people, and you should know what you're getting into. Always price gear with any training packages that might be included.

If avoiding the middleman means skipping the local instructor or school, that's usually a bad trade-off. In the long run, local support can be well worth paying a bit extra through your local dealer.

Realize, too, that costs will continue. Breaking a prop is not terribly uncommon and costs 3% to 6% of your motor's new purchase price. Wings last about 300-500 hours of sun exposure, and motors have a taste for parts.

Test Flying

Be extremely careful when trying out new gear—it can be dangerously different. Have an instructor or experienced pilot who knows the equipment help sort out its idiosyncrasies. They *all* have idiosyncrasies. See Chapter 19 for how to make the process safer.

The Wing

CHAPTER

26

Wing choice has a profound effect on your safety, success, and enjoyment of powered paragliding. It's not the place to skimp or to buy on a whim. There is no "best" one; in fact, there is a huge selection of very good choices. As with life, be leery of aggressive pitchmen claiming "mine is better than everything else!" The more aggressive they are, the less likely they have your best interests at heart.

Ease of Launch

Paragliders have come a long way over the years, especially those intended for motoring. While early reflex models expanded our safe operating range, they had sluggish handling and poor inflation. No more. Their launch characteristics have improved to the point where it's no longer relevant—it's like asking how hard a modern car is to start.

Smaller sizes, lighter fabric, thinner lines, reinforcement rods, and better design have made all paragliders better. If a normal sized, modern glider from a reputable builder is hard to launch, there's probably a problem. See Chapter 5 on troubleshooting launches. Those few gliders that *are* difficult really stand out.

This is good because foot launching a paramotor in calm winds, especially on soft terrain, is possibly the hardest thing we must master. Having better gear is a welcome improvement.

Free flight wings are subtly different. The highest performance comes in the skinniest aspect ratios, which are indeed more difficult. Thankfully, as motor pilots we have less need for that. Even free flyers have flocked to more benign, easier kiting wings, judging from what sells best.

Paraglider manufacturers are always looking for ways to improve efficiency and behavior. This shows how nylon rods are being used in the leading edge to improve airfoils and maintain shape.

Wing Loading: Choosing Size

Wing loading is weight divided by the wing's flat area and is the single most important selection criteria. Use this chart to help find an appropriate size for your mission. New pilots should start on school wings in the 8 to 9 pound/m² range while a seasoned competition or acro pilot leans towards 14 and up. At those high loadings roll rate becomes *extremely* high and dive recovery time goes way up. Needless to say, so does risk.

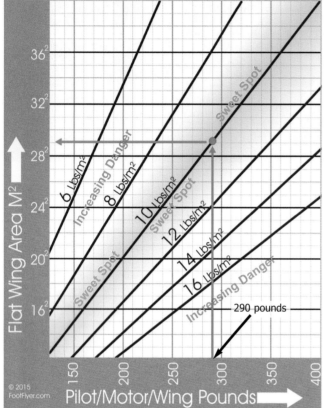

To find a wing size that puts you in the "sweet spot," start with your all up weight, including fueled motor and wing then go up to the desired angling blue line. Draw left to see what wing size that takes.

In the example shown (green line), pilot, motor, and wing weigh 290 pounds. Draw a line up to the 10 Lbs/m² line then go left to the size, which is just over 28 m² in this case.

Being over Placard

Most instructors consider it OK to be 10 to 20% over maximum placard weight on certified gliders. Realize, however, that certified gliders are only tested at their certified weights. Gliders that allow loadings much above 10 Lbs/m2 will almost certainly not be certified.

The bigger a wing is and/or the higher its aspect ratio (see page 223), the more difficult it tends to launch. The drag from large sizes makes it hard to get speed, and really high aspect ratios are more likely to come up crooked because a tip inflates late. Big wings' longer lines take more time to get overhead. The highest performance models also tend to be "slippery" while kiting—once they start sliding off to the side or yawing, it takes more to corral them back without folding a tip.

Age slows down even the best inflating wings due to line shrinkage and increasing porosity. That's a big reason *not* to go cheap on a wing.

Size (Wing Loading)

Flat wing area is the size of a glider when spread out flat. Projected area is the area of an inflated wing's shadow, usually about 15% less.

Wing loading is the weight per flat area, normally reported as Lbs/m² or Kg/m². You could use projected—it's more accurate in some ways—but we standardize on flat area because wing makers use it more.

Heavier pilot/motor combinations need bigger wings but size has trended downward as technology and preferences played out. Wings have a recommended weight range (*placard weight*) that says a lot about how they're intended to be used.

For example, while a 16 m² race wing may list a huge max weight of 250 pounds for a wing loading of 15 Lbs/m², a *certified* standard glider of 25 m² will list closer to 200 pounds or about 8 pounds/m². Most free flight soaring pilots stay closer to 8 pounds/m². At higher elevations, larger wings are desirable.

Heavier loading (smaller wings) tend to be:

- More dynamic, more responsive to control inputs, have a higher roll rate, and take much longer to level out from a dive.

- Faster but with a slower climb rate and higher power-off sink rate.

- Easier to inflate but require a faster launch run and more brake pull to lift off.

- Less likely to enter parachutal stall and more resistant to collapses, but far more violent if either one happens.

Lighter loadings (larger wings) have opposite effects and different risks.

Use the chart at left, but rely heavily on your instructor's recommendations since he'll know your skill set. Resist the urge to go too small. Physics and physiology don't change at the rate of morphing norms.

Reflex

Reflex airfoils allow higher speed with greater safety at those speeds (see Chapter 22 for more on the airfoil). There are some control caveats, namely the need to avoid using normal brakes while in reflex mode. Also, it is dangerous to use the speedbar on some reflex models while trimmed slow, even though this is a common practice among free flyers using standard wings.

Regardless of wing type, collapses at higher speed will be more dramatic.

Depending on design, speedbar and/or trimmer use changes the airfoil shape, taking the wing into reflex mode for higher speed. That's why different models may have different handling limitations in different configurations. For example, if letting the trimmers out *only* decreases the wing's angle of incidence without changing the airfoil shape, it may not prohibit using brakes. It may, however, go into reflex mode on speedbar which means there *would be* a restriction on using brakes with speedbar. That's why it's so important to read the manual.

The much higher speed range is why essentially all pylon type racing and cross country motor wings are reflex.

Fuel burns while reflexed are higher but, since you're going faster, they will be offset somewhat by the higher speed. Fuel burn per *mile* will only be a bit higher and, in much headwind, could be less. So if you're going cross country, especially with a headwind, reflex wings shine.

Glide and Sink Rate

The lower the sink rate, the less power you'll need to stay up. The higher (better) the glide ratio, the farther you'll go on a gallon of gas. And because the speed range is so small, wings with a low sink rate will likely also have a good glide ratio.

Overall, wings with a better glide ratio will be easier to land because you'll have more flare authority after the initial pull for landing.

Stability

Stability, described in Chapter 22, usually refers to collapse resistance when talking about wings as opposed to its more technical meaning of resistance to upset.

Beginner-type certified wings are generally more passively collapse resistant and recover more predictably than advanced wings. Of course they must be flown within their placarded weight range to realize that benefit. The tradeoff is that they can become boring for thrill seekers. But for new students with uncertain responses, these "boring" wings are *dramatically* safer during training.

Beginner gliders tend to have fewer cells which helps expedite recovery from upsets and longer brake travel to reduce the likelihood of pilot-induced oscillation.

A high performance glider in highly experienced hands is no different in collapse resistance than a beginner glider. That's because the pilot will automatically dampen the surges and twists that precede and contribute to most collapses. The higher performance glider is, however, more likely to suffer a complication on recovery.

2 Ways To Speed Up

Speedbar and/or trimmers employ a combination of the below methods to make a glider go faster.

Reduce Angle of Incidence

Change to Reflex Profile

Reflex Steering

For most reflex gliders, using brakes when fully reflexed (highest speeds) is undesirable. So designers employ various methods to "steer" around the problem. Most common is tip steering. It may be just a toggle to a line going to that side's trailing edge at the tip. There are some variations as shown below.

1. This approach uses a double action "2D" brake system where the pilot can engage either the center trailing edge, the tip trailing edge, or both based on how he pulls the brakes.

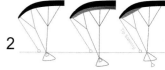

2. This method uses two toggles, one inside the other, where the smaller toggle controls the tip while the main toggle controls all the brake lines as usual. Pulling the main handle pulls the small one as well.

Many reflex gliders also have stabilo steering where a toggle or small handle (like a ball) allows for pulling down the stabilo line to turn. It has little control authority but the least amount of airfoil disturbance.

Handling

Responsiveness to brake input is the biggest element of handling. Being heavy on a wing makes it more responsive. Here are other items that affect handling:

- **Brakes**. The brakes should be in a comfortable position and tug the trailing edge within 2 to 3 inches of pull. Besides being more responsive, it ensures full brake travel for landing. When brake application crumples the tip slightly, it confers more responsiveness and dive tendency, which some pilots like.

- **Linearity**. The response should be incremental throughout the range with no significant dead spots or unexpected reactions. A little pull does a little and more pull does proportionally more.

- **Dive**. All wings descend faster when banked but some, especially smaller sizes, tend to enter a dive easier than others. Having short lines makes this more noticeable. Nimble handling can be a fatal flaw for the ham-fisted, or a joy to the master. All wings can be turned flat, but some models require more flying finesse to do so (see Chapter 16 on coordinated turns).

- **Heaviness** is how hard you must pull to achieve the result. Tandem wings flown with two people are going to feel heavy. Small wings will tend to have higher brake pressure but are more responsive, reacting quickly to even short pulls.

Some wings are "twitchy," meaning they move around a lot in turbulence. If you're into active flying this may be okay. These tend to also have sporty handling.

Speed

Advertised speed will be given at the maximum listed weight which is why certified gliders have lower maximum weights—they must pass certification at that weight. Generally speaking, given the same size, highly reflexed wings will be 20% faster.

When comparing wings of about the same efficiency, fast models tend to require more fuel burn per hour than slow ones. You won't stay up as long on a fast wing but will go the same distance in less time. If you fly with others who have slower wings, though, you'll give up the speed advantage while circling to wait for them.

Speedbar

A speedbar is nearly universal on both motoring and free flight wings although most motor pilots don't regularly hook it up. Almost all free-flight wings have a speed system so they can speed through sink faster and fight strong winds.

Different arrangements exist that trade off foot pressure for travel. Since the speedbar pulls down the highly loaded A's and B's, using pulleys provides mechanical advantage. Having only one pulley means the pilot does not have to press very *far* to get full travel, but he must push *hard*. Having two pulleys lowers the foot pressure but increases the foot travel required.

Trimmers

You'll want trimmers. Fortunately, most motor wings have them. Trimmer range for the more advanced reflex wings is huge, reflecting their larger speed range. We cover trimmers on advanced risers later this chapter.

Center Cell Visibility

It's generally helpful to see the wing's center cell easily; first, to know that you're centered on it for takeoff, and then to see if it is centered overhead.

Don't worry about this if you use the technique of looking sideways on launch to check the wing. Otherwise, being able to see the center cell will be helpful.

Speedbar/Trimmer Interconnect (STI)

A feature of some competition wings is the Speedbar/Trimmer Interconnect (STI). It uses a pulley arrangement so pushing the speedbar also lets the trimmers out (up) at the same time. It's frequently called a PK System after Paap Kolar, the first one who came up with it (covered next page).

Speedwings

Speedwings are designed to drop. Quickly. Flyers relish the ability to follow steep terrain, pulling brake to fly away at will, frequently on skis. They especially appreciate being able to stick to the snow, then when ready, pull some brakes and pop up.

For us, though, speedwings, especially the smaller sizes, go from a controlled fall to a poor glide. That means they require lots of thrust. You *can* fly them on motors but it will take a lot of power, leaving that much less for climb or play.

Like paragliders, a lot depends on size.

Given enough wind and/or big enough size, they can be foot launched, even soared if it's blowing up a decent hill.

Handling is extremely responsive which is one reason why new pilots should get training and work down to smaller sizes gradually. They have proven very unforgiving of errors in handling.

Just like flying small regular paragliders, a little brake does a *lot*—get askew of this control input and you'll be upside down before you know it. Experienced pilots do rolls at 50 feet while careening down mountains on these wings at 50 mph.

They roll more than turn. In actuality, their turn rate is like all other aircraft: based entirely on bank and speed, but the fast roll rate makes it seem otherwise.

One manufacturer wisely recognizes the effect of weight in their selection chart (Image 2 right). It shows that even their "beginner" speedwing, when flown at high weights, should be flown by advanced pilots. It's an informative chart that could be applied to every maker's line of wings.

Foot launching a speedwing

1

by Jeff Hamann

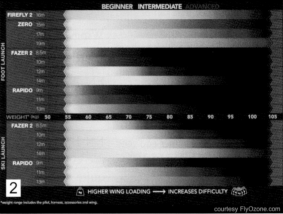

2

courtesy FlyOzone.com

1. Wind and a steep hill make foot launching speedwings easier.

2. Calling a speedwing a "beginner" glider is like calling a jet fighter trainer a "beginner" airplane. But everyone has to start somewhere. What they mean by "beginner" is an experienced pilot who is transitioning to speedwings.

The reference to ski launch suggests that those models are too fast to be safely foot launched. Looking at those sizes, we can't be surprised.

Certification

Certification by a recognized body suggests how a wing will behave in certain defined circumstances. Most commonly, flight and strength tests are done to European Normalization (EN) standards that assign a letter, A through D, where A has the most passive safety and D the least. You'll also see DHV and other certifications that use numbers, where 1 has the most passive safety and 3 the least.

Wings rarely get tested with a motor because there's little demand. Behavior is essentially the same with a motor, and more importantly, the much larger free-flight market wants testing geared towards their use. Testing can reveal bad behav-

LABORATOIRE FFVL AEROTESTS					
4 rue de Suisse					
06 000 NICE - France					
laborest-ffvl@wanadoo.fr					

<table has certification placard details>

CONFORMITY NUMBER / N° de conformité EN 926-1 & 926-2 VL 2009/014 **CATEGORY / catégorie** B **DATE** 20-janv-09

GLIDER / aile

MANUFACTURER / constructeur	AXIPARA		
MODEL / modèle	PLUTO 2	SIZE / taille	XS
Date de fabrication	SERIAL NUMBER N° de série		
MAXIMUM WEIGHT / poids maximum	70 kg		
MINIMUM WEIGHT / poids minimum	55 kg		
MODEL WEIGHT / poids du modèle	4.5 kg	AREA / surface	20.07 m²
NUMBER OF RISERS / nbre d'élévateurs	A, A, B, C, D		
ACCELERATOR / accélérateur	18 cm		
TRIMS / afficheurs	N		
CHECK EVERY / contrôles	After 100 hours of flying or two years		

HARNESS during test / harnais lors du test

TYPE	ABS	BRAND NAME / marque	SUP AIR
MODEL / modèle		EVO XC 2	
DISTANCE BETWEEN TOP MIDPOINT OF CARABINERS	Weight	Min	42 cm
Distance entre le milieu des élévateurs	Poids	Max	42 cm

WARNING BEFORE USE REFER TO THE USER'S MANUAL
ATTENTION avant utilisation lire le manuel de vol.

The wing above is certified in the EN B category—suitable as a beginner wing although EN A wings are better for brand new students. Some manufacturers have the placards filled in with magic markers at the factory, an unfortunate practice that can be hard to read after a few years.

Some modern "beginner" wings have the same performance as competition wings from 10 years ago but with greater safety.

Certification & Trimmers

It's harder to get a trimmer-equipped glider certified. That's because a glider with trimmers, must be tested at its fast and slow settings, making it harder to get into the safer categories—a minus for sales.

So they may either have a small trimmer range, or the trimmers are locked into one position, usually neutral. After purchase, the user can then undo some stitching, or other trick to unlock the wing's full speed range. That, of course, takes it out of certification. This is more likely to be seen on reflex wings.

iors that must be corrected before getting the certification. That's why new pilots should stick with certified wings.

Reflex gliders are usually only tested with trimmers closed (slow) because these gliders concentrate on collapse *resistance* in their accelerated condition. Small wings (higher wing loadings) are almost never certified because they are too dynamic during deflations. Certification testing is expensive, so it's common that only the popular sizes of a glider get tested.

A certified wing will have a label stating, among other things, its certification level, make, model, size, and weight range, usually in kilograms. No label means no certification. Avoid uncertified gliders unless you're an expert who can verify their behavior. Labels are usually located near the wingtip or center cell.

Testing involves putting the glider into various maneuvers and collapses, then letting it recover on its own with no pilot input. Time to recover is measured, and fast recoveries get better grades. Those that take a long time, or require pilot input to recover, get lower grades (a higher letter).

Wings with trimmers have special challenges as described in the left sidebar.

Certifications

EN A (DHV 1, AFNOR Standard) gliders are good for new pilots. They're less likely to collapse and generally recover quickly on their own. You can still get into trouble, of course, but it takes more turbulence or pilot buffoonery to do so.

EN B (DHV 1-2, AFNOR Standard) gliders still have good passive safety and are considered suitable for students although they won't recover from collapses quite as quickly as EN A's.

EN C (DHV 2, AFNOR Performance) gliders have moderate passive safety but could be a handful during turbulence, requiring high level active flying skills.

EN D (DHV 3, AFNOR Competition) gliders are for experts and the risk tolerant. They are mostly flown by competition soaring pilots wanting to maximize performance at some increased risk.

Kiting Only Wing

There are many good deals to be had if you're just learning and want a wing for kiting only. Plus, you spare your main wing all that UV exposure.

Older, out of date models are perfect. Expect to work harder at inflation but that will just make you better.

Smaller wings are better because they'll take less effort to kite and can safely handle a higher wind range. Try to find one with good inflation (they get harder with age). It can't be too beat up since you don't want it coming apart if you simply get lifted in a gust.

Some companies sell wings *intended* for kiting only which work great but are pricey. They're especially handy in higher winds by virtue of being as much as half the size of a regular wing.

Resist the temptation to fly a kiting-only wing.

Advanced Risers

Chapter 2 covers the basics but here we show advanced risers like those found on most reflex wings. You'll benefit from reading any wing manual but even more so with these.

For starters, a wing should have its original risers unless you know how the new risers will behave. Soaring wings are sometimes fitted with motor risers to accommodate higher hang points and/or add trimmers—a change that undoes the certification.

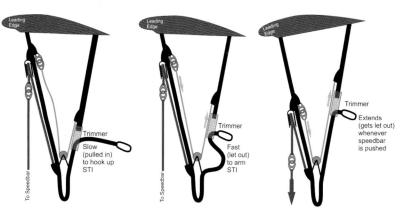

There's a lot going on that can be confusing. But seeing them in their different configurations helps makes sense of all the lines and pulleys. They set the airfoil shape, angle of incidence, and anchor all the controls. Frequently there are several types of steering available, and some wings have different ways of hooking things up.

The illustration below shows how various control combinations work their magic on a competition wing. Envision an airfoil attached to these quick links.

STI is used on the risers below but not on the next page. STI appeals most to competition pilots and videographers who relish the ability to have full speed control at their feet.

Those Clever Risers

Pictured above is a Speedbar Trimmer Interconnect (STI) or PK System schematic. Below shows STI on a real glider.

Imagine wing lines attached to the A, B, C, & D risers to see how the airfoil changes with each configuration.

When it's hooked up, the front and back of the glider teeter-totter across the STI pulley (see #1). Since there's much more load on the A's, when no speedbar is pushed, The leading edge goes up and the trailing edge stays down. Speedbar action pulls the front down, allowing the rear to go up around the STI pulley. The wing goes into reflex mode once the trimmers are released. Speedbar action mostly changes the angle of incidence (see sidebar pg. 259), that is, it just tilts the wing further downward.

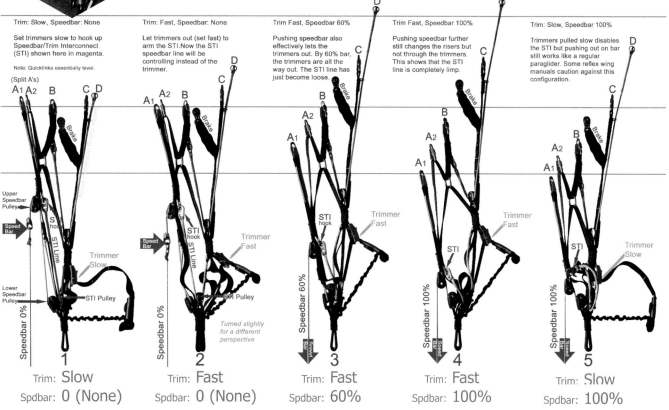

1 — Trim: Slow, Speedbar: None
Set trimmers slow to hook up Speedbar/Trim Interconnect (STI) shown here in magenta.
Note: Quicklinks essentially level.
Trim: Slow Spdbar: 0 (None)

2 — Trim: Fast, Speedbar: None
Let trimmers out (set fast) to arm the STI.Now the STI speedbar line will be controlling instead of the trimmer.
Turned slightly for a different perspective
Trim: Fast Spdbar: 0 (None)

3 — Trim Fast, Speedbar 60%
Pushing speedbar also effectively lets the trimmers out. By 60% bar, the trimmers are all the way out. The STI line has just become loose.
Trim: Fast Spdbar: 60%

4 — Trim Fast, Speedbar 100%
Pushing speedbar further still changes the risers but not through the trimmers. This shows that the STI line is completely limp.
Trim: Fast Spdbar: 100%

5 — Trim: Slow, Speedbar 100%
Trimmers pulled slow disables the STI but pushing out on bar still works like a regular paraglider. Some reflex wing manuals caution against this configuration.
Trim: Slow Spdbar: 100%

The illustration below shows the individual controls in yet another way. There are many variations, and different manufacturers have different names. Stabilo, for example, is also called "stabilizer"—it's the lines that go to the very tip. Usually gliders have something that only goes there. In the case of the glider below, Stabilo steering is intended only for minor turning in cruise flight. They call it a torque compensator, but of course, it also works for just turning, albeit very slowly.

In the illustration below, tip steering lines are in purple, stabilo steering is in blue and main brakes are in red. This glider has multiple pulley positions to accommodate either high or low hook-in machines. Most wings have some option to accomplish that.

At right, you can see where on the wing each control goes. Stabilo steering has the least effect on the reflex profile, tip steering has a small effect, and the brakes have a lot. Designers use various means to adjust how much of each control does what. Some wings require ONLY using Stabilo Steering (they'll call it something else) when fully reflexed. Always check the manual.

Control designs can vary dramatically; the glider at left, for example, has interconnect lines that actually pull some opposite trailing edge.

Many control variations exist. This is an unusual arrangement of interconnect lines (purple) to the brakes.

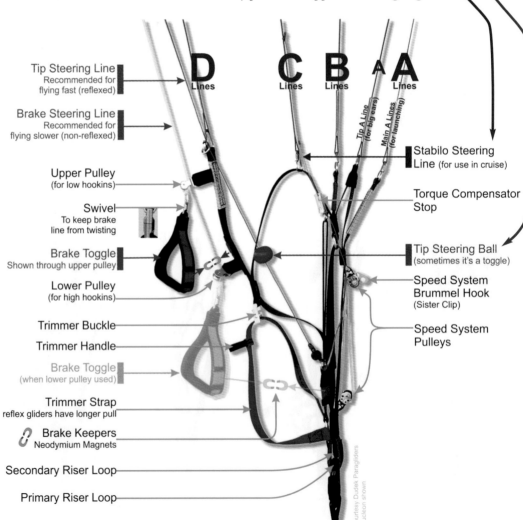

The Motor Unit

27

The perfect machine for one person may be another's nightmare. It depends on desires and dimensions; petite Patti will struggle with heavy motors as much as a big Al will struggle with being underpowered. There is no "best" machine; they are all compromises. Anyone telling you otherwise is selling snake oil—steer clear.

Trying new gear can be risky, especially for new pilots. Check out Chapter 19 for tips on minimizing that risk.

Some relics *should* be relegated to leaf blowing, having long been supplanted by better designs, but they're still shamelessly hawked to unwitting marks. Always dig beyond the slick brochures, websites, and fast talkers.

Don't buy a powerful machine thinking you'll be taking passengers up. In the U.S. and most other countries, that's far more regulated than solo flying. It's harder, too. Foot-launched tandem is demanding since you're managing a motor and wing powerful enough to lift two people. Carts are much easier and safer for tandem, but may not be legal in your country or may require special certification.

Be suspicious of advertised weights. Some companies don't include the weight of the prop, harness, or other necessary parts and may not say so in advertisements. It's true that different harnesses and props can be used, but when comparing, find out what's included and how much it *all* weighs.

These considerations are for choosing your *second* motor. Work with your instructor for your first machine unless you have very specific circumstances (like you inherited your mother's motor, for example).

Many design decisions go into each paramotor. This unit uses vanes to redirect some airflow to reduce torque at the source. Plus, the airfoil-shaped supports are less draggy than tubes so thrust loss is likely negligible.

Tradeoffs are made, and clever solutions occasionally solve two problems at once, but most improvements come in small increments.

Chapter 6 explores wheeled options and their considerations.

Weight

Anything intended to be foot launched should be on the lighter, more powerful side of the Thrust vs. Motor Weight Graph below. Electric-start machines can be only a bit heavier, even with a starter and battery. Thankfully battery weight has dropped a lot for the same energy.

How the machine hangs is another major concern. If it hangs low and cannot be raised on your back, or if the weight is far from your back, even a lightweight unit can feel awkward and heavy. If wearing the machine strains muscles after only a few minutes, it won't be comfortable on the ground.

Purveyors of heavy, awkward gear will argue that you'll only feel it briefly before launching. That might be true for experienced pilots, but for others it can be miserable. Plus, some pilots enjoy landing, messing around on the ground, and taking off just for the fun of it.

Don't get an underpowered unit, though, in search of lightness. That can be equally frustrating.

The charts below can help determine desirable power and motor weight for your particular situation. When comparing manufacturer weights, be sure they include the prop and harness. A motor that has a lot of power for its weight is said to have a good "power to weight ratio."

Trike attachments will typically add between 30 and 55 pounds. Use dry weight (no fuel) for comparison.

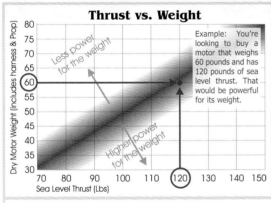

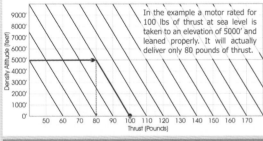

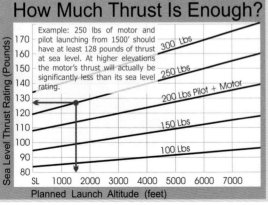

Comfort

There are many elements to comfort, both on the ground and in flight. On some physiques, bars or straps may get in the way of either visibility or movement—you have to try it, at least in a simulator. The motor should balance comfortably without pulling you back excessively or interfere with running. Its seatboard should slide all the way back against the frame.

Try to assess comfort only after adjustment by an instructor or another pilot who knows the machine. Frequently, a motor will be utterly underwhelming until it's adjusted properly.

Can you stand up with it? Do you have to sit on the ground? Does that bother you? Talk to someone—preferably the dealer—about how it's intended to be used. Some motors can seem impossible to maneuver comfortably on the ground until you know the "trick." Very, very few machines are completely horrible.

Thrust

Generally, more thrust is better, up to a point. Beyond that point, too much thrust is dangerous. Thrust helps 1) power through the inflation during a *power forward*, 2) makes launch runs shorter, 3) improves climb, and 4) allows flight at higher elevations. The downside is increased torque—high thrust machines can be dangerous for light pilots unless they are experienced at handling the torque. A lightweight pilot on a powerful machine can twist all the way around unless the machine is *really* well adjusted.

The chart at left gives a good indication of thrust required. All machines will advertise their sea-level thrust. Try to use numbers culled from published tests at fly-ins or by independent organizations. Balance them with advertised numbers and, if there's a big discrepancy, ask why.

Power decreases with height. If you'll be flying in Denver, the sea-level thrust rating must be greater. For every 1000 feet above sea level, increase the desired sea-level thrust by 3 to 5%.

On carts, more power is almost always better. Up the thrust requirements by at least 10% if you plan on adding wheels. If you won't be foot launching, then there is little penalty to having more power since weight will matter less.

Quality

Like anything built by humans, some machines are better made than others; most call it the "fit and finish."

Quality inhabits many forms. If things don't fit together, that's a sign of sloppy production. Well-made machines will interchange parts easily—the cage frame from one machine will fit fine on another like-model as long as neither has been damaged. It is rare, however, that a frame is not just a bit "tweaked" from transportation bumps or small falls.

Welds should look solid and be built to last without being overly heavy. Too much use of wire ties and hardware-store parts may be a bad sign; however field-repairability is important. Hardware store parts are OK in places where they're not critical to structural integrity.

Powerplant Considerations

We want smooth, quiet power that's easy to start, has a linear throttle response, sips cheap gas without pollution, and weighs nothing. As long as we're dreaming, it should be maintenance-free, cheap, and provide beer on tap. Or how about electric power? Three hours of flight time on a 10 minute charge would be about right. Waking up, now, we find ourselves in the reality of two-strokeville and its *many* tradeoffs.

Electric Start vs. Pull Start

Pushing a button to start is nice, and doing so while wearing the motor lessens your exposure to starting injuries, but there are tradeoffs.

Most models come with either electric or manual start but not usually both. Only a few models can charge the batteries in flight, and even those will probably require some charging at home to really be ready.

Flash starters are a manual mechanism with a second spring that winds up as you pull. It releases at the end of its reach, spinning the motor for start. These are more common on larger, clutched motors since there is no propeller to act as a flywheel, like on belted models. They tend to be needy of maintenance, especially earlier editions that traded a bit too much strength for weight.

Electric Start Pros: It's convenient, reduces some propeller/body contact risks associated with having to pull start, and enables easy in-flight restarts for soaring or aborting a landing.

Reliability

"Why can't my paramotor be as reliable as my car?" you ask. Good question given how little trouble most cars have in spite of heavier use.

There are three big reasons: weight, production quantity, and vibration.

1. We have to carry it on our back so we demand light weight for the push provided. Parts are built out of lighter material with narrowed strength margins.

2. Even the best-selling motors see fewer than a thousand units per year. They're all essentially hand-built with minimal, if any, automation. That's not enough volume to justify mass production facilities.

3. Even the best balanced motor is imparting a powerful torque pulse with every power stroke. There's no way to eliminate its weld-rending vibration.

Recessed Start Button

Kill Button

This is how most electric starts are set up. Somewhere on the frame there will be a master switch to enable the starter system. It usually also serves as an alternative kill switch: turning off the master also shuts off the motor. This arrangement reduces the chance for an accidental start by requiring two hands.

Another approach is using the same button on top for starting *and* stopping the motor. That makes it quick to restart in the air but easier to start accidentally on the ground.

Electric Start Cons: Having only electric start means more ways to be grounded. Namely, the battery and starter have to work. They're heavier than pull-starters by a few pounds, cost a bit more, and will likely require extra maintenance—not that pull-starts are maintenance free. There is a *small* increased fire risk, especially with "Lipo" batteries. They also add the risk of injury from an accidental start.

Number of Cylinders & Displacement

Nearly all PPG motors have only one cylinder to minimize weight. Twin or multi-cylinder motors may be smoother but will usually weigh more and offer more opportunity for mechanical problems.

1. Small engines are lightweight, more efficient, and generally less expensive. They are also more likely to have a clutch; although bigger machines do have clutches, thanks partially to the advent of flash starters.

Like motorcycles, displacement is measured in cubic centimeters; it ranges from 80cc up to about 312cc. Beyond that, the human frame starts requiring more maintenance (think "back strain"). Larger sizes typically power tandem units, heavy pilots, trikes, or those flying from high elevations.

2. Water cooling on this powerhouse is spent increasing horsepower. The pilot must watch the temperature because, like losing a cooling fan, water system failure would soon cook it.

Longevity & Reliability

Longevity is a measure of overall robustness. How many hours, how many cycles (start, fly, shut off) can you expect of the motor with no problems? It is notoriously difficult to predict. For one thing, it depends on how hard the motor is run. A small motor, run constantly near its peak, will wear out quicker than a larger one minimally tasked. Aviation is rife with examples of this; motors that run near their peak design limit have shorter recommended times between overhaul (TBO) than de-rated motors (max power artificially reduced).

3. This optional shroud convinces more air to pass through the motor's cooling fins.

Another aspect of longevity is support for the brand after the purchase. Obscure motors may be fine while everything works but finding replacement parts could be challenging. It's handy to have a common motor that enjoys good support.

Efficiency

Just like cars, small motors are more miserly. 80cc machines have won competitions where efficiency matters. You don't have to carry as much gas, or you can fly longer on the gas you have.

Efficiency is how much fuel is burned per hour, *at a given thrust*. For example, a big motor may burn 0.7 gallons per hour (gph) to generate 50 pounds of thrust while a small motor may only burn 0.5 gph to generate that same thrust.

Efficiency also depends on the fuel/air mixture: running leaner (less fuel per volume of air) than ideal will burn less fuel at the expense of higher temperatures. So any comparison should be done with the same relative fuel/air mixture.

Charging Ability

Some motors output a current for charging batteries. That's nice if you plan to run other 12 volt accessories, such as an aircraft strobe, but only connect those devices to the battery, *not* the motor's output.

Air Cooled vs. Water Cooled

The vast majority of motors are air cooled—it's simpler and there's no water to leak out. A very few water-cooled models use convection transfer to eliminate the water pump, but that doesn't cool as well as its more complicated pump-driven brethren. Not surprisingly, pumps are the norm.

Water Cooling: The ability of a motor to produce power is tied significantly to its ability to dissipate heat, and water does that well. The improved cooling can be used to either increase power or increase longevity by letting it run cooler. That comes at some cost in complexity, weight, and cost.

Air Cooling: Some air-cooled models, especially the smaller ones (80-125cc), use a fan to improve cooling efficiency. If the fan breaks, it's just like losing water: the motor is headed for a meltdown.

Two-Stroke vs. Four-Stroke

Simple 2-stroke motors power the bulk of our fleet. They are popular for the same reasons they are used on weed-eaters and such: weight (see Chapter 12 & 23).

Four-stroke motors are quieter, cleaner burning, and more efficient than their two-stroke counterparts. You don't have to mix oil since the motor carries its oil inside, just like a car. But they're heavier for the power and more complicated.

On average, a four-stroke motor will burn between 10 and 15% less fuel than a two-stroke at the same thrust. The two-stroke is consuming fairly expensive oil with each gallon of gas burned, while the four-stroke uses almost no oil. The four-stroke typically weighs about 15-25% more than a comparably powerful two-stroke but efficiency means you'll require less fuel weight be carried.

Inexpensive four-stroke engines have been successfully employed on carts. These have proven highly reliable and affordable. Since there is no intent that they be foot-launchable, the carts are made big enough to swing huge props, thus getting lots of thrust from their engine's limited horsepower.

1. Electric motors are available but mostly for soaring pilots who just want to get up to altitude, shut the motor off, and soar. Endurance isn't good enough yet for typical powered flying.

2. If a motor makes launching hard, it could be extremely frustrating.

For example, lines must slide smoothly up the cage during forward launches. Flexible cages may not tolerate power forwards with big wings and/or heavy pilots.

Ease of Launch

The paramotor design can have a significant affect on how easy it is to launch. A number of factors come into play with varying importance based on your location and experience.

All other things being equal, more thrust will make it easier to launch, up to a point. More thrust also means more torque, which must be managed. Excessive torque effects probably stem from poor adjustments (see Chapter 12), but when actual thrust exceeds about 70% of the pilot's body weight, torque effects become more problematic. Of course the pilot can learn to not use all the power which would eliminate this risk, but that takes practice.

Highly flexible cages can make launch somewhat more difficult if they prevent using power during initial inflation. You must get the wing nearly overhead by yourself before going to power—a technique recommended by some instructors regardless of cage type but generally more difficult than using power assistance.

Hang style, covered shortly, is likely the next most important element. A motor that sits higher on your back will be easier to manage and be less fatiguing while walking around with it. Motors that hang low tend to pull your shoulders back.

Fuel Tank Styles

Typical - by far the most common arrangement.

Bladder - Lightweight, transportable, no need to vent.
courtesy Air Conception

Above Engine - Easy fill, balanced on back, away from prop.

Integral To Frame - Minimal extra weight.

Metal - Doesn't melt, no discoloring or degreading.

Custom Formed - Max capacity, keeps fuel away from prop.

Ease of Maintenance

Complicated or proprietary shapes and pieces make repairs more difficult and expensive. Having pieces that can be readily replaced is handy, too, especially when you're out in the field.

The more parts that can be replaced, or repaired by readily available hardware, or easily stored spares, the better. Consider what "dinging" the cage (fairly common) will entail. It may be worthwhile to ask what each cage part costs if it's damaged.

Regardless of the hype permeating online forums, any motor will likely be damaged in a fall or other crash. So be leery when hearing "you won't need parts because my brand holds up so much better." Such nonsense should raise your skeptic flag into the stratosphere.

Fuel Storage

Almost all fuel tanks are made of a translucent white plastic that allows easy viewing of the fuel level and easy removal. Aluminum tanks are expensive, require a "sight tube" or quantity indicator, and are more difficult to repair, but they don't melt or discolor.

Fire risk is not affected by whether fuel is stored above or below the engine. In fact, the biggest risk for fire is a prop slicing into the tank during launch.

Ideally, fuel tanks will: 1) keep fuel away from the prop and exhaust parts, 2) be forward for balance, 3) hold as much fuel as possible, 4) be easy to fill, 5) hold a lot of gas, and 5) be lightweight.

Propeller Size and Style

In almost all cases, the largest prop will produce the most thrust with the least noise. But that might not be the most convenient for transport because it requires a proportionally larger cage.

A three- or four-bladed prop is normally less efficient than a larger diameter two-blade prop. If the blades themselves are more efficiently shaped they will make more thrust. Carbon fiber or adjustable pitch props will be more expensive but tend to be more consistent. Powerful motors sometimes employ more blades to push out good thrust without needing a mammoth cage.

A few machines can accommodate a variety of prop sizes just by purchasing different cage pieces. This would be something to check on since, if you purchased it with the small prop but then needed more thrust, you could get it without buying a whole new machine. The tradeoff is that such machines may not be ideally engineered for each size.

Attachment Points & Spreader Bars

Spreader systems, introduced in Chapter 2, keep the front portion of the harness from pressing against the pilot's chest (see Page 17). We'll expand on that here.

Human geometry and balance dictate that there are effectively only two types of hook-in (attachment) points.

Low

If the riser's pivot point, when viewed in flight, is below the pilot's shoulder, it's a low hook-in machine for our purposes. The pivot point is where the riser and any flexible attachments connect to metal.

Most motors with low attachments are trying to mimic a free-flight harness to some extent. They appeal to pilots who also own free-flight harnesses which nearly always have low hook-ins points for maximum weight-shift. Soaring wings typically have longer risers that work on low attachment machines without needing to adjust the brakes.

Some models, those with the lowest hang points and pivoting bars, are able to achieve significant weight shift. They allow moving the risers differentially about 6-8 inches through various combinations of arm swing, machine tilt, and hip action.

Low attachment machines that have no pivoting bars are probably trying to avoid weight shift and the looser feeling it invokes.

The pivot point is on a metal part of the frame (not the harness) with some kind of safety strap as a back-up.

High

If the pivot point is above the pilot's shoulder it is a high hook-in machine.

Weight shift, if offered, is via pivoting distance bars or a sliding strap arrangement. Pivoting arm units have the front harness segments attached to a free-moving pivot arm. Sliding strap types allow the front harness segments to slide through a cutout as the pilot moves a leg up or down in the seat—it doesn't move quite as freely as a pivot bar, but gives similar weight shift.

A very few, mostly older models, use fixed, over-the-shoulder J-bars. Since weight is so far below the hang point, they tend to reduce how much turbulence gets transferred to the pilot. That smoother ride sacrifices some feel. The J-bars dampen out uneven pull from the risers as each side of the wing flies through slightly different air currents. On weight shift units, this uneven pull is transferred to the seat board, which the pilot feels.

"Floating" J-bars (pictured above right), that either move or float, serve as spreaders while allowing some amount of weight shift. If the ground handling straps on pivoting J-bar machines are not properly adjusted, the J-bars can ride uncomfortably on the pilot's shoulders.

The term *mid-attachment* refers to high hang point machines where the carabiner attaches directly to harness webbing. Underarm bars of some sort will be located beneath the pilot's arms. They're called "mid" because of how they look on the ground when hooking up but, in flight, their geometry is that of a high hook-in. It can be under a 2-inch difference between high and low.

Legacy "Floating" J-bar system

Low Hook-In

This machine, like #1 on the next page, is a low hook-in system that attaches high enough to keep the thrust line below the pivot point. That allows good weight shift but with less fore-aft tilting than machines having lower attachment points.

courtesy Blackhawk.com

1. These S-shaped, or *goose neck*, pivoting arms raise the pivot point enough to be *on* the thrustline instead of below it. That reduces fore-aft tilt during power changes.

2. This high hook-in machine has pivoting underarm bars that provide some weight shift. The hang point is only a few inches higher than the common S-arm low systems.

3. This low hook-in machine uses older-style, flatter pivoting bars. The lower the hook-in, the more fore-aft tilt is felt with throttle changes and the more weight shift you get by tilting the whole machine along with differential bar movement.

Hybrid

At least one model (pictured right) starts with high hook-in points during launch, then mechanically moves them down and forward as the pilot pushes out on a bar. It gives a more laid-back posture in flight to more closely approximate free flight and improves weight shift at the expense of an increase in complexity and weight.

Hybrid hang point

Weight Shift

The entire goal of allowing weight shift is to move one riser down while the other goes up (see Chapter 18). There are several ways to do this.

Not everybody will like the active nature of highly weight-shiftable machines, especially the lowest hook-in styles with their "busier" ride in turbulence. Plus, the fore/aft tilt of some machines can be annoying.

Good weight-shift means over 6 inches of riser travel. Those that aren't designed for it will get less than three inches of travel with a fair amount of effort. Any fixed J-bar system with high hook-ins has an inch or so with great effort. Bigger pilots or more effort will get a bit more.

Sliding strap

This system, described on the previous page, works well as long as it slides easily. Being able to weight shift is a by-product of the design's original goal which was to make getting in the seat easier.

Whole-Machine Tilt

On machines with low enough hook-in points, the pilot can tilt the entire machine right and left to accomplish the riser movement. Just having low hook-ins is not enough; they must be *very* low. If intended to have weight shift, this arrangement will invariably have pivot bars, even though each bar generally moves only a few inches in flight. These types will get over 6 inches of riser travel and are closest to the way free-flyers achieve weight shift.

Having the CG this low tends to make the machine feel "loose" since its pivot point is so close to the center of gravity. They tend to swing around in turbulence both fore/aft and left/right. Pilots acclimate, but it can be disconcerting at first.

If the machine has no pivot bar, it was probably not intended to have significant weight shift and will only get an inch or two of travel.

Pivot Arm Only

Machines with high hook-ins can get decent weight shift using a pivoting arm. Even better are models where the action of one arm going up makes the other arm go down. These "Wally Shifters," named after the original designer, get the same riser travel as low hook-in systems, but the gearing mechanism is fairly heavy and adds another consequential point of failure.

Transportability

See Chapter 31 for ways to transport; this is about types of transportability. What's ideal depends on how you'll travel.

Going by airliner means the machine must break down to a very small size, even if it takes more time. Some are made for this purpose—both the cage and frame pull apart easily, usually with poles for radial arms that pull out. Such a machine will become a headache, though, if all you need to do is get it in a van. For that, you'd be better off with a cage where the top half comes off, even if it doesn't break down as far. It depends on the mission.

Unless you do it all the time, expect to spend a good hour getting your airline-transportable machine back together; whereas the simple 4-piece cage may go together in 10 minutes. Ideally, the airline-transportable machine can *also* let you remove just the top cage easily.

Machines made to squeeze into a suitcase will likely present a bit of a Rubik's Cube every time. Once you know the trick, it goes lickety-split, otherwise, grab a bottle of water. What the experienced dealer can do in 5 minutes will likely take the owner, who hasn't done it in months, many times that.

Packing any machine for shipment, if it doesn't have a case built for the purpose, will take a good hour regardless of model until you get it dialed in.

The smallest paramotors are direct drives. These loud little buggers have small props and cages that can be carried in cars (or airplanes or helicopters) without *any* disassembly. The one pictured above fits, even if barely, inside a small helicopter. But these machines aren't even sold anymore because they're just too noisy with too little oomph.

Support—Parts and Expertise

Make sure you can get parts. Unless you're a tinkerer, you'll want support for your particular machine. Cages and frames can usually be fixed by local welding shops, but not the engine itself. The motor and its unique accessories are the important pieces that are not likely to be locally available. Check around to see if other pilots have had good luck getting support for the motor you're considering.

Having a popular engine means having expertise *and* parts availability. If lots of a particular motor are "out there," most of their problems have probably been identified and solutions found. Even if the manufacturer doesn't have the fixes, the pilot community probably will. More people are around to answer questions and there's a bigger market for dealers to profitably stock parts.

If you have a local school or shop that can support what they sell, consider the enormous value of their proximity. It may well be worth several times what you pay for the gear in frustration avoided.

1. Many motors' top cage half comes apart quickly. This may be handier than having a style that breaks down farther but takes longer.

2. A motor that goes into a suitcase is great if you travel abroad a lot. Even though most airlines won't carry them as checked luggage (find out before you go), they're great for shipping. This is a safer way for transporting and certainly is the easiest to lug around. Allow enough time to shoe-horn it all in.

3. This machine was made to travel. It fits comfortably in the stout shipping container shown and includes everything but the wing. The box is bigger but that makes packing easier.

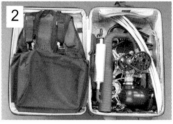

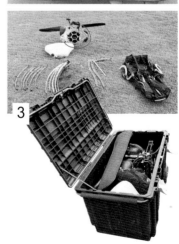

Paramotor Safety

At least one manufacturer offers "SafeStart" to reduce starting risk. During start, if the motor suddenly goes above a certain RPM, SafeStart will shut it off. After 5 seconds or so full RPM is allowed.

Nothing is perfect but, like seat belts in cars, there's enormous safety benefit in trade for minimal hassle.

Placard that should adorn every paramotor. It would be nice if they could have *some* brains.

Hopefully, equipment improvements will someday reduce our sport's biggest risk: the propeller. It causes the most serious injuries, many of which could be prevented with a well-designed cage system (see below) or a SafeStart-type mechanism. Done properly, such a design would impose minimal penalty on performance and weight while adding little cost.

There are other ways to make our machines safer, but it will ultimately be up to consumers. Safety features are expensive. They must be designed, built, tested, adjusted, etc. Then pilots have to buy them. Consumers insisting on more-sane, safer gear will drive innovation.

There is no perfectly safe machine nor will there ever be, but they can sure be improved. In the meantime, it's up to us to use best practices, to be vigilant when starting or working near running paramotors, and to fly in ways that let us keep flying. More importantly, it's up to us to protect non-participants who may blunder into harm's way.

A Better Paramotor

Reality is that humans, even conscientious ones, make mistakes. If we learn anything from airline safety, it's that we **must build better machines**. That means accounting for human factors. Search for "A Better Paramotor" on FootFlyer.com for more.

1. The cage, including its bottom area (4), should keep an open human hand out of the prop at high thrust. An inner hoop, 1" less than the prop diameter, can be added to existing units.

2. Props should break reasonably easily to lesson injury potential. This also tends to be lightweight which improves spin-up.

3. Pull starter ergonomics should keep hands safe and allow the motor to be well supported if it goes to power.

4. This bottom area must block hands and throttle cable.

5. An auto-cutoff start system (SafeStart, for example) to prevent a sudden, unexpected power-up within 5 seconds of start. To be effective it must be always-on, with no pilot intervention required, and have no effect on air restart.

6. Fuel tanks need clearance from exhaust for normal flight and from the prop in case of a crash. Bottom mounted tanks need at least 6 inches of clearance from prop tips (less for short props, under 45").

7. Harness and frame should eliminate most torque twisting effects. That can be done by offsets, weight, hang points, airflow redirection, and other methods.

8. Air bag protection (like free-flight harnesses) for vertical impact protection.

9. Stable platform that doesn't tip easily and provides some protection. It should be curved enough to avoid catching on small ground protrusions during inevitible slide-in landings.

10. The motor, specifically the prop, should be as close to the pilot's back as possible for comfort on the ground and other balance issues.

11. Minimize how far the prop sticks out behind the cage to reduce line snags during aborted launches. This trades off having the prop farther from its cage.

12. If the fuel tank has insufficient prop clearance, it should be reinforced so a prop strike can't breach the tank.

13. Pivot points should minimize fore/aft tilt during throttle up and allow for an upright posture on takeoff and landing.

14. Seatboard should fold up completely to allow easy running and be easy for the pilot to get into the seated position without letting go of a brake.

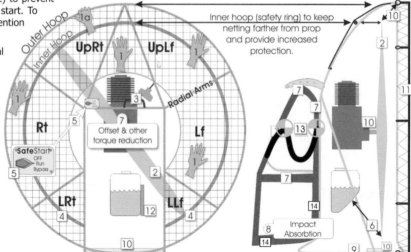

By Scott Adair

Accessories

CHAPTER

28

We've covered the basic accessories in Chapter 2, but this offers more detail on what pilots frequently add to a basic PPG package.

It's nice that you can accessorize with minimum fuss providing safety is minded. A lot can be attached, carried, or used in conjunction with our craft, but some goodies add more risk than utility. They cause distraction and yearn for the propeller: anything that can reach the prop eventually will. Accessorize carefully.

Reserve

There are two primary choices: rounds and steerables.

Steerables, which are mostly Rogallo-shaped have an improved descent rate, weigh slightly more, pack about the same size, and glide about 2:1 after releasing the brakes. Opening speed and reliability is about the same, provided they're installed correctly, which is more critical since there is a left and right. Get help from a competent instructor who is familiar. Obviously, being able to steer away from Earth's bad things is a huge benefit.

Rounds, usually Pulled Apex types, are simpler to install and easier to repack but attention must be paid to ensure the pilot lands level: there is no steering at all.

Rapid opening makes paraglider reserves completely unsuitable for free-fall—they would likely come apart in a high speed (terminal velocity) opening.

Factors affecting choice are size, reliability, opening speed, and steerability. Sink rate varies by size and you'll want to be within the weight range. Unlike paragliders, where pilots frequently fly heavy (small wing), a too-small reserve will not do its job properly.

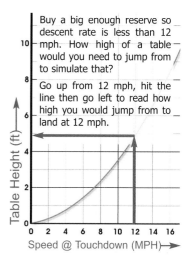

Buy a big enough reserve so descent rate is less than 12 mph. How high of a table would you need to jump from to simulate that?

Go up from 12 mph, hit the line then go left to read how high you would jump from to land at 12 mph.

Adding Wheels

Chapter 6 covers most rolling options, but here are some thoughts on wheels as accessories. If possible, choose a cart that's made for your motor—the mounts and balance will have already been optimized and tested for its frame. If you use a different motor or harness, do a thorough hang test. In the U.S., single place wheeled craft are still ultralights. In some coutries they become regulated aircraft.

The choice of wheels depends on where you fly. Balloon tires are great in sand and other soft surfaces but have more rolling drag. Skinnier, larger diameter tires work well on firm surfaces but don't slide left and right as well, making them more tippy on those surfaces. Plus tall wheels add height, which aggravates the problem.

Sitting close to the ground helps keeps the center of gravity low which helps resist toppling, but small wheels won't handle taller grass or rough ground. Having lower hook-in points reduces rollover tendency at the expense of wobbliness in flight.

A strong cage is a must to keep lines from flexing the hoop during inflation, possibly hitting the prop. There's always some flex, more with a trike, so cages should be a bit stronger or have more prop clearance.

The simplest add-ons don't have much occupant protection—a safety tradeoff. However, if your motor's cage is strong and the mount stout, it will give some minimal protection. The comfort bars on most paramotors are *not* designed to support your seated weight during a bumpy roll so the trike should have some support under the pilot seat.

On tandem carts (check legalities), look for protection of the front seat occupant. There should be some structure extending beyond the front person's legs so that the frame absorbs a head-on impact, not the passenger.

A functional trike is easy to build, but engineering good handling and crash protection takes thought. As always, there's more than meets the eye.

Stability

Stability, in this context, means resistance to tipping over sideways or backwards during launch and landing. In flight it refers to how much the cart moves around in turbulence and power changes. Here are some beneficial characteristics.

1. Widely spaced wheels dramatically reduce the tipping tendency. Quads with widely spaced wheels are the most stable but, if they have sled type steering, any bump that hits only one wheel will try to turn the cart in that direction.

2. Low center of gravity reduces the tendency to tip over sideways.

3. Moderately lower attachment points reduce the tipping tendency but increase the cart's wobbling around during turbulence.

4. Mass should be concentrated near the center to reduce rotational inertia which can make for some large swings in trubulence once it gets going.

5. The thrust line should be vertically close to, or below, the wing's pivot points so throttling up won't pitch the cart down. Thrust should also angle up enough to keep from ruffling the wing at idle.

Most carts use a trike configuration with single pivot steering where left pedal press turns right.

Single Pivot Steering Trike (most common)

Quads are the same although a few have incorporated dual pivot steering like a car. You still use your feet but each wheel turns independently like a car. The advantage is that uneven ground doesn't tend to turn the cart when only one side hits a rough spot. The drawback is weight and complexity which is why this type is so rare.

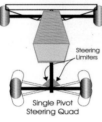

Single Pivot Steering Quad

Car-type steering Dual Pivot Steering (rare)

Extra wheels can enhance stability, reducing the likelihood of either rolling over or flipping back on the cage (turtling). These are primarily used during training on tippy carts.

Rear Stabilizing

Side Stabilizing

The ultimate convertible. This trike accepts either a hang glider or paraglider wing but is powered by a paramotor.

Helmet, Hearing & Communications

A helmet should protect both your head and hearing while allowing easy radio communications. If it has no ear protection then use ear plugs with at least 25 dB noise reduction to prevent permanent hearing loss. Even full face motorcycle helmets don't have enough hearing protection. Plus, they limit your peripheral vision and ability to see the wing overhead.

The more head and neck coverage the better since it must also protect from propeller shards.

Radio Compatibility

In the U.S., Family Radio Service (FRS) radios are common, so most helmets can be made compatible with them but each brand is different. Make sure helmet and radio play together.

It's almost a given that helmets designed to work with FRS radios will not work with aviation radios. Some makers do allow this using special *pigtails* where different plugs can be hooked into an in-line connecter. But even these can have compatibility issues.

The key to a good-sounding radio for inflight use is its microphone. A high quality dynamic, noise cancelling mic will make a huge difference. Not all microphones work with all radios, though. A dynamic mic requires power and expects the radio to provide it. Some do, some don't—you must check first. 2-meter radios, which are becoming more popular due to higher quality, usually do, but they require a license to use, at least in the U.S.

Audio mixers are available that allow music and radio communications to coexist. Music gets turned down when the radio sounds. Ideally this capability is built into the helmet because connections are always bad for reliability. Another handy, but rare feature is *sidetone*. You hear your own voice when transmitting which 1) helps keep you from shouting, and 2) lets you know that your microphone is working.

Paramotor ignition circuits generate electronic noise that can interfere with radio and other electronics. It causes static that changes with motor rpm but can be reduced by using a resistor spark plug or cap. Never combine the two—it will affect the motor's operation. A braided wrap around the spark plug wire (shield) will also reduce the noise.

Free Flight Radios

U.S. free flight pilots use VHF radios on specially designated channels in the 2-meter band. The Hang Gliding and Paragliding Association (USHPA) manages the licensing for the Federal Communications Commission (FCC). These radios are far more reliable, with better range and sound quality, but do cost more. The trick will be getting your flying buddies to use them.

Aviation Radio Setup

Pigtail, or adapter harnesses, are available from aviation radio maker, provides standard plugs for aviation headsets.

Aviation headsets have a fairly standard set of plugs: 1/4 inch "phone" plug and a smaller mic plug. Mic plugs into PTT, if one is being used.

Special helmets are available to go over top of aviation headsets.

A push-to-talk (PTT) add-on goes between the headset and aviation plugs. This is great for formation flying or filming where you really want to keep hold of the brakes.

Note: "**Jacks**" are what "**plugs**" go into. The term is used more often in audio applications.

Courtesy Icaro Helmets

Helmet Types

1. Motorcycle helmets can work, and this one includes a voice-activated communications apparatus designed for bikers. When the pilot talks, it transmits using FRS (Family Radio Service) channels or Bluetooth. Try it first to make sure it can handle our noisy environment. And beware that these helmets usually don't have enough hearing protection.

2. Purpose-built helmets like this are expensive but work well. They can frequently be ordered with plugs for your radio model, and some models allow for a bluetooth music input. The transmit button is usually on the side of an ear cup.

3. A full face helmet offers the best protection. It can prevent injury in a face plant or other head-on mishaps.

Music

Now that your phone doubles as a music player, there is nothing extra to carry. If your helmet doesn't have a music input, wear ear buds below the helmet's ear cups. Now you'll have radio comms and music for no extra cost.

Above is an older version of what's in Chapter 2, showing its cabling. Soaring pilots will love having a variometer (climb/sink rate) in addition to engine indications.

Courtesy www.Hobbico.com

Wind Indication

Hunter's Smoke is a fine powder that's great for visualizing really light wind.

Anemometers (wind meters)

Courtesy wtbShop.co.uk

Engine Indicating

Chapter 2 covers the basics for engine RPM (tachometer) and temperature, but there are some other choices and considerations.

Most tachometers count sparks, and since some motors fire two sparks per revolution and others fire only once, you must have the correct tach (or setting) for your motor. If your tach reads half or twice of what you expect, it's the wrong type. Of course it will work fine; you just need to adjust the reading mentally.

Installation is simple, run the detector wire up to the spark plug wire and wrap it around 4 times or according to the instructions. The ground wire should be hooked to a ground, although most tachs work without it connected to anything.

Optical tachometers are handy for working on motors that don't have a tach. You point it at the prop and read its rpm directly. Inexpensive units are available at model airplane (hobby) shops but these need to be held close to the prop. More expensive units, built for airplanes, can be held farther away.

EGT, CHT

Heat is the scourge of 2-stroke motors and our application can be particularly brutish, so it's valuable to know how much heat is building up.

As covered in Chapter 2, an EGT (Exhaust Gas Temperature) gauge responds quicker to temperature changes than a CHT (Cylinder Head Temperature) gauge. But EGT probes are more involved to install and lead shorter lives in the harsh, hot exhaust stream.

There are two types of gauges, digital and analog. No battery is required on analog dial types since the probe generates its own voltage to run the gauge. Anything with an LCD-type display will require batteries. Multipurpose models can come bundled with other indicators that combine temperature, sink rate, rpm and more.

The Cylinder Head Temperature (CHT) is far more common since it just sits underneath the spark plug like a washer and is quite durable. It doesn't respond as quickly to temperature changes because the cylinder head must heat up; that makes it unusable for adjusting the mixture.

Like the EGT, most CHT's generate their own voltage to move the needle (unless it is part of a digital readout).

Wind Indicators

Chapter 7 covers several simple, purpose built and natural wind indications, but we like gadgets, and the choices abound.

Wind speed indicators, or *anemometers*, have the advantage of quantifying what you feel so you can equate that to values. With practice, you'll be able to estimate the winds within 10% or so. Models for phones work either by sound, having tiny rotating parts, or other more esoteric methods.

A few models may allow mounting on a tripod so they can remain in the field and record maximum gusts. That's handy since higher gust intensity, and sharpness equates directly to stronger turbulence.

Airspeed Indicator

An airspeed indicator tells how fast you're flying through the air. They are rarely found on PPG's because it's difficult to mount them clear of the motor's interfering thrust field. Wind speed indicators (anemometers) can be hand-carried to give an indication, at least while the motor is idling. Some variometers, made for soaring, have an airspeed probe that hangs below the pilot—beware of the prop.

GPS

Common among drivers, hikers, and cruise missiles, GPS tells us far more than direction and distance to home. Its most useful feature is displaying speed and direction over the ground. That lets you get an idea of the wind aloft by turning a slow 360° circle to see where the wind is from. The direction of slowest ground-speed equates to the wind direction and the difference from slowest to fastest represents twice the wind speed.

Technology has improved such that they are accurate to within about 10 feet horizontally and within 50 feet of altitude—an amazing feat given that the signal comes from space. You'll prefer units that display altitude, groundspeed and direction simultaneously. Some include a barometric altimeter but accuracy of the GPS-generated altitude is usually sufficient.

Strapping it to your leg is ideal because you can see it easily and the antenna has a clear view of the sky.

Phone apps have made knowing what airspace you're in very easy. The free application shown at right, Avare, requires no subscription and shows your position on a current Aviation Sectional Chart.

A must-have for flying in remote areas is a *personal locator beacon* (*satellite locator*) that can transmit distress signals from anywhere in the world. Press a button and it sends your location and trouble to a satellite rescue network.

For a monthly fee, you can add satellite messaging (most use the Iridium constellation).

Fig. 28.50

Fig. 28.54   Fig. 28.55

1. Wearing GPS nav on your wrist is convenient and accurate. Some also have barometric altimeters.

2. This basic hand held GPS has a primitive moving map. Like most, it plugs into your computer for planning or to upload your flights and see them on Google Earth.

3. The Avare phone app provides navigation on the cheap (free). If you have data, you'll even get current radar reports.

Digging Deeper: Altimetry

We live underneath an ocean of air where pressure is highest at the bottom, decreasing as you go up. That's what barometric altimeters measure: pressure.

Nearly all altimeters, including the wrist variety, have a way to set current barometric pressure. It is called, cleverly enough, *altimeter setting*. You now don't have to know your elevation—by setting that barometric pressure, your altimeter will accurately display its altitude above sea level. Some models will initially set themselves using GPS altitude.

At sea level, the standard barometric pressure is 29.92 inches of mercury (abbreviated Hg), and it decreases one inch for every 1000 ft altitude increase. Take a barometer that was reading 30.00" Hg at sea level and drive it up to Atlanta, GA (elevation 500 feet) and it will read 29.50 Hg. When meteorologists say the barometric pressure in Atlanta is 29.92, what they mean is that, *corrected for elevation,* the pressure is 29.92. The actual pressure is 29.42.

If you set an altimeter to the current field elevation and come back a few days later it will have changed, going up or down as the atmospheric pressure changes. A low pressure area will make it read higher and vice-versa for a high pressure area.

You may run into the terms QFE (Query Field Elevation) and QNH (Query Nautical Height). QFE is the pressure that results from setting your altimeter to zero. As you climb it reads height above field elevation. QNH is simply setting the barometric pressure. Your altimeter then reads altitude above sea level.

Emergency Kit

What you carry depends on where you'll be, but start with a fully charged cell phone and, in more remote areas, a foldable solar charger. Besides basic tools (see Chapter 12), consider a lighter, regular knife, and bug repellent. For serious cross country flights there's more to consider based on terrain.

Fig. 28.60

If you fly beyond reach of shore (See Chapter 19) the whole machine needs flotation that keeps it upright after ditching. The Agama (Fig 28.60) is one approach—it inflates automatically three seconds after submersion. *You* need flotation too, of course. A thin life jacket is reliable and requires no action, but a CO_2 powered vest is more comfortable while flying. Get the kind with automatic inflation in case you've checked out before hitting the water. Another option is a small, portable breathing system (Fig. 28.60), but it must be within easy reach and requires some practice using, especially if you're not a scuba diver.

A tree rescue kit is essential if you spend much time over woodlands. There are two approaches. One helps others get a rope up to you—basically 80 feet of dental floss (or similar) with a metal clasp at the end. The clasp is lowered so rescuers can tie a larger rope to it. You haul up the larger rope then lower yourself down. The floss should be at least as long as the highest trees in your area. The other approach, described at left, is for self rescuing—a much better plan if you go forest flying beyond phone or radio range.

Possibly the most valuable kit for remote flyers is a personal locator beacon (see Fig. 28.50). Using GPS and special satellites, it can relay your location and status to emergency services. For a monthly fee, advanced models are almost like a satellite phone with texting capability.

Use common sense in equipping yourself for the mission and be prepared to handle being stranded by an engine failure.

Cold Weather Gear

Nothing saps the joy of flight quicker than being cold. Essential accessories include warm inside layers, a windproof outer layer, good gloves, and face protection.

Full face motorcycle helmets with a visor are wonderful, but make sure you can open the visor in flight to keep it from fogging up.

Every part of your body must be covered but scarves are a verboten—it's too easy to forget a loose end and have it stream prop-ward. Commercial flight suits are great but a cheaper option that also works are basic cold-weather overalls or snowmobile suits.

Big gloves are a necessary evil and a real pain to launch with—everything is difficult to feel. Some pilots have had luck with heated gloves and other garments but that entails more complexity. Chemical hand warmers, available from department or sports stores, can also be helpful.

1. This self-extracting tree rescue kit incorporates a belay device that works with 105 feet of 6mm Perlon rope and a sewn sling. You should get instruction and practice before needing it. And don't skimp on rope size—40% of the rated strength disappears with the first knot—heat and rough deceleration can eat up any remaining margin.

2. You can launch on frozen lakes, but it's not for the faint of foot. Landing on them isn't so bad as long as the ice holds. Plan on being done after landing, though; it may be too slick to re-launch.

By Ulf Nyström

Home Building

29

An entire organization, the Experimental Aircraft Association (EAA), has grown up around regular people building airplanes. There are, in fact, several thousand homebuilt airplanes plying U.S. skies at speeds upwards of 500 mph. Burt Rutan, pioneer of the first private ride into space, started off as a home builder. So building your own paramotor is reasonable for some people.

But it's not for everyone.

There is a *whole* lot more to it than meets the eye. For one, there is enormous risk for anyone not taking it seriously—your life depends on sound design and execution. Very, very few people that set out to build a paramotor on their own, from scratch, and without previous aircraft building experience, ever actually fly it. On the other hand, those who build from respectable kits or plans usually *do* succeed in flying their creation. PPGPlans.com was set up to provide reliable information on the topic. We then bought the only viable plans on the market and put them online for those willing to get proper training. There is no need to be duped by inadequate plans especially since the PPGPlans set is free.

Don't build your *first* paramotor. For one thing, you'll be throwing away much of your ability to customize because you'll have no idea what you'll like. Buy an existing machine, learn on that, then build your masterpiece. It will allow forming ideas of what is *safe* to change along with what you'd *like* to change. The information in this book will help you know what *not* to change.

Build your own paramotor because you like to build, not because you want to save money. Even a well implemented kit will take 50 hours depending on what comes assembled. If it has little or no prefab, expect up to 4 times that much.

Jeff Baumgartner is flying the proto-type Skybolt. Its no-weld design was eventually turned into for-sale plans. After dozens of plans were sold and paramotors built, rights to the plans were bought by us, Footflyer.com. The plans are available for free at PPGPlans.com.

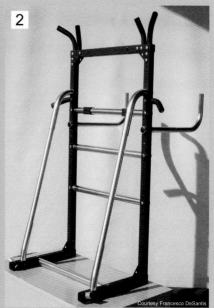

Courtesy Francesco DeSantis

1. Welding aluminum is far more difficult than welding steel and should not be taken lightly. That's why almost all plans or kit machines do not require any welding. The machine above (see PPGPlans.com) uses fittings wherever tubes meet or cross and a very clever key-ring-through-hoop idea to secure the netting. Wheels pop on and off easily for hauling of the machine, wing, helmet etc.

2. When this kit was available it used rivets and gussets to fasten the pieces together. Nearly the same technology is used in regular aircraft; it worked well if done right and with plenty of rivets.

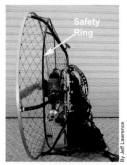

Safety Ring

By Jeff Lawrence

This is a case of modifying existing plans to suit a different suspension system. Notice the over-shoulder bars. Adding the safety ring dramatically reduces prop injury risk.

As with any machine, make sure you have an instructor that is sufficiently familiar with it and is willing to teach you on it. Most will, provided they feel the machine is reasonably safe and appropriate for your weight. The worst possible combination would be a marginally trained pilot trying to fly an untested, homebuilt motor.

Don't be fooled by the build-time estimates. They might be accurate for highly skilled mechanics but certainly don't include time for redoing parts, multiple runs to the hardware store, or other surprises that invariably emerge.

Building Your Own Design

There's a lot more to paramotor design than meets the eye. The process should include an experienced paramotor pilot who understands the constructs, limitations and choices involved. It takes flight experience on different machines to know what ramifications each design feature will have. Experienced builders of other things will still need expert help or extensive paramotor flying experience to sort out paramotor design elements. Even long time designers get flummoxed when their great ideas don't always pan out, so don't be surprised when some super new feature you devised only makes matters worse. See the end of Chapter 27.

If you *do* have broad paramotor experience, like to build, can work with simple tools and have time on your hands, then building your own design could be quite rewarding. The best approach is to model an existing machine as closely as possible. Find one that you like and learn why it's built that way. Look closely at how the harness attaches to the motor, where it hangs in a simulator and how the motor is mounted. Settle on the same type of motor to keep it balanced and stick with the same geometry. If you innovate, do so with great care.

Surprisingly small changes make big differences. For example, the weight shift bars common on high hook-in machines must be positioned just right. It was found, early on, that positioning the pivot point just 2 inches back (towards the propeller) made them far more effective.

There are many, many factors that likely went into a tried and true design, one that people are actually flying. Change them at your own peril. In the past, small changes to geometry or function have hobbled a machine to the point where it became unsafe. Pilots have been injured in such efforts. Be ready to deal with that and do lots of testing in the simulator before taking any new creation aloft.

After settling on a design—a time-consuming process that will probably involve many adjustments—the time and tools required to build a machine should be about the same as building from plans.

Building From Plans (Scratch)

If the plans are for a machine you've never seen fly, there's probably a reason. Find other plans that have been built and flown!

Buying plans from the back of a magazine or internet site was a bad idea before today's options existed. It's completely unnecessary now.

One of the biggest challenges will be acquiring all the parts. You'll need a harness, fuel tank, throttle, aluminum, motor mounts, fuel line, motor, netting material, throttle, etc. Good plans will have a current and thorough source list.

Tools: It depends on the design, but you may require aluminum welding which, unless you're quipped for it, adds difficulty and expense. You can expect to bend tubes, cut thick aluminum (fine tooth jigsaw can be used), rivet and/or fabricate various fittings. Anyone considering this should already have a normally equipped shop with the skills to use it. Some reputable plans don't require welding or you can buy the welded parts separately.

Expect to take from **100 – 500 hours** total building time from start to first flight—more if the plans don't describe accurately what's needed. Visit FootFlyer.com to see what kits are recommended. Nearly worthless plans have been foisted on unsuspecting buyers for years; buy something that comes recommended.

Building From A Kit

This is, by far, the best way to build it yourself. Even so, it should only be done with a proven kit that has examples flying in the field. Make sure you can watch or talk to pilots who have built the kit too. Any reputable seller will offer a list of customers to talk with. Even if they cherry pick the customer list it would be preferable to having no other information. Internet groups devoted to the machine provide another valuable resource.

Most kits do not require aluminum welding. Instead, they provide the welded pieces so the builder is mostly just assembling, riveting or bending tubes.

Kits may use pop rivets. They're cheap and, on a properly designed machine, are plenty strong. The key is to make sure no individual rivet carries much load, and have a lot of them, spreading out that load. Metal airplanes have been holding

1. As with all kits, the rivets and gussets of this machine must be done according to plan. In this case, it must be gusseted properly (the angled reinforcements).

2. Attaching cage netting is just as challenging for homebuilders as it is for manufacturers. On styles where the net is strung through frame members, it is cumbersome when a line breaks. The ingenious method shown below sidesteps that problem by riveting loops and having the netting line go through those. Restringing is a piece of cake.

By Jason "Sky Monkey"

Since you build it, you can make it safer. This shows the safety ring drawn onto Jason's homebuilt, dramatically improving cage protection.

Test your creation thoroughly. Hang it in a simulator where an instructor can go through the completed assembly. Make sure you can get in the seat, reach all the controls, etc.

together for years this way.

Tools: Generally you will already have what is needed: A drill, small hand tools, and a vice. The process is more assembly than fabrication which is especially good for the critical dimensions regarding motor mounting and frame alignment.

Time: Expect to take from **20 – 80 hours** total building time from start to flight. These times depend on the kit's level of completion.

Testing & Changes

There's always something. It may seem simple, but strange interactions and problems invariably show up during testing. Some are dangerous. Be ever mindful of the prop while going through the process. Some pilots (or would-be pilots) have been mangled after the briefest moment of inattentiveness. Have your instructor present when first starting the motor.

Like any new machine, your preflight should make sure there's nothing within reach of the prop that could get sucked in. The cage must have good prop clearance and the fuel system should be leak free with a good vent. These cautions go for changes to existing designs, too. Have your instructor or an experienced pilot check it out for you.

Consider what would happen in a crash. Can components skewer the pilot? Will the prop flex down enough to slice through the fuel tank, spraying fuel around and potentially igniting a fireball?

Will the change allow the risers to come together, causing riser twist in flight? Will the cage come forward on the risers and allow the brakes to go through the prop? These things have all happened and many other possibilities exist.

Hang the system by its carabiners to make sure you can get in and out of the seat easily. Install a kick-in strap and practice until it's second nature. Have an alternative (besides the kill switch) way to shut off the motor that doesn't involve reaching too close to the prop. When everything checks out, run it up on the simulator and see if any problems creep up.

Keep those first few flights close to home and check the condition of everything carefully after each flight. This is no different than buying a new machine or one that has recently been apart. Postflight is always a great time to inspect, but is even more important on a new machine or design.

Tinkering: Not all bright ideas in paramotoring come from manufacturers; many come from users, especially experienced pilots looking to get the most out of their gear.

Tinkerers have devised both doozies and duds. Wally Hines' counteracting weight shift, where one bar's upward travel pulls the other bar down, was a doozy as an aftermarket for certain brands.

Another creation, pictured right, didn't go so far. While not a complete dud, this retractable foot rest never caught on. It stowed for launch or landing and could be extended whilst cruising. He soon decided that the weight didn't quite justify the benefit. But it sure was comfy once airborne!

Section
VI

Getting the Most out of Powered Paragliding

Section VI

Getting The Most Out of PPG

Now that you're flying an aircraft that can travel with you, the list of possibilities is enormous. While a powered paraglider is wonderful for enjoying your *local* slice of heaven, there's a lot more out there.

Being able to take the gear frees you from the road; family vacations can become a whole different experience. Business trips can become an excuse to explore from above, and family visits can include "demonstrations." And as you'll see, there are even more ways to enjoy this amazing craft.

Other Uses

CHAPTER

30

What can be done with a paramotor is fun and surprising. It certainly is more amusing than practical but, who knows, one person's amusement may spawn another person's practical application. Be mindful of the risks; never forget that it's still an aircraft with that oh-so-effective spinning *fingerlator* on the back.

Stan Kasica combined two of his favorite sports, powered paragliding and water skiing. He launched from dry ground, hopping into the ski after doing a reverse inflation. This water was less than two feet deep but, be careful, drowning is paramotoring's most common fatality.

Using PPG for Transportation

Yeah, probably not. Exceptions may indeed allow using a paramotor to get somewhere but fickle weather, limited conditions, and slow speed conspire against us. However, if you're flexible, on nice days, there is no cooler way to arrive!

Ideally, your launch is close to home (better yet, at home). Portability means that, after you get there, it can be folded up for the ride back, especially since one-way trips are better. Like any cross country, you'll be happier with a faster wing.

If you have an airplane (you'd be surprised how many paramotor pilots do), this can be a great way to get back and forth to pick it up from maintenance. The same is true for cars if your shop has a nearby field. You may even need to choose your shop differently now.

Be leery of planning a round trip, though. If the paramotor is your only ride home it will be extremely tempting to push the limits and fly when you would otherwise pass. "Get-home-itis" has been the fatal flaw in many general aviation flights where pilots took on marginal conditions and lost.

If you have good sites at both ends of a planned trip, plenty of fuel, a legal route (not congested), and have good weather, the PPG *is* a fun way to get there.

Planes, Lanes and Helicopters

Before discovering PPG, I had a helicopter (*Ellie*). It required yearly inspections at a shop some 35 miles away. Dropping it off involved an onerous drive through nasty traffic. Twice. Then along came paramotoring. In spite of living in a suburb, I had an uncongested air route from my house and, of course, the shop had a helipad (middle picture, below). The pad wasn't much, jutting out into a swamp and all, but it would do.

So when the next inspection came due, I loaded my paragear into the helicopter and headed out. Flying there was pretty quick—while helos are slow by aircraft standards, they're greased lightning by paramotor standards. After landing, Darryl Oliver, the shop owner, spirited *Ellie* into his repair lair. Then he got some friends to come over and watch the crazy PPG pilot (me) launch. He thought I was nuts.

With the swamp before me, and the wing laid out carefully behind, I was ready. Nervous, too; if the motor quit, or I couldn't climb well enough, that swamp would be no fun. So I psyched up, powered up and went for it. The edge came quickly; I lifted off just before the water and held my feet up to clear the longer shoots of swamp grass. Easing up on the brakes let me accelerate and climb. Whew! *That* was satisfying. Darryl later admitted that he half expected to fish me out of the muck.

Flying home was almost magical.

A couple weeks later I reversed the process—paramotoring up to the helipad and flying everything home. Boy did that beat driving. And landing at the helipad seemed brainless compared to launching there.

Another fun example of usefulness was retrieving a motorcycle after maintenance. How convenient it was that the shop had a field next door. I'm sure the employees got a kick out of that sight. And yes, a helmet *was* worn, both on the road and in the air.

Flags & Banners

Flags and banners can be fun to fly but do add some risk. Attaching anything to the wing adds drag which slightly increases the chance for parachutal stall and makes the wing that much more difficult to inflate. Attached stuff may also impede recovery from malfunctions. Risk has proven minimal but avoid rough weather, excessive brake usage and follow the connection guide below.

When connecting a banner or flag, you want to 1) minimize turning tendency, 2) keep it out of the lines and prop, and 3) make sure it flies fully.

There are several ways to attach banners to the wing. Regardless of the method, put it near the center (to minimize turning pull). Since it can't be exactly centered, attach it to the opposite the side that your motor naturally torque turns. So if the motor makes you turn left, put the flag on the right side.

Use the most center brake line since that is the most rearward and will minimize turning tendency. You'll feel the flag flapping through your brake handle so some pilots will use a D-line (or C on 3-riser wings) instead.

You will have two lengths of 1/8" nylon strings that

are tied to the top and bottom of the banner's leading edge (2 & 3 at right). The top line gets tied to where the brake line connects at the wing (1) and the bottom line connects where the brake line cascades from below (4). The length of each line, plus the flag's height should be slightly longer than the brake line distance between attachment points. This will let the flag "bow" out without crumpling in the middle.

Put fishing clips (called snap swivels) on each end to make removing the flag easy.

Before launching, make sure the flag is on the ground and clear of the other lines. Generally just making sure it is on the ground and lines are on top of it is enough. After inflating make sure the flag is not hung up on anything before committing to flight—easy to do on a reverse inflation and a bit more challenging on a forward.

Hanging Banner

Hanging the banner works well if you want to fly somewhere before deploying it or if no-wind conditions make the inflation difficult.

Tie a weight (3 pounds should suffice, more for a bigger banner) to the banner's leading edge bottom (6) then tie a line to the top and secure that to a Velcro strap. Attach the Velcro to a low-hanging part of the frame or to your foot (5). It should attached so that a snagged banner would only peel the Velcro off.

The pilot launches with the banner stowed and then, after reaching a safe altitude, throttles back and drops it. The banner could foul the propeller so be careful; it's better done with the prop stopped. Be over landable terrain in case of problems.

With the banner in tow, don't fly near people who could get hurt if the banner dropped accidentally. Be mindful of how low it hangs and avoid the possibility it could get snagged on a part of your machine.

Before landing, either drop the banner or stow it back in a bag.

Cattle Herding

Don't laugh, a paramotor "round-up" has been done and the rancher loved it. In fact, he asks the pilots to help out regularly. Of course you can't get paid but you can earn another flying site, or at least a welcoming place to fly over.

Coordination is a must but it's mostly a matter of flying in such a way as to keep the cattle moving in a desired direction. Simply going out and finding strays helps a lot and the PPG, with its unrestricted view and slow speed, is perfect.

The coordination comes into play when two or more pilots are working one group of cattle. It also helps when working with people on the ground.

Be careful since it's easy to get so distracted by the mission that you fly right into wires, fences or the ground. It takes discipline to build a scan that regularly looks where you're going, not getting too focused on the mission target. Make no mistake, this adds risk; and doing it down low increases the risk dramatically.

Where cattle graze is usually landable terrain, but not everywhere. Be mindful of your engine-out options whenever spending attention away from flying. It's easy to get caught up in an activity and then be surprised by a motor failure. Surprise is decidedly unhelpful when only seconds remain before touchdown!

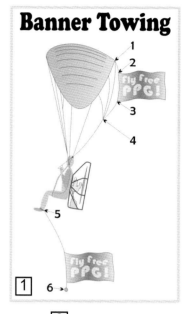

1. This shows 2 ways to connect a banner, one on the wing and the other on your foot. Of course there are other ways, but these have proven reliable.

2. Fishing tackle clips are a good way to fasten the banner line.

2. The same New Mexico group that has pioneered rescue work has also been called on for cattle herding. This pilot is working a small band of separated cattle along the Rio Puerco, West of Albuquerque. Legally, these uses fall under allowed recreational use and there would probably be no question unless you were getting compensated in some way.

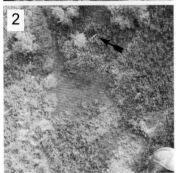

1 & 2. Looking for lost models can be tedious. There's no guarantee they'll be immediately visible and you must fly a search grid from different altitudes. I spotted this one from 500 feet or so. Notice how very close to the road this model was and how nearly impossible it would have been to see from the ground. From above, though, it was pretty obvious in spite of blending in with other yellow vegetation.

3. On this occasion the model's remote control quit working and the pilotless plane wandered almost a mile away before crashing with little damage. It, too, proved easy to spot from the air while being impossibly hidden from ground searchers.

Search and Rescue

Our high perch is also useful for search and rescue. Although cell phones and GPS's have reduced the need for such efforts, people still get lost. While we can't do much if they're wandering the woods, we can certainly cover open areas, including difficult to inspect crop lands. This should only be pursued by experienced pilots who generally make launches on their first try.

Contact your state Search and Rescue director (if available) or the local fire and police departments to offer your services. It would be on a volunteer basis and is a great show of community support.

Be up front with them about your capabilities and limitations. The worst thing to do is exaggerate what you can do and then wind up needing a rescue yourself. Most important, explain the limited weather conditions you need to operate in and time of day constraints—don't expect to do this on mid-summer afternoons.

Finding Model Aircraft

A great way to befriend the local Radio Control flying club is offering your search services for their lost airplanes. Give them your telephone number and explain your capability.

When those planes go down they can be nearly impossible to find from the ground and they have quite a range. Tall grass is ideal to find planes by PPG—they're almost impossible to locate from below but frequently pop out from above.

The flying is obviously simple: Pick a pattern and fly it while scanning the ground. Pick different altitudes too. If the airplane is buried in deep grass, you might have to be nearly over it. Going up high puts you farther away but provides the vertical angle that may enable a better view.

Once the plane is located, identify nearby landmarks that you can find from the road (or hack a GPS). It is best if you go out personally to get the plane because you know where it is. The nuance of location can get lost in a translation.

Public Relations & Exhibition

Flying in airshows can be difficult. You may need a rating (PPG2 is required for most insurance), approval by airshow management, and must work with the "Air Boss" who's in charge of all flight operations. They have exemptions from certain rules but that means all pilots flying under the exemption must be specially qualified. It's a potentially lengthy process that PPG ratings can smooth out.

At smaller gatherings, or even some airshows, it can be great public relations to have your craft out there with some basic information brochures (www.USPPA.org). They may even let you fly since it would keep the audience interested.

Motor Madness

The motor has turned up some surprising uses. For one, it is the monster of all leaf blowers. Of course a regular leaf blower won't cut your arm off but, for those willing to try it, there's no better way to move a big volume of air on very little gas. Only do this stuff wearing the motor on your back and don't let that cage near anything. Props find bystanders just as tasty as pilots. Be careful!

Traveling with Gear

31

The ability to travel so readily with your aircraft is unique to powered paragliding. It's not always easy, but it's almost always worth the effort. Free flyers have it even easier, but being able to motor to the where of your wishes is an extraordinary capability.

Shipping

PPG's can be boxed and shipped around the world using common consumer freight carriers, but there are caveats. These tips may help.

First off, if there is obvious gas in the tank or carburetor then it's considered hazardous materials and may not qualify to be carried even via ground shipping. Make sure it's *completely* drained, including carburetor bowls or chambers. Removing the gas tank then running the motor until it quits is a good way to get most gas out.

Preparing the Motor

The machine must be completely free of fuel, fuel odors, and packed well enough to endure rough handling. At least one major carrier requires 3 inches of padding between the box's edge and your contents; any part that touches the cardboard will likely be damaged.

If there's any fuel present, anywhere, it must be declared as hazardous materials ("hazmat"), opening Pandora's Box. You may luck out and not have your motor inspected but, for everybody's sake, don't risk it.

Remove the harness and clean everything. Yes, fuel works well for cleaning, but not now. Use a sweet-smelling degreaser that doesn't harm aluminum. Spray-type carb cleaner gets rid of grime in hard-to-reach areas. Brake cleaner is good on exposed metal surfaces but brutal on paint. It's nice in that it leaves no residue.

by Jeff Hamann

courtesy TrikeBuggy.com

Some machines are made to travel. Key elements are 1) no single piece too long to fit in normal sized checked luggage, 2) it must assemble/disassemble quickly, and 3) the engine must be easy to remove so it can be packed separately.

The machine above has its engine mounted to a piece that's only slightly bigger than the engine itself. Everything else snaps to that—no bolts required.

Other solutions involve an engine that detaches quickly from the frame, which itself breaks down easily. Parts commonality helps by reducing extra things that must be carried for those wanting some backup capability. There's nothing worse than arriving at the world's coolest flying site only to have your pull starter come out in your hands.

Puzzle props, shown above, are used to cut their size nearly in half for better packing.

Be leery of assembly times claimed by sellers. They are frequently based on someone who has done it many times on a perfect machine— one that hasn't been tweaked by rough handling or oopses. Reality reveals that it can easily be three times what the manufacturer says.

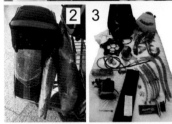

Packing gear in two hard-sided pieces of luggage makes it easier for airline personnel, but gives you twice the chance of being stranded. If they lose only one piece, you're still out of luck.

Older luggage without the handle and wheels provides more room.

1. World traveler Matt Minyard arrived to find that his well-wrapped motor had been inspected by the TSA. Thankfully it was there, and it was *all* there.

2. Matt's motor, shown here among other parts wrapped to go, fits in two suitcases.

3. Here are all the parts spread out post-travel.

If you have an air filter, now is a good time to replace it. Otherwise, double bag it and squeeze out excess air. Clean the air box thoroughly. Wash the tank out with soapy water, then deodorize it with a product like ZorbX (shown previous page). If time permits, dry the fuel tank completely. When there isn't a hint of fuel vapor, it's legal for transport, but airlines may still not take it.

Remove as many attachments as possible—muffler, reduction drive, air filter, carb, etc. If the motor *can* be removed from the frame easily, do so. Usually only the throttle, fuel line, kill switch and battery line must be disconnected. Having pull-apart electrical connections speeds things up. Being compact is better for motor shipping and probably a lot cheaper. Plus, keeping the motor separate reduces the chance of a careless drop bending the frame.

Packaging

Using just one single hard-sided case makes packaging easier while giving the freight company less to lose. Pack it to survive a drop from several feet high. Moderately firm foam of at least 3 inches, including a softer layer next to the motor, should line the box. Foam can be purchased from fabric shops (and elsewhere) in sheets.

A few models come apart enough to fit in an airline-legal hard-sided suitcase, but all airline luggage is now screened in some way. So, unless you *know* the carrier will accept it, have another plan in case it's refused.

Another padding option is forming foam—a material that sprays out from a can and forms to your object (*Great Stuff Foam* is one brand) then hardens. It can be re-used in new boxes as the old ones wear out. Put your gear in a plastic garbage bag first.

Once the heavy pieces are secure, everything else can be added and packed in bubble wrap. Limit this box to necessary flight gear. Lighter is better. A good idea, for example, is to wrap the muffler, carburetor, and gear box (heavy items) in plastic wrap and put them in with the wing that you will check on the airline. That saves shipping costs, but remember, the fewer boxes you need to have for an airworthy machine at the destination, the better your odds will be of getting airborne.

Propellers fit nicely in gun cases. Even the cheap ones from discount stores work well and accept two wooden props up to 50 inches long. *Puzzle props*, those that come apart at the hub (previous page), are great since they fit into your other boxes, negating the need for a separate prop container.

Wings conveniently squish into a sleeping-bag sized, easily checked item. It can be good for packing other things with since the fabric serves as its own protection. Just be sure that nothing sharp protrudes and that no fuel or oil can get on it.

Having more boxes may be easier to deal with for one person but every additional box is an additional chance of losing a required flight item. One big box is more likely to get there than several smaller ones. Find out about maximum weights, though, since some shippers may not take heavy or oversized boxes.

Airlines

Most U.S. airlines prohibit motors, even though there is no federal regulation that mandates it. And not having crankcase oil (as in 2-strokes) won't help. Motors that have never been run *may* be allowed which is why cleaning *really* well is so important. Nearly all carriers follow IATA (International Air Transport Association) guidelines. Include a letter stating that you comply with IATA guidelines (provided you do) and place it in view of those who will invariably inspect your stuff.

Some pilots *have* succeeded at getting motors on airlines, even regularly, but it's still a gamble. Non-U.S. carriers may be more tolerant. Taking the engine farther apart (exhaust, redrive, cylinder, carb, air box) and calling it "parts" (which it is) may help.

Even if an airline *does* allow your motor, it probably *will* be x-rayed and inspected. If they smell any fumes it will **not go**! Don't think that plastic wrap will solve the problem—officials will probably open that it up too. Consider having a contingency plan. Think about the return trip, too.

For best results, remove the engine and ship it alone in the smallest box possible—it's cheaper, safer for the motor, and doesn't annoy the baggage gorillas as much. Then check everything else on the airline. It'll be a big, but manageable box with the motorless frame, clean gas tank, harness, muffler, prop, redrive, and so on. Expect to pay an oversize or excess baggage fee.

Props may need their own box—rifle cases work well. Larger frames with rigid cage pieces may need 2 boxes and should be lightweight to minimize damage potential.

1. A smaller box for just the engine makes damage and confiscation less likely. It also makes everything easy to carry.

2. Hard-sided cases are always best. They add weight but the protection is worth it. Props fit nicely in gun cases.

3. This shows a temporary box handle made with strapping tape.

Put the wing in a stout bag before boxing to add protection in case the box gets punctured.

Pet carriers and large plastic storage boxes work well—put a couple of cheap tie-down straps around them for strength.

Freight Carriers

Hazardous material requirements limit what cargo airlines can accept but they're more liberal than passenger lines. The box is still likely to be opened so don't leave fuel in anything—doing so endangers all involved. Plus, it's a federal offense and more shippers are inspecting contents, including removing gas tank caps.

Each shipping company has its own pricing structure. Some airlines have freight divisions but the cargo usually goes on passenger flights. If it's going to a foreign country, it must clear Customs and may be delayed up to three weeks while incurring steep customs fees (usually refundable once you take the gear back out of the country.) It can be quite the paper chase, too. These are reasons for taking the gear on your international passenger flight, if allowed.

Many freight companies offer less-than-truckload (LTL) options. Search "LTL shippers near me." You drop your motor off at their warehouse, they palletize it, ship it; then you pick it up at a warehouse near your destination. It may take 3 weeks, though.

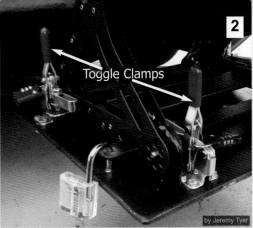

Toggle Clamps

by Chris Santacroce

by Jeremy Tyer

TUMBLEWEED

by Martin J. Henderson

By Eric Sansli

by Jeff Hamann

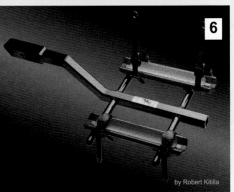

Uses a
Universal Joint

by Robert Kitilla

by Timothy Garvey

by John Winkopp

On The Road

A few of the many ideas from some very clever humans

For the latest transport ideas and links to resources, Google "Footflyer paramotor transport." Here are some good ones to start with:

1. This commercially available rack has an option (see inset) to swing out for vehicles with a tailgate. It doubles as a runup rack and place to sit while putting the machine on.

2. Quick release locking clamps work well.

3. Having a trailer to put gear in has all kinds of advantages if you can tow and store the trailer. Having a wagon that allows transporting the motor and accoutrements gives even more convenience for some situations like when it's a long walk from the parking lot.

4. A roadable trike negates the need for a platform or trailer.

5. Off the shelf platforms come in many sizes. This one fits two motors; most fit one. There are several sizes of receivers and hitch balls, but since our gear is pretty lightweight, we don't stress even the smallest sizes.

6. Another commercially available solution that uses bicycle mount hardware to make quick work of securing a paramotor. It's available for one or two paramotors.

7. Welders own the world. This custom motorcycle platform is the simplist solution that doesn't involve wearing your machine. It has a universal joint to keep the motor upright while managing dips in the road.

8. Pedal power can be used for short distances as this kayak carrier attests to.

Basic Cautions

All carriers should support the motor near the prop to minimize fore/aft bouncing on bumpy roads. For short trips, it may not matter, but if it's held only by the frame legs, they may crack or bend.

Sun is hard on harness fabric and cage netting. If the motor will be exposed for long it should be covered, ideally with something that goes all around including the bottom. That will minimize dust and road grime.

Paramotors get stolen—have a good lock attached to a visibly stout cable that's secured to the vehicle.

Transporting via Road

Transporting by car is what most of us do, so it ought to be convenient. Plus, breaking it out on long journeys makes for an exhilarating new perspective on travel.

Tall vans are ideal: they keep the paramotor upright and out of bad weather. Trucks are next best but their high beds can make handling awkward. Trailers are great if you have storage space and a tow vehicle, but the most common solution is some kind of platform. They work on all vehicles and have *many* clever implementations.

Using the Platform

A platform lets you carry one or more motors fully assembled outside your vehicle. It usually attaches to a receiver that can be installed at many trailer stores (like U-Haul). The two common sizes are 2" for heavier loads and 1 ¼ inch but our gear doesn't stress even the lighter one. Trailer lights are not normally required (check your state's laws), but the license place must be visible.

Secure the motor with at least two means in case one lets go. Secure free-spinning props (clutched units) to reduce bearing wear. A bicycle cable and lock provides some security and, if the motor falls off, will drag its remains to your next stop. Try to avoid that. A cover protects from sun, dust, rain, and prying eyes, but road dust gets into anything that's not sealed up, including from the bottom. Large grill covers work, but purpose built paramotor covers are easier to use.

Be careful; gear can easily get damaged in transit for those who travel a lot. Plus, constant bouncing around is hard on everything. If possible, put hard foam on the bottom to absorb some of the jostling.

Making or Selecting the Platform Mount

A paramotor mount must be strong and durable, of course, but why not make it convenient? Have everything fit together like a puzzle where the last piece holds it all down with a single toggle clamp, bolt, or other locking device (opposite page, #2).

The wood and aluminum Rube Goldberg below is an example. Numbers indicate how the paramotor is mounted. Secure its top to prevent fore/aft bouncing with a strap, or some kind of vertical piece. Bicycle mounts can give some ideas. Here is how it fits together.

1) Slide the paramotor's bottom, rear crossbar under the angled aluminum and between screwed-down wood strips that keep it from moving around.

This clever prop cover primarily protects the prop. But it also prevents spinning during transport *and* provides some start protection (on clutched machines). Check with the maker before assuming it's good for the engine-starting, hand protection mission.

Receiver & Platform

Bolts to car, search for "trailer hitch receiver." 2 inch is the most common size but 1 1/4 inch is plenty strong for our use. Think bike rack.

courtesy Lowes.com

Platform, available at many hardware and automotive supply stores. Make sure the tongue size matches your receiver.

2) Slide a pre-drilled 2x4 into the U-bracket (colored cyan for clarity) and the other end over a captured bolt (3).

3) Screw a nut and washer onto the captured bolt to hold everything together. In this case, there is no vertical stand to support the motor from fore/aft motion so a ratcheting strap goes over the frame's top.

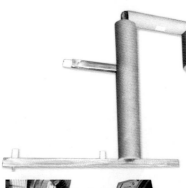

Gas & Oil

Some travel modes (airlines, freighters) prohibit gas containers that have had fuel in them, so it may be easier just to plan on buying one on arrival and leaving it behind.

Unless you're flying a 4-stroke or electric, you'll need 2-stroke oil. Although it's not considered a hazardous material, most airlines still prohibit it, even in checked baggage. Motorcycle and go-cart racing shops usually have the best selection of oils. Hardware stores frequently carry it for chain saws, and gas stations sometimes stock outboard blends—not ideal, but it works in a pinch. In most cases you'll be OK since your motor is completely emptied on each end of your trip.

See Chapter 4 for more on choosing 2-stroke oil.

Bus Lines

Some pilots have had good luck using commercial bus lines. You must drop everything off at the bus terminal and pick it up at a designated spot, but sometimes arrangements can be made for delivery service. Check with the line to see if they'll take your gear.

Customs & Declarations

The problem here isn't fuel, it's taxes and tariffs. Registering your motor with an organization and having the documentation may help to show that it's yours. Some countries (not the US) require registration with the government. The border folks fear that you may be importing the motor for sale so it's more suspicious if you're traveling with more than one. They may also fear some nefarious use so having a picture of it in flight may be helpful. You already look sketchy with all this kit.

If you're traveling with a group, it may be best to have the frame in a box with the prop separated. That attracts less attention.

The most appropriate declaration is "Sporting Equipment" or "Paragliding Equipment" for personal use. It's true, and it's not evoking the horror of something so bold as "aircraft" or even "ultralight."

by Vince White

The Minimalist

Vince White has created a minimalist solution for cars with a trunk (or boot) but no hitch. It's similar to some bike mounts which are a great source for paramotor carrier ideas. The PPG's frame legs sit in nylon or plastic holders.

When not in use, these mounts pull up off the bumper and stow away flat to conserve space.

It can also be helpful if you have a local person there to help deal with issues, especially if you don't speak the language.

In the U.S., anti-terror laws may not allow individuals to ship using airline cargo services—you must go through a *freight forwarder* who ships using the cheapest means, most likely a freight airline for rapid delivery. Otherwise, you must be certified as a *known shipper*. Your dealer may have already acquired that status and be able to help.

The large freight companies can be used (FedEx & UPS) but are expensive depending on the destination. They do handle the customs issues but don't be surprised if there is a very large charge at the end. Some countries can be "creative" with charges which is why it's good to enlist the help of a local. Some charges verge on extortion.

In any case, your best advice will come from other pilots who have already traveled to your intended destination. Seek them out on the Internet and give kudos to modern communications.

Enjoy our immense opportunities.

Photography

32

What an amazing platform for capturing pictures and video—it provides perspectives that just aren't practical with any other craft—and in a form you can bring along. Rules in many countries may limit commercial use (see Chapter 8), but there's still a lot you can do with it.

Distraction is a major concern, requiring discipline to remain aware of your surroundings and ensure a clear flight path—concentrating too much on the shot, especially while flying low, adds tremendous risk. Collisions *have* happened.

Paramotor flying is a harsh environment for gear so pay close attention to how it's secured. Use a long enough camera leash to allow movement while making it impossible to get anything into the prop or engine. Looping the camera strap through a harness piece is better than looping it around a body part. Hanging the camera strap around your neck, for example, could allow it to get caught in the propeller or other moving parts which has happened. If you *do* launch with anything around your neck make sure it is cinched up tight. Once in flight you can attach it to some part of the machine if necessary.

Still Photography Basics

Photography merits its own shelf of books but these few tidbits will help you get great shots, even ones worthy of magazine covers.

Quality

There's a lot more to quality than pixel count; check out *Pixels and Pictures* on page 303. What matters most is the lens and sensor, image stabilization, rapid fire (high burst rate), and others we'll cover shortly.

Higher quality gear also does better in low light, like sunrise and sunset, which pro-

Top: Phil Russman was an early pioneer in helmet cam flying.

Just above: Enormous capability lurks in the developing realm of high quality, stabilized camera drones. They bring immense capability, including capturing paramotor pilots performing their art. Drones will take increasing roles as their versatility is explored and exploited.

Having a separate camera operator can put Hollywood quality aerials at your fingertips.

Courtesy www.GeorgeSteinmetz.com

The Killer Shot

Photog George Steinmetz has shared incredible views of the world through the pages of National Geographic. He's got an eye for what's interesting and knows how to capture it—"a photographer who flies" as he describes himself.

His paramotor has become a tool that sometimes has no equal, especially in the lesser accessible places that he so frequently visits. It can easily be the only practical way aloft. And he gains access to flying sites the same way most of us do: asking politely for permission or, on occasion, forgiveness. He offers that being respectful is important; never be annoying or arrogant—advice that has served him well.

When asked to share some wisdom with aspiring photographers, he offers: "I do a lot of research before I go. But I always find interesting, unexpected things when I arrive. With close ground support, I can scout a lot by boat, car or camel, but it always looks different from above."

This shot of the Gobi Desert's "Empty Quarter" shows several principles at work. First, of course, you have to know it's there. Then get to the right place with the right equipment and finally, set up the shot. In this case, having the horizon in view adds greatly to the sense of size. Having an interesting foreground helps a lot too. Try shooting during the low sun of morning and evening—fortunately, our best times for flying, too.

vides some of our best opportunities. If your goal is putting the pictures in print, they will appear at 300 dots per inch (DPI)—far more than what's needed for a computer screen, and even basic phones have the necessary resolution. Other desirable aerial camera traits are: 1) a remote (for specialty shots), 2) decent zoom, operable with one hand, and 3) good image stabilization to reduce camera shake blur.

Unless you're into high quality control, use the default compression format, JPEG (or JPG). It sacrifices some minor quality degradation (unnoticeable in most uses) for a significantly smaller file size. *Fineness* describes the level of compression—more *fine* means less compression.

If your pictures are intended for magazines or other published media, use the highest resolution and fineness available. Even though cheaper cameras tend to make bloated, grainy images at their highest resolutions, it's better to reduce them later rather than wish you had higher quality settings. Only use a lower setting if memory is an issue. For the highest quality, photographers shoot RAW, which does no processing at the camera but requires more work later on a computer with special software.

The best cameras have removable lenses and fast burst rates with good optical stabilization. Mirrorless models, as opposed to DSLR, are handy because they're smaller. High quality video is a welcome byproduct. Sensor size is less important in the brighter light, and infinity focus settings we tend to use flying. Tilting LCD displays let you hold the camera away from your cage while framing.

Focus

Any picture is essentially worthless if the main subject is blurry. Most cameras have an autofocus that works well but it has limits, the worst of which is focusing on the wrong thing. Equally useless is a slow autofocus that balks when your subject moves into position and doesn't take the shot because it's "hunting" for focus. You may be able to reduce this by setting focus to "center spot." Then point to the center of the subject, press the button down halfway, reframe it, and push the button down all the way to snap it. That keeps the camera from focusing on something real close like your own risers or cage. As long as you're shooting with no zoom (the subject looks far away), you can set most cameras to remain on infinity where everything farther than about 8 feet is in focus. There's nothing worse than discovering your perfect shot of a spiraling pilot to be a perfectly focused shot of your leg.

In low light situations it gets harder for the camera to focus. On most models, holding the shutter down half-way makes it "calculate" the shot—setting shutter speed, focusing, and other parameters. Then when you press the button fully, it takes the picture right away. So if it won't focus on your subject, point it towards something with better contrast but the same distance, push the shutter button half-way, point it back to your subject and press the button all the way.

Sharp Subject, Blurry Background

Professional photographers value blurry backgrounds to make their subject stand out. There are two primary ways to do this:

1. **Panning**. Carefully track the moving subject so the background is zipping by, causing it to blur. The slower the shutter speed, the more dramatic the effect. Of course a slow shutter speed makes it harder to keep the subject sharp too.

2. Narrowing **depth of field**. The in-focus distance range is called *depth of field* *(DoF)*. A large DoF means that most everything, distant and near, is in focus. A small DoF means that only objects at the focused distance are sharp, while everything else is blurry. Zooming in on a nearby subject decreases DoF, making the background more blurry. Opening up the aperture (lower f-number) also narrows DoF. A wide aperture (smaller f-numbers mean larger aperture) lets in a lot of light which means that shutter speed will be quite high. A camera with a large aperture lens (goes to a smaller f-number), and larger focal length (MM on lens) will be better at blurring the background (narrower DoF).

1. Depth of field blur. Zoom and an open aperture helped create this.

2. Motion Blur. To get this effect, zoom a bit, pan the subject and use the slowest shutter speed possible.

For most cameras, controlling shutter speed and aperture require being in their "Program" (P) setting.

Digging Deeper: Exposure, Getting the Light Right

Exposure tells a lot about a picture; underexposed is dark and over exposed is too light. Anytime you have to correct something later, information is lost so always try to have the best settings. Three notable attributes affecting exposure:

ISO the camera's sensitivity to light. A lower ISO number means less sensitivity. A high ISO, say 3000, is very sensitive meaning it can take pictures with very little light. More sensitivity though, means more noise—pictures are splotchy or grainy when enlarged. As sensor technology improves, sensitivity increases without being noisy.

Shutter speed is how long the shutter stays open. Longer times mean more light. So 1/60th of a second gathers more light than 1/250th but the faster shutter speed will have less motion blur. Really fast shutter speeds can "stop the action." A good rule is to use the lens's focal length in MM as the shutter speed fraction. So a 50 MM lens would be 1/50th of a second. Double that to 1/100th of a second or more if there's much motion (like while flying, especially in bumpy air).

Aperture is how big the opening is where light comes through and is expressed as "f stop" where larger numbers mean a smaller opening. So an f-number of f1.8 is wide open (many cameras can't go that big) and f5.6 is a smaller opening. The bigger the aperture, the more light can pass. That allows shooting in lower light at faster shutter speeds.

Most cameras automatically choose aperture and f-number based on lighting when you press the shutter button down halfway. Almost all models, beyond the most basic, let you change one setting while it adjusts the other. For example, if you want to stop the action in a shot, set a faster shutter speed and let the camera choose an optimum aperture. Auto logic may also adjust the ISO depending on how the camera is set up.

Other Settings & Tidbits

Fortunately the auto setting on most cameras does a decent job in our usual bright light conditions. Using auto leaves you free you to frame and fly.

Use the highest quality settings available. The bulk of your effort was getting there so don't waste it on low quality. Here are some basic tips to help capture images from a PPG. There are no hard and fast rules so these are just general guidelines:

1. Including part of yourself or frame in the shot can add interest. It gives perspective while letting the viewer know what it was taken from.

For air-to-air work, cameras with an external display are handy. If you are forced to look through a view finder, shots like this are difficult.

2. Self portraits can make for interesting angles. In this case, Red Bull acro pilot Chris Santacroce mugs for his "Hairy Leg Cam." Page 304 has ideas on where to mount cameras.

by Chris Santacroce

- Use the auto setting unless you really know what you're doing and the camera allows quick adjustments. One exception might be setting focus to infinity unless you're doing *very* close work.

- Have sufficient light. Once the sun gets too low you must be very steady for pictures to be sharp. In poor light it might be a good tradeoff to set the camera's *ISO* to a higher number. This increases the sensitivity at some expense in *noise*—a distortion that's visible when zoomed way in to the image.

- Unless the background *is* the star, frame your subject large—around 50% of the shot as a rough guideline.

- Be leery of zoom. Autofocus gets confused more easily if you're not centered on the subject, and even slight movement of the camera will blur the shot. Good optical stabilization negates some of this.

- Use zoom when appropriate. You need bright light for a fast shutter speed, but it's usually better to zoom now than to crop later. Take multiple shots at different zooms if that's practical.

- Skip *digital zoom* where the camera simply makes the pixels bigger but has fewer of them. Cropping later does the same thing but gives you more control.

- Try wide angle lenses, especially for self portraits. Positioning these on your frame or wing and shooting remotely can yield spectacular shots.

- 4k or higher resolution for video. That's enough for their frame grabs to fill a magazine cover.

- Be close and get your subject to do banks and dives for added interest. Of course you must keep flying the craft! This is extremely risky since you're not only flying close, you're thinking about the camera.

- Generally, try keeping your subject down sun. But sometimes cool effects can be had when shooting into the sun, especially in hazy conditions.

- It's usually more interesting to see the pilot's face, especially if he's looking at you. There are exceptions, of course, and experimenting is half the fun.

- Unless you have specific scenery in mind, try to get a human subject in the shot, especially another PPGer.

- Have something or someone of prominence in the foreground to add interest and scale.

Video

One of the hardest things to get while flying is good video. Start off with appropriate equipment—essentially as good a quality camera as you can afford. Quality has improved so that consumer equipment is only about 5 years behind its professional predecessor. Bigger is better for lenses, too, and make sure the camera can accept a wide-angle adapter. A wide-angle lens, about 0.5x, captures the pilot and glider in the same shot without being too far away.

Steady is king. The absolute worst thing you can do is subject your viewer to jittery video. Everything else is secondary. Gyro stabilizer technology has revolutionized this arena. Cameras now rival the smoothness available with an external stabilizer. Optical stabilization is remarkably effective but doesn't work well with certain types of shots (see your camera's manual).

The camera can be handheld but is better with some type of gyro stabilization. Weight shift steering is a plus here.

Occasionally, use the widest angle lens that you can afford. You have to be very close (risky) to the subject, though, or they'll appear too far away.

A helmet with sighting viewfinder, either visual or electronic, is a great tool. Besides freeing your hands up to fly, it will yield much better shots—you must be able to see what you're framing. It can be as simple as bending a coat hangar for the sight and taping to the helmet. Skydiver accessory suppliers have helmets ready-made to accept a camera and framer (search "skydiving ringsight").

Hanging small cameras from your wing or other locations can add interest. Be careful launching—making sure you're balanced and the camera stays put. Page 300 has some ideas on placement.

When flying close, as required with a wide-angle lens, be aware of the extreme collision risk and include extra precautions. Plan to avoid wake turbulence, too, when working around other flyers.

Here are some tips to improve your in-flight video recording:

- Be smooth. If it wiggles, it won't likely make the cut. Choose smooth air whenever possible. Gyro stabilization is great but smooth air is best.

- Be leery of zoom. Even more than stills, inflight video rarely looks good when zoomed because it's too jittery. Only zoom with calm conditions when you can hold the camera extremely steady. Even then be ready for throw-away footage.

- Use the widest angle you can get if you're close enough to the subject.

- Frame your subject close. Little gliders, far away, are rarely interesting. They

Helmet cams are great because your hands are free. For best results you need an eyesight for targeting, a steady head, good stabilization, and a wide-angle lens.

Phil Russman had the mother of wide angle lenses (1 and 3) while John Phillips (2) makes use of a helmet mounted consumer camera.

When filming other pilots, having a push-to-talk (PTT) in your hand helps tell other pilots what to do without needing to move your hands from the brakes: you keep the shots steady while playing director. This image was taken during a lull in filming *Risk and Reward*. Phil had to hang out of the harness in order to keep the risers out of frame.

Digging Deeper: Pixels and Pictures

Pixels are the little colored dots recorded by your camera and displayed on monitors or printed pages. Resolution is the number of pixels horizontally and vertically. Generally, more is better. A one megapixel image has a resolution of 1200 by 800 (1200 dots across by 800 dots down). That fills up an older monitor, which uses 72 dots per inch (DPI) but is only 4 inches wide when printed since print needs 300 DPI.

Your eye has amazing resolution—it takes a 25 megapixel camera to approach the quality available through an open human eyeball.

can be, but it has to be for a really good reason.

• Vary the shot. Vary the angle, the zoom, the background, the subject, bank angles, etc. Edited shots rarely last longer than 2 to 5 seconds.

• Have something in the shot moving relative to the rest of the scene. For example, occasionally having the subject flying by from right to left may be more interesting if you *don't* follow him. Point the camera so that he flies into and out of frame where the background is stationary or slides by slowly.

• Have interesting audio, preferably well-paced narration. Never, ever, *ever,* subject your viewers to continuous motor noise.

Some of the best PPG video is shot on the ground. It's not as much fun to shoot, but does capture the frequently-entertaining launches and landings. Getting experienced pilots to play around on objects is also fun.

Have someone record your own flights for later review and critique. It's an invaluable tool for learning.

More than anything, though, capturing our passion in action is yet another great reason to exercise that passion. So go out, capture carefully, capture frequently, and revel in the fantastic freedom afforded by our incredible platform.

Mounting the camera in different places adds interest for both stills and video. (Top picture below) Jeff Hamann had a line-mounted setup to take this shot with a very wide angle lens.

Right-side pictures: helmet mounts are great tools provided you can see what you're framing and talk to your subjects. Having a hand-held PTT helps to direct them for better shots.

The coolest video usually comes from getting close. That's the riskiest way, too. Be extremely careful!

By Jeff Hamann

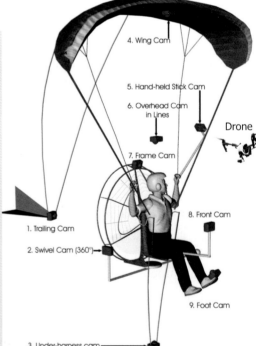

4. Wing Cam

5. Hand-held Stick Cam

6. Overhead Cam in Lines

Drone

7. Frame Cam

8. Front Cam

1. Trailing Cam

2. Swivel Cam (360°)

9. Foot Cam

3. Under-harness cam

Here are some places pilots have mounted cameras in order to get different and interesting angles. Be careful anytime you're connecting something to the frame or wing since that may change its behavior. And consider what could happen in an accident.

A wing cam can be mounted using neodymium magnets on 2 pieces of coroplast. One piece goes in the wing's cell, the one holding the camera sticks to it from below. Tie a back-up string on the camera.

Checklists are on the inside back cover of the book for quick reference or for cutting out and using in the field. It's impractical to use a paper checklist in most of the training environment so don't expect to. Your instructor will have some routine for you to memorize that hopefully includes these elements and adds what's appropriate. These checklists are a good starting point and can be used after you leave training if it has been a while.

For the pre-launch checklist, use it like this: once you're standing there, ready to launch, but before you've grabbed the A's, run through it by memory. When you get to "brakes and biners," hold out the brakes to see that they're clear to the pulleys without being wrapped up in anything. After doing it by memory, look at the list to see that you've covered everything. Soon you will not need to keep referring to the paper.

If you make your own checklist, it should be compact and easy to remember or else it will eventually be discarded. That means it must be brief—covering only what's important and rolling easily off the tongue. It's useless if it's not used.

The gold standard of checklist use in airline flying is the "challenge-response" method. One pilot reads while the other pilot checks and responds. The reader checks, too. So have your flying partner read the checklist... OK, nevermind, that's not practical here, but you get the idea—try to be vigilant.

The Pre-Launch and Pre-Landing checklists have been designed with a "memory aid," sing-song cadence to improve recall. Use a paper copy until you're thoroughly familiar with the routine. Try to do it by memory; then refer back to the checklist to see if you've missed anything. It's worth practicing at home once you've had enough training to know what's being checked. Stand there imagining being ready for takeoff and going through the motions. "Leg, leg chest and chin," for example, starts the pre-launch checklist.

Items may be different based on your machine but these checklists give a good basic plan. If you do not recognize a part name then it probably doesn't apply to you. For preflight checking the motor, start with your carabiners and proceed around. Look for the most obvious items: loose, missing or damaged parts, broken safety wire, etc. If a machine has just been assembled, do a post-assembly inspection as well as a good once-over before flying. A paramotor preflight takes only a minute, and you'll be surprised at what gets uncovered every now and then. Don't skimp on inspections when borrowing gear, either—it's a useful minute.

After flying, clean the machine so you can see cracks or leaks early on. Do a thorough postflight inspection to find problems *now* so they can be fixed before your next session.

These checklists will help know what to look for. Once you're familiar with the flow then the paper checklist can be used optionally.

Remember, more propeller-strike injuries happen while starting or test running a motor than at any other time, so treat the machine with enormous respect. Hard to start motors are particularly problematic because pilots lose respect. And that helmet can protect you in case of a disintegrating prop while also providing ear protection.

Checklists on inside back cover

Appendix - Resources

Fuel/Oil Mix Chart

Consult your engine maker for recommended types of gas, two-stroke oil, and desired mixes. There are different requirements for breaking in a motor (seating the rings properly) which is normally considered the first 5 hours. This table shows how to mix some common fuel/oil ratios (32:1, 40:1 and 50:1) using the markings on many oil and fuel containers. This may be helpful when the gas and oil container markings are not uniform.

For this many units of fuel	Add this many **ounces** of oil:			Add this many **milliliters** of oil:		
Ratio→	at 32:1	at 40:1	at 50:1	at 32:1	at 40:1	at 50:1
1 gal	4.0	3.2	2.6	118	95	76
2 gal	8.0	6.4	5.1	237	189	151
5 gal	20.0	16.0	12.8	591	473	379
1 ltr	1.1	0.8	0.7	31	25	20
2 ltr	2.1	1.7	1.4	63	50	40
5 ltr	5.3	4.2	3.4	156	125	100
10 ltr	10.6	8.5	6.8	313	250	200

Note the crazy English volume units: 1 US Gal = 4 quarts = 8 pints = 128 ounces = 3.785412 liters = 0.832 UK gallons
Metric units: 1 Liter = 1000 milliliters = 0.2641721 US gallon

Repair

The best resource for replacement or repair is the dealer where you bought the gear. It's likely that they know where to look, or what can be substituted. They will also know best whether replacement is necessary. Visit www.FootFlyer.com for updates to resources along with other new information relating to powered paragliding.

Instruction

A valuable resource is www.USPPA.org which lists certified paramotor instructors, including those who are actively giving ratings. That's desirable. In the USA, solo pilot certification programs are run by the U.S. Powered Paragliding Association (USPPA) and U.S. Ultralight Association (USUA). Tandem exemption programs may be run by the USPPA or other organizations but check out their website. FootFlyer.com maintains a section on the current status of training exemptions under Educational, Chapter 1. Check with the organization for your country to find a certified instructor for solo or tandem training.

Welding

Aluminum welding is very specialized and not all shops do it. Even fewer will do it if they know it's for a flying machine. Look in the yellow pages under welding—even if they don't do aluminum, they should know who to call.

When you do find someone to weld, avoid describing its primary function unless it comes up. Some pilots have tried calling it by one of its auxiliary uses such a glorified leaf blower, ski & skate power for the vertically challenged, etc.

2-Stroke—A valveless motor with a power stroke every time the piston goes down.

4-Stroke—A valved motor with a power stroke every other time the piston goes down.

A Lines—The first row of paraglider lines; they go from the A riser to the leading edge of the wing.

Absolute Altitude—height above the terrain if you could measure it with a long tape measure.

Accelerator—System used to accelerate the wing using a foot bar connected to the risers, through the harness. The pilot activates it by pushing the bar out with both feet. Also called Speedbar.

Active Flying—The fine control inputs required to keep the wing exactly overhead in turbulence or maneuvering, damping both left/right oscillations and fore/aft surges.

A/FD—Airport Facility Directory. On internet: "digital A/FD"

AGL—Above Ground Level.

ACPUL—Association des Constructeurs de Parapente Ultra Legers. European association that developed test standards for paragliders later adopted by AFNOR.

AFNOR—Association Française de Normalisation, French organization that does certification of paragliders (among many other things).

ASL—Above Sea Level.

ATC—Air Traffic Control, which consists of Approach Controls, Control Towers and Air Route Traffic Control Centers (just called "Center").

Airspeed—Speed through the air. A GPS reads groundspeed; the pilot feels airspeed.

Aspect Ratio—Ratio of the wingspan (projected) to the average chord.

Asymmetrical Collapse—When one side of the wing deflates and not the other. It is the most common paraglider malady that results from turbulence.

Asymmetric Blade Thrust—see P-Factor.

Asymmetric Spiral—A spiral dive where the bank on one side of the circle is shallower than the other.

B Lines—The second row of paraglider lines; they go from the B riser to the wing.

B Line Stall—A condition where the wing is stalled by virtue of the pilot pulling the B-lines down to his chest. Descent rate is usually about 4 times normal.

Big Ears—A maneuver where the pilot pulls the outer A lines such that the tips of the wing fold downward to increase descent rate.

Brake Lines—Lines that go from the brake toggles, through a pulley or loop on the rear riser, and up to the trailing edge of the wing.

Brake Toggles—The handles used by the pilot to control the craft. They attach to the brake lines.

C Lines—The third row of lines; goes from the C riser to the wing.

Canopy—Another name for the wing.

Carabiners—Metal fasteners that attach the wing, through its riser loops, to the harness.

Cart—Wheeled assembly that allows for a rolling launch.

Cascade—The split in a wing's lines where it spreads from one line to several as it goes up to the wing. This design feature reduces the total line count and resulting drag.

Cells—A single sewn section of a wing containing air that makes up the airfoil shape.

CEN—Comittee of the European standards organization that set certification standards for paragliders (among other things).

CHT—Cylinder Head Temperature.

CIMA—International Microlight Commission of FAI.

Clip-In Weight—The pilot weight plus motor, fuel, and any accessories necessary to fly. Aka hook-in weight.

Chord—The distance from the leading edge to trailing edge at any point along the span.

Collapse—What happens when part or all of the wing deforms (aka fold or deflation) due to turbulence or pilot input.

Constant Stall—see Parachutal Stall.

Crab—Heading some amount into the wind to maintain a desired ground track.

Damping/Dampen—Control input required to reduce roll or pitch oscillation.

Deck Angle—see Pitch.

Deflation—see Collapse.

Density Altitude—Altitude adjusted for pressure, temperature, and humidity. Hot, humid air hurts aircraft performance—it is said to be at a higher density altitude. Aircraft performance is based on density altitude, not the actual altitude as read on an altimeter.

DHV—German Hanggliding and Paragliding Federation "Deutcher Hangeleiter Verband." They certify free-flight paragliders, harnesses and related equipment in Germany. This is the most common service used to certify paragliders.

DULV—German Ultralight Flight organization that certifies paramotors and paramotor wings designed for paramotoring.

Downwind Demon—Series of illusions that frequently lead to a pilot pulling too much brake when low to the ground and turning downwind.

EN—European Standards organization. See also CEN.

FAI—Fédération Aéronautique International. The world's Air Sports Federation. See also CIMA.

FAR—Federal Aviation Regulations; governing law for paramotor pilots in the USA.

Float Bowl Carburetor—A type of carburetor that uses a float to regulate fuel level in the bowl.

Fold—See collapse.

FPM—Feet Per Minute. A measure of climb or descent rate.

Full Stall—An extreme maneuver where the pilot pulls enough brake to deform the wing so much that slows dramatically and deforms the glider and is characterized with a very high descent rate.

Forward Inflation—Any inflation done while facing away from the wing and into the wind; usually done in light winds.

Front Tuck—see frontal.

Frontal—A wing deformation where the leading edge folds downward. Maintained in this state, the wing will descend about 3 times the normal rate.

Free Flyer—One who flies without a motor; a paraglider pilot. They generally seek out natural lift sources and launch from high places or get towed in aloft.

GA—General Aviation; all aviation that is not military, governmental, or scheduled airlines.

Gyroscopic Precession—The characteristic of any rotating mass whereby a force acting perpendicular to the direction of rotation will cause the reaction 90 degrees in the direction of rotation.

Harness—The combination of fabric and straps that holds the pilot up in flight through an attachment to the wing and also what the motor is attached to.

Glossary

Helicopter—One of several aerobatic maneuvers where the pilot is spinning around an axis other than the center of the wing.

Latitudinal (Lateral) Axis—An imaginary left/right line around which the PPG pitches up or down. The extended arms of a seated pilot represent the lateral axis direction, but the axis itself is between the pilot and wing.

Leading Edge—Front of the wing where the cell openings are.

Longitudinal Axis—An imaginary front-to-back line around which the PPG rolls (banks).

Horseshoe—When referring to a paraglider, the wing deformation where the wing tips come forward and may touch each other. Descent rate is usually about 4 times normal.

Loop—A high energy aerobatic maneuver where the pilot uses speed from a steep spiral to fly over the top of the glider.

Maillon—see quick link.

Membrane Carburetor—A type of carburetor that uses a membrane to regulate fuel flow.

Mechanical Turbulence—Random swirls of air downwind of a solid object (building, hill, mountain, etc.).

MSL—Mean Sea Level. Usually is used in reference to altitudes above sea level (ASL).

NOTAM—Notice To Airmen.

Outlanding—Landing somewhere other than intended, usually after an engine failure.

Over-The-Nose Spiral—A spiral dive where the wing is pointed nearly straight down. Recovery can be difficult.

P-Factor—Assymetric force caused by a prop that is not acting perpendicular to the relative wind.

PK System—see STI.

Parablend—An expensive Nylon/Kevlar cocktail, stirred by prop; usually prepared after an aborted launch.

Parachutage—see Parachutal Stall.

Parachutal Stall—A stall where the fully-formed wing stops flying forward and descends like an old round parachute.

Parasite—Location where powered paragliding takes place.

Pendulum—The left right swinging action that occurs whenever the glider is upset laterally.

Pitch—Motion around the PPG's latitudinal axis. The pilot is said to Pitch up when power is added.

PLF—Parachute Landing Fall.

PPG—Powered Paraglider

Pressure Altitude—Pressure represented as an altitude, assuming a standard atmosphere. It is also the altitude indicated on your altimeter when set to 29.92 in Hg. See also Density Altitude.

Propeller—The long skinny blade that provides propulsion.

Quick Link—The steel ring that connect the wing's A, B, C, or D lines to their respective riser. The usually use screw-together gates.

Rear Riser—The aftmost riser. On 3-riser wings, it is the C riser. On 4-riser wings it is the D riser.

Reverse Inflation—Any inflation started while facing the wing instead of the wind. Usually done in stronger wind.

Riser Loops—The loops at the very bottom of each riser where the carabiner goes through.

Riser Set—The combination of individual A, B, C and D risers and their corresponding loop for each side of the wing that connect to the harness through a carabiner and lines through quick links.

Roll—Motion around the PPG's longitudinal axis.

Rotor—The swirling air that results from wind blowing around an obstacle.

S.A.T.—"Safety Acrobatic Team" maneuver where the glider and pilot appear to be rotating around each other.

SHV—Swiss paraglider certifying agency of the Swiss Hang gliding Association.

STI—Speedbar/Trimmer Interconnect, aka PK System.

Speedbar—see Accelerator.

Spiral Dive—An extreme banked turn where the wing is angled towards the ground. See also "Over-The-Nose" spiral dive.

Stall—see Full Stall.

Surge—The characteristic of the wing to overfly the pilot under some conditions. It can be induced by pilot action or turbulence.

Stabilo Line—Line that goes to the wing's tip, usually a B line.

Tell Tale—A small wind indicator, usually a streamer of some sort.

Torque—The property of a motor/propeller that makes the motor, and its harnessed occupant, want to twist in the opposite direction of propeller spin.

Torque Induced Lockout—A condition where angled thrust pushes the pilot sideways, and into a bank the other way. Lockout is reached when brake pressure alone cannot compensate for the resulting turn.

Trailing Edge—The rearmost part of the wing when in flight.

Trimmers—Mechanism of some risers (usually on motoring wings) that allows changing the rear risers to increase speed. The pilot pulls a "Trim Tab" to effect the change.

Trim Speed—The speed that results when flying with no brakes applied, trimmers in their cruise setting, and no speedbar.

True Airspeed—Actual speed through the air as opposed to what it feels like to the pilot. At high elevations, the pilot must move faster through the air to get the same feel as at lower elevations.

True Altitude—Altitude above sea level if you could measure it with a long ruler. see also absolute altitude.

Turtle—The occurrence when a pilot falls backwards such that he is lying on top of the motor, unable to move until un-clipping from the unit.

Vertical Axis—an imaginary top-to-bottom line around which the PPG yaws (twists left or right).

Virga—Precipitation that evaporates before reaching the ground.

VOR—Very High Frequency (VHF) Omni Directional Range used for navigation or reference points by airplane pilots.

Waypoint—point on the surface used for navigation.

Windmilling—The spinning of a prop due solely to the relative wind blowing through it.

Wind Shadow—A calm that exists downwind of obstructions.

Wing—The means to our magic.

Wing Fold—see Collapse.

Wing Over—A series of turns in concert with the natural pendular bank rate of the glider.

Yaw—Motion around the PPG's vertical axis. If the PPG rotates to the left without banking it is said to yaw to the left.

Index